THE MAKTOUMS

LEGENDS OF THE TURF

Caresse d'orchidées par Cartier

Cartier

www.cartier.com - Cartier Boutiques: UAE Abu Dhabi: Hamdan Street – 02 627 0000, Dubai: Emirates Towers Boulevard – 04 330 0034, BurJuman – 04 355 3533

The Maktoums
Legends *of the* Turf

SEVENTH EDITION

PO Box 29997, Dubai, United Arab Emirates
29 Harley Street, London, Great Britain

Copyright © 2006 Media Prima. All rights reserved.
Printed by Ibdaa Printing Press, Dubai

Foreword from
HH Sheikh Hamdan bin Rashid Al Maktoum
UAE Minister of Finance and Industry, Dubai Deputy Ruler

An Emirati poet once wrote that; "Good horses are few, like good friends, though they may appear many to the inexperienced eye."

Almost three decades ago, my brothers and I embarked upon a journey that, observers have said, would lead us into the annals of racing history. This, the seventh edition of *Legends of the Turf*, is a record of not just the good, but the great horses who have played such an important role in the fabric of modern thoroughbred racing.

I was taught to ride by my father, the late Dubai Ruler Sheikh Rashid bin Saeed Al Maktoum, almost as soon as I could walk. Riding, like hunting and falconry, were seen as prerequisites of our upbringing on the Arabian Peninsula. But for my father, and my brothers and I, our involvement with horses was never simply about their iconic value. It was part of a shared passion and a deep affection for the animal itself.

As I have written before, my father taught me that in the animal kingdom there was no creature so intelligent and noble as the horse. Throughout my life I have never had cause to question such an assertion.

As children, I recall my late brother Sheikh Maktoum, Sheikh Mohammed, Sheikh Ahmed and myself enjoyed wonderful, innocent times in the desert surrounding Dubai, during a period when Dubai was simply a small but thriving trade entrepot. From our stables at Al Fahidi Fort, and later Sheikh Maktoum's stables at Al Ghusais and Sheikh Mohammed's stables at Za'abeel, we would strike out into the interior. It was a truly liberating time, a moment of freedom in a life that would later become dominated by national duty.

Yet — as every Arab horseman knows — there is a great deal more to the Arabian horse than an animal of pleasure. To the Bedouin especially, there is a zeal when it comes to breeding. The Bedouin valued purity above everything in Al Khamsa — the five. Stories of great courage, endurance or speed always accompanied the recitation of the genealogy of a given animal, such as the mighty Kehilet Al Krush, the Kehilet Jellabiyat and the Seglawi of Ibn Jedran. Each of these mares carried with them stories of amazing battles and intrigue. Their daughters were sought after by the most powerful Kings but often remained unattainable.

To my brothers and I, four young horsemen, these dramatic stories were enchanting and sowed the seeds for a passion that would last a lifetime.

Almost inevitably, this passion would lead us to thoroughbred racing. In 1976, Sheikh Maktoum and Sheikh Mohammed began our association with the sport when purchasing three horses at Tattersalls in Newmarket. During the intervening period, some 30 years, we have enjoyed being part of this noble pastime.

Life as an owner can be cruel just as it is, at times, euphoric. For every success there are disappointments. Losing a race is a matter of sportsmanship — losing a horse is like losing a part of me.

The highs, however, are always what one draws upon when recalling the last three decades. The indomitable Nashwan, the devastatingly fast Dayjur, the class of Almutawakel, Salsabil and Sakhee, a few of the many wonderful thoroughbreds which I have been privileged to have represent me. Often I have been asked how long my brothers and I will continue. We have won nearly everything in the sport, what still motivates us to continue striving for success?

Quite aside from the passion that we have for the sport, and the animals that represent us, my answer is simple. The excitement of being on the gallops when one of my horses puts in a fine piece of work, or the anticipation of the birth of a well-bred foal, or the thrill of the moment when one of our horses crosses the finish line. In 30 years these feelings have never dimmed, and I am delighted that my sons and many nephews and nieces have followed our lead and become enthusiastic about horses and equestrianism.

I think of a comment by Sir Winston Churchill, who stated; "There is something about the outside of a horse that is good for the inside of a man."

It has been an honour to have these magnificent creatures in my life.

The Jewel of the Desert

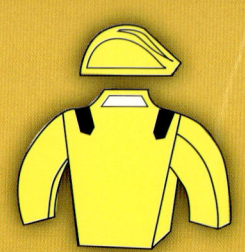

JEBEL ALI RACECOURSE

RACE TRACK

It is a right-handed, horse-shoe shaped track of 2200m (a11f). There is also a straight 1400m (a7f) track that joins the round track at the 900m (a4½ f) pole. From the 2200m (a11f) pole the horses meet the rising ground up to the 1950m (9¾ f) pole, whence it levels out to the 1600m (a8f) pole. From the 1600m (a8f) pole horses race downhill to the bend at the 1200m (a6f) pole, whence it levels out and joins the straight course at the 900m (a4½f) pole. The track levels out from the bend to the 400m (a2f) pole where there is an uphill climb to the winning post. The surface of the track is a mixture of special desert sand and oil. This track is considered to be one of the best all-weather tracks in the world.

RACING PROGRAMME

Jebel Ali Racecourse takes pride in hosting three stakes races during the Emirates racing calendar and has contributed towards making the UAE a centre for international racing.

Jebel Ali Stakes	(Listed)	1950m (a9¾f)
Jebel Ali Mile	(Listed)	1600m (a8f)
Jebel Ali Sprint	(Listed)	1000m (a5f)

LOCATION

Situated 15 minutes from the city of Dubai, opposite the Dubai Internet and Media Cities. Located off the main Dubai - Abu Dhabi highway (Sheikh Zayed Road), beside the Emirates Golf Club.

BRIEF HISTORY

Following specifications laid down by HH Sh Ahmed bin Rashid Al Maktoum and Dhruba Selvaratnam, the construction of the racetrack and grandstand commenced in November 1990.

An upper level was added to the existing grandstand to accommodate sponsors and corporate hospitality guests in 20 boxes. The VIP grandstand was constructed in 1993

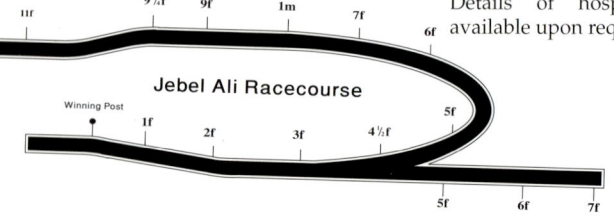

ADMISSION

General admission is free with car parking facilities available for 3500 cars.
From the public car park, racegoers are shuttled by coach to the public enclosure reached via a short walk through the 'Faltaat Tunnel' which was built in 2001.

HOSPITALITY

Details of hospitality packages are available upon request.

Clerk of the Course: *Karthi Selvaratnam* - **Racecourse Secretary:** *Emma J. Campbell*

P.O. Box 53135 - Dubai, United Arab Emirates Telephone: (971 4) 347 4914 - Fax: (971 4) 347 2478 - Email: jblalist@emirates.net.ae

Contents

Milestones	**14**	**Shadwell Farm**	**95**	**Sheikh Mohammed**	**181**
Ajdal	26	Daylami	106	Hatta	186
Al Bahathri	28	Diminuendo	108	Height of Fashion	188
Alhaarth	30	Dubai Millennium	110	High Hawk	190
Aljaber	32	E-Dubai	112	High-Rise	192
Derrinstown Stud	**35**	**Road to the DWC**	**115**	**An Equine in Time**	**195**
Almutawakel	44	Electrocutionist	140	In The Wings	214
Ameerat	46	Erhaab	142	Indian Skimmer	216
At Talaq	48	Ezzoud	144	Intrepidity	218
Bachir	50	Fantastic Light	146	Island Sands	220
Legacy of Godolphin	**53**	**Sheikh Hamdan**	**149**	**Sheikh Ahmed**	**223**
Balanchine	72	Favourable Terms	154	Jalmood	228
Barathea	74	Firebreak	156	Jazil	230
Bernardini	76	Grandera	158	Jet Ski Lady	232
Cadeaux Genereux	78	Green Desert	160	Jeune	234
Sheikh Maktoum	**81**	**Shadwell Estate**	**163**	**Gainsborough**	**237**
Cape Verdi	86	Haafhd	172	Kayf Tara	242
Crimplene	88	Halling	174	Kazzia	244
Dayflower	91	Harayir	176	Lahan	246
Dayjur	92	Hatoof	178	Lammtarra	248

continued on next page

continued from previous page

Sheikh Ahmed	**251**	**Godolphin Enigma**	**286**	**Sheikh Ahmed**	**324**
Ma Biche	256	Oh So Sharp	294	Shantou	326
Marienbard	258	Old Vic	296	Shareef Dancer	328
Mark of Esteem	260	Opera House	298	Singspiel	330
Moon Ballad	262	Pebbles	300	Snow Bride	332
Darley	**265**	**Sheikh Hamdan**	**302**	**Sheikh Maktoum**	**334**
Moonshell	270	Refuse To Bend	306	Soviet Star	338
Mtoto	272	Rule of Law	308	Street Cry	340
Mubtaker	274	Sakhee	310	Sulamani	342
Sheikh Rashid	**276**	**Kingwood House**	**312**	**Sheikh Mohammed**	**344**
Mutafaweq	278	Salsabil	316	Sure Blade	346
Mutamam	280	Shadayid	318	Susu	348
Nashwan	282	Shadeed	320	Swain	350
Nayef	284	Shamardal	322	Touching Wood	352
				Sheikh Saeed	**354**
				Unfuwain	356
				Wassl	358
				Zilzal	360
				Acknowledgements	**362**

A revival of classical artistry in fine furniture today.

In the small town of Romano d'Ezzelino, near Venice, Italy, over a hundred artisans work daily to create individual furniture pieces that are veritable works of art.

The fine Italian craftsmen are part of Francesco Molon, a family-owned business dedicated to the revival of furniture artistry in classical European style.

The world of Francesco Molon offering high-end residential furniture, is now exclusively showcased in our dedicated showroom at Pyramid Centre, Dubai.

To make an appointment for a private viewing of this unique showroom, please call 04-3345596.

FRANCESCO MOLON
Live well.

Phone: +971 4 334 5596, Fax: +971 4 334 5669,
P.O. Box 31071, Dubai, U.A.E.,
E-mail: fmolon@emirates.net.ae - www.francescomolon.com

Milestones

The Maktoum family's 30 years in thoroughbred racing

1976 The first Maktoum sales draft. Among the three yearlings purchased through the Tattersalls sale ring by the Curragh Bloodstock agency is the filly Hatta *(pictured below)*, knocked down for 6,200 guineas.

1977 Hatta competes a four timer of successes with the Maktoums' first pattern win in the Group Three Molecomb Stakes at Goodwood.

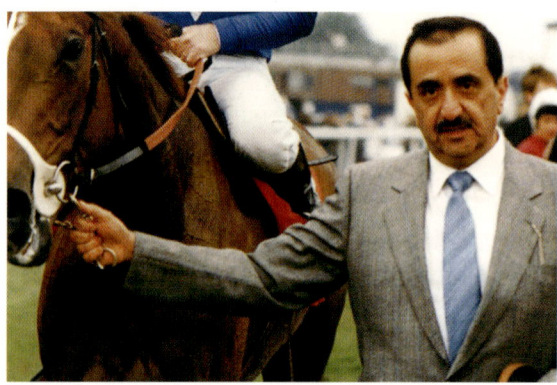

and three-years-old he comes to hand as a four-year-old and the Busted colt achieves four successes, including a victory in the high profile Gordon Carter Handicap.

1978 Sheikh Mohammed enjoys four victories during this campaign with Haddfan, Swanlinbar and Le Silentaire, the latter winning twice.

1979 Sheikh Maktoum's first racecourse representative, Shaab, arrives in the winner's enclosure. After blank seasons at two

1980 Sheikh Hamdan gets off the mark as an owner with juvenile Mushref. After one maiden success, the son of Key to the Mint finishes second in the Listed Champion Two-Year-Old Trophy.

1981 Noalto is the first Maktoum-owned performer to be placed in Group One company when Easter Stakes winner finishes third in the Sussex Stakes at Goodwood behind Kings Lake. Sheikh Mohammed's Jalmood collects third in the William Hill Futurity, while the owner enjoys 10 wins that summer.

Chopard

"Passione"

The Mille Miglia GMT Chronograph. Mechanical passion, technology, power, distinctive character, flowing curves: a these are just a few of the striking parallels between automotive engineering and watchmaking. Forming a bridge between these two worlds, the legend of the Mille Miglia is alive and well. A race that is now reserved for classic vehicles that have taken part in one of the historical editions of this competition, the Mille Miglia offers a concentrated blend of performance and passion. Chopard has been the sponsor and official timekeeper of this event since 1988.

GMT for Greenwich Mean Time. When it appears on a watch, this symbol signifies the addition of a second time zone.

The Mille Miglia GMT chronograph: certified chronometer (COSC), available in stainless steel (ref. 16/8992) or gold (ref. 16/1884). Also available with a stainless steel bracelet (ref. 15/8992).

أحمد صديقي وأولاده
AHMED SEDDIQI & SONS

Wafi City Burj Al Arab
Tel: 04 3241010 Tel: 04 3489595

www.seddiqi.com

Sheikh Hamdan enjoys his first pattern success, when Ghadeer takes the Group Three Prix Carlo Porta in Italy. The Lyphard colt also finishes placed in three other group race in Italy and Germany.

1982 For the first time Dubai sponsors the end-of-season Dubai Champion Stakes (Gr. 1) today one of the longest ongoing commercial deals in horseracing.

Sheikh Mohammed again reaches double figures as an owner in Britain. His seasonal tally reaches 30, headlined by black type earners Awaasif and Jalmood.

Top class filly Awaasif notches Sheikh Mohammed's first Group One success in the Yorkshire Oaks on York's Knavemire track. The filly subsequently adds a classy third place in the Prix de l'Arc de Triomphe behind Akiyda and Ardross.

The Tom Jones-trained Touching Wood *(pictured)* becomes the first Maktoum-owned Classic winner when claiming the St Leger in the colours of Sheikh Maktoum. Earlier the son of Roberto had finished second to Golden Fleece in the Epsom Derby, won the Welsh Derby at Chepstow, and, after Doncaster, added the Irish St Leger to his haul.

1983 France-based filly Ma Biche adds a third Classic for Sheikh Maktoum when taking the 1000 Guineas at Newmarket under Freddie Head. The filly also scores in the Group One Prix de la Forte at Longchamp in October.

A fourth Classic in three seasons comes the way of Sheikh Maktoum when trainer Michael Stoute *(right)* saddles Northern Dancer son Shareef Dancer to claim the Irish Derby at the Curragh, in doing so defeating the great Caerleon. Shareef Dancer also wins the King Edward VII Stakes (Gr. 2)

In Sheikh Ahmed's first season as an owner his colours achieve Classic success as Wassl scores in the Irish 2000 Guineas. The son of Mill Reef is also prepared by John Dunlop to take the Greenham Stakes (Gr. 3) and makes third spot in the Sussex Stakes (Gr. 1).

Sheikh Marwan is the fifth member of the Maktoum family to make an impact in racing when, in his first season as owner, his Nophe wins the Acorn Stakes and is placed in the Cherry Hinton (Gr. 3) and Queen Mary Stakes (Gr. 2).

1984 The first season that Sheikh Mohammed scores with over 60 individual winning horses, among them pattern stars Head For Heights, Kanz, Local Suitor, Optimistic Lass and Royal Lorna. A great deal is thought of Henry Cecil-trained Juvenile Oh So Sharp after she takes the Fillies Mile (Gr. 3) and Solario Stakes (LR).

Sheikh Mohammed's Deceit Dancer is the first horse representing the family to take a graded race in America, one of five seasonal success including the My Dear Stakes (Gr. 2). The filly later wins the Fury Stakes (Gr. 3) and is placed in the Canadian Oaks.

Sheikh Hamdan's first Group One success as At Talaq claims the Grand Prix de Paris. The Roberto colt is also placed in the British and Italian Derbies.

1985 Sheikh Mohammed is champion owner in Britain for the first time when his 71 winning individuals muster 115 races, including 16 Group races in Britain alone. This eclipses all previous records and begins an unparalleled championship winning streak for the Maktoum family.

Clive Brittain *(below)* trained Pebbles wins the Eclipse Stakes and Champion Stakes (both Gr. 1) before a success in the Breeders' Cup Turf.

Maktoum horses win an unprecidented four of the five British Classics — three fall to Oh So Sharp (1000 Guineas, Oaks and St Leger) and Sheikh Maktoum's Shadeed trains on from his Houghton Stakes success as a juvenile to score in the Craven Stakes and then head home a Maktoum 1-2 in the 2000 Guineas from Sheikh Mohammed's Bairn.

Sheikh Hamdan enjoys his first Classic success courtesy of Al Bahathri in the Irish 1000 Guineas, after the filly has followed Oh So Sharp home in the English version.

1986 Sheikh Hamdan's At Talaq breaks new ground for the family when saddled by

Colin Hayes to take the biggest race in the Southern Hemisphere, the Melbourne Cup.

Following on from a pair of pattern victories as a two-year-old Green Desert blooms into one of the finest horses ever to represent Sheikh Maktoum. The Michael Stoute trained star takes the July Cup (Gr. 1), Sprint Cup (Gr. 2) and Free Handicap (LR), also finishing second in the 2000 Guineas.

Sheikh Mana is the sixth family member to taste racecourse success, most notably when colt Zajal takes the Clarence House Stakes.

Another of Sheikh Mohammed's golden years, with 18 British black type winners among them the prolific Adjal, Indian Skimmer and English and Irish Oaks heroine Unite.

1987 Four-year-old Mtoto *(pictured above)*, probably the finest thoroughbred ever to represent Sheikh Ahmed, fires home a trio of Group race wins. In addition to success in the Coral-Eclipse (Gr. 1) he is saddled by Alec Stewart to claim the Prince of Wales's Stakes (Gr. 2) and Brigadier Gerard Stakes (Gr. 3), before going on to finish placed in the Prix de l'Arc de Triomphe.

1988 Drama in Ireland, as Sheikh Mohammed's English Oaks winner Diminuendo fights out a finish in the Irish Oaks with his second string Melodist. The pair flash past the post together and are judged to have dead-heated, the first time this had happened for 40 years and the first time that two horses belonging to the same owner had dead-heated in a Classic anywhere in Europe.

1989 A remarkable four of the five English Classics fall to Maktoum horses: Musical Bliss, the 1000 Guineas; Nashwan *(pictured below)*, the 2000 Guineas and Epsom Derby; and Snow Bride, the Epsom Oaks.

Sheikh Hamdan's Nashwan, already a double Classic winner, goes on to become arguably the best Maktoum-owned horse of all time, when

EMERGENCY

Dubai Breitling Boutiques:
Deira City Centre: 2954109, Mall of the Emirates: 3411165,
Wafi City: 3243530, The Ritz-Carlton: 3995741, Le-Meridien Mina Seyahi: 3993090,
Sheraton Dubai Creek Hotel & Towers: 2284739
Abu Dhabi: Emirates Palace Hotel: 6812286, Marina Mall: 6814122,
E-mail: brietl@emirates.net.ae

INSTRUMENTS FOR PROFESSIONALS™

saddled by Major Dick Hern to victories in the Coral-Eclipse (Gr. 1) and King George VI and Queen Elizabeth Diamond Stakes (Gr. 1).

1990 Following the middle distance exploits of Nashwan the previous summer, Sheikh Hamdan's season is headlined by the explosive sprinter Dayjur. The son of Danzig powers his way to wins in the Sprint Cup at Haydock, the Nunthorpe Stakes at York and the Prix de l'Abbaye de Longchamp. In a moment of terrible drama, during the latter stages of the Breeders' Cup Sprint in America Dayjur looks to be cruising to a remarkable success when he leaps over a shadow on the track, losing his chance and finishing second.

Salsabil becomes Sheikh Hamdan's second double British Classic winner when posting success in the 1000 Guineas and Oaks, before she is shipped to Ireland to defeat a field of colts in the Irish Derby. She is the first filly to win the Irish Derby since 1900.

French-based colt In the Wings, following success in the Coronation Cup at Epsom and Grand Prix Saint-Cloud, claims the Breeders' Cup Turf under Gary Stevens.

1991 Weeks before the British season gets under way, Sheikh Mohammed inaugurates racing at a new track in his home country of Dubai. The new Nad Al Sheba *(pictured)* has a soft opening in February before a full-blown meeting in April including appearance of Willie Carson and Lester Piggott *(pictured)*. During the same period Sheikh Ahmed opens Jebel Ali Racecourse *(opposite page)*.

1992 Professional racing under rules gets under way in the Maktoum home state of the United Arab Emirates. The season is headlined in the inaugural in Dubai International Jockey's Challenge, which brings together top jockeys from all over the world. American pairing Gary Stevens and Kent Dersormeaux take the overall trophy.

1993 After a quiet winter preparation in Dubai, filly Dayflower and colt Blush Rambler return to Europe in the spring, running in the colours of Sheikh Maktoum. Trainer Satish Seemar saddles Dayflower to a close up fifth in the 1000 Guineas and the filly goes on to become the first UAE-trained winner of a western race when winning a conditions event at York.

1994 Godolphin appears in the Classic record books for the first time as Balanchine takes the Epsom Oaks and then the Irish Derby. The Godolphin licence holder is Hilal Ibrahim who earlier becomes the first UAE national to train a winner in Europe. Other major performers include Cezanne (Irish Champion Stakes) and Lovely Millie (Solario Stakes).

More Breeders' Cup success for Sheikh Mohammed when Barathea claims the Mile at Churchill Downs courtecy of a blistering late run close to home.

1995 New Godolphin licence holder Saeed bin Suroor *(pictured)*, a former policeman, wins his first Classic when Moonshell claims the Oaks. The global nature of Godolphin's ambitions is clear as Heart Lake wins the Yasuda Kinen in Japan, Red Bishop the Queen Elizabeth in Hong Kong and San Juan Capistrano Handicap in the United States.

Lammtarra *(pictured)* becomes the third Maktoum Derby winner and a first major winner to a member of a new generation. His owner is Sheikh Saeed bin Maktoum Al Maktoum, eldest son of the Dubai Ruler. Lammtarra is the first horse since 1918 to win an Epsom Derby in his first race of the season.

1996 The Dubai World Cup is inaugurated. With a $4 million purse this is the richest race on the planet. The first running attracts American star Cigar—at the time probably the greatest racehorse on dirt in the world. Cigar wins the first running of the race.

Godolphin's Halling completes a remarkable big race double-double, winning Coral-Eclipse (Gr. 1) and Juddmonte International Stakes (Gr. 1) for a second consecutive year, while Mark of Esteem scoops the 2000 Guineas

1997 Godolphin's Swain claims the first of two consecutive King George VI and Queen Elizabeth Diamond Stakes successes.

1998 High-Rise wins the Epsom Derby for Sheikh Mohammed Obaid Al Maktoum, cousin of the Maktoum brothers. An owner and enthusiast for many years, this is Sheikh Mohammed Obaid's first big race win in Britain

For Your Eyes Only gets Sheikh Rashid bin Mohammed Al Maktoum, the eldest son of Sheikh Mohammed, off the mark as an owner in Britain, highlight of the season for the gelding being success in the William Hill Mile at Goodwood.

1999 Godolphin trainer Saeed bin Suroor, having won major races all over the world, finally wins his domestic showpiece, the Dubai World Cup, with the Richard Hills-ridden Almutawakel.

The Maktoum family and Dubai are pivotal in creating the first team style competition in horseracing, the Shergar Cup. Fought out between horses belonging to owners from the Middle East and Europe, the concept breaks new ground.

Even by Godolphin's high standards few have witnessed anything like the remarkable September day when the team wins the Man o'War Stakes in America with Daylami, the English St Leger with Nadawi and the Irish Champion Stakes with Swain.

2000 Dubai World Cup day on March 25 sees a purse of $6 million on offer, with $3.6 million going to the winner. The complete seven race card will carry $12 million prizemoney, including the Dubai Duty Free and the newly-inaugurated Dubai Golden Shaheen, a six furlong sprint worth $1 million.

After his name was changed before making his debut the previous season, Dubai Millennium returns in 2000 with expectations high and Sheikh Mohammed predicting great things. After routing his opponents in a top class prep race at Nad Al Sheba, Dubai Millennium

gallops his opponents in the Dubai World Cup into submission. After a similarly spectacular win in the Prince of Wales's Stakes at Royal Ascot, the colt *(pictured)* suffers a tragic injury and is retired. He later dies prematurely.

2001 Fantastic Light dominates much of the summer with successes in the Tattersalls Gold Cup in Ireland, the Prince of Wales's Stakes and Irish Champion Stakes. But then another elite Godolphin star emerges in the shape of Sakhee, who runs away with the Juddmonte International Stakes and the Prix de l'Arc de Triomphe.

At the Breeders' Cup meeting in New York Fantastic Light adds the Turf to his tally while Sakhee goes within a whisker of claiming the Classic.

2002 Tragedy strikes when Nashwan, one of the great racehorses of the modern era, dies at Shadwell Stud. The son of Blushing Groom was humanely destroyed after suffering complications following what was expected to be a minor operation on his right hind leg. The loss of Nashwan is a second severe blow to Shadwell Stud, who earlier had lost his half-brother Unfuwain.

2003 A landmark success for Dubai's elite Godolphin when, in the 21st renewal of the Grade 1 Arlington Million at Arlington Park, Sulamani claims the organisation its 100th Group or Grade 1 win. Racing manager Simon Crisford says: "Having won 100 Group One races on three different continents, in 11 countries over 10 years has been quite an accomplishment..."

2004 Winning his fourth British Champion Trainers' title Saeed bin Suroor saddles eleven Group One race winners, his stable stars including Doyen, Papineau, Sulamani and Refuse To Bend.

2005 This year marks the tenth running of the world's richest race, the $6,000,000 Dubai World Cup. In addition to the feature race, there are a further five Group races and a Group One for Purebred Arabians, ensuring the day is one of the most significant in global racing. A total of 989 horses from 21 countries are entered for world's richest day of racing, which boasts $15,250,000 in prize money, making Dubai World Cup day the most cosmopolitan anywhere on the planet.

2006 Unprecedented Maktoum success in America's prestigious Triple Crown as first Sheikh Mohammed's Bernardini claims the Preakness Stakes and then Sheikh Hamdan's Jazil *(pictured)* the Belmont Stakes.

Ajdal
b. c by Northern Dancer – Native Partner (Raise A Native)

Versatile is surely the word with which one could sum up Ajdal, who went from Epsom Derby hope to top-class sprinter as a three-year-old, also proving trainer Michael Stoute as one able to think what is nowadays virtually unthinkable.

Sheikh Mohammed's Northern Dancer colt was unbeaten in three starts as a juvenile, claiming the Mornington Stakes and then the Group One Dewhurst Stakes.

The following spring Ajdal reappeared in the Craven Stakes and continued to impress in defeating another of 1986's top juveniles, Don't Forget Me.

The 2000 Guineas, however, proved his undoing. The colt was travelling well throughout the mile contest, but after receiving an unwelcome bump late in the race, he recovered to finish one length fifth to Don't Forget Me.

The two reopposed in the Irish 2000 Guineas, with Ajdal looking set to take the race one furlong out only for Don't Forget Me to get up by a length from Ajdal in third.

Despite having no appeal over a longer distance, Ajdal subsequently ran a cracking race in the Epsom Derby to finish fourth by seven lengths to Reference Point.

Even before his charge's heroics over a mile and a half, Stoute had entered him in the six-furlong July Cup and at Newmarket proved Ajdal far better suited to the shorter trip. Facing 10 established sprinters, Ajdal was always up near the head of affairs and went on in the dip to take the lead to finish a head winner from Gayane with Bluebird a further length away in third.

Bluebird reopposed Ajdal in York's Sprint Championship the following month, over a minimum trip which had proved Bluebird's optimum. But again Ajdal found speed and jockey Walter Swinburn drove him into the lead from the outset for an all-the-way victory. Haydock's six-furlong Sprint Cup was his next point of call, where Ajdal trounced another Group One field.

Having already been syndicated to stud, he rounded off a remarkable season with a trip to contest France's premier sprint, the Prix de l'Abbaye, in October, where firm going seemed to play a decisive role as he showed little of his previous form.

	Nearctic	Nearco
Northern Dancer (b. 1961)		Lady Angela
	Natalma	Native Dancer
AJDAL (b. 1984)		Almahmoud
	Raise A Native	Native Dancer
Native Partner (b. 1966)		Raise You
	Dinner Partner	Tom Fool
		Bluehaze

Al Bahathri

ch. f by Blushing Groom – Chain Store (Nodouble)

While not Sheikh Hamdan's first British group race winner—that honour fell to Princes Gate in Group Three Westbury Stakes in 1982—Al Bahathri was the first star name to represent the owner.

Trained by Tom Jones, the $650,000 yearling opened her account on her second trip to the track in a Newmarket maiden. She then went on to complete a six furlong hat-trick of successes by adding the Listed Princess Margaret Stakes and then York's Group Two Lowther Stakes.

Looking to become the Champion two-year-old filly of 1984, Al Bahathri finshed third in the Cheveley Park Stakes and went into the winter as a leading contender for the spring classics.

Having proven herself a natural front-runner, with a good cruising speed and flowing movement, it was therefore a surprise when connections favoured holding her up, when returning to the track in April for the Fred Darling Stakes. Her surprise defeat when odds-on ensured a quick return to the pace-setting tactics.

In the 1000 Guineas, Al Bahathri was allowed to join the front rank from the moment they left the stalls, was still there in the late stages and looked to have secured the honours when easing ahead of Bella Colora. Only subsequent triple crown heroine Oh So Sharp denied Sheikh Hamdan's filly, with a lightning late burst.

The filly next started in the Ireland 1000 Guineas, with the soft ground seemingly against her and a good class field assembled. Again dictating the early shape of the race, Al Bahathri came under severe pressure entering the straight when pressed by four for the lead, but through sheer tenacity stayed on to claim the race.

Routed to the Coronation Stakes during Royal Ascot, the filly produced an excellent run. Dictating the race from the front, she shook off the field rounding the last turn and—even allowing for a momentary loss of action when her back end slipped away—she stayed on, reaching the finish with one length to spare from Top Socialite.

Looking better than ever, Al Bahathri also claimed Newmarket's Child Stakes, giving weight away and crossing swords with older horses. After below-par runs in the Nassau Stakes and Sun Chariot Stakes she was retired.

AL BAHATHRI (ch. 1982)	**Blushing Groom (ch. 1974)**	Red God → Nasrullah / Spring Run
		Runaway Bride → Wild Risk / Aimee
	Chain Store (b. 1972)	Nodouble → Noholme II / Abla-Jay
		General Store → To Market / Generals Sister

Alhaarth

b. c by Unfuwain – Irish Valley (Irish River)

Home bred by Sheikh Hamdan, Alhaarth had one of the best juvenile seasons of any Maktoum horse over the last 25 years. Trained by Major Dick Hern, he opened his account in a maiden at the Newmarket July meeting, fighting out the finish with the well-regarded Mark Of Esteem. In beating the subsequent 2000 Guineas winner by a neck—the pair four lengths clear of the third—Alhaarth confirmed high hopes and stepped up to pattern company for the remainder of the summer.

His second appearance was in the Vintage Stakes, an event previously used as a stepping stone by the likes of Dr Devious and Eltish. The race proved Alhaarth very much in the same mould. Despite his inexperience, the colt's success was remarkable and stamped him as one of the finest of his generation.

He returned to action in the Solario Stakes at Sandown, showing more improvement to take his second pattern race with conviction. The Solario Stakes was an even better example of his apparent class, Alhaarth conceding 10 pounds and easily defeating Staffin.

After a suspect win in a falsely run three horse Champagne Stakes at Doncaster, Hern dropped his Classic prospect into the year's hottest two-year-old contest, the Dewhurst Stakes, next time out. Alhaarth silenced all his critics. Facing another small field, Alhaarth put in his most devastating performance.

He wintered as a Classic front-runner but returned the following year a shade disappointing, although managing fifth in the Epsom Derby and placings in the Sussex Stakes and Celebration Mile. Alhaarth completed his three-year-old season with a deserved pattern success, however, in taking the Prix Rond-Point at Longchamp in October.

After wintering in Dubai with Saeed bin Suroor Alhaarth showed improved form to finish second to Bosra Sham in the Prince of Wales's Stakes. In the same grade he returned to the winners' enclosure a fortnight later, taking the International Stakes at the Curragh, before another placed run behind Pilsudski and Desert King in the Irish Champion Stakes.

Alhaarth was shipped to Dubai for a second winter, and returned to Europe the following summer in good heart. In five starts he added to his tally the Budweiser American Bowl International Stakes in Ireland and the Prix Dollar at Longchamp.

ALHAARTH (b. 1993)	Unfuwain (b. 1985)	Northern Dancer — Nearctic / Natalma
		Height of Fashion — Bustino / Highclere
	Irish Valley (ch. 1982)	Irish River — Riverman / Irish Star
		Green Valley — Val de Loir / Sly Pola

Aljabr

gr. c by Storm Cat — Sierra Madre (Baillamont)

Aljabr was Godolphin's juvenile winner in 1998, the first of many, but almost as soon as he had completed a four-length success at Sandown he was being spoken of as something special. His classy performance was enough to warrant a reappearance in the heady class of the Lanson Champagne Vintage Stakes at Goodwood, with much the same result. Aljabr won by three lengths from Raise A Grand.

If this was a pointer in class, then his next outing was nothing short of a confirmation. Facing 2000 Guineas ante-post favourite Stravinsky in the Prix de la Salamandre at Longchamp, Aljabr put in a superb performance. With the pair clear in the latter stages, Aljabr suddenly found Stravinsky pulling alongside. He lengthened and went on again near the line to claim a half length victory. Stravinsky was subsequently dissqualified.

Wintering in Dubai, now a leading fancy for the 2000 Guineas, the next the world knew the classy grey was heading for a far different engagement, the Kentucky Derby, after finishing close up behind Worldly Manner in a Nad Al Sheba private trial race.

During the spring he improved further and was quietly fancied in some quarters. According to plan, he shipped to the US and was training well when, the day before the race, all was not well and he was later found to be lame in a hind leg. Returning to Britain soon after this, he reappeared in the St James's Palace Stakes at Royal Ascot and finished an excellent second to the top class colt Sendawar.

His next outing came in the Sussex Stakes, against the best milers of his generation and older horses, where he won gamely by a length from Almushtarak. After a disappointing fourth in the Prix du Moulin du Longchamp it was discovered that he had cracked a knee.

Aljabr returned the following May looking superb in the Juddmonte Lockinge Stakes at Newbury, making all to win by two lengths, and followed this with below-par runs in the Queen Anne Stakes at Royal Ascot and attempting a repeat in the Sussex Stakes.

Nevertheless, Aljabr remains in elite company having won a Group One race in each of his three seasons on the racecourse.

ALJABR (gr. 1996)			
	Storm Cat (b. 1983)	Storm Bird	Northern Dancer
			South Ocean
		Terlingua	Secretariat
			Crimson Saint
	Sierra Madre (ro. 1991)	Baillamont	Blushing Groom
			Lodeve
		Marie d'Irlande	Kalamoun
			La Ferte Milon

Derrinstown Stud

A major force in the industry for almost a quarter of a century, Sheikh Hamdan bin Rashid Al Maktoum had his status confirmed as one of the greatest owner/breeders in history when, on the first Saturday in May 2004, Haafhd flew home to win the 2000 Guineas from half a dozen other Group One winners. As if this weren't enough, the imposing chesnut son of the Sheikh's homebred Alhaarth then returned to Newmarket's straight Rowley course in October to land the Group One Champion Stakes (sponsored by the Emirates Airline) defeating the likes of Chorist, Azamour, Refuse To Bend and Doyen - all prolific winners in the highest grade.

To breed and own the winner of the world's most prestigious mile Classic for colts is a major achievement, but that's only part of the story. Back in 1983, Sheikh Hamdan made a very shrewd decision to purchase the high-class Group winning filly, Height of Fashion from The Royal Studs. She was to breed six Group and Stakes winners, including Nashwan (Derby Stakes and sire of brilliant Prix de l'Arc winner Bago), Nayef (Champion Stakes), and Haafhd's grandsire, Unfuwain.

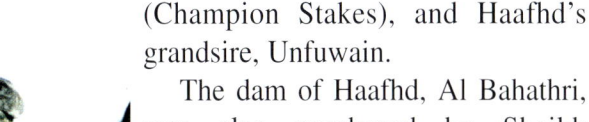

The dam of Haafhd, Al Bahathri, was also purchased by Sheikh Hamdan as a yearling. She won the Group Two Lowther Stakes, at York as a juvenile and trained on to become Ireland's Champion Filly at three, winning the Irish 1000 Guineas and the Group One Coronation Stakes, at Royal Ascot. Haafhd is one of her seven winners to date.

Buying the best blood available is one thing; securing the best available conditions to breed Champion racehorses is another. Sheikh Hamdan purchased Derrinstown from Anne, Duchess of Westminster in 1982, a farm consisting of 375 acres, near Maynooth in Co. Kildare. The Duchess was famed for her ownership of Arkle, by far the greatest steeplechaser of the modern era.

Is there another place in the world blessed with the soft rains which blow in from the Atlantic and fall on the limestone rich pastures of the 'Emerald Isle'? Add to this the natural flair of the Irish horsemen and you are well on the way to breeding top-class thoroughbreds.

Derrinstown Stud was built from scratch to the highest standards and, even though its dimensions have since swelled to encompass ten farms and more than 2,000 acres, that principal has always been adhered to.

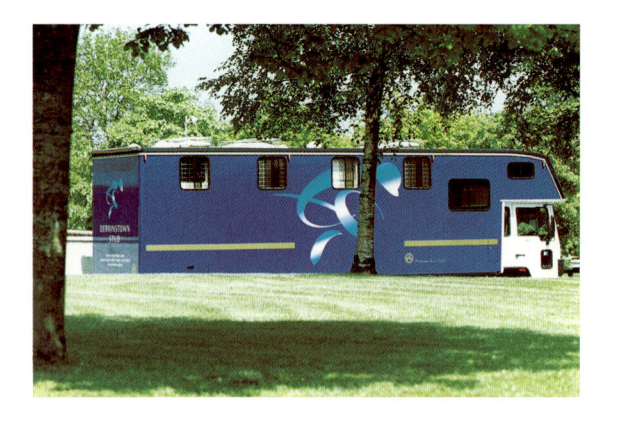

Only the best will suffice. Such selectivity has also been applied to the staff and Sheikh Hamdan quickly gathered around him many of the top horsemen in the industry, including General Manager Stephen Collins. The six stallions currently under his care at Derrinstown could grace any stud in the world. As befits horses owned and raced by Sheikh Hamdan, they all have impeccable pedigrees as well as boasting impressive records on the track.

The eldest, Marju, is a Group One winning three-parts-brother to Champion Filly Salsabil. He is established as one of Europe's top stallions who regularly weighs in with a fistful of top class horses each season. Up to the end of June 2006, he has been responsible for more than 35 individual Group winners, including Group One winners Soviet Song, Marbye, My Emma, Sil Sila, Viva Pataca and Marju Snip. Marju is not only good, he is consistently good and in all his progeny have won or placed in over 216 Stakes races around the world. It is hardly surprising that he has been fully booked since retiring to stud.

Homebred Alhaarth, a Champion Two-Year-Old by Unfuwain, won seven Group races, including the Group One Dewhurst, Group Two Champagne Stakes, Prix du Rond-Point and the International Stakes at The Curragh. His stud career kicked off in similar mode and he was one of Europe's Leading First Crop sires in 2001.

Alhaarth has carried on the excellent work since

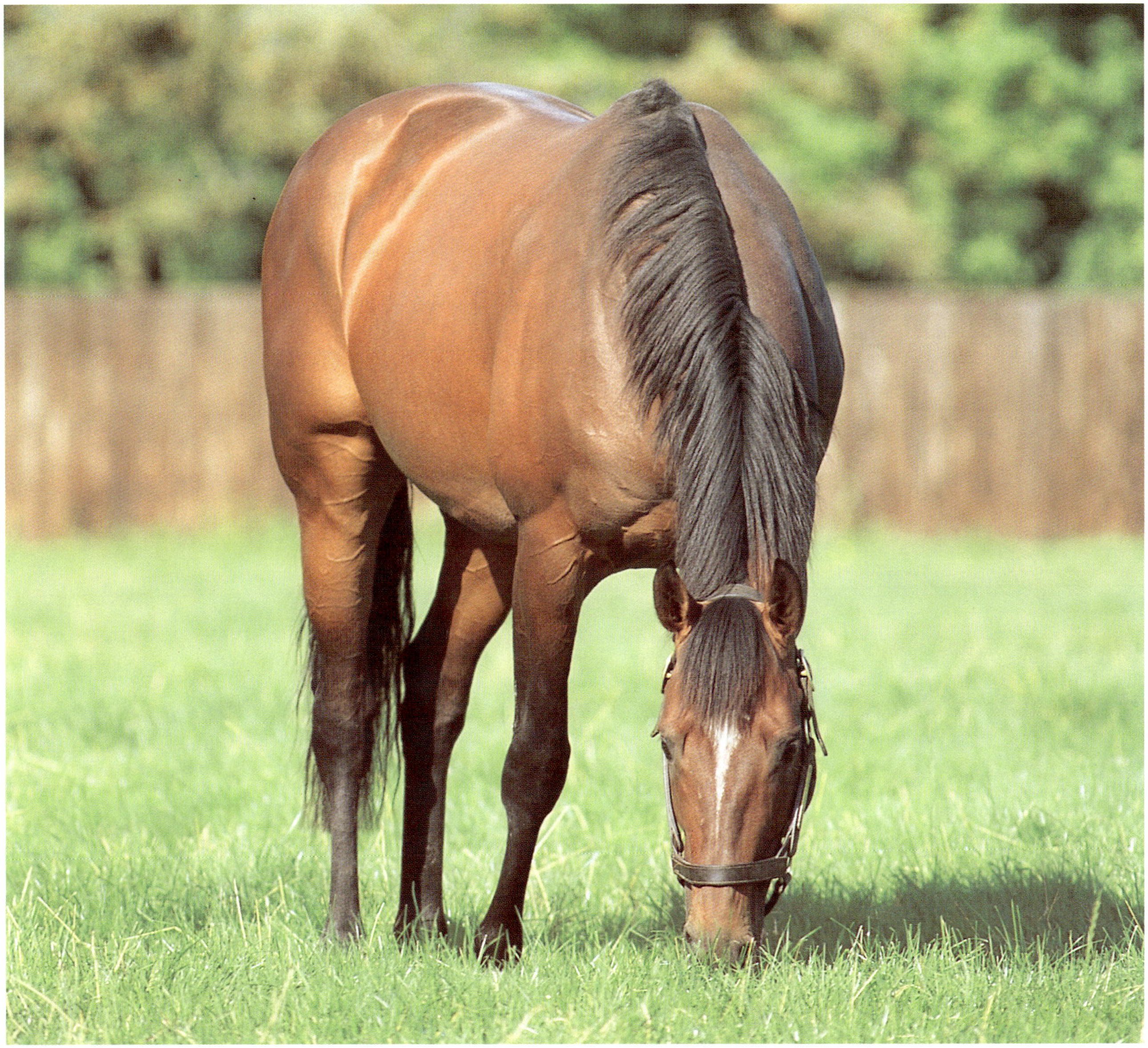

and his major successes include the aforementioned 2000 Guineas and Champion Stakes winner Haafhd, and the globetrotting multiple Group One winner Phoenix Reach. He has established himself as one of the most exciting young sires available in Europe with further Group and Stakes winners such as Bandari, Birdie, Dominica, Hoh Buzzard, Maharib and Misterah. The latter was also clear cut winner of the Gr.1 Dubai Sheema Classic in 2005.

Intikhab, a World Champion Miler and record-breaking Royal Ascot winner by Red Ransom, had sixteen individual first crop winners in 2003, including the Group One winner Paita and Group winner Toupie.

Intikhab has since continued the excellent work and his 2006 successes have included the multiple Black Type winner Moon Unit, the outstanding two-year-old Hoh Mike and the impressive Royal Ascot winner Red Evie.

Almutawakel - like Alhaarth, bred and raised at Derrinstown - is no stranger to racing fans. Winner of the Gr.1 Dubai World Cup in course record time, he also gained Group One honours in Europe by taking the Prix Jean Prat at Longchamp. He is by sire of sires Machiavellian, who had been European Champion at two, and is out of a Green Desert mare. His full-sister Muwakleh won the UAE 1000 Guineas at Nad Al Sheba and was runner up in the 1000 Guineas at Newmarket, so he lacks for nothing on the breeding front.

He got off to a flying start with his first crop of two-year-olds in 2004, siring 14 individual winners of 19 races, including Stakes winners Liset and Silver Cup and Salsa Brava. He has been to some extent an "unsung hero" ever since, not only producing an impressively high percentage of winners to runners, but also some of quality like Wahid and Silver Cup (a Classic winner in Europe and now a triple Group Two winner in the States).

Elnadim was a dual Champion Sprinter and brilliant winner of the Group One July Cup at Newmarket. He comes from one of the most successful families in the stud book with seven individual champions appearing beneath the first and second dams, including the incomparable champion Dubai Millennium.

With credentials like that, Elnadim can hardly fail to make his mark as a stallion and he too has achieved a high strike rate with his progeny. The sire of thirteen individual first European crop winners in 2005 - in addition to the Group Two winner and Group One placed Pendragon in Australia - he has continued to impress in 2006 with 40 per cent two-year-old winners to runners in Europe (to 4 July).

Bahri (previously in Kentucky) has his long-awaited European first crop yearlings passing through the sales ring in 2006. A European Champion, Bahri was one of he very best milers of the 1990s and his American-sired foals have included the outstanding colt Sakhee (winner of the Group One Prix de l'Arc de Triomphe); the high-class fillies Alshakr (Group Two Falmouth Stakes) and Secret History (Group Three Musidora Stakes), and this year's Zetland Gold Cup winner, Chantaco.

All the above stallions give mare owners from all over Europe the chance to use the very best blood available on the most reasonable terms. Sheikh Hamdan also supports local breeders, and the industry in Ireland in general, by buying yearlings at Goffs and Tattersalls sales each autumn.

As a horseman himself, Sheikh Hamdan also had the vision to see how important it was to encourage young staff working in the training stables in Ireland by sponsoring the ever-popular Derrinstown Stud Apprentice Series. Now firmly established in the Irish racing year, it has had the effect of encouraging trainers to give riding opportunities to young lads who might otherwise have been overlooked. The 35 races throughout Ireland are keenly contested and culminate in a valuable and prestigious final at the famous Curragh racecourse in October.

Prize money for the apprentices extends down to sixth place, while the winner's Master also receives a prize, as does the trainer of the most individual winners during the series. Last year, a special prize was also instigated for the 'Rookie of the Year' and awarded to the most successful first season apprentice.

All this is ample evidence indeed of Sheikh Hamdan's, and Derrinstown Stud's, continued commitment to the industry which supports the sport we all love and live for.

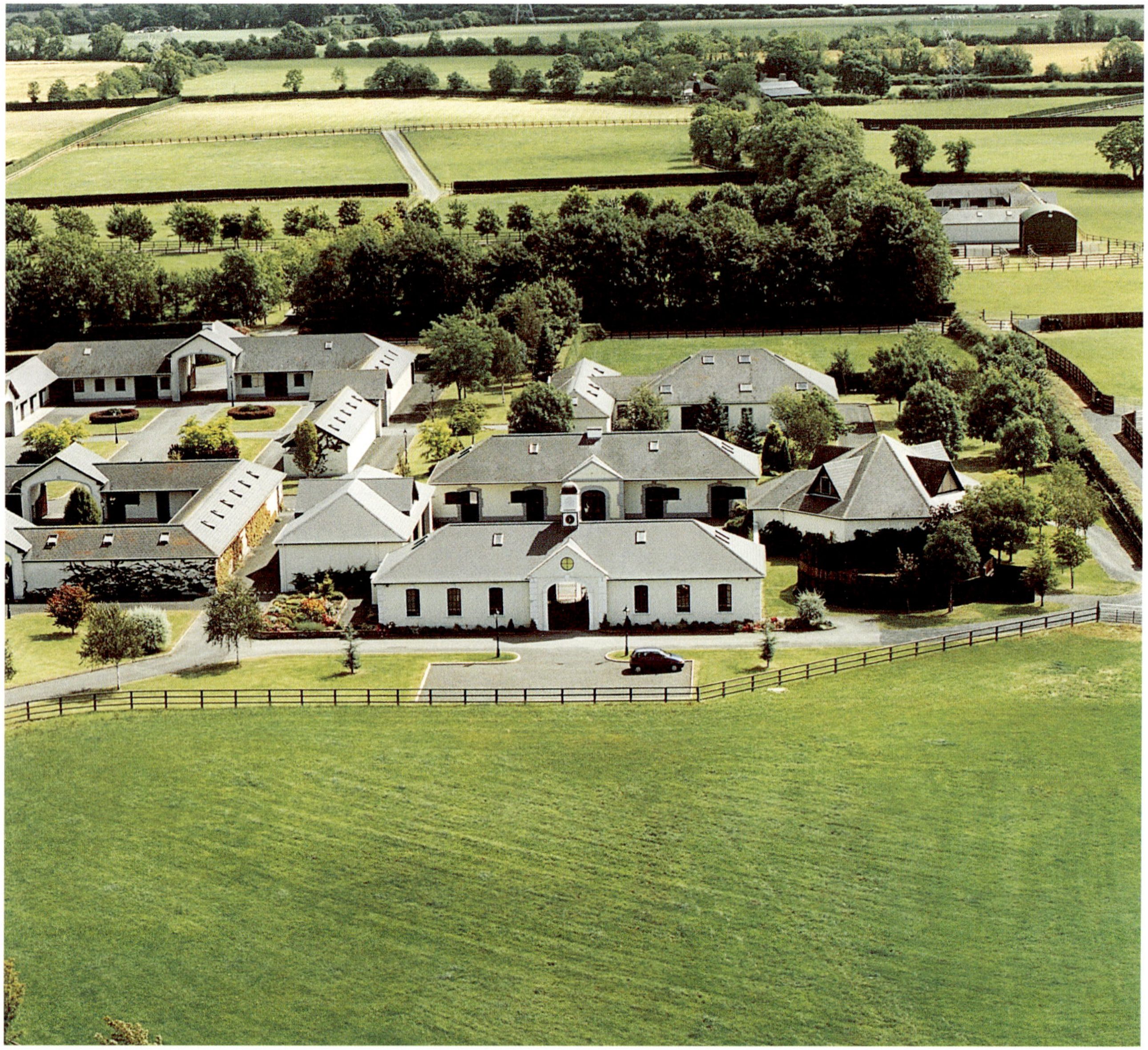

Alhaarth

European Champion 2yo by Unfuwain, winning seven Group races, including a defeat of Danehill Dancer in the Gr.1 Dewhurst Stakes. Quickly established himself as a top European Classic Sire with such winners as HAAFHD (Gr.1 2000 Guineas & Gr.1 Champion Stakes). PHOENIX REACH (Gr.1 Sheema Classic & Gr.1 Canadian International) and mutiple Group winners BANDARI, DOMINICA, etc. Winner of 8 races, including 7 Group races and £374,467, incl:

Won	Gr.1	**GENEROUS DEWHURST STAKES**, 7f, Newmarket.
Won	Gr.2	**LAURENT-PERRIER CHAMPAGNE STAKES**, 7f, Doncaster.
Won	Gr.2	**PRIX DU ROND-POINT,** 8f, Longchamp.
Won	Gr.2	**BUDWEISER AMERICAN BOWL STAKES**, 8f, The Curragh.

Almutawakel

Bred and raised at Derrinstown, Almutawakel won the world's richest race – the Gr.1 Dubai World Cup in a new course record time. Also Gr.1 winner in France. By the great sire of leading sires Machiavellian, he is out of a Green Desert mare and is a full-brother to Muwakleh (UAE 1000 Guineas and runner-up in 1000 Guineas, Newmarket). Almutawakel is already sire of SILVER CUP (Gr.2 Italian 1000 Guineas and a triple Gr.2 winner in U.S.A. in 2006) and WAHID (dual Gr.1 winner in New Zealand). Winner of 4 races and £2,196,551 at 2, 3 and 4 years (7-10f), incl:

Won	Gr.1	**DUBAI WORLD CUP**, 10f, in track record time, Nad al Sheba.
Won	Gr.1	**PRIX JEAN PRAT**, 9f, Chantilly.
2nd	Gr.1	**GRAND PRIX DE PARIS**, 10f (btn. nk), Longchamp.
2nd	Gr.1	**WOODWARD STAKES**, 9f *(btn. nose)*, Belmont Park.

Bahri

European Champion Miler, by Champion Sire Riverman. Winner of 3 races at, £481,090 over 6 to 8f. His victories in the Gr.1 St James's Palace Stakes and the Queen Elizabeth II Stakes (by 4 and 6 lengths respectively) ensured his championship status. Retired to Shadwell Farm in Kentucky, he moved to Derrinstown in time for the 2004 season. Sire of European Champion SAKHEE (Gr.1 Prix de l'Arc de Triomphe & Gr.1 Juddmonte International), ALSHAKR (Gr.2 Falmouth Stakes) and SECRET HISTORY (Gr.3 Musidora Stakes). Won 3 races and £481,090 at 2 and 3 years (6-8f), *viz:*

Won	Gr.1	**QUEEN ELIZABETH II STAKES**, 8f, by 6 lengths, Ascot.
Won	Gr.1	**ST JAMES'S PALACE STAKES**, 8f, by 4 lengths, Royal Ascot.
Won		**SHERWOOD STAKES**, 6f, by 6 lengths at 2, Nottingham.
2nd	Gr.1	**SUSSEX STAKES**, 8f, Goodwood.
2nd	Gr.1	**JUDDMONTE INTERNATIONAL STAKES**, 10.5f, York.

Elnadim

A Group One winning son of Danzig, Elnadim is a dual Champion Sprinter, including the Gr.1 July Cup and Gr.2 Diadem Stakes. Retired to stud at Shadwell in Kentucky, he relocated to Derrinstown in 2002. His first European crop of 2yos included an excellent 13 individual winners. Also sire of Australian Gr.2 winner PENDRAGON (also Gr.1 placed twice). Over 80 per cent of his second European crop ywo-year-olds have won or been placed to date.

Won	Gr.1	**JULY CUP**, 6f, Newmarket, in new course record time of 1m 9.7s, by 2 lengths.
Won	Gr.2	**DIADEM STAKES**, 6f, Ascot.
Won	LR	**HOPEFUL STAKES**, 6f, Newmarket.

Racehorses of 1998: 128 ..."*an imposing colt...*"

TIMEFORM'S CHAMPION SPRINTER OF 1997 AND 1998

Intikhab

World Champion Turf Horse and Champion European Miler. Earned an annual rating of 135 after beating a top-class field in the Gr.2 Queen Anne Stakes *(now Gr.1)* at Royal Ascot, by 8 lengths. Established as a successful stakes sire incl. RED EVIE (unbeaten winner of 5 races in 2006, incl. LR Sandringham at Royal Ascot), HOH MIKE (2nd Gr.2 Norfolk Stakes, Royal Ascot), etc. Earlier winners include PAITA (Gr.1 Criterium de Saint-Cloud), TOUPIE (also 2nd Gr.1 French 2000 Guineas), MOON UNIT, etc. Winner of 8 races, £233,395, at 2, 3 and 4 years (6-9f):

Won	Gr.2	**QUEEN ANNE STAKES**, 8f, Royal Ascot, by 8 lengths.
Won	Gr.3	**DIOMED STAKES**, 8.5f, Epsom, by 5 lengths.
Won	LR	**JOEL STAKES**, 8f, by 2 lengths.
Won	LR	**FORTUNE STAKES**, 8.5f, Epsom.

Racehorses of 1998: 138

TIMEFORM'S CHAMPION OLDER HORSE OF 1998

Marju

Firmly established as one of Europe's most consistent stallions. On the racecourse, Marju won the Gr.1 St James's Palace Stakes and was runner-up to Generous in the Gr.1 Derby Stakes, at Epsom. At stud Marju is sire of such high-class performers as SOVIET SONG (Gr.1 x 5 and Gr.2 Windsor Forest Stakes, Royal Ascot, 2006), and other Group 1 winners MY EMMA, SIL SILA, MARBYE, MARJU SNIP and VIVA PATICA *(in 2006)*. Won 3 races, £282,640 at 2 and 3 years, from 7-8 furlongs:

Won	Gr.1	**ST JAMES'S PALACE STAKES**, 8f, Royal Ascot.
Won	Gr.3	**CRAVEN STAKES**, 8f, Newmarket.
Won		**NEW ZEALAND STAKES**, 7f, York unextended by 6 lengths – only start at 2.
2nd	Gr.1	**DERBY STAKES**, 12f, Epsom.

Almutawakel

b. c by Machiavellian — Elfaslah (Green Desert)

This Godolphin juvenile first appeared in the racecourse in a July 1997 Sandown maiden, winning the event, added a Newmarket conditions race and finished second in the Stardom Stakes. Almutawakel then appeared in the Royal Lodge States, where he finished fifth.

Almutawakel wintered in Dubai and progressed enough to warrant the status of Godolphin second string in the 2000 Guineas. Relatively unfancied, he ran a brave race in the Classic in claiming seventh, just five lengths off King of Kings. After a win in the Prix Jean Prat at Chantilly and second in the Grand Prix Du Paris, he returned to Dubai.

It was February before it became clear that Godolphin thought Almutawakel a potential runner in the Dubai World Cup. In the weeks before the race he was to play second-fiddle to Epsom Derby star High-Rise, but come the evening of the world's richest race, jockey Richard Hills went to post on a colt that was quietly fancied.

In the event, Almutawakel looked very much at home on the Nad Al Sheba sand surface. When Hills asked for an effort the response was both breathtaking and immediate. Challenged late by US raider Malek, Almutawakel quickened again to claim a thrilling home victory. For the 30,000 people at Nad Al Sheba that evening, Almutawakel had provided a fairy tale finish, amid scenes of emotion that even the most hardened racing follower had to admit were unique.

Success in Dubai and Almutawakel's obvious liking for a dirt surface led to his shipping to the US the following September, after a seventh on turf in the Juddmonte International Stakes at York.

Back on his favoured surface in America, Almutawakel began to shine in a campaign designed to take him to the Breeders' Cup Classic, finishing second in the Grade One Woodward Stakes at Belmont Park.

At the same venue in October, dropped down to a sharp nine furlong trip for the Jockey Club Gold Cup, he finished an excellent third. Finally, he ended his career with a superb fifth in the Breeders' Cup Classic.

Halo	Mr Prospector	**Raise A Native** / Gold Digger
	Coup De Folie	**Machiavellian** / Raise The Standard
ALMUTAWAKEL (b. 1995)		
Elfaslah	Green Desert	Danzig / Foreign Courier
	Fair Of The Furze	Ela-Mana-Mou / Autocratic

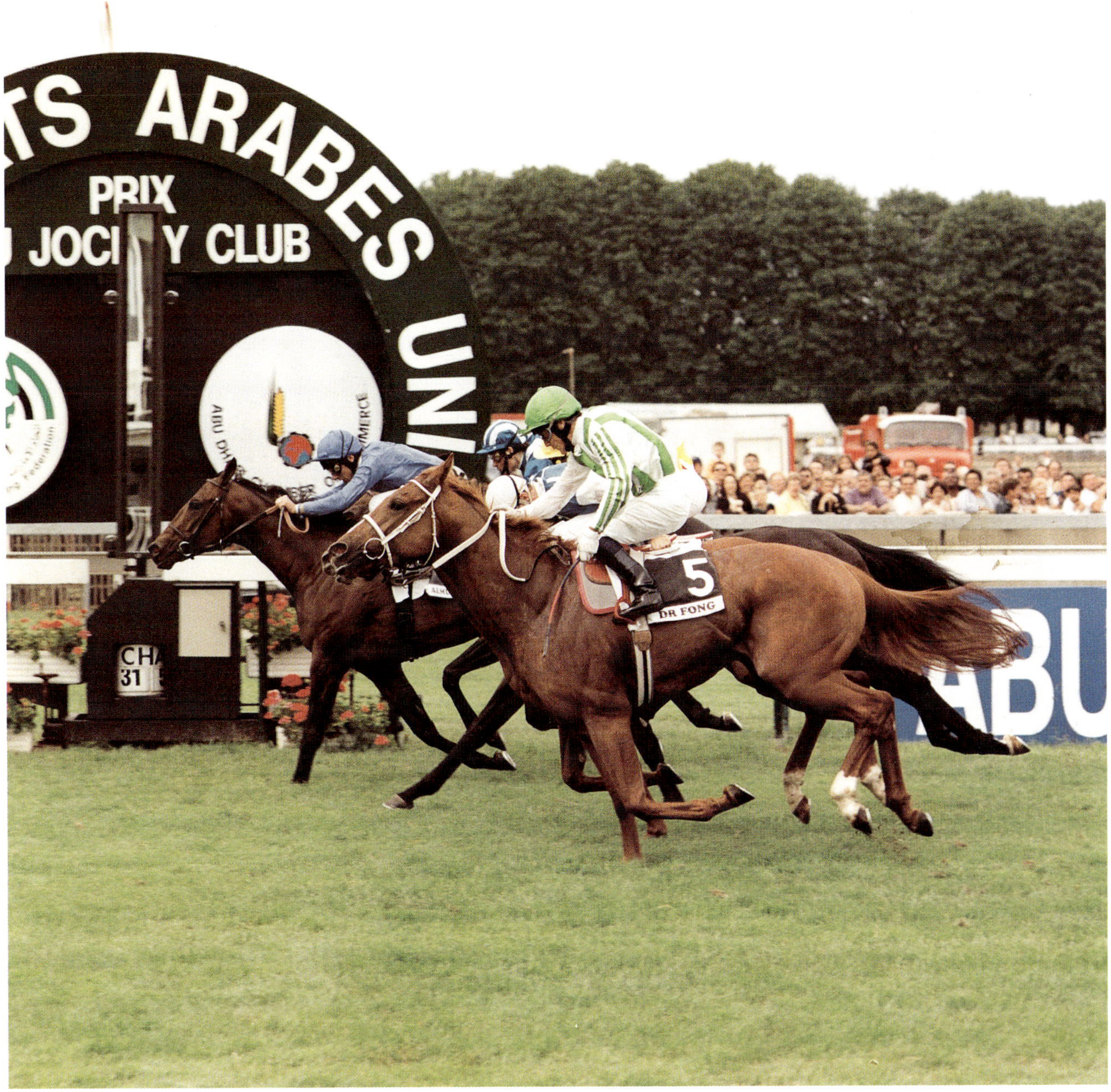
TS ARABES UNI
PRIX
U JOC Y CLUB
5
DR FONG
ABU

Ameerat
b. f by Mark of Esteem - Walimu (Top Ville)

Ameerat has the best possible start to her racing career. She was bred in the purple, by Godolphin campaigned champion miler Mark Of Esteem. She was also heavily influenced by the greatest stallion of modern times. Mark Of Esteem's dam was a grand-daughter of Northern Dancer. Ameerat's granddam Summer Impressions is also a grand-daughter of Northern Dancer.

As a two-year-old her class on the gallops at home was enough to ensure a big name even before she set foot on a racecourse. After a maiden success, trainer Michael Jarvis routed her into better company. She took a glowing reputation to Goodwood in August and an easy win there showed further improvement.

Next came a stern test against some of the best of her generation. Stepping up to Group Three company for the Rothmans Royals May Hill Stakes at Doncaster, Ameerat was always moving well throughout and when asked for an effort a success looked likely. One was better, however, although an excellent one length second to Karasta ensured that she would end the campaign with hopes for 2001 high. An end of season 106 rating on official figures rubber stamped her progress and confirmed that she was considered one of the very best fillies of her generation.

Despite no-prep race that spring, Jarvis had his charge in superb condition for the 1000 Guineas. She had trained on and looked a picture in the Newmarket parade ring. And on the racecourse, her looks were equally matched by her outstanding performance.

Well fancied Goldolphin filly Muwakleh, the mount of Frankie Dettori, had led from the start and looked to make all. Muwakleh looked to have victory in her grasp as they met the rising ground, but Sheikh Ahmed's familiar yellow and black silks were now prominent. Ridden by Philip Robinson, Ameerat made a brilliant late surge to win the classic by a neck, taking the lead only in the dying strides.

Robinson had won the race on Sheikh Mohammed's Pebbles in 1984. It was Jarvis' first English classic in 33 years as a trainer.

Ameerat would run well, but never quite reach such heady heights again that season. But her place in the history books was already asured.

AMEERAT (b. 1998)	**Mark of Esteem (b. 1993)**	Darshaan — **Shirley Heights** / **Delay**
		Homage — **Ajdal** / **Home Love**
	Walimu (b. 1989)	Top Ville — **High Top** / **Sega Ville**
		Summer Imp's — **Lyphard** / **Roussalka**

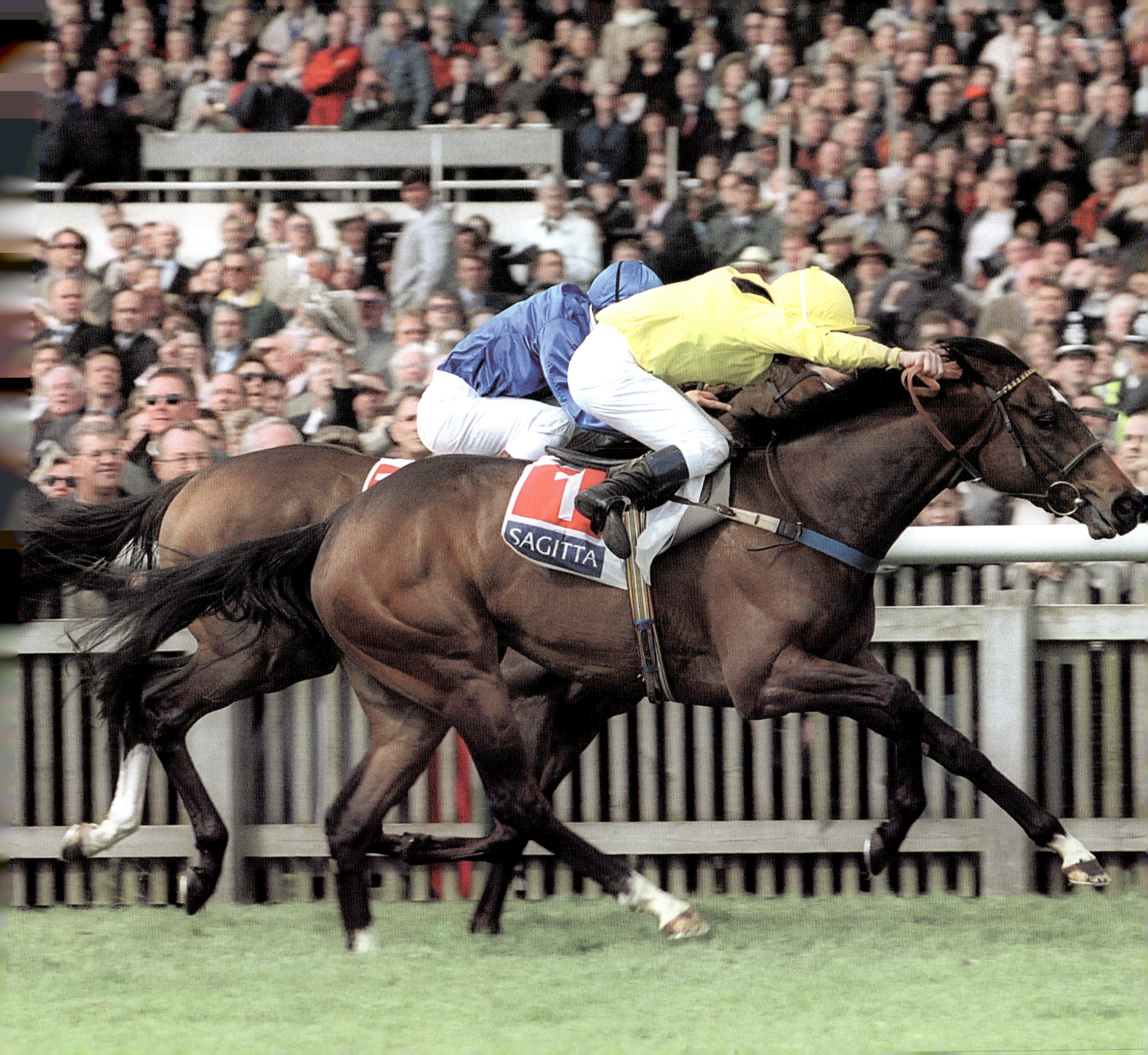
SAGITTA

At Talaq

b. h by Roberto - My Nord (Vent Du Nord)

While the Maktoum empire blossomed in Europe during the mid-1980s, Australian opportunities had not gone unnoticed. An early bearer of Maktoum colours in the Southern Hemisphere was At Talaq, who had more than proven himself in group company in Britain, tackling top class races in nearly all of his 12 starts and winning the 1994 French St Leger at Longchamp for trainer Tom Jones.

It was Jones who believed his charge suitable for Australia and proposed this to Sheikh Hamdan's main trainer down under, Colin Hayes, when they met at Keenland in 1985.

The colt debuted in Australia in a mile event at Moonee Valley early the following year, finishing fourth over what was for him a sharp trip. Just a fortnight later he contested the Group One Queen Elizabeth II Stakes over a more suitable 2,000 metres, and finished an eye-catching third to Tristarc.

Placed in his third start, at Victoria Park, At Talaq faltered in his fourth outing, finishing 11th of 12 in a minor event. He was subsequently found to have a virus. After a period sidelined, the colt returned to the track with a Cups campaign firmly in Hayes's mind. At Talaq let nobody down.

Showing improved form, he ran a succession of good races in Group One and Group Two company, including runner-up in the Caulfield Cup in October.

That performance put the horse firmly on course for the Melbourne Cup, at Flemington, a track which the trainer believed suited his charge like no other on the continent. His final prep race for the big event was in the LKS Mackinnon Stakes, at Flemington, in which he finally got his head in front at the wire beating the useful colour page.

This victory brought At Talaq into consideration for the Melbourne Cup, Australia's biggest race. Given a superb ride by Michael Clarke, At Talaq did plenty of work at both ends of the race, leaving his rivals with no room for excuse as he outstayed placed finishers Rising Fear and Sea Legend.

Continuing his form, At Talaq added the C F Orr Stakes three months later, completing a hat trick of successes.

Aimed at the Australian Cup in early March, At Talaq found only Bonecrusher too hot to handle, finishing second. He was retired following a fourth in the H E Tancred Stakes in April.

	Hail to Reason	Turn-to
Roberto (b. 1969)		Nothirdchance
	Bramalea	Nashua
AL TALAQ (b. 1981)		Rarelea
	Vent du Nord	Vandale
My Nord (br. 1973)		La Caravelle
	My Alison	Courtly Delight
		Stellar Role

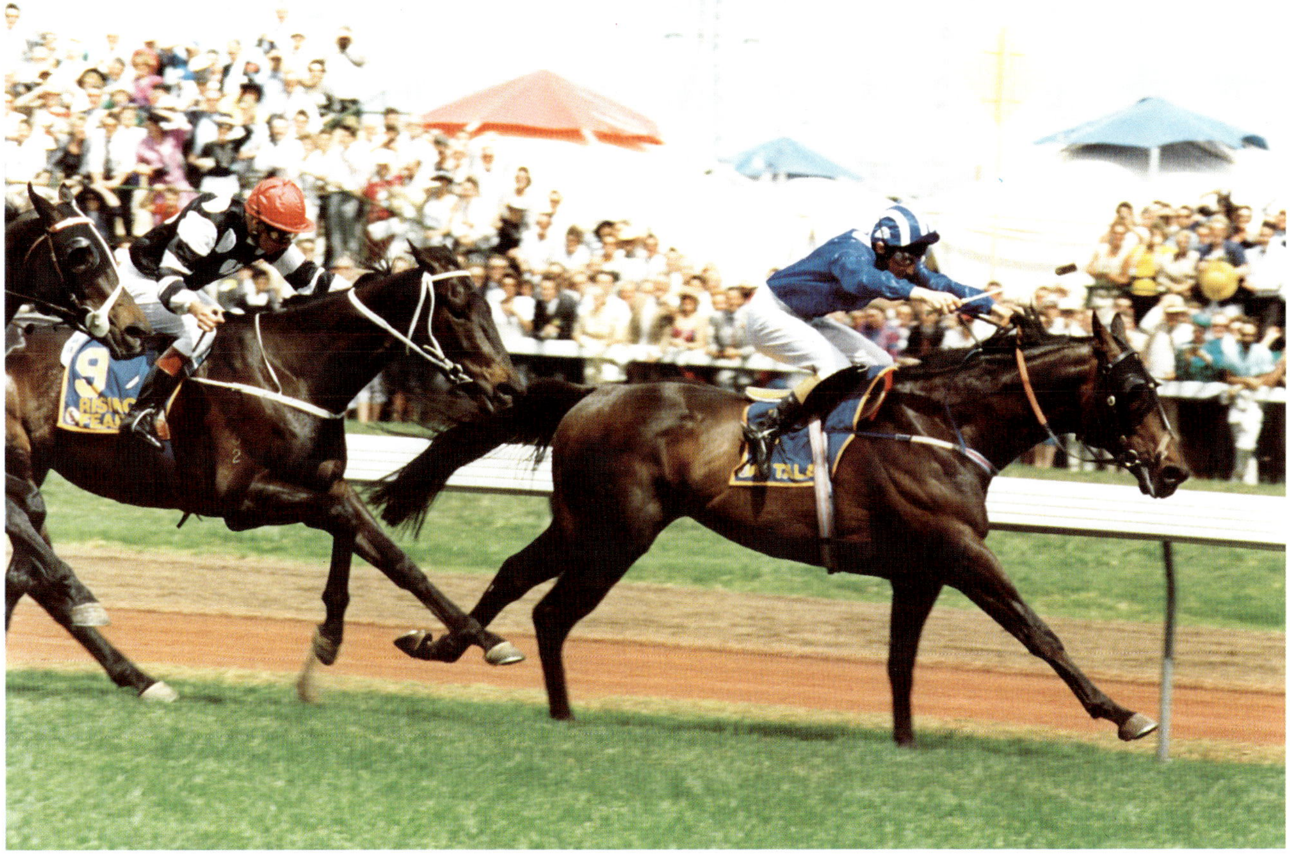

Bachir

b. c by Desert Style - Morning Welcome (Be My Guest)

Bachir was a classic, *pun intended*, example of the brilliance of the Godolphin team and its programme. Snatched from his British base following a classy, but not top drawer, campaign Bachir bloomed in Dubai and returned to Europe to make history during his three-year-old campaign.

Bred from the female family line of Pitcairn, and from the first crop of Desert Style, who represented Dubai's Ruling family on the racecourse, Bachir was a coup for his stallion. Highlighting the likes of Northern Dancer and Sadler's Wells, Tony Morris wrote in the *Racing Post* in 2000 that; "the horse starting out at stud with a first-crop son who surpasses him in achievement, and out of a mare of no particular distinction, allows hope that he might develop that admirable habit."

Bachir went into training with John Gosden. He burst onto the scene with a pair of successes in his first two starts. The opener came in a relatively minor six furlong median auction event at Chepstow.

But, thereafter, Bachir was to be campaigned in only the highest company. His second success came in the Group Two Richmond Stakes where he won well for Sheikh Mohammed, Gosden and jockey Frankie Dettori. Two Group One thirds ended his juvenile campaign, in the Prix Morny and Prix de la Salamandre. In the latter contest, at Longchamp, he finished four lengths behind Giant's Causeway.

The colt reappeared for his three-year-old season showing improvement to claim the Khor Dubai at Nad Al Sheba, and then finished second in the UAE Derby to stablemate China Visit, perhaps failing to stay an extra furlong.

He was dropped back to one mile for his seasonal bow in Europe, the Gainsborough Poule d'Essai des Poulains, the French 2000 Guineas, at Longchamp. In Paris he proved one and a half lengths too powerful for Berine's Son.

Two weeks later Bachir claimed a slice of history and a piece of revenge. Despite facing stiffer opposition in the Irish 2000 Guineas at the Curragh, Bachir pulled off a unique classic double, making all to defeat the redoubtable Giant's Causeway by a neck.

After below par performances at Royal Ascot and Goodwood, Bachir was then retired.

	Green Desert	**Danzig**
Desert Style (b. 1982)		**Foreign Courier**
	organza	**High Top**
BACHIR (b. 1997)		**Canton Silk**
	Be My Guest	**Northern Dancer**
Morning Welcome (ch. 1989)		**What A Treat**
	Dawn Is Breaking	**Import**
		Brief Chorus

Bachir runs second to China Visit in the UAE Derby.

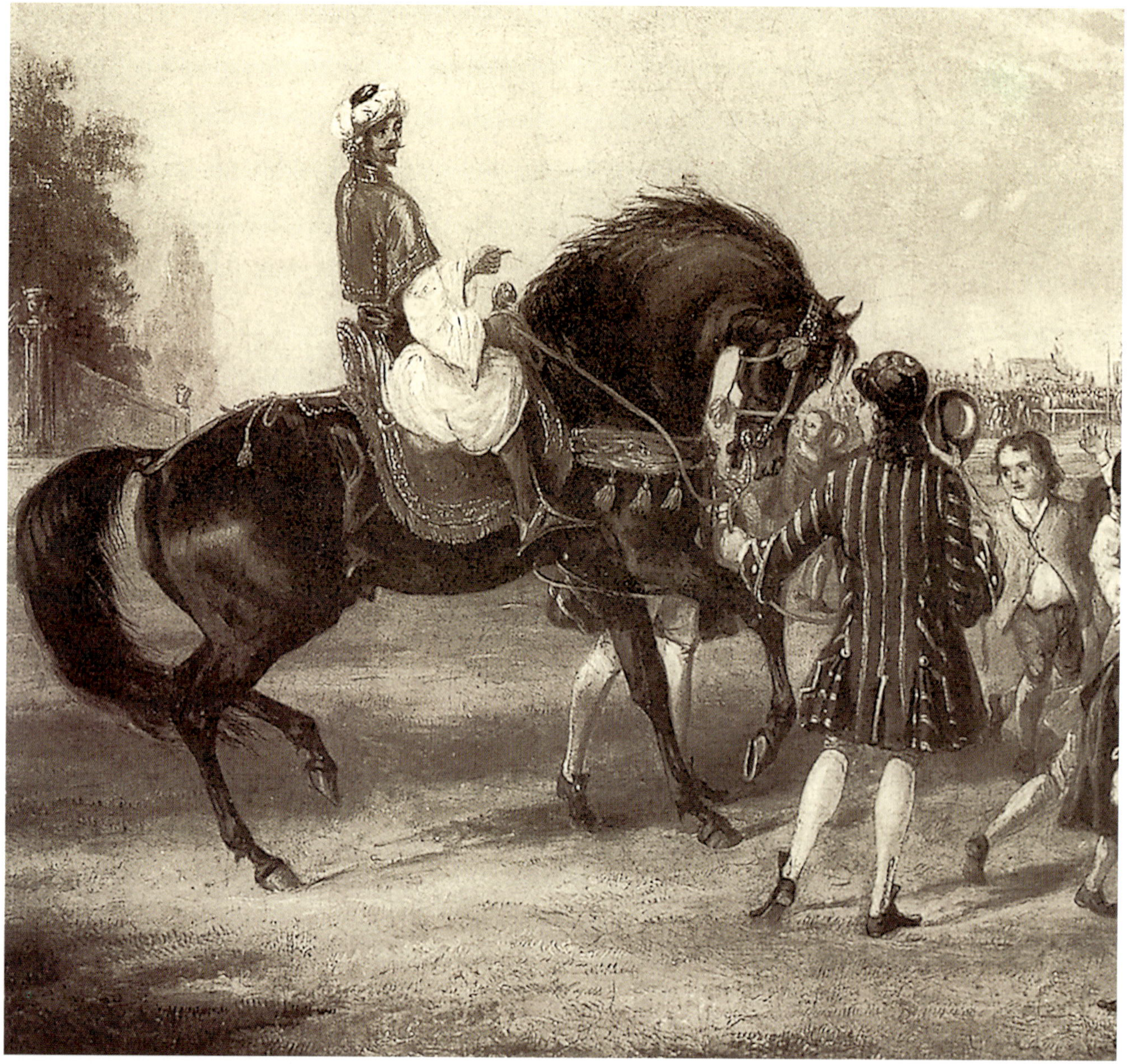

The Legacy of Godolphin Arabian

His proud neck arched, his bold eyes flashing and his nostrils flaring, an Arab stallion walks with prancing gait. He is bridled and reined with silken cords; tassels hang from his breastplate and saddle. His rider sits on him somewhat nonchalantly, trusting his fiery steed to the firm hold of two attendants, clad in the livery of jockeys of the eighteenth century, for the ground that he is pawing is not the hot sand of Arabia but the turf of the Knavesmire or Newmarket.

The rider, both by his dress and his demeanour, is evidently a stranger to these parts for he hold out a pointing finger, apparently asking the way to the starting post, where three horses can be seen waiting in the background. Edgar Wallace wrote a short story about a small boy, dangerously ill, who wished to see before he died what he described as a 'proud horse'. The horse depicted would have been just what the doctor ordered. The proud horse is Sham, the Godolphin Arabian.

The picture *(left)*, Turner's front piece to Eugene Sue's fantasy about the Godolphin Arabian, may be as highly imaginative as the book itself and may depict a casting director's notion of the ideal Arab, but it may also be a good likeness according to those who saw Sham in life.

Sham, the name if pronounced to rhyme with 'charm' not 'ham' was a dark bay brown with a white mark on the inside of his off hind coronet. He was a horse of great beauty with a wild haughty appearance. He had the head of the typical Arabian, full of fire and character, though more masculine than pretty, which is probably why one writer describes a certain plainness of head and ears.

His head was set on a beautifully curved neck with a pronounced crest, 'the knight of the Wonderful Crest' Nimrod called him. He was a short-backed horse with muscled loins and a high, broad croup. The muscles of his loin were 'inserted into his quarters with great strength and power than any horse yet seen of his dimensions. He stood 14.2 hh. One critic states that he was narrow in front and rather on the leg, but the Vicomte de Manty, who saw Sham when he was in France, writes:

'He was of beautiful conformation, exquisitely proportioned with large hocks, will let down, with legs of iron, with unequalled lightness of forehand - a horse of incomparable beauty whose only flaw was being headstrong. An essentially strong stallion type, his quarters broad in spite of being half starved, tail carried in true Arabian style.'

What one writer describes as 'narrow in front'

appears to another as 'unequalled lightness of forehand'. In any case to be narrow in front might well have been a virtue, for of all the breeds of horses the thoroughbred is the narrowest in front and a stallion of this thoroughbred evolution.

Sham was foaled in the dark ages before Volume One of the General Stud Book had been published and of all the horses of that era of myth and legend none has been the subject of more fantasies than Sham. Lady Wentworth, by far the most reliable source, has carefully presented all the evidence, factual, written and hearsay, as to the origins of this Arabian. It seems that he was of the Jilfan blood of Yemen, and was exported via Syria to the stud of the Bey of Tunis. In 1730 the Bey presented four Arabian horses to the King of France. Three of these were turned out in the forests of Brittany to improve the local stock and the other, who was Sham, was sold to Edward Coke, the proprietor of St James's Coffee House, for his stud at Longford Hall in Derbyshire.

One of the myths concerning Sham tells of the Arabian pulling a water cart during his stay in France, a story often repeated in print. It appeared in Professor Ridgeway's treatise on the origins of the thoroughbred, and Theo Taunton in Famous Horses writes that the Godolphin was believed to have been stolen and subsequently bought from the owner of a water cart.

This is nonsense but every legend springs from a well of truth, however distorted it may become in the re-telling. The Vicomte, writes:

'The horses arrived in poor condition and were very thin and, though put in the Royal stables, were despised and neglected and the grooms disliked them because they were quick and fiery and hard to ride. One of these was Shami, a bay brown with reddish mottle and very little white on his hind feet.'

Here, then, is the origin of the tale. It would be a small step from saying 'in poor condition' to 'half-starved' to 'looks has if he has been pulling a cart'. The description of his temperament destroys the truth of the truth of the story as effectively as Sham would have broken up the cart.

In 1733 Mr. Coke died and bequeathed his mares to the second Earl of Godolphin, who then bought Sham from Roger Williams, who had inherited the stallions of the stud. And so Sham became the Godolphin Arabian, and remained so for at least a hundred years, as it was then that Nimrod, the best-known Turf historian of the period, wrote, 'In his reign (George II's) the Godolphin Arabian appeared, the founder of our best blood.' Then suddenly, with as little evidence as there is to attribute the works of Shakespeare to Bacon or Marlowe or Lord Tom Noddy, some writers decided that the Godolphin Arabian was a Barb. This conclusion was reached on two premises – portraits of Sham and the 'failure' of the Godolphin line. The chief 'barbarian' was a Captain Upton, who wrote:

'The original portrait of the Godolphin Arabian I have not seen. All the prints of him do not correspond; but the impression of the countenance and the outline of the head as generally depicted would lead me to the supposition that he was a horse of Northern Africa (commonly called a Barb) and not of pure or unmixed blood, which can be further strengthened by the drawing of the ears, which are shown as lopping outwards.'

The gallant captain was right to say that all the prints do not correspond. Most of them do not even show the correct markings and are not even of the horse. However, the eventual compilers of the *General Stud Book* took Captain Upton's venture in art criticism seriously and inserted the following in the Stud Book:

'Whether he was an Arabian or a Barb is a point disputed (his portrait would rather lead to the latter supposition) but his excellence as a stallion is generally admitted. There is an original portrait of the horse in Lord Cholmondely's collection at Houghton. Comparing it with Mr. Stubbs' print of him, it will seem that disproportionately small limbs as represented in the latter do not accord with the painting.'

Another to have been misled by this picture more recently was Martin E. Eversfield, contributor to *Thoroughbred Breeding of the World*, published in Germany in 1970. He writes:

'this brown Barb standing about fifteen hands (looking at his picture we are tempted to accept the fact of his Moroccan origin) was so prepotent in his stud career that he rivaled for the leadership with the other two 'legs of the tripod' the Byerley Turk and the Darley Arabian ... Students of the effect left on the thoroughbred by both Arabian and Barb believe that the "Godolphin" was possessed of a lesser degree of prepotency because he was not a horse of pure Arabian origin, the latter being credited with more outstanding prepotency'

This is an extraordinary surmise. Does the writer suggest that the Alcock Arabian, Gibson's Grey Arabian, the Honeywood White Arabian, the Malcolm Arabian, the Bloody Shouldered Arabian, Bell's Arabian, the Woodstock Arabian, the Lonsdale Bay Arabian, Oglethorpe's Arabian, the Oysterfoot Arabian, the Cyprus Arabian, Litton's Chestnut Arabian et al could not have been Arabians because they possessed 'a lesser degree of potency' than did

Sham if Sham was a Barb?

The portrait at Houghton is not an original but a copy of what is alleged to have been an original painting by David Morier. The Houghton painting was not painted from life and it seems it might have been painted many years after Sham's death because it bears the inscription:

'Esteemed one of the best Foreign Horses ever brought to England. Appearing so both from the country he came from and from the Performance of his Posterity. The being Excellent both as Racers and Stallions and Hitting with most other Pedigrees and mending ye Imperfections of Their Shape. And is allowed to have refreshed the English Blood more than any Foreign Horse ever imported.'

Whoever worded the inscription begged the question of the horse's breed and origin. He must have been puzzled, for the horse depicted was undoubtedly a Barb, while at that time there was no suggestion that Sham was anything but an Arabian.

Now Lord Godolphin *(right)* had a Barb, in fact he had two Barbs. One was a grey and the other was a brown, the same colour as Sham except that he had a star. It seems possible that David Morier asked to paint the Godolphin Arabian when he had become so famous after his death, may have used Lord Godolphin's Brown Western Barb as a model, painting in Sham's markings and his famous crest. There is a portrait of the Godolphin Arabian painted by Wootton, signed by the artist and dated 1731. The horse is Arabian and is undoubtedly Sham.

C.M. Prior, who wrote so many books on the early history of the thoroughbred and who had in his possession the manuscript stud books of both Edward Coke and Lord Godolphin, wrote:

'In case any doubt should still exist after the written testimony of both his owners and anyone should persist in saying that the Godolphin was a Barb, the evidence of Osmer should be conclusive on this point. He knew the horse better than any other writer, as he was personally well acquainted with him, and invariably alluded to him as an Arabian, further mentioning that: "Barbs may in general easily be known by an observant eye."

The suggestion of failure of the Godolphin line might similarly be said of the St Simon line, since both stallions dominated the breed of the thoroughbred in their time. The impact of the Godolphin Arabian on the breed is amazing considering how sparingly he was used; he sired ninety foals in a stud career of twenty-two years. The veterinary surgeon, Osmer, mentioned above, writing shortly after Sham's death says; "it was a pity that he was not used more universally for better mares."

Despite this, the Stud Book (1858) states: 'It is remarkable that there is not a superior horse now on the Turf without a cross of the Godolphin Arabian, neither has there been for many years past.'

The Godolphin arrived at stud a generation or so later than many of the other great Eastern horses. Gossip about him started right away. It was said that he was used as a teaser for Hobgoblin, and that it was only after the latter refused to cover Roxana that Sham was used. Lady Wentworth has given her vision of Eugene Sue's description of the mating from his extravaganza, which is worth repeating for her footnote. 'We have the melodramatic story of his fight with Hobgoblin for the lovely Roxana; the horses trying to stun each other with furious charges.'

Lady Wentworth's delightfully malicious comment is; 'Sue's foster mother as a child was a nanny goat, which perhaps explains his primitive ideas of fighting by butting.' C.M. Prior discounts the whole story on the grounds that, firstly since Hobgoblin was racing in 1730 and 1732, it is unlikely that he would have been brought back to stud in 1931, and secondly there is no record in Lord Godolphin's stud book that Hobgoblin covered any mares in 1735. On the other hand the reverse might be true, i.e. that he went to stud in 1731 and, because of his failure to do his duty, was brought back to racing in 1732. Whether the story is true or not is immaterial. The Godolphin Arabian was mated with Roxana and the result was the good racehorse, Lath.

Lath was the best racehorse of his day. He beat Squirt, who was to become the grandsire of Eclipse, in the Great Stakes at Newmarket. Although there is no record of the distance over which this race was run, all the runners carried the same weight of 8 stone 7 lbs and they were all of the same age so it might be said to have been a forerunner of the classic as we know them today, although this race was for four-year-olds. It was not until 1858 that the ages of racehorses were reckoned from New Year's Day and in the old days, much more sensibly and more naturally, their official birthday was the first of May, it was a mistake to have changed it. As the Great Stakes (a splendid name – I wonder why it is not used today?) was run at the end of April, the classic contenders were almost five-year-olds.

A son of the Godolphin Arabian with not such a splendid name was Cripple, but Cripple's son had a name that is almost as well known today as that of Matchem. This was the little dark grey horse, Gimcrack – 'the sweetest little horse that ever was' as Lady Sarah Bunbury declared when she saw Gimcrack win. 'and the sweetest little horse he has remained to every lover of the Turf from that day to this,' as Sir Thomas Cook has added. This great stayer raced for eight seasons and won twenty-five races all over the country, but oddly he was beaten the only two times he ran at York, where the race baring his name is run and where the owner of the winner is allowed a free rein at the Gimcrack Dinner to tell the guests how racing should be run. Gimcrack must have been one of the first racehorses to have crossed to France. As his wins over long distances prompted Count Lauraguais to buy him to win a bet that a horse could cover 22 1/2 miles in an hour; the Count won his bet and Gimcrack returned to England to continue his winning ways. As he only stood about 14 hh he was always a good thing in give and take races, which were handicapped by height so he made a speciality of them.

Another of the progeny of the Godolphin is commemorated by a race to this day – the Selima Stakes for two-year-old fillies at Laurel. Selima was exported to the States in 1750 and was unbeaten there. In addition to the stake money for the Selima Stakes there is a cup bearing the inscription: 'This cup is presented by Belair Stud (William Woodward, owner) in memory of Selima (by the Godolphin Arabian) imported to Belair in the reign of George the Second, Selima the ancestress of Hanover, Foxhall

PATEK PHILIPPE
GENEVE

Begin your *own* tradition.

You never actually
own a Patek Philippe.

✧

You merely look
after it for the *next*
generation.

Men's Annual Calendar
Ref. 5146J by Patek Philippe.

AHMED SEDDIQI & SONS   أحمد صديقي وأولاده

Wafi City Tel: (04) 3243030, Burjuman Centre Tel: (04) 3559090
www.seddiqi.com

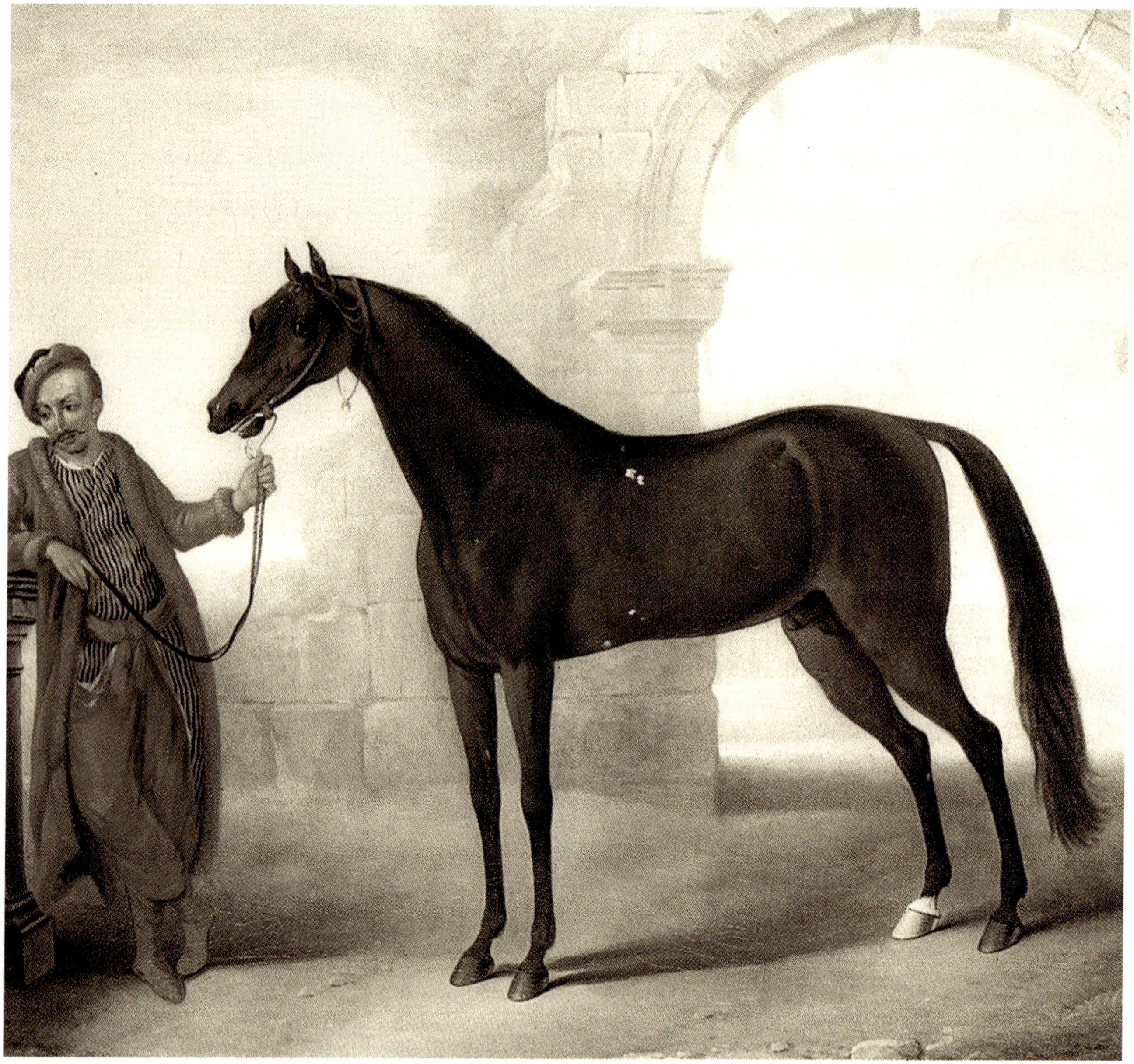

and many fine racehorses.'

Regulus, whom Sham got in 1739, won seven Royal Plates and was never beaten. He is a most important link in the chain of thoroughbred inheritance as he is the sire of Spiletta, the dam of Eclipse. It is recorded in the General Stud Book that "Eclipse was so called, not because he eclipsed all his competitors, but from having been foaled during the great eclipse in 1764."

He was bred by Duke of Cumberland, who did not live to see what great horse his famous stud had produced, and was sold to a Mr Wildman when little more than a yearling. Wildman turned up late for the sale but found it had started too early, so with his eye on Eclipse, insisted that the lots be resold. He did not race the colt until he was five. Eclipse won his first heat and it was after that Dennis O'Kelly made his famous bet of "Eclipse first and the rest nowhere". His bet came off as, in the second heat, Eclipse outdistanced the others, a distance being 240 yards. O'Kelly bought a half-share in the horse, who throughout his career showed himself to be head and shoulders above any other thoroughbred. Eclipse won every race he contested with astonishing ease, he was sound in wind and limb, and could carry big weights; in addition to his speed and stride he could stay, and was never thoroughly tested.

Another daughter of Regulus was the dam of MacHeath, who in seven weeks travelled and raced 500 miles winning six four-year-old plates. One of the first thoroughbreds to make a name for himself in the United States was Brutus, a roan son of Regulus and Miss Layton. Miss Layton, also known as Lodge's Roan Mare, was descended from a Barb mare given by the Emperor of Morocco to Lord Arlington when he was Secretary of State for King Charles II. Edward Fenwick, a relation of the breeder of Matchem, had established a large stud in South Carolina and imported a number of stallions and mares from England. Naturally, in view of his family's successes with the son of Cade, he was very keen on the blood of the Godolphin Arabian *(left)*. Brutus was most successful there.

Babraham, another son of the Godolphin, was far more typical physically of the line as we have known it in this century than the little grey Gimcrack. He was 'a fine, strong horse, 16 hands high and master of 18 stone'. So near to the original Arab source this was an exceptional height and he is the only horse whose height comes in for specific mention in the General Stud Book. He won numerous races in 1748 and managed to cover fifty-three mares in the same season. He met defeat at the hands of another son of Godolphin, Bijazet, over six miles at Newmarket, each carrying 12 stone.

The Godolphin bred another successful sire, particularly of broodmares, in Blank. The phenomenal success of the Duke of Grafton's stud owed a lot to Blank's daughter, Julia. Mated to a daughter of Regulus he bred Rachel. This mare, who was inbred to the Godolphin Arabian with no free generations (2 x 2), bred the unbeaten Highflyer, who was born beneath the Highflyer walnut trees in the paddocks of Sir Charles Bunbury, who won the first Derby with Diomed. He was buried at Highflyer Hall, built near Ely by Mr Tattersall, where the memorial stone reads:

'Here lieth the perfect and beautiful symmetry of the much lamented Highflyer, by whom and his wonderful offspring the celebrated Tattersall acquired a noble fortune, but was not ashamed to acknowledge it.'

The great Highflyer was not named immediately, which was unfortunate and would have saved a deal of argument as Highflyer's unbeaten record depends on the records of two races. Firstly, a race over the Beacon course at Newmarket, won incidentally by a son of Gimcrack, with Sir John Moore's bay colt by Herod unplaced. A racegoer present stated, 'over a bottle of port' it is written, that this bay colt was subsequently named Highflyer. As it does not say after how many bottles of port, the evidence must be suspect!

The second race in which Highflyer is alleged to have been beaten, was in a race from 'The Ditch In' won by Quicksand, 'Lord Bolingbroke's colt by Herod was unplaced'. Lord Bolingbroke owned a colt by Herod out of Marotte and it seems probable that this is the colt referred to on both occasions. The first volume of the Stud Book reads: 'Highflyer never paid forfeit and was never beaten. The author is induced to deviate thus far from his general plan, at the request of an old sportsman, from whom he learns that many bets have been made on this fact, owing to an error in the Index to the Racing Calendar of 1777, wherein Highflyer is confounded with a colt of the same age, got by Herod out of Marotte.' Well, thank heavens that horses have to be named today before they can run and that we have the *Calendar* and *Timeform* and *Raceform Up-To-Date* et al.

Highflyer bred three Derby winners in four years: Noble, Sir Peter Teazle and Skyscraper.

Rachel had another successful son in Mark Anthony, who won twenty of his twenty-eight races. He sired a Derby winner in Aimwell, the only horse to win the Derby who is not descended from the three great foundation sires – Godolphin *(above)* and Darley Arabian and the Byerley Turk. He was descended from the Alcock Arabian.

Yet another daughter of Blank bred Goldfinder, who was never beaten, and was to challenge the great Eclipse. The excitement awaiting the meeting of these two unbeaten horses for the Kings Plate in 1770 was intense, but, unfortunately Goldfinder broke down at exercise shortly before the race.

The year after producing Lath, Roxana died foaling Cade, the son of the Godolphin Arabian who was to hand on the line, to be reared on cow's milk. Cade was not as good a racehorse as his full brother, Lath, but he was a very good stallion, who besides Matchem, got another branch of the line that ran for a few generations. His son Changeling got Le Sang, sire of Bourbon, winner of the St Leger, and of Duchess, winner of the Doncaster Cup; Le Sang himself was out of a mare called Duchess, winner of the Doncaster Cup; Le Sang himself was out of a mare called Duchess. Bourbon won the St Leger in 1777, the year before the classic was named after Lt General Anthony St Leger of Park Hill. Presumably the Park Hill Stakes, the equivalent of the fillies' St Leger, is named after his residence. The progeny of Le Sang ran first and second as Bourbon beat a filly Ballad Singer by Le Sang. He was ridden by a well-known Yorkshire jockey called John Cade.

Cade's famous son, Matchem, gave his name to the male line of the Godolphin Arabian just as did Eclipse to that of the Darley Arabian (*pictured*)) and Herod to that of the Byerley Turk. The name he gave to the line is often spelt Match'em but it is recorded in the General Stud Book that in 1748 the Partner Mare (Mr Crofts 1733) bred a bay colt called Matchem by Cade. Around this time they were not too particular about giving horses a name as there are ten Partner Mares in the stud book belonging to Mr Crofts and another eight belonging to other breeders! Bred way up in Northumberland at Bywell, where Lord Allendale now lives, by William Fenwick, Matchem made a winning first appearance at York then won again in his home county. He won three times the next season and then went, unbeaten, South of Newmarket, where he beat a good horse in Trajan by Regulus, with the others distanced. In this race Trajan had shown the better speed and his defeat was put down to lack of condition, a suggestion that William Fenwick immediately countered by challenging for the Whip.

The Whip, which is said to have been carried by Charles II when he rode at Newmarket, hangs over

64

the fireplace of the coffee room in the Jockey Club rooms. Round the handle of the trophy and also in place of the keeper are hairs from the mane or tail of Eclipse. A challenge for the Whip was decided over 4 1/4 miles. Matchem, ridden by the Yorkshire jockey, John Singleton, started favourite but Trajan was a hard puller and went so far in front that long odds were laid on him, but Matchem got up to his opponent and went on to win easily. He won one other race before going to stud at only 5 guineas.

The first of his offspring, Caesario, proved a good one. From then on his fee went up and up to keep pace with his numerous winners year after year. He was still going strong in his old age, getting the St Leger winner, Hollandise, when he was twenty-six and Teetotum, winner of the Oaks *(left, Epsom)*, when he was twenty-eight.

In 1772, his progeny won 15.5 per cent of the stake money on offer during the season! The St Leger that Hollandaise won was the first to first to be run after the race had been named. She was a grey filly and was ridden by George Herring, who was later tragically killed at Hull. The Doncaster *(pictured below)* meeting should have seen a great double for Matchem as his son, Magog, also a grey, would almost certainly have won the Doncaster Cup had he not been most brutally got at by having his tongue nearly severed. The race was cancelled. Despite his injury he, like Sea Cottage who was shot in the quarters, came back to win several more races.

Pumpkin was one of the very best sons of Matchem and at Newmarket he beat Firetail and Conductor, the son of Matchem that was destined to carry on the line. Stubbs painted Pumpkin many times, being very fond of his characteristic head and face with its big blaze. Conductor was the winner of ten races. He was a chestnut and got ten foals out of a mare called Brunette, recorded as a brown filly. Five of these foals were black, among them Trumpator. A columnist who wrote under the name of 'Matchem' states that 'Matchem was a racy black horse whereas most of his well-known representatives are chestnuts. As I have written above, Matchem is recorded in the stud book as a bay, but that is no certainty as black coat colour in the thoroughbred is difficult to follow. Firstly, because it is sometimes mistaken for brown and vice versa and, secondly, because for some reason the colour appears to be unpopular, with the result that blacks are often registered as browns. Black is somehow associated with temperament, a belief that gentle 'Black Beauty' and those sedate plumed horses carrying people to rest have done nothing to allay ('neither shies he nor is restive' as Kipling describes 'The Undertaker's Horse'). However, many of the best horses of the Godolphin line were black.

The black Trumpator stood 15.2 hh, i.e. a hand higher than his grandsire. His mating with Prunella was an alliance that had an immediate and enduring effect on the history of the Turf. Prunella, by Highflyer, is named by Dennis Craig as the greatest 'cluster' or foundation mare known to racing. Within six generations she produced among her direct descendants in the female line ten winners of the Derby, seven winners of the Oaks, three winners of the St Leger, eleven winners of the Two Thousand Guineas and eleven winners of the One Thousand Guineas. To Trumpator she bred the wonderful mare Penelope. Not only did she win sixteen races but she proved herself a very great broodmare. She found her ideal mate in Waxy to whom she threw eleven foals and then proved her own prepotence by breeding a classic winner to Rubens. Among the firmest believers in inbreeding to the Godolphin Arabian was the Third Duke of Grafton (1735-1811), for many years as enthusiastic a foxhunter as he was a racing man. While Prime Minister from 1766 to 1770 he was mercilessly pilloried by the anonymous writer of 'The Letters of Junius', who denounced him as 'profligate without gaiety'. An extraordinary character, the Duke *(pictured)* outraged the undemanding morals of Georgian society by flaunting his lovely mistress Nancy Parsons at the races before becoming a strict Unitarian in old age, and devoting himself to the writing of religious tracts. He mated Penelope to Waxy 'for the reason that she, being herself inbred to the Godolphin Arabian of whom there were five strains of her, would be most suitably mated if put to a horse in whom there were three strains of the Godolphin Arabian. 'The Duke had a very different idea from the 'barbarians', who decried the Godolphin Arabian and described him as a Barb, as to the advisability of using horses and mares of the Godolphin line. The matings of Waxy and Penelope produced wonderful results, among them Whalebone, Web, Woful and Whisker.

Whalebone was one of the great forefathers of the thoroughbred. He founded three great sire lines of Eclipse through his sons Camel, Defence and Sir Hercules that carry through to this day. His groom said of him 'he was the lowest, longest and most double – jointed horse, with the best legs and the worst feet.' That well-known writer 'the Druid' agreed about his feet and says, 'Whalebone was as shabby as old Prunella herself. He was broad and strong with a shortish neck. He stood just over 15 hh and was a mottled brown horse with an off-hind white fetlock. He won many races including the Derby of 1810. Besides the great male families he founded he bred Lapdog and Spaniel, both of whom won the Derby, and Caroline, who won the Oaks.

Web was a good broodmare and a great foundation mare. She bred Middleton, who won the Derby in 1825, and would have foaled another Derby winner in Glenarthey had he not been pulled to let his stable companion, Mameluke, win. Her daughter, Filigree, was dam of Riddlesworth, winner of the Two Thousand Guineas, in 1831, and of the great mare Cobweb, who won the One Thousand Guineas and the Oaks herself in 1824 and then foaled three classic winners.

Woful was a good race horse and sire, who won twelve races and sired fifty-eight winners before going to Germany. He got Theodore who won the St Leger in 1822. Theodore was desperately unsound and was so lame when produced for the Leger that his owner sold his book and all his chances for £200. The odds against him were fantastic: £1000 to a walking stick being laid and the official starting price was 200-1. He jumped off in front and was never headed.

Woful's did well winning four classics. Augusta won the Oaks in 1821, Arab the One Thousand in 1827 and Zinc both of these races in 1823.

'Whisker was as near perfection in looks as anything could be with the exception of being a little calf-kneed,' so wrote 'The Druid'. Whisker won the Derby in 1815 by a 'whisker' as he just got up in the last stride to beat General Gower's Raphaei with the same owner's Busto a neck away third. Whisker was probably lucky to win the Derby, as had not Busto been sent out on a peacemaking mission, he must surely have beaten Whisker as he had done before at Newmarket. Whisker won three races the next season but was not a great racehorse and retired to stud at a modest 15 guineas which quickly rose as he made a name for himself in his new role. He founded a sire line which ran through Economy, Harkaway, and King Tom, second in the Derby and leading sire in 1870 when his son, Kingcraft, won the Derby. Harkaway is not a horse of the Godolphin line but he had more of the Arabian's blood in him than any horse standing during his generation. Two of Whisker's sons won the St Leger, the Colonel and Memono. The Colonel also ran a dead-heat with Cadland for the Derby but lost the run-off. Whisker was a great sire of broodmares. The most famous of them was Emma, who bred two winners of the Derby in Munding and Cotherstone and was grandma of the Triple Crown winner, West Australian, one of the greatest of the male descendants of the Godolphin.

Prunella had been a granddaughter of the Godolphin's granddaughter Rachel and when Trumpator was put to anther granddaughter he got Paynator. Paynator was very similar in looks to his sire, but not so lengthy. He stood about 15.2 hh and his stock had remarkably good legs and neat heads.

The Paynator branch of Matchem might, but for bad luck, have carried on in tail male to this day, and, through her son, Newminster, in the male line of Eclipse.

Trumpator's son Paynator, who was out of a Mark Anthony mare, got a little horse standing 15 hh, Doctor Syntax. Because of his size his owner decided to have him cut as a hack for his son. It was a very hot day when the vet came so it was decided to postpone the operation. The trainer, John Lonsdale, called in and was so taken with the yearling that he persuaded his breeder to part with him. He a horse of great character with an eye 'as full and bright as a hawk's' and a head very broad at the base of the nose with wide flairing nostrils. His hind quarters fell away rather sharply from the croup and he was rather short-quartered. Mouse in colour he was remarkably short-coated, so that a brief canter would bring his veins standing out like a network. Nimrod wrote that Doctor Syntax was descended from 'our very stoutest blood'.

He needed to be from 'our very stoutest blood' not only to make up for his lack of inches but because he was raced for ten years, during which time he won twenty Gold Cups. It was said of him that 'he was shod with gold cups' and an attempt was made to make this come true. He liked to make his own running and cut his opponents down. In anticipation of his eighth successive victory in the Preston Gold Cup a set of golden shoes was prepared, but he never got to wear them. Bob Johnson his usual jockey could not ride him. The pair had built up a legend something like Brown Jack and Steve Donoghue did in the Queen Alexandra Stakes between the two world wars. Johnson understood the old horse, who would have nothing to do with whips or spurs, and would coax him on by talking to him or in moments of extreme urgency, by hissing at him. Doctor Syntax took an instant dislike to his substitute and tried to savage him. The old horse needed to be at his best to win the Preston Gold Cup as he was opposed by two formidable rivals, both winners of the St Leger, Reveller and Jack Spigot. He was in one of his very worst moods and his new jockey could not get him to do his best and he was beaten by Reveller. Doctor Syntax finished his career by winning the Richmond Gold Cup but collapsed twenty yards past the post. He never ran again. He had been a legend in his time, always way out in front, making the running; he won twenty-four races. Despite his fame and popularity he was neglected at stud because of his small stature and uncertain temper. It was a great pity as he turned out a first-class sire and he might well have founded another line of Matchem had he gone to stud earlier.

Doctor Syntax got one in his own image, for if 'the Doctor' was the Brown Jack of his day, his daughter Bee's-Wing was the Brown Jill of hers. She was a bay mare with black points, 'light of bone and small, but well ribbed up and had good broad hips and the sweetest of heads.' Bee's-Wing not only took after her little sire in looks but she had a deal of his temperament too, for she was a tremendous kicker in the stall, although a sweet ride. Doncaster was her favourite stamping ground. She won the Champagne Stakes, was third in the St Leger and won the Doncaster Cup in 1837, 1840, 1841 and 1842. In the year of her last victory at Doncaster her admirers wanted her to contest the Ascot Gold Cup. Her owner, William Orde, was enthusiastic about it but her jockey, Bob Johnson, was not at all keen; 'let south coom to't North if they want to be beat; not we gang to them.' Nevertheless they went and the Ascot Gold Gup joined all the other trophies. In all this wonderful mare won fifty-two races, including the Newcastle Cup in her home county six times.

Those who deplore hard racing for future broodmares might expect that the last might have been heard of Bee's-Wing when she went to stud. Apparently she was used for a hack for a bit and so was not asked to produce a foal until she was ten-years-old. She then bred eight foals in nine years. This wonderful mare transferred her success on the racecourse to the paddocks as her first-born, Nunnykirk, won the Two Thousand Guineas and ran second to the famous racehorse, The Flying Dutchman, in the St Leger. Nunnykirk, inherited his mother's head for he is described as having 'a sweet head and a still sweeter action'. His brother, Newminster, had this good action too. Although he was not so pretty a horse as Nunnykirk, he was better ribbed up and 'he went near the ground with great leverage behind and his style of creeping along without any bustle was quite beautiful to see.' But he was such a shocking walker that there were no takers when offered for £1200. His trainer had a lot of trouble with his teeth and his feet and he had to miss the Derby and York, and even at Doncaster had not got him to his liking. Nevertheless he won the St Leger easily by three lengths. Newminster never won again but at stud, unhandicapped by his physical disabilities, he proved a great sire getting such as Hermit and Lord Clifden.

Through the former was handed on the line of descent from Whalebone and through the latter was handed on a branch of Eclipse that leads to Hyperion and it is not surprising that in those "professional chefs-de-race" as Son-in-Law and Bayardo runs the blood of that great staying mare Bee's-Wing. In tail female are descended from Bee's-Wing numerous classic winners of this century: The Panther, Herringbone, Brown Betty, Tideway, Sunstream, Mid-Day Sun, Royal Lancer and Singapore

The unbeaten Galopade was a son of Doctor Syntax and inherited his sire's Midas touch, for he won four Gold Cups on his only four outings. The Doctor's best son was Ralph, who inherited his sire's fine velvety skin as he seemed to have no hair except on his mane and tail. He fulfilled his promise by winning the Two Thousand Guineas in 1841. He credited Doctor Syntax with his second Ascot Gold Cup in succession when he won that race the year after Bee's-Wing's victory, but pulled up in distress. Poor Ralph had been got at and died. With him died a chance of handing on a branch of the Matchem line.

The value of such horses of the calibre of Doctor Syntax and Bee's-Wing, or for that matter Brown Jack and Secretariat *(pictured above)*, cannot be assessed in their winnings. Every victory they score is a moral tonic of the Turf cancelling out the bad reputation earned for it by dopers and others trying to make a quick buck.

Reproduced with the kind permission of Mourdant Miller

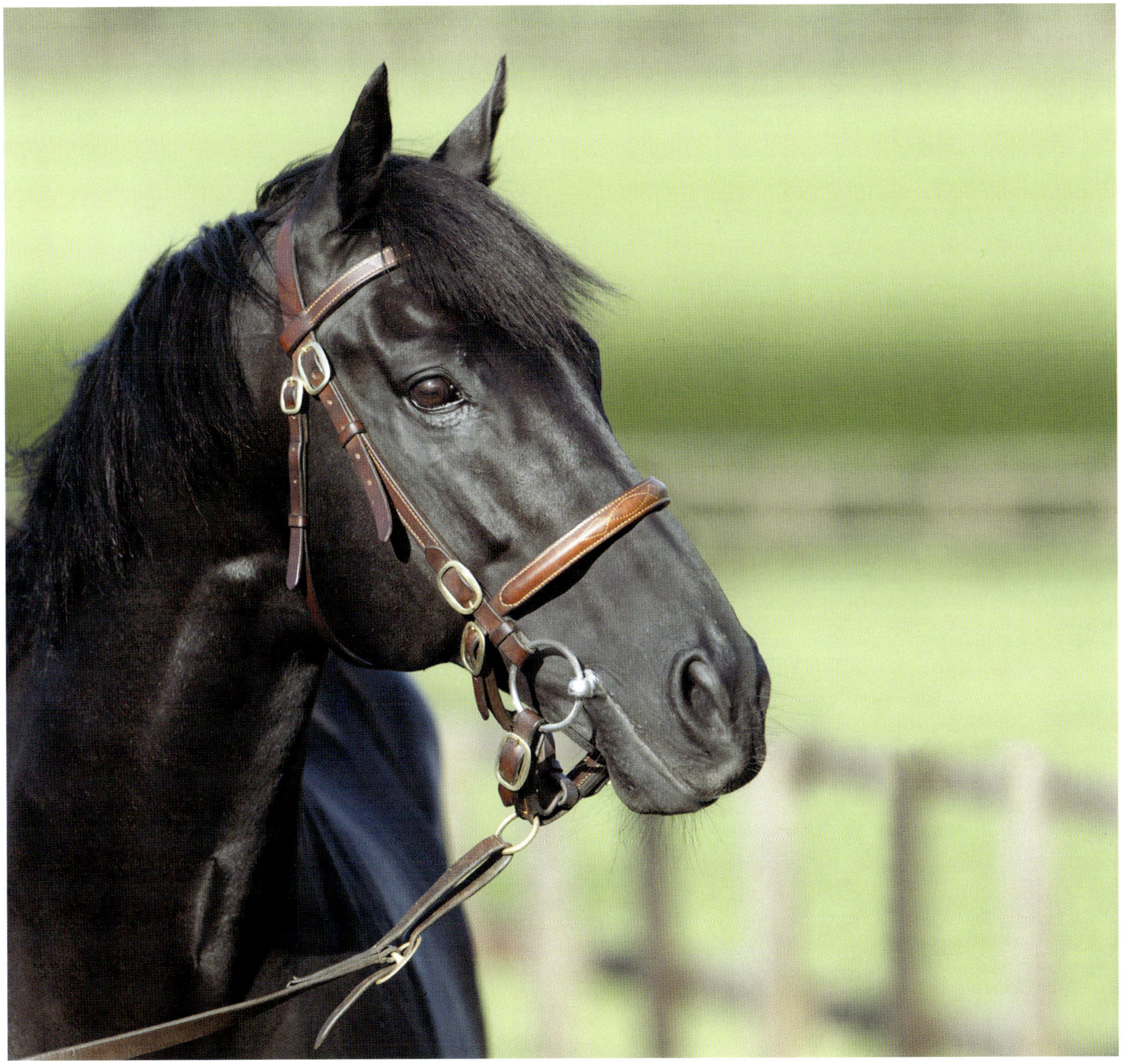

Balanchine

ch. f by Storm Bird — Morning Devotion (Affirmed)

If one horse can be said to have sealed the argument on international training, she is Balanchine. An impressive Newbury maiden winner, she also took a minor Salisbury event as a juvenile before going into the winter viewed by trainer Peter Chapple-Hyam as an interesting prospect.

The filly changed hands soon after as part of a group of four sold by Robert Sangster to Sheikh Mohammed and was subsequently shipped to Dubai. She returned to Britain under the care of Sheikh Mohammed's newly-formed Godolphin operation and immediately made an impact of her seasonal debut in the 1000 Guineas. Clearly one who relished further than a mile, Balanchine showed true tenacity when missing out to Las Meninas by a fraction of an inch, the official minimum distance of a short head being a poor reflection of the closeness of the pair.

One month later, over rain-softened ground at Epsom, Balanchine claimed Godolphin's—and her own—first Classic with an uncompromising relentless gallop.

Immediately following her success at Epsom, Balanchine was targeted for the Irish Derby where she would be taking on the leading colts of her generation. Despite facing a class field at the Curragh, Balanchine was, if anything, showing even better form. Moving well in the early stages and looking comfortable, the filly began a run three furlongs out and, on hitting the front, had the race won.

One furlong from home she was fully in command and finished comfortably in front of King's Theater. In doing so she became only the third filly to win the Irish Derby this century.

Tragically, mid-July changed the whole complexion of her dual Classic-winning career when Balanchine was struck down with a life-threatening bout of colic. She recovered, but was again under a cloud in August when she suffered a second, milder attack.

Plans for the latter end of the season were shelved in favour of a second winter in the Gulf. However, when Balanchine returned to Europe the following spring she was not the same filly.

After finishing out the frame in the Prince of Wales's Stakes at Royal Ascot, another layoff ensued, following which she ran a promising second in the Prix Foy to Carnegie. A tenth position in the Prix de l'Arc de Triomphe proved to be her final race.

```
                              Northern Dancer    Nearctic
                                                 Natalma
            Storm Bird (b. 1978)
                              South Ocean        New Providence
                                                 Shining Sun
BALANCHINE (ch. 1991)
                              Affirmed           Exclusive Native
                                                 Won't Tell You
            Morning Devotion (ch. 1982)
                              Morning Has Broken Prince John
                                                 A Wing is Rising
```

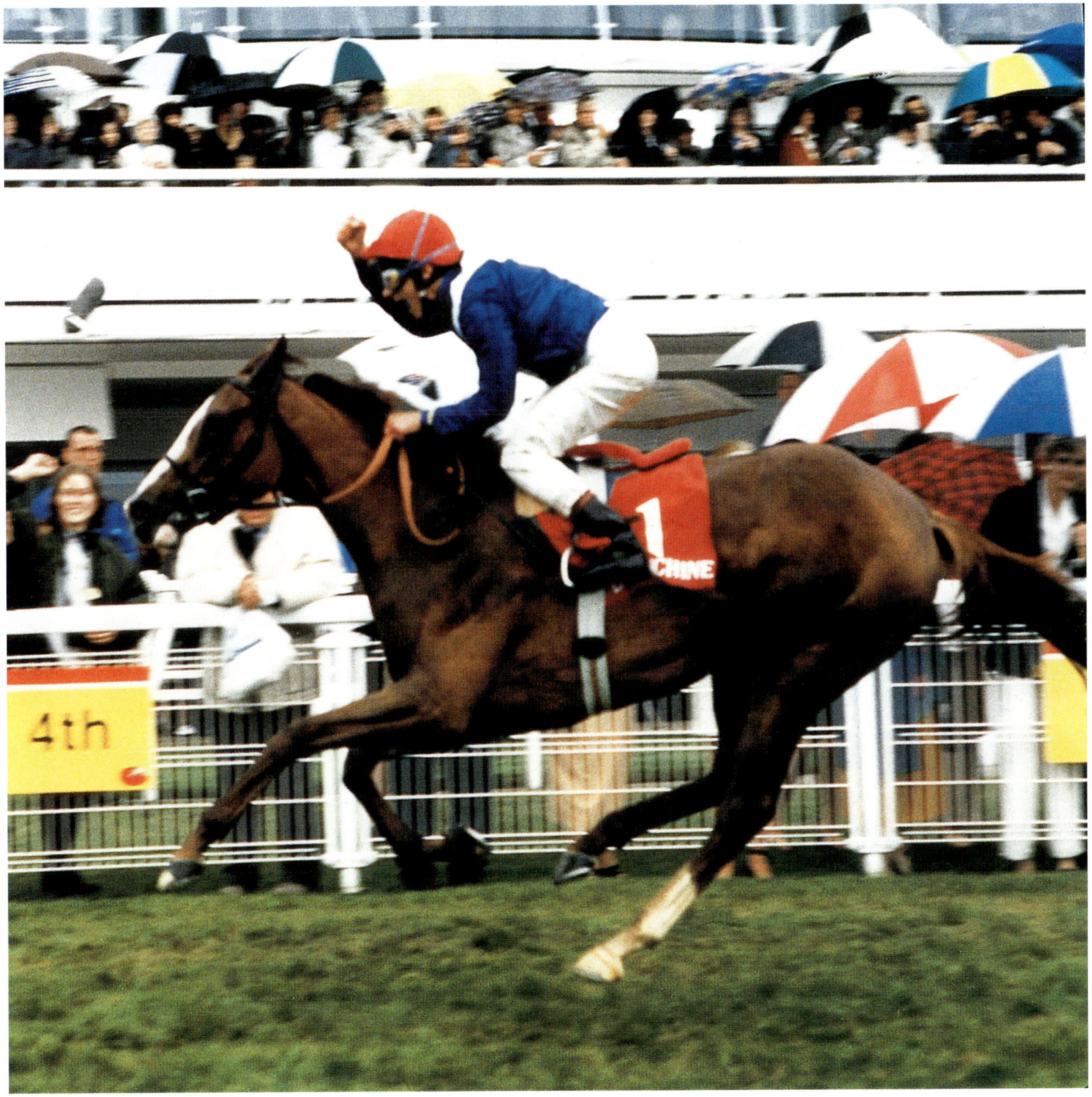
4th
1
CHINE

Barathea

b. c by Sadler's Wells — Brocade (Habitat)

After just two racecourse performances as a juvenile, Barathea had all the embodiments of the talent that was take him all the way to the top in his final start two seasons later. He began with victory in the second division of a Newmarket maiden and followed up in the Houghton Stakes, a race often used as a stepping-stone to better things.

Reappearing at three to finish a close fourth in the Craven Stakes, Barathea went in to the 2000 Guineas shading the well thought of Zafonic as favourite. After finishing second by three and half lengths to that rival, he travelled to Ireland where he won the Irish 2000 Guineas

Apparently needing further, the colt was moved up to 12 furlongs for the Epsom Derby. The Blue Riband found him out when, after travelling strongly for much of the way, he faded in the late stages to finish fifth, nine lengths adrift of winner, Commander in Chief.

On his next start he took on 10 furlongs, and the favourite tag, in the Eclipse Stakes, but again faded into fifth after travelling well early. Trainer Luca Cumani then campaigned his charge back over a mile for the remainder of the summer, finding limited results in the Prix du Moulin de Longchamp, Queen Elizabeth II Stakes and Breeders' Cup Mile.

He returned to the track the following year in the Queen Anne Stakes, giving weight to all his rivals and regained a winning thread. After a surprisingly competitive sprint performance in the July Cup, in which he finished fourth by only one length to Lochsong, he returned to a favoured mile trip in the Sussex Stakes. This time Barathea had all the hallmarks of a winner in the latter stages when surging clear below the distance. Only a sustained challenge from Distant View could overhaul him in the final strides.

After failing to headline in the Prix Jacques le Marois at Deauville and second to shock winner Maroof in the Queen Elizabeth II Stakes at Ascot, he was again pointed towards the Breeders' Cup Mile. Arriving at Churchill Downs his future was already decided, having been purchased for stud duties for a reported £5 million. Always travelling well in the big race, he entered the short home run just behind the leaders and when unleashed came with a superb run to claim the race.

BARATHEA (b. 1990)		
Sadler's Wells (b. 1981)	Northern Dancer	Nearctic
		Natalma
	Fairy Bridge	Bold Reason
		Special
Brocade (b. 1981)	Habitat	Sir Gaylord
		Little Hut
	Canton Silk	Runnymede
		Clouded Lamp

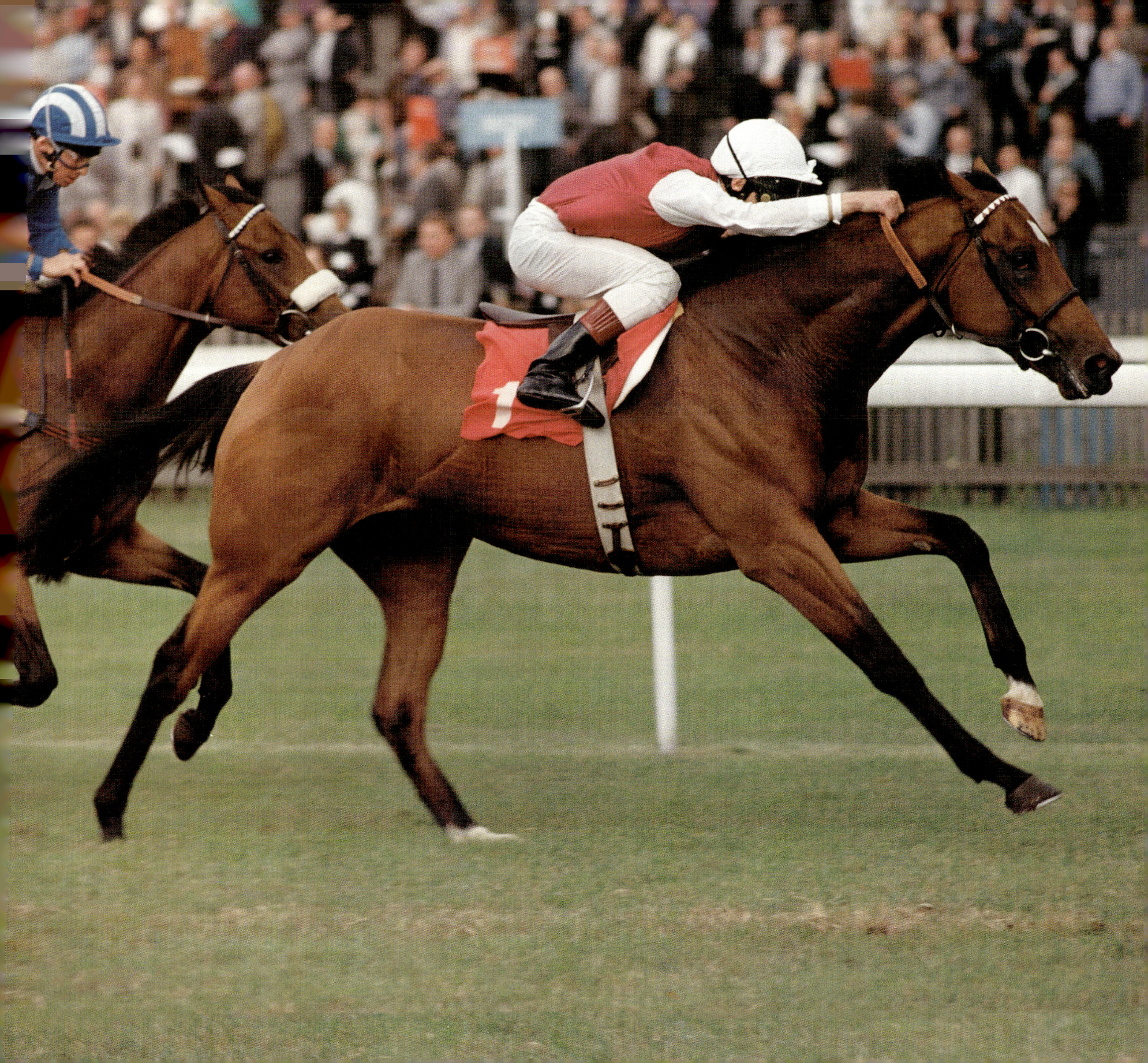
1

Bernardini

b. c by A P Indy — Cara Rafaela (Quiet American)

Homebred by Sheikh Mohammed's Darley operation, Bernardini made his debut in the January of his three-year-old career. Introduced in a six-furlong Gulfstream Park maiden, he was to suffer his only defeat at the time of writing when finding the trip too sharp. Almost two months later he was stepped up to a mile, also at Gulfstream in maiden company and opened his account in great style. Elevated to Graded company after that effort, he was the easy winner of the Grade Three Withers Stakes, over a mile.

The Preakness Stakes, middle leg of The Triple Crown, was to be his next port of call and he was to win the race by over five lengths. Having sat behind the pace in fourth, jockey Javier Castellano decided he could wait no longer as the field rounded the home turn. His mount soon opened up a commanding lead and galloped all the way to the line to win well.

Bernardini is trained by Tom Albertrani, formerly part of the Godolphin team but now back in his native USA as a trainer in his own right

This is clearly a colt of huge potential and it was no surprise connections elected to miss the concluding leg of The Triple Crown, the Belmont Stakes, given that all four of his career runs had been in 2006.

He justified that decision by winning the Grade Two 2 Jim Dandy Stakes on his fifth start before returning to Grade 1 company for his sixth. If there was any doubt regarding his talent before the Travers Stakes at Saratoga, they were soon dispelled.

So easily did he win that Castellano was actually patting him with half a furlong of the 10-furlong race left as they won by almost eight lengths to record the biggest winning distance in the race since 1979.

With over $1.6million in prize money to his credit, Bernardini owes connections nothing and looks sure to be a major player on Breeders' Cup night 2006.

A P Indy (dkb/br. 1989)	Seattle Slew	Bold Reason
		My Charmer
	Weekend Surprise	Secretariat
BERNARDINI (b. 2003)		Lassie Dear
Cara Rafaela (gr. 1993)	Quiet American	Fappiano
		Demure
	Oil Fable	Spectacular Bid
		Northern Fable

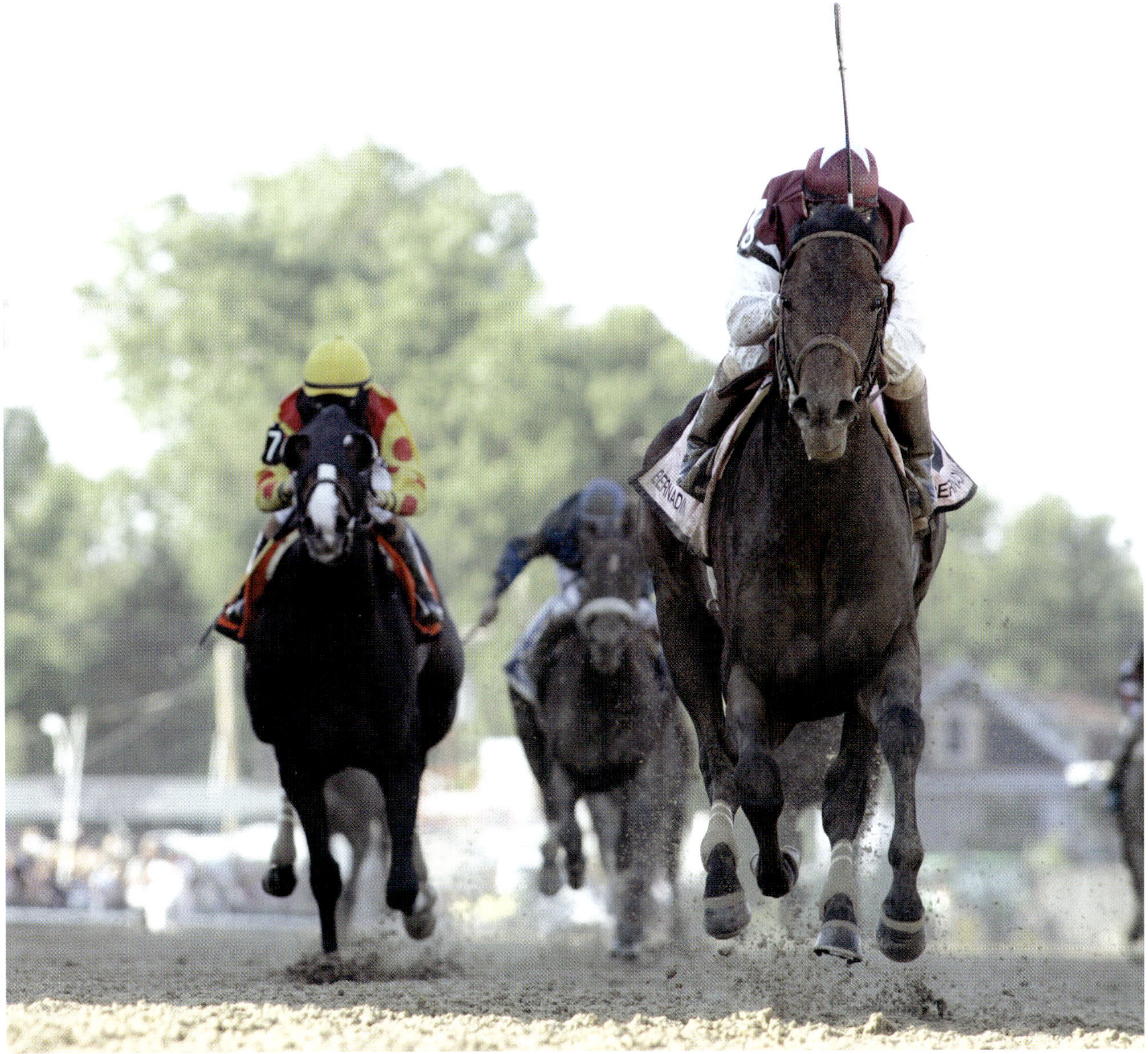

Cadeaux Genereux

ch. c by Young Generation – Smarten Up (Sharpen Up)

Uninspiring in two racecourse appearances as a juvenile, this 210,000 guinea yearling became arguably one of Sheikh Maktoum's finest sprinters during his years as an owner in Britain.

Opening his season with a relatively simple success in a graduation event at Pontefract and then a six-furlong win in a Newmarket handicap, Cadeaux Genereux reappeared in the William Hill Golden Spurs at York, where he took the race after a tough challenge from Silver Fling, going on by half a length.

The colt returned to Headquarters facing the highly-regarded Salse in the Van Geest Stakes in June. The two fought a thrilling finish over the last furlong, Cadeaux Genereux edging to the front and holding off a renewed challenge to record a short head victory.

Defeated in his next two starts, in the Prix Maurice de Gheest and the Sprint Championship at York, Cadeaux Genereux resumed his winning ways in superb fashion in the Diadem Stakes in September. Established as top class over six furlongs, he returned to five furlongs in one of Europe's hottest contests, the Prix de l'Abbaye de Longchamp. Held up early, Cadeaux Genereux unleashed a previously unwitnessed turn of foot to join the leaders and go on into a three-quarters of a length lead, holding the classy Handsome Sailor by a head. Unfortunately this superb win was expunged from the record books as the colt lost the race in the stewards room for causing interference.

He returned as a four-year-old with a disappointing third on his reappearance in the Temple Stakes at Sandown and an unplaced outing in the Kings Stand Stakes at Royal Ascot.

An easing in his workload at home was the apparent key to a spectacular return to form for Cadeaux Genereux, who silenced doubters next time out with a dramatic success in the July Cup in which he shaved more than a second off the course record, set by Ajdal during the July Cup of 1987.

Having added the Sprint Championship at York next time out, Cadeaux Genereux then finished third in the mile Prix du Moulin de Longchamp. Soon after he sustained a tendon injury and was retired.

	Balidar	Will Somers
Young Generation (b. 1976)		Violet Bank
	Brig O'Doon	Shantung
CADEAUX GENEREUX (ch. 1985)		Tam O'Shanter
	Sharpen Up	Atan
Smarten Up (ch. 1975)		Rocchetta
	L'Anguissola	Soderini
		Posh

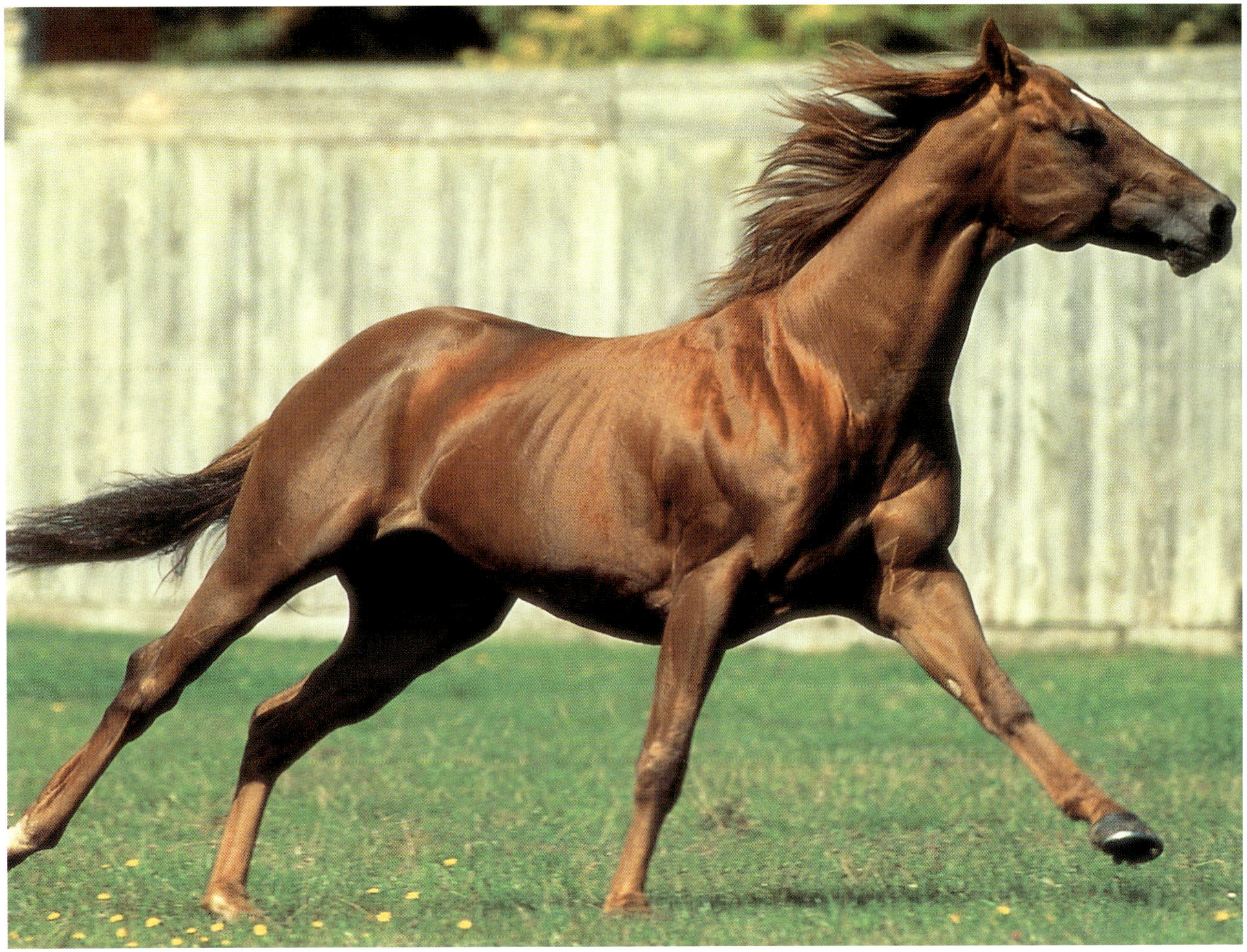

Chronograph watch
Automatic Quartz Movement
Diamonds embedded on bezel and case
Leather strap

www.damasjewellery.com

damas
Les Exclusives

Toll Free: 800 4916

Sheikh Maktoum bin Rashid Al Maktoum

The death of Sheikh Maktoum bin Rashid Al Maktoum in January 2006 not only robbed Dubai of a ruler but the world of a great politician and, more relevantly for this publication, a leading racehorse owner/breeder. Vice-President and Prime Minister of the United Arab Emirates and Ruler of Dubai, his blue silks with a white chevron were among the most instantly recognised in the sport the world over, while his Gainsborough Stud was a major player in the breeding world.

In fact, Gainsborough Stud were also a major sponsor within the industry with both the French 1000 and 2000 Guineas being obvious examples of such generosity.

It was Sheikh Maktoum who was, in fact, the first of the Maktoums to own a Classic winner in both the UK and Ireland when his Touching Wood won both country's St Legers in 1982. His Gainsborough Stud also bred Lammtarra, winner of the 1995 Epsom Derby in the green silks of his son Sheikh Saeed, as well as breeding 1996 Dubai Duty Free winner Key of Luck, who also carried the same green silks.

The list of great horses who carried his own infamous silks over a 25 year span is endless. Hatoof, Fantastic Light, Cadeaux Genereux, Storming Home and Jet Ski Lady spring immediately to mind. A co-founder of Godolphin with his brothers Sheikh Mohammed and Sheikh Hamdan, as well as Sheikh Ahmed to a lesser extent, it was he who supplied many of their greatest moments – Fantastic Light and, more recently Shamardal, being obvious examples.

In 1994 Balanchine, often credited as Godolphin's first major success, won both the Epsom Oaks and the Irish Derby in Sheikh Maktoum's blue silks. Pictavia, a recent Godolphin winner, was third in the Oaks in 2005 for Sheikh Maktoum.

He was also highly supportive of the concept of international racing and the creation of the Dubai World Cup meeting, the world's richest race day.

At the time of his death he had over 200 horses in training around the world, divided between 10 trainers and former champion jockey Joe Mercer, his racing manager for almost 20 years, led the tributes: "It's absolutely awful," he said.

"We had hundreds of great horses - Cadeaux Genereux, Royal Applause, Fantastic Light, Hatoof, Shadeed, Shareef Dancer - dozens and dozens of them.

"He really enjoyed his racing. He knew what was going on and was a very good man to work for. He was a good loser and a good winner. He had 10 trainers throughout the world including Sir Michael Stoute, Ed Dunlop, Barry Hills, Mark Johnston, Andre Fabre and Criquette Head in France and Neil Drysdale in America.

"He had over 200 horses in training and a lot of yearlings still to come in. The whole family have done a remarkable job for English racing. They bought stallions at the right price and invested a tremendous amount of money into the bloodstock business.

"They have been great for the industry."

Middleham trainer Mark Johnston lost his main owner: "Obviously it's a great shock. It's terrible and unbelievable and I had no inkling anything was wrong with him.

"He did a huge amount for racing, not just in Dubai but worldwide. Along with Sheikh Mohammed, he was instrumental in changing the whole shape of my yard and helping move me to a different level.

"There have been no yearlings allocated yet this year but most years I have had about 30 of his horses with me - he was my biggest owner."

In 2005 his colours were carried to a Group 1 victory in France by Court Masterpiece and his last winner in the UK was Easy Air, a half-brother to Court Masterpiece, who won a juvenile maiden at Lingfield in November. His Gainsborough Stud colours were seen in the winner's enclosure at Jebel Ali two days before Christmas when his Sparkford won a maiden for Rod Simpson - so perhaps fittingly his last winner was seen in the UAE.

Of course, his love for the horse came with his heritage and his love for racing, from that affinity with the horse. Always an avid horseman, a young Sheikh Maktoum was taught to ride a horse, hunt with a falcon - skills traditionally handed down through the generations from father to son. His father, the late Sheikh Rashid bin Saeed Al Maktoum, taught his son these essential traits to a young Arabian noble.

83

A close family friend, Hamad bin Sukat, recalled: "We quickly saw in Sheikh Maktoum many of Sheikh Rashid's traits. Both had an affinity for animals, were skillful horseback riders and hunters."

As with his brothers, it was during education in the late 1960s, in the UK, that he had his first taste of western thoroughbred horseracing. He completed his schooling at the elite Gordonstoun school in Scotland having become Heir Apparent to the Dubai Crown upon his father's accession to the throne in 1958.

On his return to the UAE in 1969 he developed the first local racecourse on a sight now occupied by Dubai International Airport. A tight oval sand track, it was a far cry from what was to be achieved in the future but he was able to arrange several open meetings each winter for Purebred Arabians and imported thoroughbreds.

When the Federation of the UAE was created in 1971, Sheikh Maktoum was appointed as the first Prime Minister for the seven United Arab Emirates and worked closely with Sheikh Zayed bin Sultan Al Nahyan, the UAE President, to develop the fledgling state.

Hunting and riding remained his main leisure interests until, in 1976, he purchased his first thoroughbred racehorse, Shaab, at Tattersalls in Newmarket. Shaab was entrusted to John Dunlop and finally came good in 1979 when winning four times, including the Gordon Carter Handicap. The horse won eight times in total and remained one of his owner's most prolific winners and was soon followed by the likes of Shareef Dancer, Ma Biche and Touching Wood.

In 1982 and 1983 he won no less than four Classics, and after Touching Wood took the St Leger at Doncaster, a delighted owner explained what it was like to win his first Classic: "I could not feel my legs. I did not know if I was sitting or standing!"

We have already listed just some of his other leading horses and breeding achievements but, perhaps remarkably, in his homeland he was a leader who will be remembered for his philanthropy as opposed to his thoroughbred racehorses. In the UAE and Dubai alike his generosity remains legendary, including the funding of a Dhs100million centre for the handicapped. But it was arguably best publicised during Bob Geldof's *(pictured)* 'Live Aid' appeal in 1985 when both he and Sheikh Mohammed helped organisers raise millions of dollars for drought savaged Ethiopia. Touched by the pictures of malnourished children, the brothers pledged $1 million late in proceedings, by far the largest single donation, to help boost the amount raised.

A UNICEF statement stated: "... this provided the world with an admirable example. Their action proves their belief in the common destiny for all people on earth and their effective support for the concept of humanitarian assistance from people to people, irrespective of race, colour or creed."

It is of course for his love and support of horse racing for which we racing enthusiasts will remember Sheikh Maktoum and it is fitting that his blue and white silks have remained - in the name of his Gainsborough organisation. The likes of the aforementioned Court Masterpiece and Easy Air will continue to wear these and it is perhaps fitting that he died in Australia, where he was visiting the yearling sales looking for more horses to pursue his passion of racing.

The majority of his bloodstock interests will be encompassed in Sheikh Mohammed's Darley operation, but the influence of Sheikh Maktoum will live on for a very long time - both among his people and in the world of bloodstock.

Cape Verdi

b. f by Caerleon - Afrique Bleu Azur (Sagace)

Not many fillies have gone into the almost exclusively colt Epsom Derby in recent times, fewer still with a live chance. Cape Verdi did and, although not winning the Blue Riband, presents one of the most remarkable stories of any Godolphin horse since Saeed bin Suroor first burst onto the international stage.

She began her much-touted career with success in a good Newmarket maiden in May 1997, reappearing at Royal Ascot in the Chesham Stakes, where she finished second. Two months later she enjoyed her first pattern success when landing the Lowther Stakes, a short head ahead of Embassy, before a fourth in the Cheveley Park Stakes.

In September Cape Verdi was sold as part of a group to Godolphin, and she wintered in Dubai. Her eagerly anticipated return came in the 1000 Guineas at Newmarket, where her reputation was enough to send her off as co-favourite.

Rarely has a Classic been won easily. At the dip Frankie Dettori pushed his mount along and she responded in spectacular fashion, sweeping clear and into a five length lead at the line.

The Oaks looked ripe for the taking. Yet attempting the near impossible is much of what Godolphin is about, and a crack at the Derby, won by only three fillies in the 1900s, was a tempting prospect for Sheikh Mohammed. Only 10 days before the Blue Riband she was supplemented into the race at a cost of £75,000, and the Godolphin star went to post as favourite.

In the race itself, she was to encounter plenty of problems in running and was barged twice. As they turned Tattenham Corner she was sixth but faded to pass the post in ninth.

Sadly, her season went no further. In July she was reported lame and later it became clear that Cape Verdi had suffered a hairline fracture of a hind pastern.

The filly returned to Dubai for a second winter and was back at Godolphin's Newmarket base in 1999, from where she was saddled to a third in the Falmouth Stakes, before a below-par last place in the Nassau Stakes at Goodwood.

CAPE VERDI (b. 1995)	**Caerleon**	Nijinsky	Northern Dancer
			Flaming Page
		Foreseer	Round Table
			Regal Gleam
	Afrique Bleu Azur	Sagace	Luthier
			Seneca
		Albertine	Irish River
			Almyre

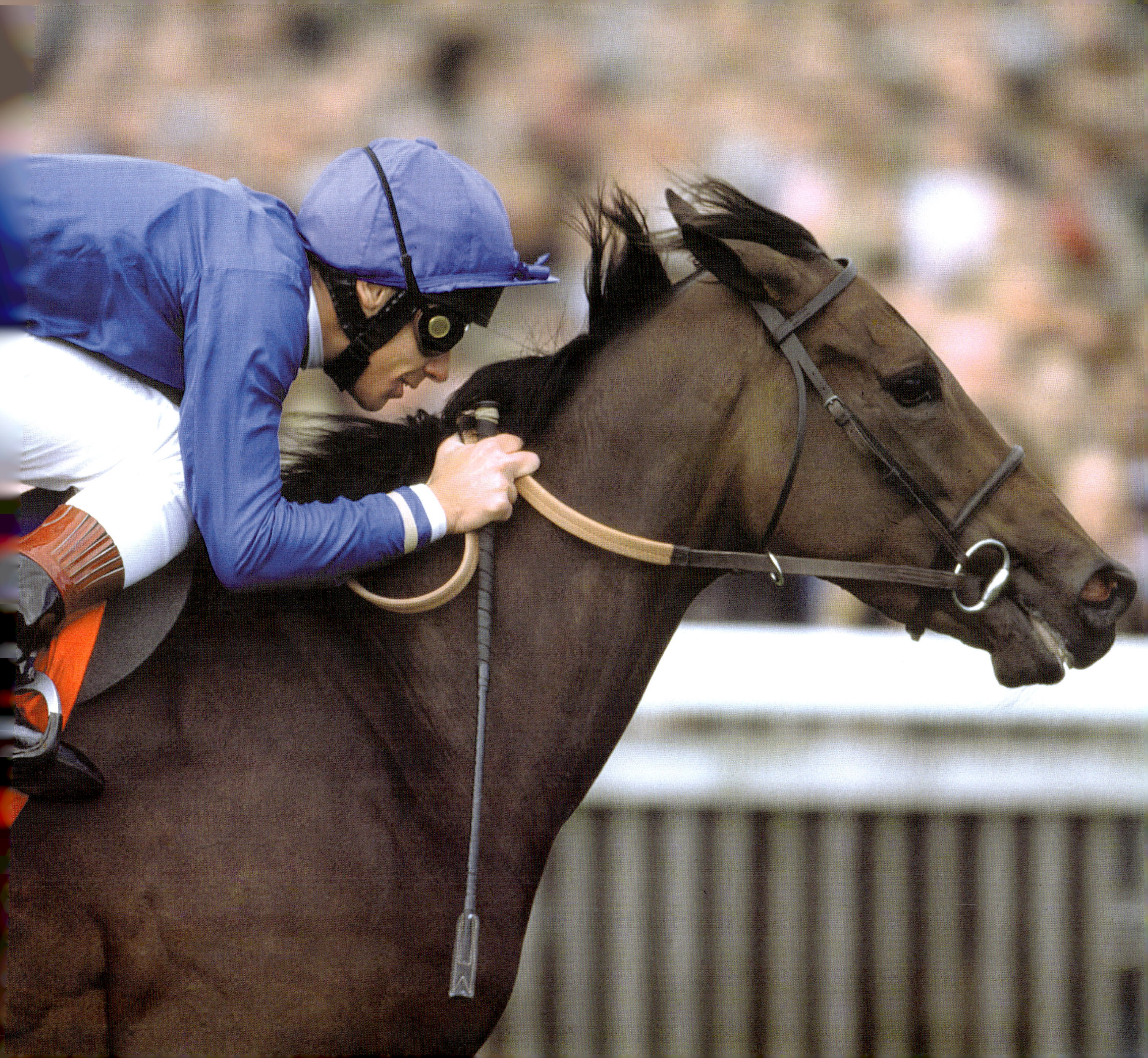

Crimplene

ch. f by Lion Cavern — Crimson Conquest (Diesis)

Sheikh Marwan Al Maktoum had his first winner in Britain in 1983 and arguably his best horse was Nomphe, group placed that year. That was until Crimplene, a dual Classic and triple Group One winner, one of the best offspring sired by Lion Cavern. Trained by Clive Brittain, the filly began her career with success in a maiden, a small Salisbury race and then finished third in the Cheveley Park Stakes, from six starts.

Her trainer mapped out a remarkable campaign for her three-year-old season, that began with a trip to her owner's home country and an entry in the UAE Derby. She finished sixth to China Visit.

Back in Britain, she began a Guineas campaign with a third in the Fred Darling Stakes at Newbury, and achieved the same result when resuming her travels to Rome for the Premio Regina Elena, the Italian 1000 Guineas. Brittain announced afterwards that she ran poorly due to the rough treatment of the Italian stalls handlers.

A week later Crimplene got off the mark for the season winning Dusseldorf's Henkel-Rennen, Germany's 1000 Guineas.

This persuaded her connections of the merit of another Classic challenge and Crimplene was then routed to the Irish 1000 Guineas. There, Crimplene was set off to do much of the work and led most of the way. One by one her opponents made a challenge, but with each demand upon her she simply stayed on strongly and eventually ran out a length and a half winner from Amethyst.

She was next seen in action in the Coronation Stakes at Royal Ascot, which attracted much of the cream of the three-year-old filly crop in Europe that summer. The race was expected to be competitive, but in the event Crimplene turned it into a procession. Always in command and never headed, as the field turned into the straight the race was hers. At the line she took the Group One by two and a half lengths from Princess Elen, with the rest toiling well behind.

Four wins in three months and plenty of travel had taken its toll however. After below par efforts in the Prix Jacques le Marois and Queen Elizabeth II Stakes, she was a surprise visitor to the United States for the Breeders' Cup Distaff where she ran a prominent three and three quarter lengths fourth. Crimplene was then retired.

CRIMPLENE (ch. 1997)	Lion Cavern (ch. 1989)	Mr Prospector — Raise A Native / Gold Digger
		Secrettame — Secretariat / Tamerett
	Crimson Conquest (ch. 1988)	Diesis — Sharpen Up / Double Sure
		Sweet Ramblin Rose — Turn-To / Velvet Rose

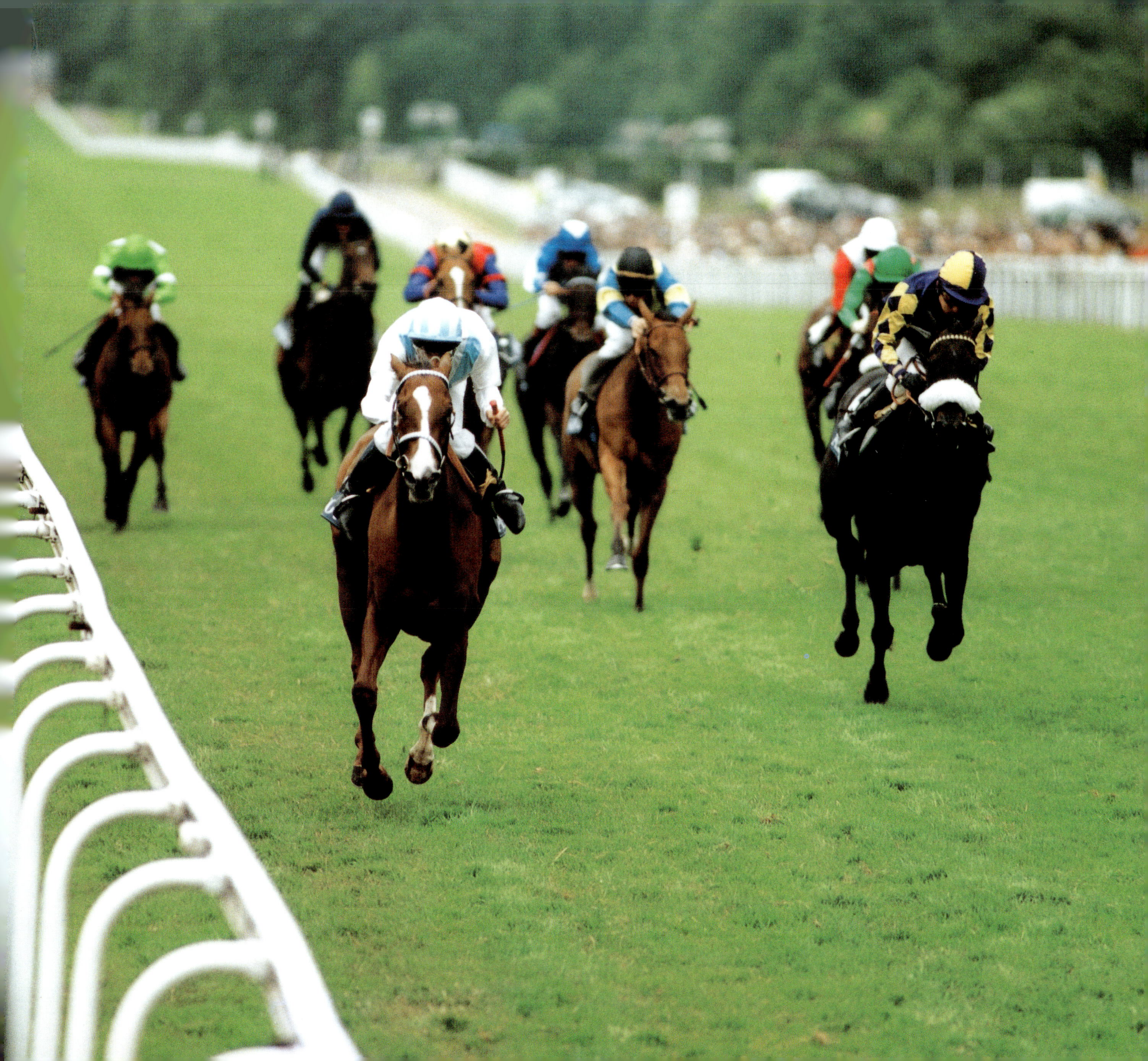

BUILDING SPEED FOR THE FUTURE

Aljabr
Storm Cat – Sierra Madre, by Baillamont

Dayjur
Danzig – Gold Beauty, by Mr. Prospector

Dumaani
Danzig – Desirable, by Lord Gayle

Intidab
Phone Trick – Alqwani, by Mr. Prospector

Kayrawan
Mr. Prospector – Muhbubh, by Blushing Groom

Sahm
Mr. Prospector – Salsabil, by Sadler's Wells

Swain
Nashwan – Love Smitten, by Key to the Mint

Rick Nichols, *Vice President/General Manager*
Kent Barnes, *Stallion Manager*
Stallion Inquiries: (859) 224-4585
4600 Ft. Springs Road   Lexington, KY 40513 USA
info@shadwellfarm.com   www.shadwellfarm.com

SHADWELL FARM

Dayflower

ch. f by Majestic Light — Equate (Raja Baba)

In horticultural terms, the Western Dayflower, *Commelina dianthifolia*, is a perennial that blooms in late July or early August. In racing terms, Dayflower is a name that will ever be defined by a filly who bloomed in the Middle East and showed herself at her most dramatic in Britain

The filly Dayflower may never have become a household name, as other Maktoum horses have managed, but nevertheless her place in history is assured. A $160,000 yearling, the attractive youngster went under the care of Henry Cecil where she soon proved a handful. Her initial racecourse appearance produced the first of many public shows of nerves when she reared in stalls and refused to start at Doncaster.

After some intensive work at home, she returned at Newmarket in July looking a great deal more relaxed, but far from perfect. After a stumbling start however, she showed potential to take up the running three furlongs out, going on to record a useful looking victory.

When Dayflower left Britain to winter in Dubai, her departure warranted hardly a mention in the racing press. Trainer Satish Seemar put her through intensive training in the stalls, and during her stint in warmer climes, she muscled up considerably. Word was certainly spreading when she made her Guineas prep race, in the unlikely surroundings of Nad Al Sheba. Her defeat by handicapper Ghurragh, while being ridden tenderly, was hardly encouragement.

When Seemar saddled his charge in the first Classic she ran as though something was amiss during the early stages, but picked up nicely as they hit the rising ground. Ending the race strongly under Frankie Dettori, Dayflower finished fifth by just two and half lengths to Sayyedati and was seen running on strongly at the finish. She returned to the track to take a small conditions event at York under Walter Swinburn.

In racing terms the event meant little, but as part of the wider picture, Dayflower's success did mean something. The following summer Godolphin would mount their debut campaign, Sheikh Mohammed's mind perhaps made up by the troublesome filly who came good.

Dayjur

br. c by Danzig - Gold Beauty (Mr. Prospector)

A $1.65 million yearling, Dayjur began his career with success in a Newbury maiden and ended his two-year-old season with a tight second in a listed event.

The following season saw him dropped to six furlongs and subsequently five furlongs, clearly his optimum distance. Running against older horses in the Temple Stakes at Sandown, he accounted for the likes of Tigani and Statoblest.

By the time trainer Major Dick Hern sent him to York for the Nunthorpe Stakes in August, Dayjur was maturing steadily. Taking on the best speed horses in Britain, the colt simply sprinted his opponents into oblivion, a display which saw him home four lengths clear, a full second inside the track record.

Just two weeks later, returning to six furlongs at Haydock in the Sprint Cup, a similar front-running performance saw the field left trailing. Dayjur was five lengths to the good when Royal Academy came with a run. He was hardly troubled to maintain a one and a half length advantage at the line.

After a further victory over the minimum distance in the Prix de l'Abbaye de Longchamp, connections sent Europe's champion sprinter to America for an October engagement in the Breeders' Cup Sprint.

The event itself proved one of the most dramatic in history of the racing. Two horses fell in early barging. Dayjur started slowly and was immediately under pressure. Entering the turn, he sat second behind US favourite Safely Kept. The two matched strides and left all but one opponent trailing at this early stage.

In the home straight it was just Dayjur and the mare Safely Kept in contention. Looking the better of the two, Dayjur began to go on, taking on a half-length advantage when disaster struck.

Striding out toward the finish, he came to a shadow of the grandstand cast over the track and tried to jump it. That momentary break in stride was all that Safely Kept needed to gain the upper hand. Even as they flashed past the post, Dayjur was shying from another shadow.

In the event, the colt won just as many plaudits in finishing second in his final start as he might have had he won the race itself.

Danzig (b. 1977)	Northern Dancer	Nearctic / Natalama
	Pas de Nom	Admirals Voyage / Petitioner
DAYJUR (br. 1987)		
Gold Beauty (b. 1979)	Mr Prospector	Raise a Native / Gold Digger
	Stick to Beauty	Illustrious / Nail to Beauty

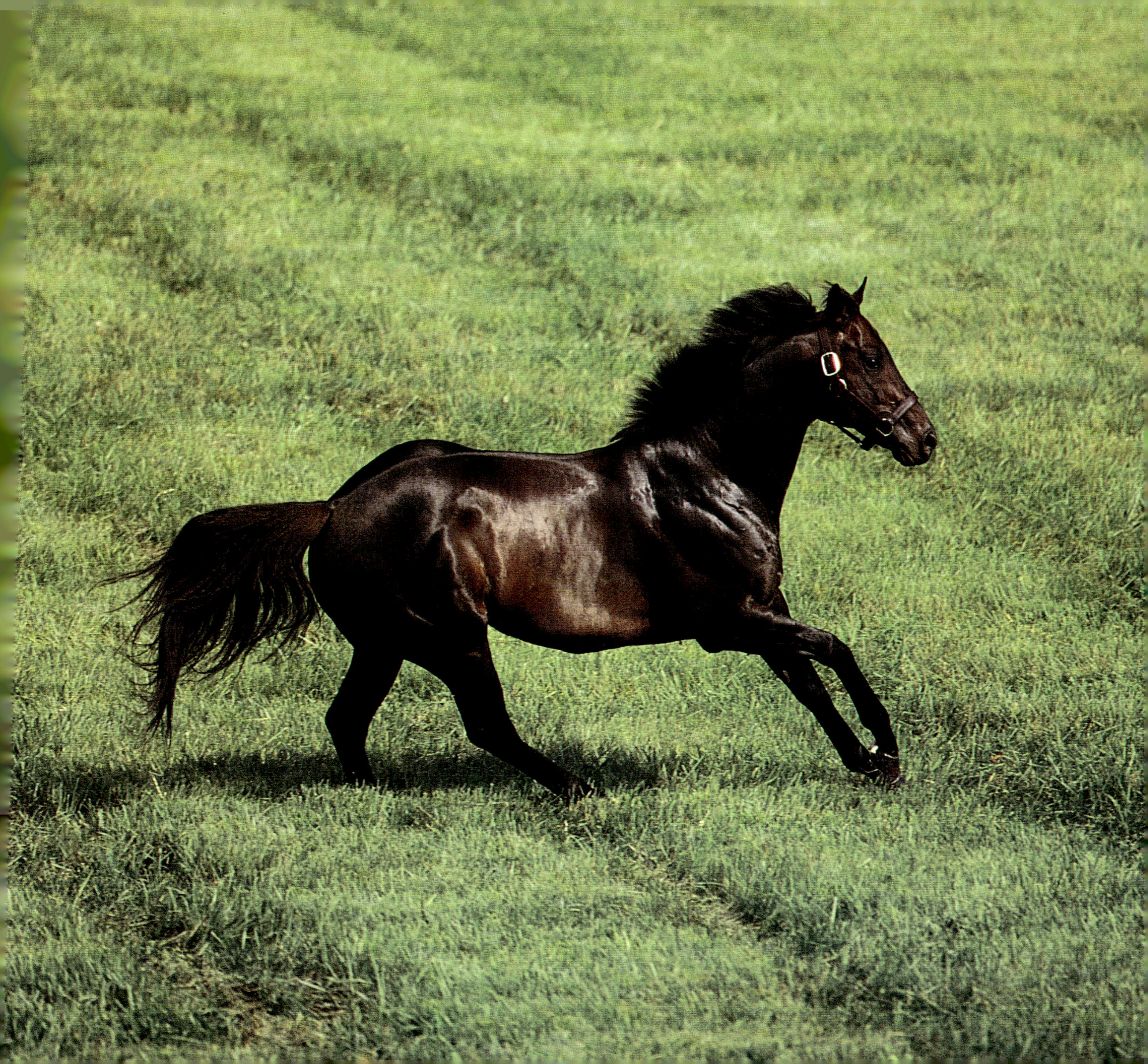

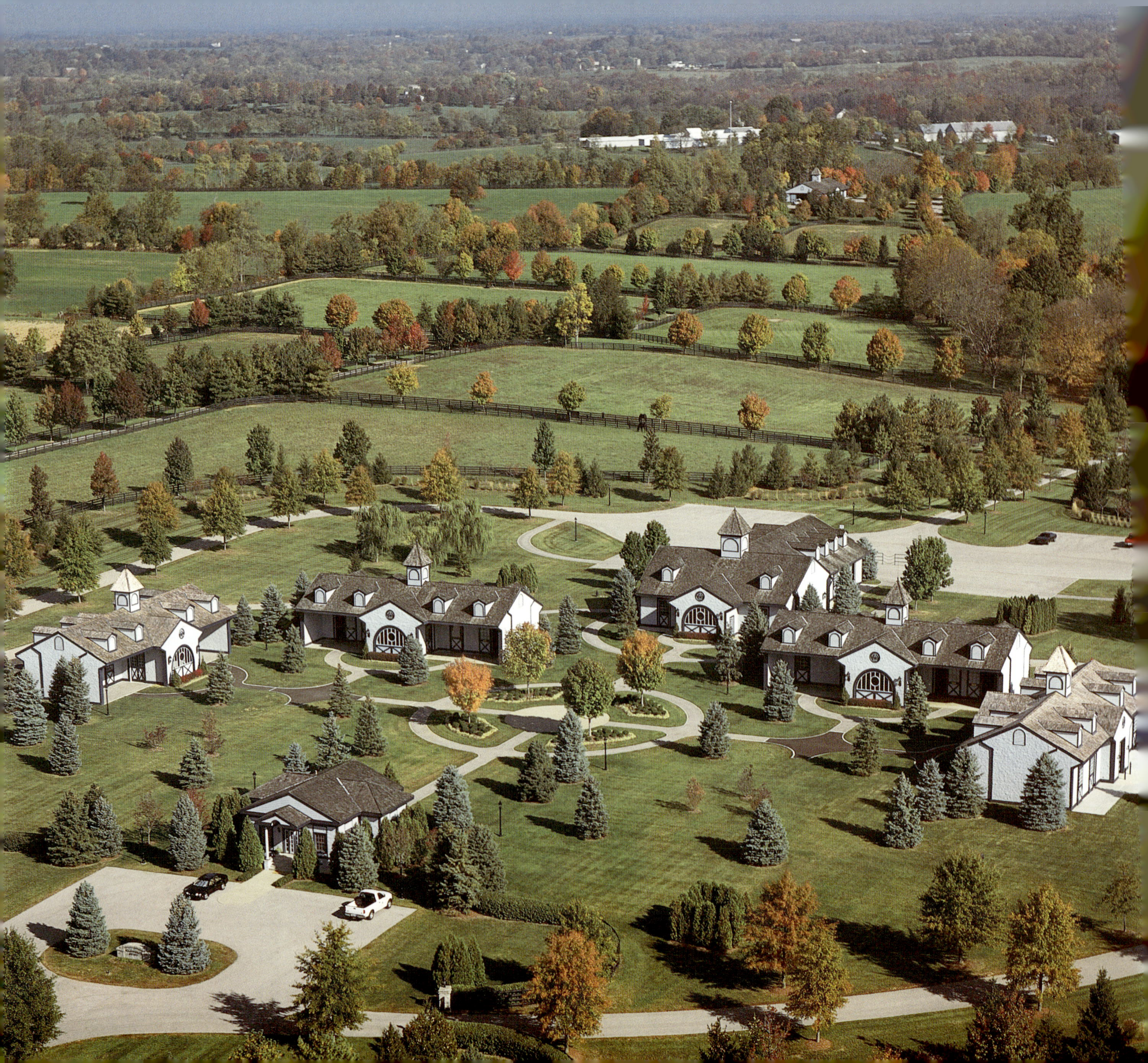

Shadwell Farm

The prime Bluegrass Region surrounding the city of Lexington, Kentucky in the center of the eastern half of the United States is where Shadwell Farm has enjoyed many great achievements. This location of limestone-rich soil and rolling hillsides has made the Bluegrass the world's premier locale for raising thoroughbreds. Here, Sheikh Hamdan bin Rashid Al Maktoum's Shadwell Farm produces an amazing array of talented runners. At the Farm's stallion division, Sheikh Hamdan offers some of his best colts to breeders to help ensure not only Shadwell's influence for generations to come but also to give breeders the opportunity to reach this same goal.

In 1984, Sheikh Hamdan selected, purchased, and began construction on 720 acres near Lexington. Today, the farm encompasses over 3,400 acres. The Farm was designed to accommodate 100 to 125 mares and their offspring through their yearling year. The wisdom of Sheikh Hamdan is apparent in every facet of Shadwell Farm. Rick Nichols, the Farm's Vice President and General Manager, comments, "Sheikh Hamdan is the best all around horseman I have met. His knowledge of the horse industry is expansive. He possesses not only a tremendous eye for a good individual animal but also superior knowledge of pedigrees and breeding concerns. His keen interest in racing is part of that success – he knows the competition well. He also understands how breeding farms operate and often visits his mares and foals. He genuinely loves his horses."

It is a great honor for Nichols to work closely with Sheikh Hamdan who personally reviews and approves ideas, or designs concepts, and plans construction. Nichols comments, "He is a great leader. Shadwell's global success is the result of his hands-on management. With racing and breeding programs in Ireland, England and America, Sheikh Hamdan pulls everything together into one successful unit."

Success has come to Sheikh Hamdan as a result of his skill at assembling all the necessary ingredients for a top-notch programme. He bought the best land available and built an outstanding facility. He owns many of the world's best broodmares and breeds them to top stallions. He employs qualified professionals and provides the necessary leadership to achieve his goals. Under his guidance, Shadwell Farm, in a short time has produced the winners of eight classic races: Epsom Derby and English Guineas winner Nashawan; Epsom Derby winner Erhaab; English One Thousand Guineas winners Shadayid and Harayir; Irish One Thousand Guineas winner Mehthaaf; English Oaks winner Snow Bride; and French One Thousand Guineas winner Ta Rib. In addition, Bahri's Arc winning son Sakhee came within inches of winning the 2000 Epsom Derby. In the winter of 2005 Shadwell acquired the Uruguayan Triple Crown winner, Invasor (Arg), who went on to capture Shadwell's first Grade One victory in the United States while winning The Pimlico Special (Gr.1) in his American debut. In his second U.S. start Invasor continued to prove his superstardom by dominating the Suburban Handicap (Gr.1). A short time later Jazil brought Sheikh Hamdan's blue and white colors to the forefront when he conquered one of the greatest American Classic Grade One races, the Belmont Stakes. It marked the first Classic victory for the Shadwell Stable as Jazil performed like a seasoned professional. To date, racehorses from Shadwell Farm in Kentucky have carried Sheikh Hamdan's famous blue and white silks to victory in more than 74 Group races.

The farm is organised into several departments, each with specific responsibilities and overseen by Farm Manager, Gregory Clarke and Assistant Farm Manager, Jody Dunlap. These crews look after one of the most prestigious broodmare bands in the world including classic winners Mehthaaf and Eswarah and classic producers Histoire and Safaanh. Of course, one mare that will always be

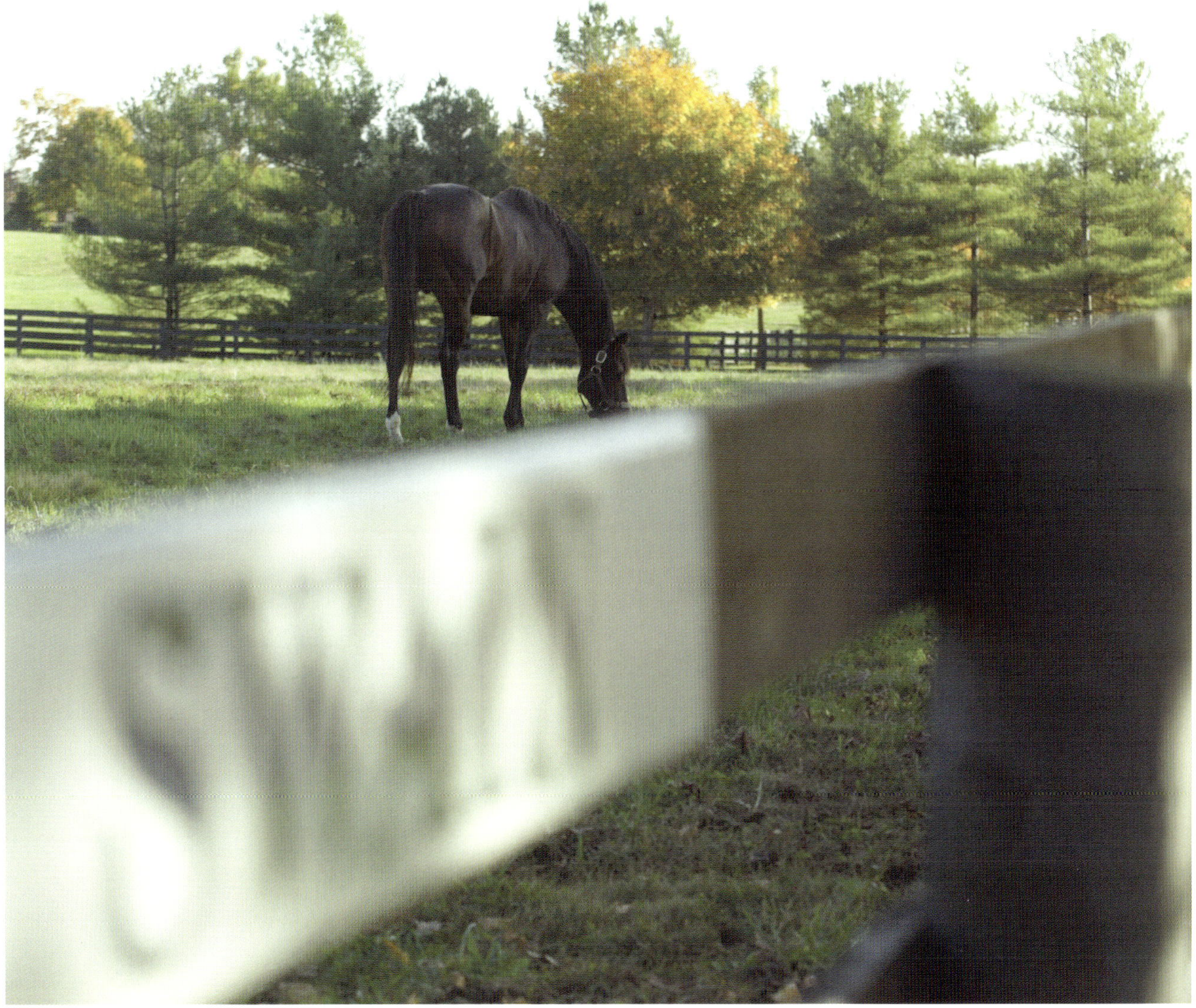

remembered is the legendary Height of Fashion who produced Unfuwain and Nashwan. Height of Fashion's legacy lives on as she proved her dominance for Sheikh Hamdan by giving him her last foal the versatile Nayef who was victorious in the 2001 Group One Dubai Champion Stakes, in 2002 the Group One Dubai Sheema Classic and the Group One Juddmonte International Stakes, and his magnificent victory in the 2003 Group One Prince of Wales's Stakes. Recently, Sheikh Hamdan has made several high caliber additions to his already impressive broodmare family. Among these are Dessert, Golden Apples (Champion Grass mare at 4), Habibti, and Magical Allure, all of which are superior Group One winners. These mares along with many more have established the prominent ranks of Shadwell's broodmare band. Nichols expresses the pride shared by the Farm's employees, "It is such a great honor to work with these royally bred animals."

The Yearling Department sprawls out over 1,500 acres and is home to foals from the time they are weaned until they are exported in September or October of their yearling year to one of Sheikh Hamdan's training centers. The Yearling Department's activities are conducted in two locations at the farm.

Initially raised on the main farm, the young horses are then sent to our Yearling Department located at Shadayid Stud, which was named in honor of our 1000 Guineas winner Shadayid. This department is a crucial element in the successful production of racehorses for Sheikh Hamdan's racing stable. This area is under the supervision of Tim Miller.

Nashwan Stud, which opened in 1991 is Shadwell's stallion facility named after the first homebred classic winner raised at the farm. Nashwan is home to seven stallions; Aljabr, Dayjur,

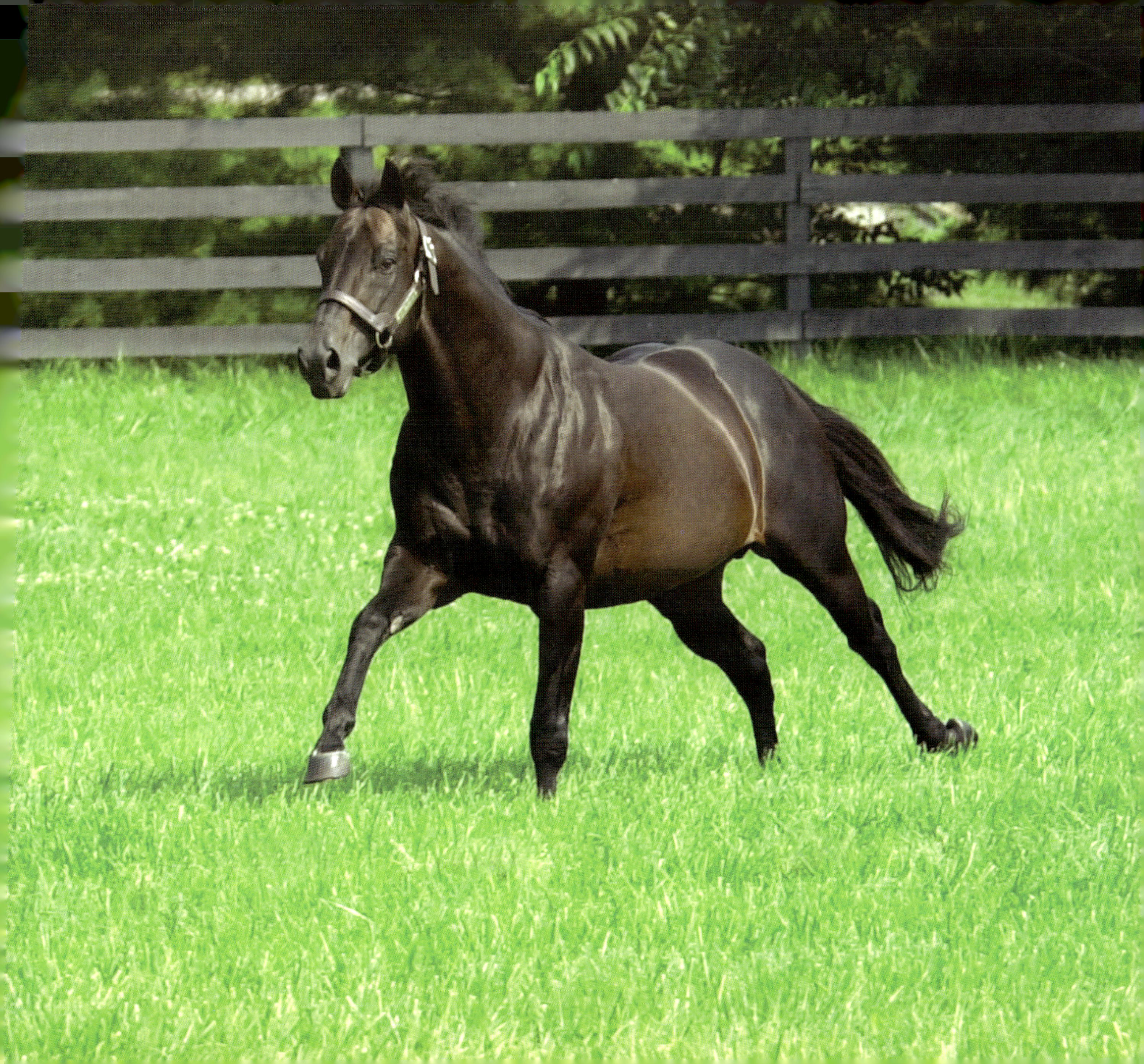

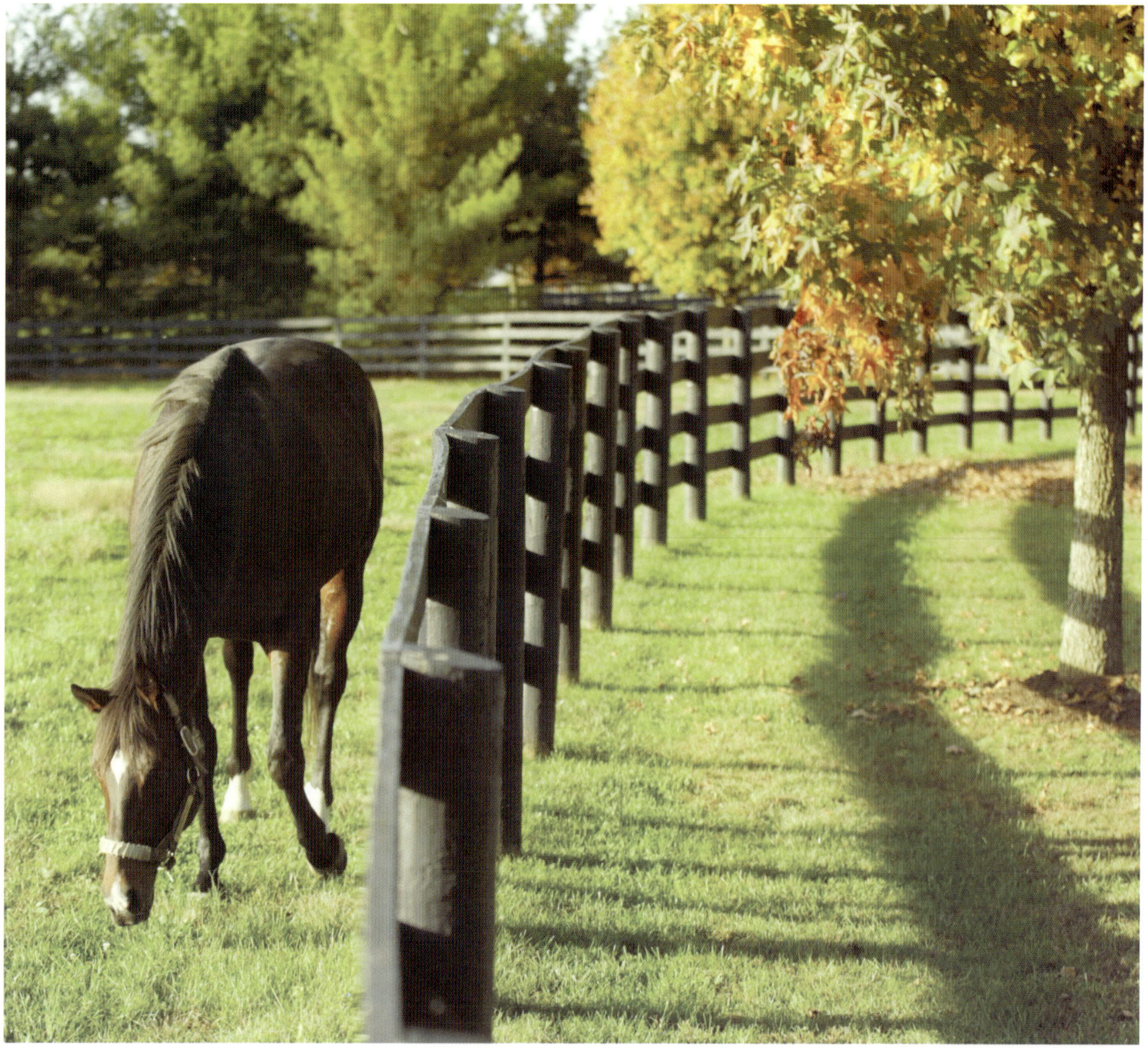

Dumaani, Intidab, Kayrawan, Sahm, and Swain and is managed by Kent Barnes. These stallions are predominately homebreds, which campaigned internationally for Sheikh Hamdan and/or Godolphin.

The tough consistent Aljabr, foaled and raised at Shadwell Farm, was campaigned by Godolphin and is still today the only son of Storm Cat to have managed the feat of winning Group One races at the ages of two, three and four.

The first stallion to retire to the new Nashwan Stud in 1991 was the exceptionally quick Dayjur. This multiple sprint champion is a son of Danzig and the American champion sprinter Gold Beauty, by Mr. Prospector. A true international sire, Dayjur has sired 50 stakes horses in ten countries, with lifetime earnings of over 18 million dollars and has made a name for himself as a prominent broodmare sire.

Dummani, another son of Danzig out of Group One winner Desirable, proved his worth by winning stakes races on three continents with earnings over $1 million dollars. His North American stakes wins include consecutive runnings of the Keeneland Breeders' Cup Mile, now known as the Shadwell Turf Mile (Gr.1).

Intidab was one of the best sprinters of his generation. The son of Phone Trick out of the Mr. Prospector mare Alqwani, won both the True North Handicap (Gr.2) and the A Phenomenon Handicap (Gr.2).

The ultra classy Mr. Prospector colt, Kayrawan, won the prestigious Tom Fool Handicap - Group Two at Belmont Park. He is out of the Group Three winning daughter of Blushing Groom, Muhbubh.

Sahm was a consistent performer on the dirt and turf, finishing first or second in ten of his eleven starts, including his record performance in the

Knickerbocker Handicap (Gr.2). He is the product of sending Sheikh Hamdan's brilliant race filly Salsabil to the great Mr. Prospector.

A multiple champion and globetrotting sensation, the incomperable Swain was foaled in Ireland and raced for Godolphin, after winning nearly $4 million dollars and accolades from the greatest races around the world.

In addition to skilled horsemen, Sheikh Hamdan employs leading professionals to ensure a safe and healthy environment for raising horses. Shadwell Farm's Agriculture and Maintenance Department is managed by Scott Clemons. His crew oversees a plethora of construction projects on the farm in addition to the somewhat awesome task of painting and maintaining miles of fence and numerous structures. The beauty of this functional and successful enterprise is a testimony to their work.

The Agricultural Department has planted well over 30,000 trees to enhance the beauty and quality of the farm, as well as contributing to the environment, and takes care of all plant life throughout the farm's 3,400 acres, including the pastures and grasses.

Sheikh Hamdan has worked very hard and carefully planned each detail of his operation. Few individuals have put into the horse business as much effort as Sheikh Hamdan. The success he derives from Shadwell Farm is well earned and very well deserved.

Aljabr

The only son of Storm Cat standing in Kentucky to win Group races at two, three and four. There are 27 winners for the third-crop sire to date, including stakes winner WHERE'S BAILEY.

Won Gr. 1	**LANSON CHAMPAGNE SUSSEX STAKES**, New Course Record, 1m in 1:35.66, defeating DOCKSIDER, ALMUSHTARAK
Won Gr. 1	**JUDDMONTE LOCKINGE STAKES**, 1m, equal top weight, by 2 lengths, defeating TRANS ISLAND, INDIAN LODGE, GOLDEN SILCA, SUGARFOOT
Won Gr. 1	**PRIX DE LA SALAMANDRE**, 7f, defeating KINGSALSA, ZIRCONI, EXEAT, ROLO TOMASI, STRAVINSKY
Won Gr. 3	**LANSON CHAMPAGNE VINTAGE STAKES**, 7f, by 3 lengths, defeating RAISE A GRAND, GOLD ACADEMY, LOTS OF MAGIC, MENSA

Dayjur

Graded Stakes Winners in the U.S., Japan, England, Ireland, and France on Dirt and Turf. Averaged over $2 million in progeny earnings annually for last seven years. Progeny include ASFURAH, FORLIPANA, SHINKO SPLENDOR, MAJOR ZEE and DAYJOB. Dayjur is also making an impact as a broodmare sire, the youngest broodmare sire on the Thoroughbred Times list of top 100 damsires.

Won Gr. 1	**NUNTHORPE STAKES,** New Course Record, 5f in 56.16, by 4 lengths, defeating STATOBLEST
Won Gr. 1	**PRIX DE L'ABBAYE DE LONGCHAMP**, 5f, by 2 lengths, defeating LUGANA BEACH
Won Gr. 1	**LADBROKE SPRINT CUP**, 6f, by 1 1/2 lengths, defeating ROYAL ACADEMY
Won Gr. 2	**KING'S STAND STAKES**, 5f, by 2 1/2 lengths, defeating RON'S VICTORY, LUGANA BEACH
Won Gr. 2	**SEARS TEMPLE STAKES,** 5f, by 2 lengths, defeating STATOBLEST, BLYTON LAD
2nd Gr. 1	**BREEDERS' CUP SPRINT**, 6f, to SAFELY KEPT, by a neck, defeating BLACK TIE AFFAIR

Dumaani

Record setting Mile and MGSW millionaire by sire of sires Danzig. Dumaani has eight stakes horses, 79 individual winners, and over $3.5 Million in progeny earnings. Among his stakes horses are BLOWIN IN THE WIND, WUDANTUNOIT, SCOOTIN' GIRL and CHARACTER WITNESS.

Won Gr. 2	**KEIO HAI SPRING CUP,** 7f in 1:21 1/5, defeating BIKO ALPHA, HOKUTO VEGA, EMPEROR JONES, HEART LAKE
Won Gr. 2	**KEENELAND BREEDERS' CUP MILE S**, 1 mile in 1:35 3/5, on the turf, defeating DESERT WAVES, DOVE HUNT, HARGHAR, BRAVE NOTE, KISSIN KRIS,
Won Gr. 3	**KEENELAND BREEDERS' CUP S**, 1 mile, on the turf, defeating HOLY MOUNTAIN, MR PURPLE, INSIDE THE BELTWAY, MANILAMAN, WEEKEND MADNESS
Won Gr. 3	**KING CHARLES II STAKES,** 7f, defeating SATIN VELVET, RAFFERTY'S RULES, ELRAFA AH

Intidab

Eleven stakes performances both on dirt and turf, including a 120 Bayer Speed Figure winning Saratoga's Grade Two A Phenomenen. From just 11 starters, Intidab has three stakes horses and eight winners, including three-time graded stakes winner GREATER GOOD.

Won Gr. 2	**A PHENOMENON HANDICAP**, 6f, defeating ARTAX, YES IT'S TRUE, GOOD AND TOUGH, RUN JOHNNY, MINT, KASHATREYA
Won Gr. 2	**TRUE NORTH HANDICAP**, 6f, defeating BRUTALLY FRANK, ORO DE MEXICO, COWBOY COP, MASTER O FOXHOUNDS,
Won	**EILLO STAKES**, 6f, top-weighted, defeating SALTY GLANCE, MAYOR STEVE, STORMY DO, STORM PUNCH, FAST DEPARTURE
Won	**ALLOWANCE RACE** at Belmont Park, 6f, equal top weight, by 3 lengths, defeating NOT SO WACKY

Kayrawan

Sensational sprinter by Mr. Prospector. Won on three continents including Belmont's Grade Two Tom Fool Handicap. His progeny include five stakes horses, 46 individual winners and nearly $2.5 Million in progeny earnings, including DUBAI SHEIKH.

Won Gr. 2	**TOM FOOL HANDICAP**, 7f, in 1:22 4/5, by 1 1/4 lengths, defeating COLD EXECUTION, LITE THE FUSE, REALITY ROAD, FLYING CHEVRON
Won	**ALLOWANCE RACE** at Keeneland, 6 1/2f in 1:16 2/5, by 2 1/2 lengths, defeating COMMANCHE TRAIL, DYNAMIC ASSET
Won	**ALLOWANCE RACE** at Belmont, 6f in 1:08 1/5, by 6 1/2 lengths, defeating REALITY ROAD, CHURKA, STREAKING NORTH
2nd Gr. 3	**MARYLAND BREEDERS' CUP HANDICAP** 6f, to FOREST WILDCAT, defeating DEMALOOT DEMASHOOT, JEALOUS CRUSADER, MEADOW LAD

Sahm

Record-setting GSW by Mr. Prospector, out of a Classic winner. The only son of champion Salsabil, the first filly in 90 years to win the Irish Derby. Finished 1st or 2nd in 10 of 11 career starts. To date he has sired five stakes horses, 46 individual winners and generated early $2.5 Million in progeny earnings, highlighted by the likes of MUSTAMEET, ADAALA and SAHMKINDAWONDERFUL.

Won Gr. 2	**KNICKERBOCKER HANDICAP,** 9f, **e**qualed stakes record, 1:48.69, defeating GLOK, LET GOODTIMES ROLL, MUSICAL GHOST
Won	**ALLOWANCE RACE**, Belmont Park, 8.5f by 4 lengths, defeating STAR CONNECTION
Won	**ALLOWANCE RACE**, Belmont Park, 7f on dirt, equal top weight, by 3l, defeating ENCRYPTION
Won	**ALLOWANCE RACE**, York, 7f, by 5 lengths, defeating TUSCANY
2nd Gr. 2	**KELSO HANDICAP**, 1m, to DIXIE BAYOU, by a head, defeating LET GOODTIMES ROLL
2nd Gr. 2	**LANSON CHAMPAGNE VINTAGE STAKES**, 7f, 2nd by half-length, disqualified for interference

Swain

Multiple Champion on Turf, brilliant Group One performances on Dirt. Won/placed in 20 of 22 Starts, including 11 Group Ones. Immediate family of Champions Fantastic Light, Kamar, Golden Attraction, Square Angel, etc. His most notable progeny include DIMITROVA, NASHEEJ, STANLEY PARK and MUQBIL.

Won Gr. 1	**KING GEORGE VI AND QUEEN ELIZABETH DIAMOND STAKES,** 12f, equal top weight, defeating PILSUDSKI, HELISSIO, SINGSPIEL
Won Gr. 1	**KING GEORGE VI AND QUEEN ELIZABETH DIAMOND STAKES,** 12f, equal top weight, defeating HIGH-RISE, ROYAL ANTHEM, DAYLAMI
Won Gr. 1	**IRISH CHAMPION STAKES**, 10f, equal top weight, defeating ALBORADA, XAAR
Won Gr. 1	**VODAFONE CORONATION CUP**, 12f, defeating SINGSPIEL, DE QUEST
Won Gr. 2	**GRAND PRIX DE DEAUVILLE LANCEL,** 12.5f, defeating ZILZAL ZAMAAN, SUNRISE SONG

Daylami

gr. c by Doyoun — Daltawa (Miswaki)

Daylami was an unusual acquisition by Godolphin, the colt being leased out of the yard of top French trainer Alan de Royer Dupre at the end of his three year old season.

Having claimed a listed race success and finished second in the Grand Criterium as a juvenile, Daylami's fourth success from five starts came in the Poule d'Essai des Poulains. He then finished placed in the St James's Palace Stakes, Prix Jaques le Marois and Prix de Moulin, before shipping to Dubai.

He returned to Europe the following spring with an ambitious programme mapped out. After easily accounting for a class field in the Tattersalls Gold Cup at the Curragh, Daylami followed this success with a second in the Prince of Wales's Stakes. In the Coral-Eclipse Stakes at Sandown later in the season, Daylami was always in control. The grey was eased down near the line and ran out a half length winner, part of a Godolphin 1-2-3. Daylami again finished in the money on his next start, in the King George VI and Queen Elizabeth Diamond Stakes, behind Swain.

He next shipped to America, claiming the Man o'War Stakes at Belmont Park, and despite not fully recovering from the US trip, Daylami finished third in the Dubai Champion Stakes.

Returning to the Gulf that winter Daylami ran credibly in the Dubai World Cup, behind Almutawakel, before arriving back in Europe and opening his account in the Coronation Cup at Epsom.

Later in the summer he reappeared in the King George, running a massive race at Ascot and from early in the straight never looked like being beaten, finishing five lengths clear of Nedawi.

Next on his agenda came the Irish Champion Stakes, where Daylami pulled out one of the most dominant performances seen on any track in Europe that summer, defeating a Group One field by eight lengths.

The grey was widely believed to have a favourite's chance in the Prix de l'Arc de Triomphe at Longchamp. But rain turned the track far too soft for the Godolphin contender and he ran well below his best.

DAYLAMI (b. 1994)	Doyoun	Mill Reef	Never Bend Milan Mill
		Dumka	Kashmir II Faizebad
	Daltawa	Miswaki	Mr Prospector Hopespringseternal
		Damana	Crystal Palace Denia

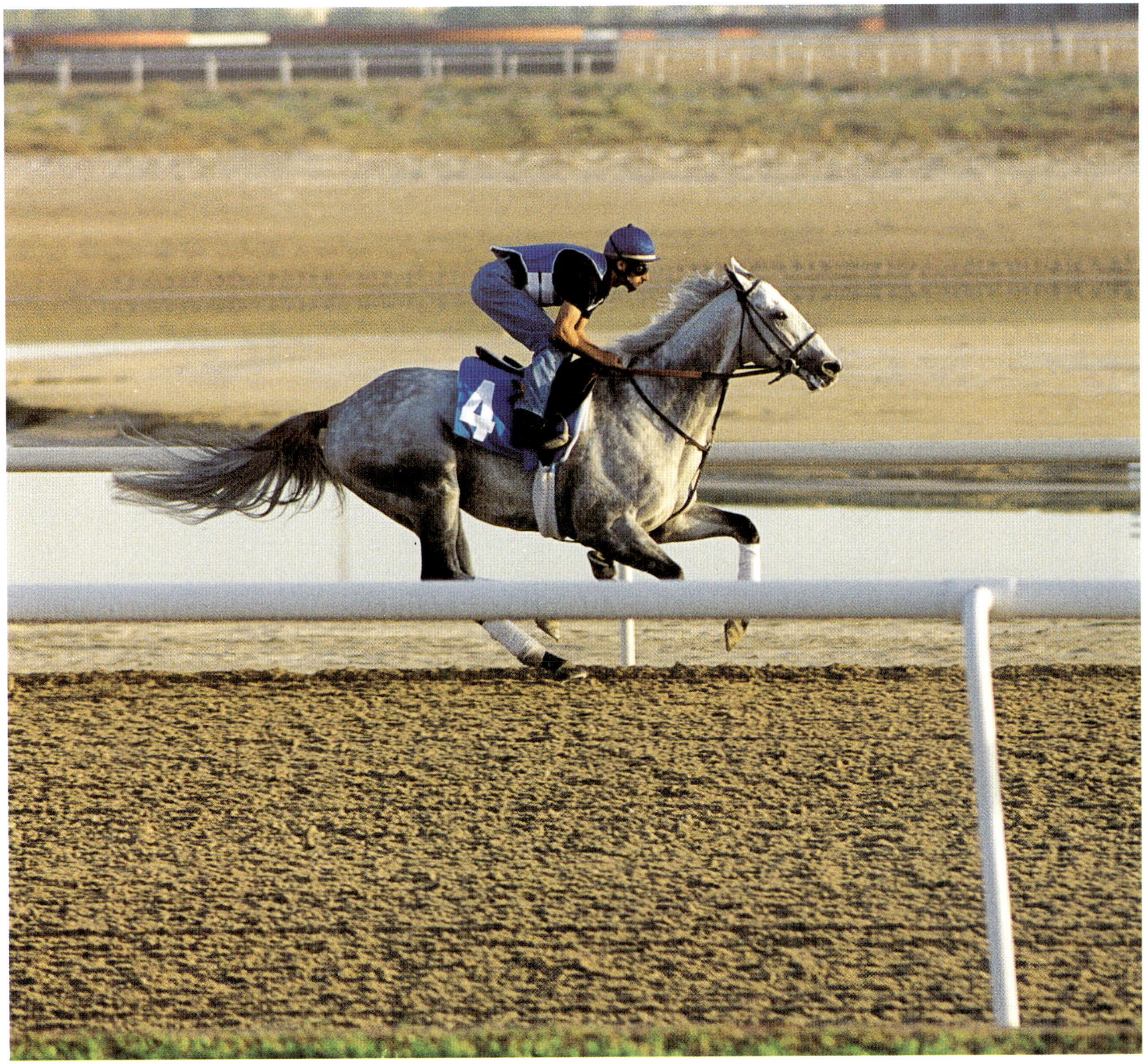
4

Diminuendo

ch. f by Diesis - Cacti (Tom Rolfe)

A $125,000 yearling from the first crop of Diesis, Diminuendo made history on her first career outing, an effortless 10-length victory in a Leicester maiden—the first racecourse success for her sire. Within a month, the juvenile was regarded as being among the leading fillies of her generation following two further successes.

Running in the Hoover Mile in September, Diminuendo unleashed a tremendous turn of foot in the last furlong to claim a comfortable win. Judged on that performance, the filly was clearly an Oaks candidate, and in-the-frame defeats in the Nell Gwyn and 1000 Guineas the following spring did nothing to diminish her standing.

When Diminuendo did take a step up in distance, in the Musidora Stakes at York, she responded by trouncing her five rivals.

At Epsom, Steve Cauthen settled his mount mid-division. There was little change in the running order until Tattenham Corner, when the principals began taking closer order. Three furlongs out there was little disguising the apparent ease at which Diminuendo was moving and when Cauthen asked, his mount displayed her turn of foot to hit the front and build a commanding victory margin.

Her next target took her to The Curragh for the Irish Oaks and seemingly an easy task compared with the field she met at Epsom. However it was not to be. Entering the straight she was again poised just behind the front-runners, but as Melodist went on, Diminuendo soon came under pressure and edged right into the whip. When she did find her stride, Melodist had already gained a strong advantage. As the line drew near Diminuendo began to reel in her rival. The duo passed the post together and the judges called a dead heat, the first in an Irish Classic for more than 40 years. Later it was revealed that Diminuendo had come into season days before the race.

Saddled in the Yorkshire Oaks where she shattered the course record, Diminuendo's final outing of the season came in the St Leger where she started odds-on against five rivals. With 200 metres to go, the Classic was a match between Diminuendo and Minster Son. Diminuendo was one length down at the distance and despite strong urging she failed to make any impression.

Diesis (ch. 1980)	**Sharpen Up**	Atan
		Rocchetta
	Doubly Sure	Reliance II
		Soft Angels
DIMINUENDO (ch. 1985)		
Cacti (ch. 1977)	**Tom Rolfe**	Ribot
		Pocahontas II
	Desert Love	Amerigo
		Desert Vision

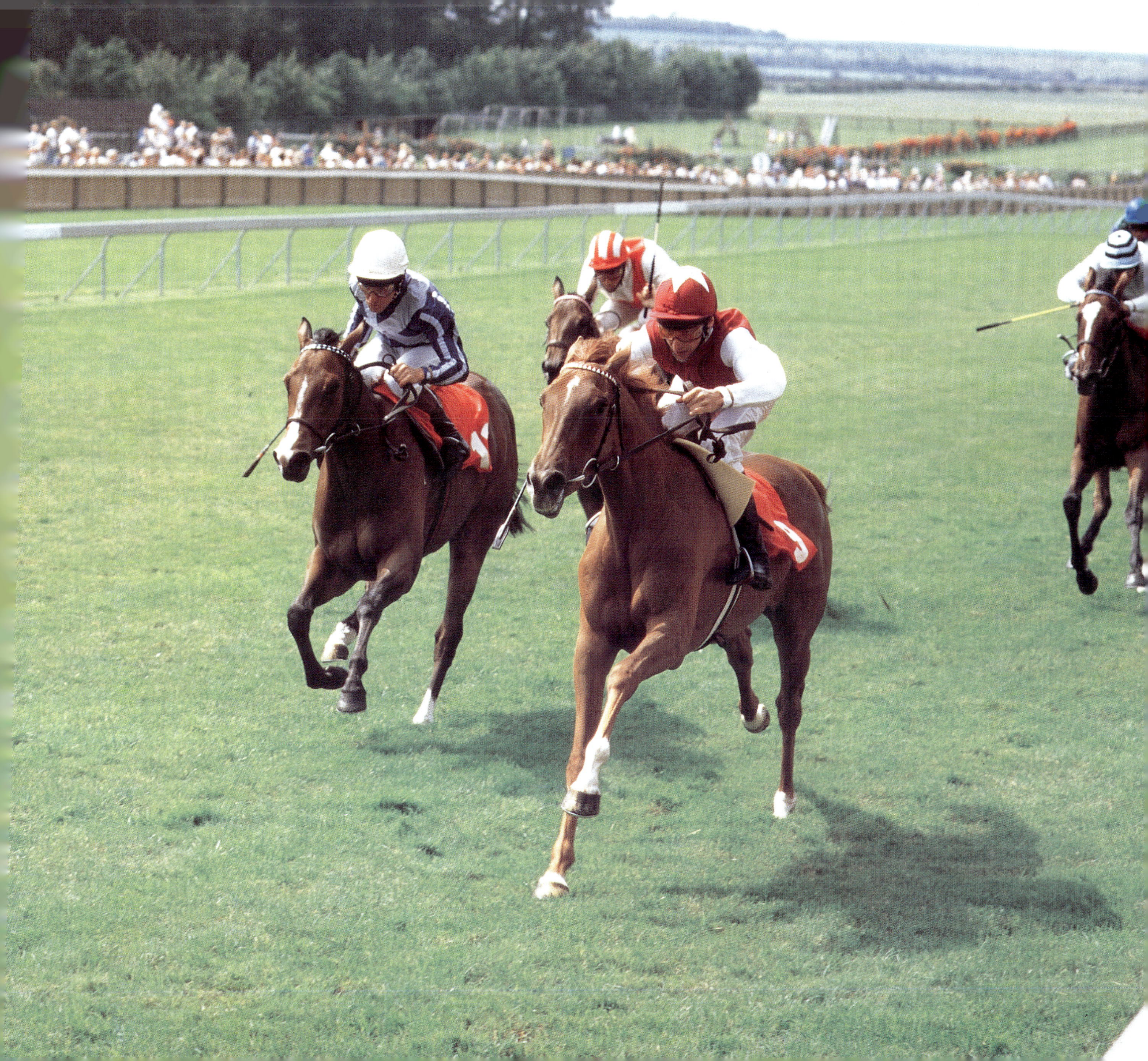

Dubai Millennium

b. c by Seeking The Gold — Colorado Dancer (Shareef Dancer)

Originally named Yaazer, the colt was renamed Dubai Millennium by Sheikh Mohammed, showing potential after going into training.

After a maiden win at Yarmouth, Dubai Millennium moved to Dubai for the winter and growing rumours of his progress led to his being installed as one of the fancies for the Guineas. He eventually missed the Guineas and was first seen out when taking a conditions event at Doncaster, and then stepping up in class to take the Predominate Stakes.

Dubai Millennium went into the Epsom Derby having registered three successes from three outings, with a combined winning distance of 17 and a half lengths. Going well during the early stages he was soon found wanting and faded into ninth.

The result of this was always going to be a drop in distance, and when shipped to France for the Prix Jaques le Marois the colt won well.

The Queen Elizabeth II Stakes was his next target, and Dubai Millennium was at his devastating best. With two furlongs remaining, he was sent on, unleashing an awesome kick to win by six lengths.

It was the beginning of March 2000 before he reappeared, for a Dubai World Cup sharpener at Nad Al Sheba. On the bridle and eased late, Dubai Millennium still broke the track record.

Against 12 opponents in the Dubai World Cup, Dubai Millennium went to the front inside the first furlong and thereafter made the world's richest race a procession, a remarkable performance.

Only one horse remained in Dubai Millennium's way on the road to being considered the greatest—Montjeu. Sheikh Mohammed proposed an unprecedented $6 million match race between the two stars. This head-to-head collapsed tragically when Dubai Millennium fractured a leg on the gallops. He was retired to stud in Britain. Worse was to follow, when, by a million to one chance, Dubai Millennium contracted the rare and often fatal equine disease of Grass Sickness and was put down humanely to prevent him from suffering further.

DUBAI MILLENNIUM (b. 1996)	**Seeking The Gold**	Mr Prospector — Raise A Native / Gold Digger
		Con Game — Buckpasser / Broadway
	Colorado Dancer	Shareef Dancer — Northern Dancer / Sweet Alliance
		Fall Aspen — Pretense / Change Water

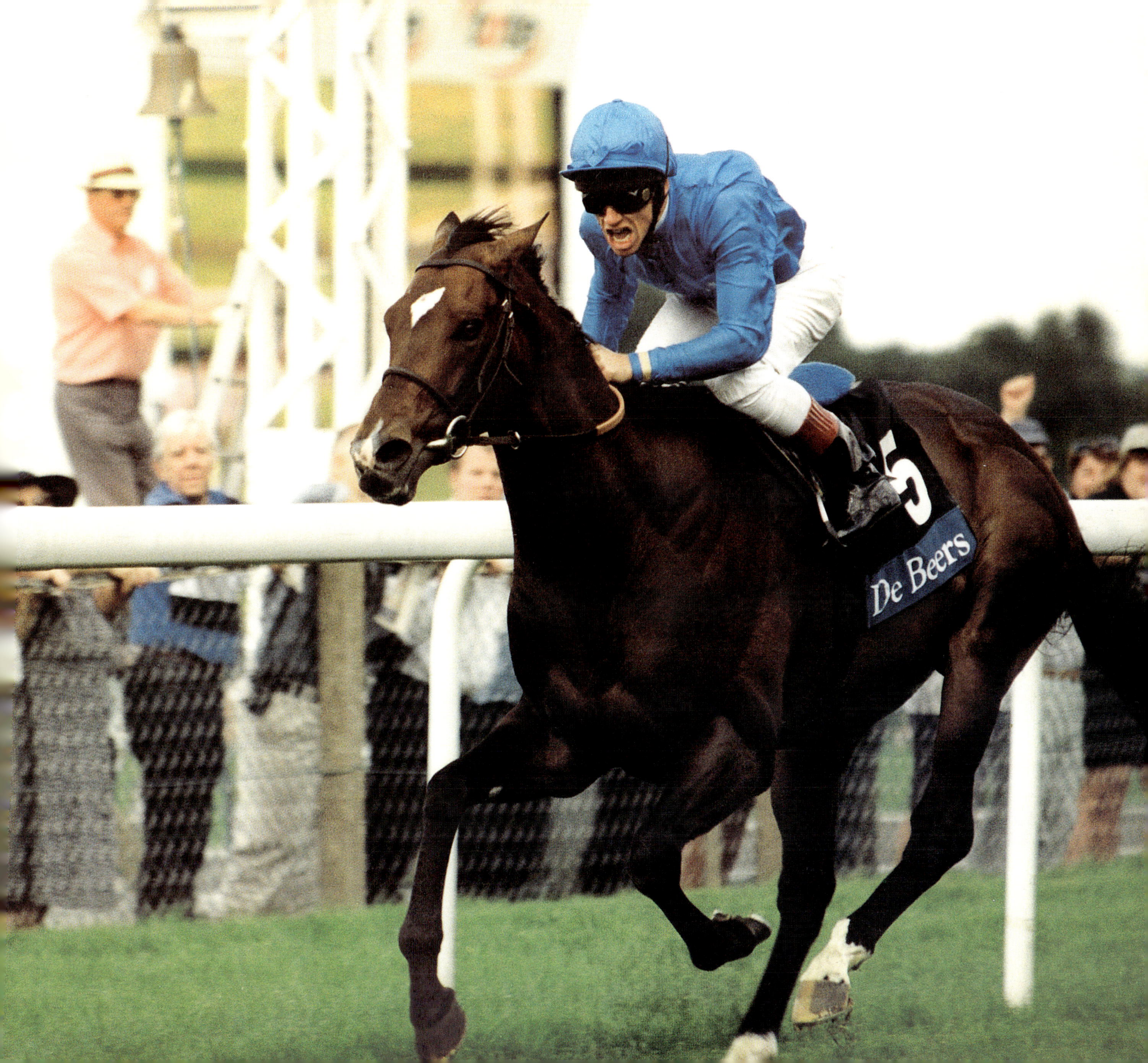
5
De Beers

E Dubai

b. c by Mr. Prospector - Words of War (Lord At War)

Bred in Kentucky by Arthur B. Hancock III and Stonerside Stable, this striking colt was purchased for $1,350,000 by John Ferguson Bloodstock at the 1999 Keeneland September Yearling Sale.

In 1999 Godolphin, having enjoyed unprecedented success in Europe, began to set their sights seriously on the United States. Worldly Manner debuted for Godolphin in the Kentucky Derby that year. Soon after the stable established a juvenile division that included 2001 Breeders' Cup Juvenile Fillies winner Tempera. In 2001 Fantastic Light, a multiple Group One winner around the world, won the Breeders' Cup Turf.

After two outings and a single victory in his juvenile season, in 2000, E Dubai spent the winter in Dubai in preparation for the Kentucky Derby. He won his only race in the Emirates and was shipped over for Derby, but never started. Instead he embarked upon two years of campaigning that would make him the most consistently successful Godolphin horse ever in North America.

As a three-year-old the colt claimed two races at Belmont Park, an entry-level allowance race and the Grade Two Dwyer Stakes. But it was to be his four-year-old season in which the son of Mr. Prospector fully bloomed.

Assistant trainer Tom Albertrani had no intention of entering E Dubai in the Grade Two $500,000 Suburban Handicap until he received a call from Belmont Park to inform him they only had four confirmed starters for the race. They needed additional horses. Albertrani offered to enter, but stated that would not run.

Only the night before the Suburban did Sheikh Mohammed approve his colt to run. It was to prove an inspired move, however. E Dubai cruised to a three-quarter length victory under John Velazquez, making every post a winning one.

In his final career start E Dubai set the pace for the Breeders' Cup Classic, but faded into eleventh place. He retired to stallion duties at Jonabell near Lexington. Retiring with five wins and three seconds from 11 starts, and $920,800 in earnings, his three runner-up efforts were all in graded company: the Travers Stakes to Point Given, the Super Derby XXII and the Peter Pan Stakes.

E DUBAI (b. 1998)	**Mr. Prospector (b. 1970)**	Raise a Native — Native Dancer / Raise You
		Gold Digger — Nashua / Sequence
	Words of War (b. 1989)	Lord At War — General / Luna de Miel
		Right Word — Verbatim / Oratorio

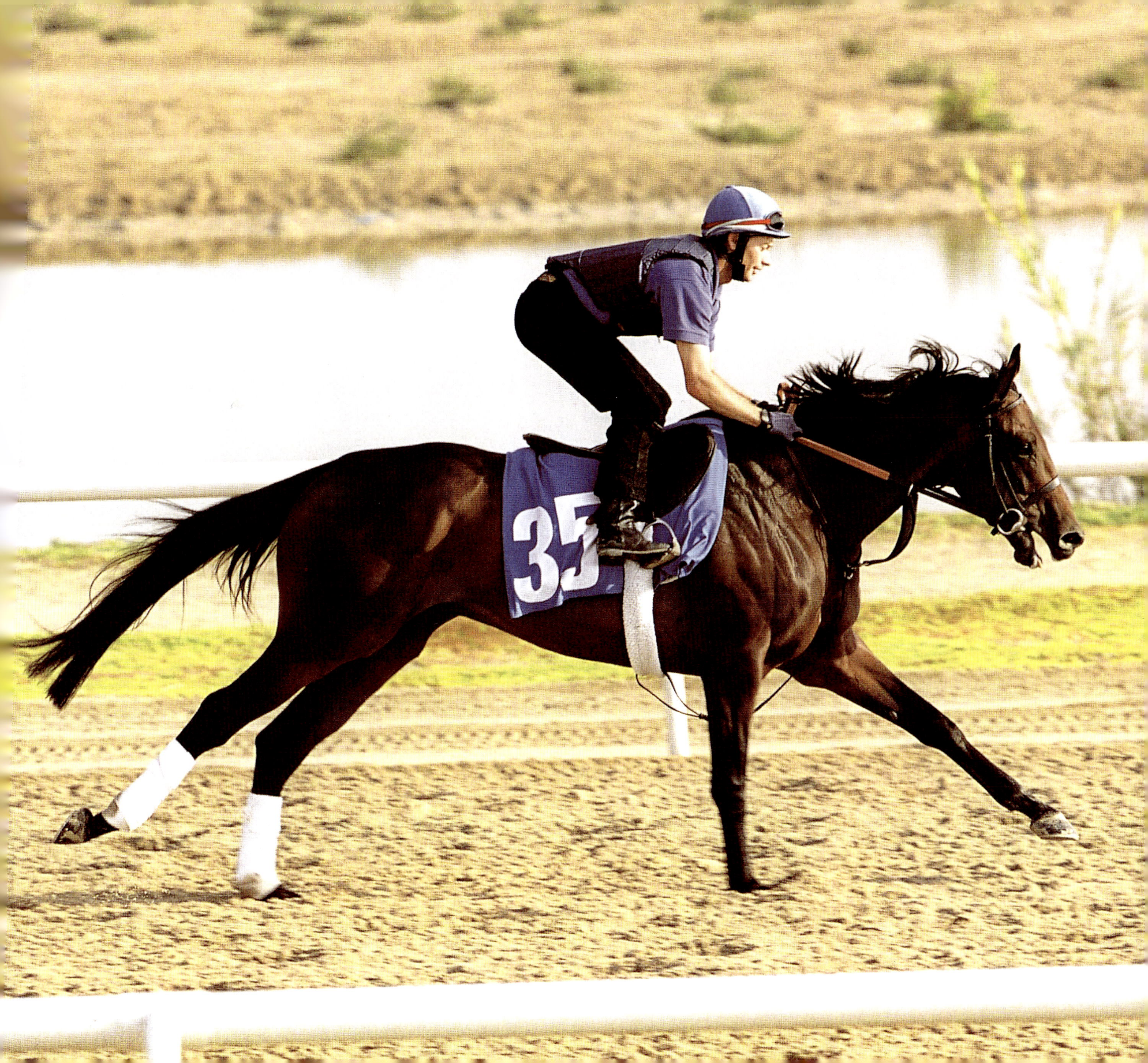
35

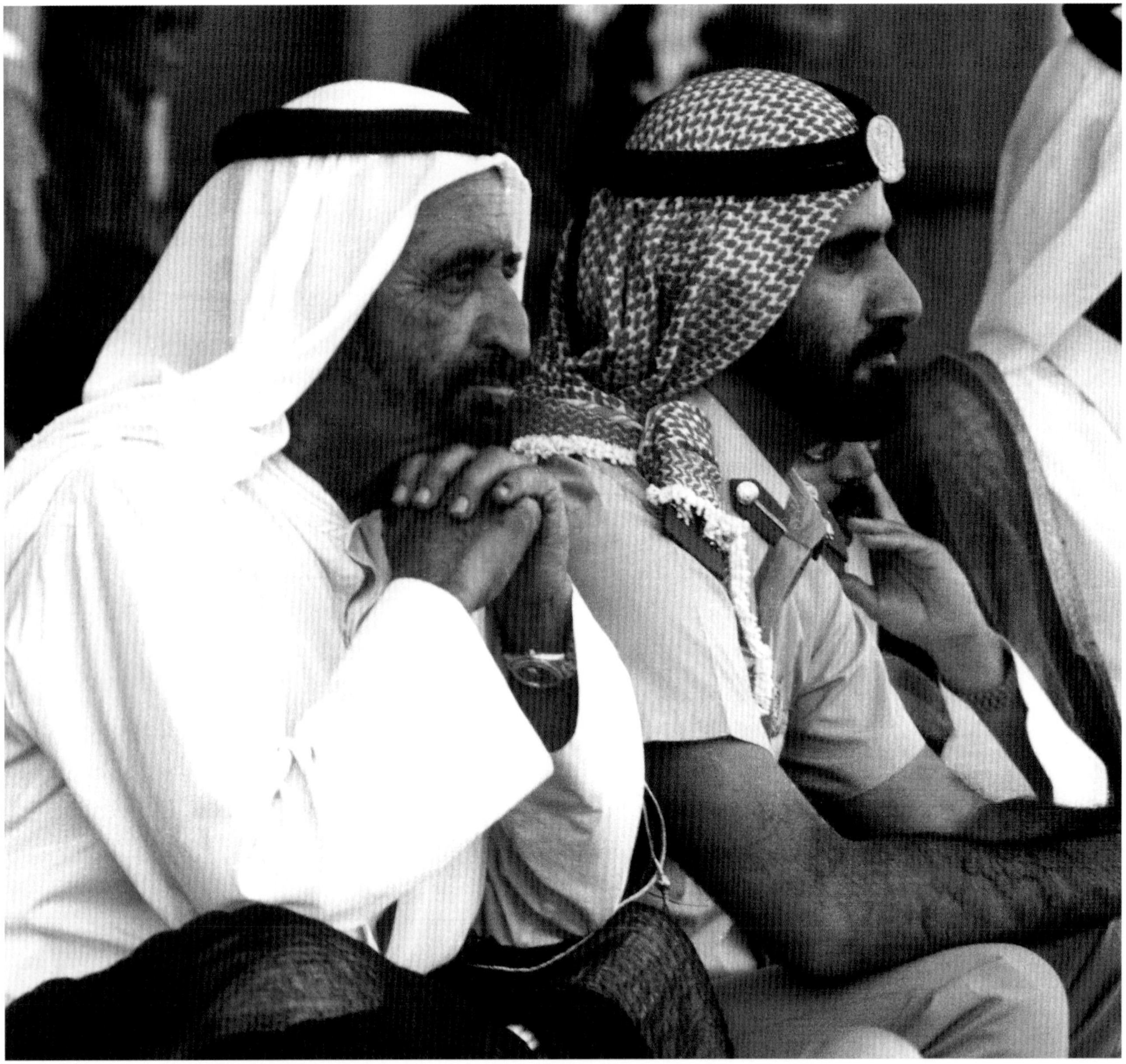

The Road to the Dubai World Cup

"There is no future, if the present is not linked to the past," said late UAE President Sheikh Zayed bin Sultan Al Nahyan. This statement is not only true in the case of all UAE citizens, but also the Arabs as a whole. The horse is a common cultural factor that unites the entire Middle East.

Although it is only in recent years that Dubai has become an international racing venue, Arab fascination with horses dates back centuries. Bedu folklore tells of tribal gatherings on important occasions such as Eid Al-Fitr, a celebration to mark the end of the Holy month of Ramadan, when sportsmen showed off their skills in falconry and shooting and matched their finest camels and horses in long distance races across the desert. The parallels between these great events and modern Endurance perhaps underpins the growth of this sport in recent times.

In the late 1920s and early 1930s, English racing was being dominated by the likes of Derby winners Gainsborough, his son Hyperion and Mahmoud. In America the likes of Gallant Fox and Omaha were achieving their own immortality by winning the Triple Crown. Half a world away, the young Crown Prince of Dubai, Sheikh Rashid bin Saeed Al Maktoum (*pictured left with Sheikh Mohammed*) was developing into a horseman of some repute locally. He loved riding and was seen in the saddle nearly every day taking his beloved Arabian, named Al Sqalawi, on a punctual mid-afternoon tour of public works and construction sites round the city-state.

His lifelong friend, Hamad bin Sukat, recalls Sheikh Rashid's fondness for horses. According to Bin Sukat, Al Sqalawi would follow at his owner's shoulder if Sheikh Rashid dismounted. Even after buying his first car, a Model-T Ford in 1934, Sheikh Rashid still preferred to ride Al Sqalawi. No surprise then, that the keen rider found time away from his relentless task of building Dubai, to tutor his sons in this noblest of Arab pursuits.

The link to thoroughbred racing came in the spring of 1967. Sheikh Hamdan and Sheikh Mohammed were based in Cambridge studying English when they observed newspaper reports highlighting the build-up to the 1000 and 2000 Guineas in Newmarket. Their interest was pricked and, on Saturday May 5, 1967 they visited a British racecourse for the first time. Training legend Sir Noel Murless won the 2000 Guineas with Royal Palace that day. The youthful brothers watched, fascinated, as a crowd of 40,000 at Newmarket erupted when the colt hit the front under jockey Gary Moore in the dying strides of the race.

It was a watershed experience for both. Sheikh Mohammed later recalled: "When we came [to England] we saw a lot of care taken, with both the horses and the racing."

Before the end of Sheikh Mohammed's second one-year tenure in Cambridge, the brothers would return to Newmarket several times and, indeed, venture to other tracks such as Ascot and Sandown. The 2000 Guineas of 1967 was the starting point in a passion shared by the four Maktoum brothers. Inexorably their interest was fanned.

Horse racing in its western form, had only begun to penetrate into the Gulf region prior to the Second World War and later. Bahrain's ruling Khalifa family began utilising their famed Arabian horses on a circular track, with a running rail, in the Sakir region of the island. In Abu Dhabi there are anecdotal stories of beach racing in the 1950s and 1960s.

In Saudi Arabia breeders from the Royal family raced Arabians and cross breds on a number of oval tracks with a running rail. The Racing and Hunting Association of Kuwait claims to have the oldest history of racing in the Gulf, on a sand track outside of Kuwait City that is said to have been operating in the 1940s.

But Gulf-wide there was no real ongoing programme of racing and standards were low.

By the late 1960s, both Sheikh Maktoum and Sheikh Mohammed maintained active stables in their home country. Their modest strings were made up of locally-bred horses, along with a smattering of thoroughbreds imported from, among others, Iraq and Pakistan.

These were raced on two tracks. In 1969 Sheikh Maktoum had instigated the construction of what could be called the first racetrack in the Emirates at Al Ghusais *(pictured right)*, Deira, on a site now occupied by the much expanded Dubai International Airport. Sheikh Maktoum's private stables were also at Al Ghusais. A block of 30 boxes was supplemented by the most advanced equine veterinary facility in the region at the time.

"Sheikh Maktoum would visit the stables nearly every day, and was a keen rider himself. Often he would go riding for hours." stated Dr. Ahmed Billah, a veterinary expert who flew in with a consignment of horses in 1969, and who remains in the UAE today. "He was very knowledgeable and most interested in reconciling modern training methods with the traditional ways that were prevalent at the time."

Sheikh Mohammed, meanwhile, also maintained his stables at Za'abeel, where former UAE champion trainer Satish Seemar is still based today. Sheikh Mohammed and his friends often rode races among themselves on a tight oval track at this site. The remnants of that circuit can still be seen today within the modern training track that Seemar added a decade ago.

It was the well appointed Al Ghusais, however,

117

which hosted some of the UAE's first race meetings on a purpose-built track during the early 1970s. These, were small affairs with only a handful of spectators in attendance. Runners were drawn predominantly from Al Ghusais and Za'abeel, with some entries from independent stables as far afield as Abu Dhabi and the Northern Emirates.

This informal and intermittent racing programme continued in the UAE throughout the 1970s with little in the way of progress being made. After 1977, of course, the Maktoums had made their entry into thoroughbred racing in Britain. The catalyst to this had been chance encounter in Dubai. Sheikh Mohammed, in his role as Head of Dubai Public Security, and Colonel Dick Warden, representing the Curragh Bloodstock Agency, in the UAE to deliver a consignment of horses for Dubai Police, had been the key. Warden had been instrumental in morphing an interest in racing to the Maktoum brothers becoming owners in Britain.

Purchased through Tattersalls in 1976, Sheikh Mohammed's Molecomb Stakes winner Hatta had set the ball rolling. Sheikh Maktoum has enjoyed success, mainly with Shaab, and, in 1980, Sheikh Hamdan had earned his first success with Mushref.

While the brothers from Dubai were becoming familiar names in Britain, the foundations of racing were being put down in their homeland. On October 1, 1981, Dubai Camel Track hosted the first meeting under any form of regulation. Three thoroughbred races, one sprint *(pictured)*, one mile and a mile-and-a-half event, were staged. This meeting is widely seen as the beginning of racing in Dubai and the UAE and they were essentially run under Jockey Club Rules.

At the time, several expatriate trainers were already established in Dubai and Sheikh Maktoum, who was particularly heavily involved with his string, was supporting Gulf-wide efforts to instigate some healthy regional and international competition.

During the early 1980s, Dubai's two main stables won races at an invitational meeting in Bombay, and dominated open events in Bahrain, which in 1979 had opened a western-style racecourse based upon the old Wolverhampton stadium and track.

Indeed, attempts to develop an annual Gulf

Racing Championship were effectively stifled by the success of Al Ghusais and Za'abeel, who dominated the 1982 Championships in Bahrain. After Dubai stables had won all five races on the card, regional interest waned.

"Ourselves and Al Ghusais were just to good," chuckles Paddy Crotty, the pioneering Irish trainer based at Za'abeel during this period. "Za'abeel won our three races by a combined margin of 35 lengths. Al Ghusais won one race by maybe 10 lengths. It was a bit one sided."

Interest around the UAE was also on the rise. Late UAE President Sheikh Zayed bin Sultan Al Nahyan was keen to promote heritage among his people. He organised a number of high profile National Day Cup meetings in Al Ain, where a semi-permanent track had been established but sadly did not continue.

In 1981 Za'abeel Stables won four of the five events in which they had runners. "That was a great day for us," said Crotty. "There was not that much racing at the time, a couple of odd meetings a year at best, so it was pretty important for us to do well."

During this period the sport was better organised. More meetings were being programmed (although not always staged) and a couple of 'proper' tracks were being developed. In 1982, the neighboring emirate of Sharjah constructed a dedicated racecourse at Sharjah Equestrian Club, which hosted a couple of meetings each season, while enthusiasts in Dubai opened the Al Met track *(pictured left)* in 1990, adjacent to the Metropolitan Hotel. These venues, along with Al Ghusais, Ajman Camel Track *(pictured above)* and a rough circuit in Umm Al Quwain, provided the basis of a small programme of up to half a dozen meetings each winter.

The development of Dubai as a commercial and tourism centre saw traffic into Dubai

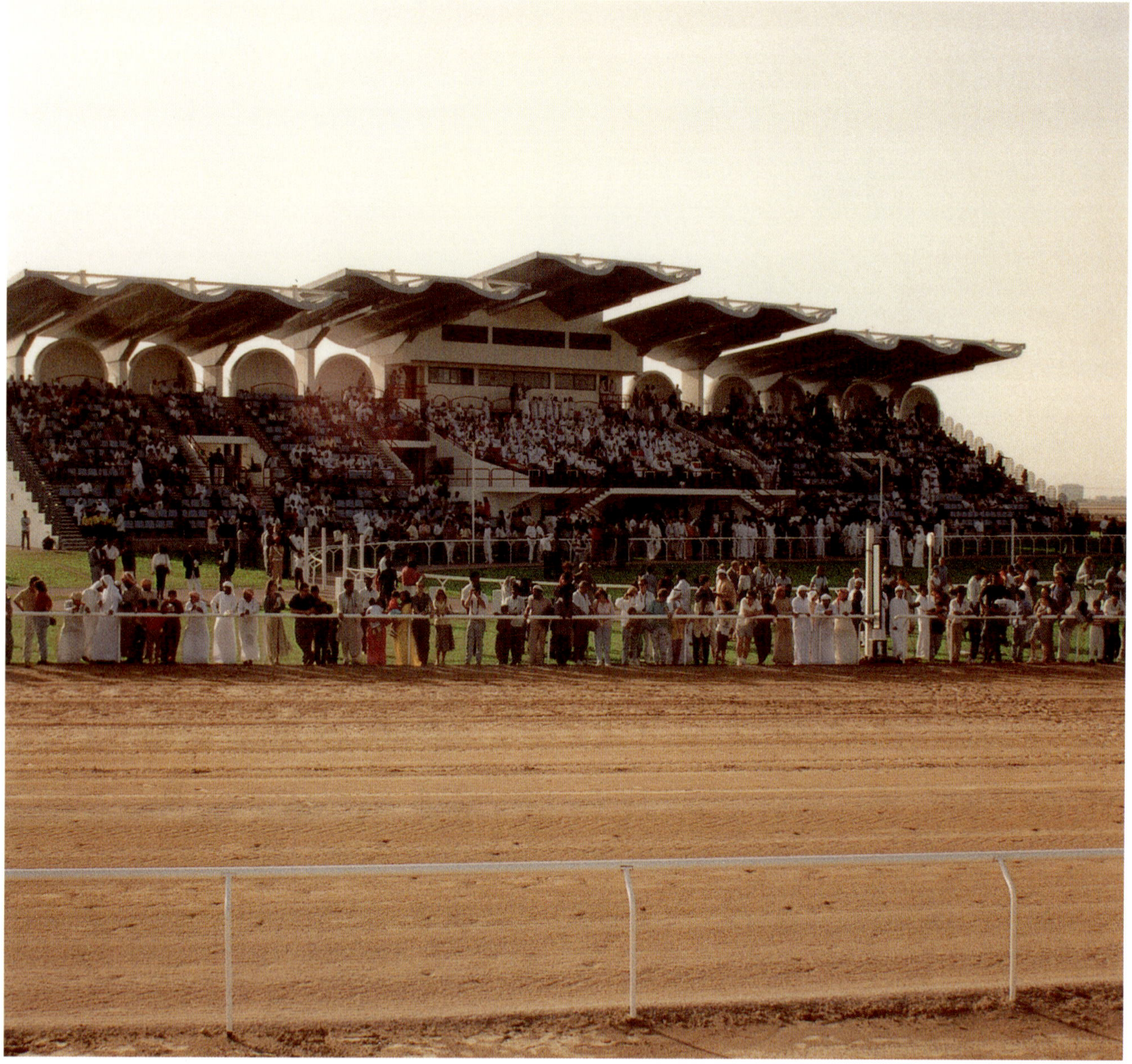

International Airport grow considerably during the early part of the decade. It was clearly no longer suitable for horses due to noise, Al Ghusais closed prior to the 1982 season. This was a bitter blow to those seeking to develop racing in the UAE further.

It was an era in which, after a gradual period of growth during the early years, the Maktoums' interest in European racing was growing. Sheikh Mohammed's burgeoning string in England burst onto the scene in 1982, with 20 individual winners, among them Yorkshire Oaks heroine Awaasif, Jalmood and Khaizaraan. The following summer he enjoyed 54.

But if Sheikh Mohammed had arrived in the spotlight, Sheikh Maktoum was hitting the very heights in 1982 through tough colt Touching Wood, a double St Leger winner and second in the Epsom Derby. Ma Biche and Shareef Dancer continued the Classic run in 1983, a year in which the brothers' combined string in Britain would number around 250.

This emerging passion for the sport was reflected in Dubai on a much smaller scale, Sheikh Mohammed was developing his Za'abeel Stables further. Sheikh Hamdan kept a string of ex-European thoroughbreds and some Arabians.

For months, Sheikh Maktoum and his advisors looked for the best site for a new facility. Hindsight is a wonderful thing, but little can Sheikh Maktoum have known what an excellent choice he was to make when he decided to relocate his Al Ghusais stables to a little known scrub desert area called Nad Al Sheba, well outside of Dubai's city limits.

Within 18 months, by early 1984, Nad Al Sheba opened. The site comprised of a flat, sand training track with a plastic running rail and little else. The original eight-hundred-seater grandstand *(pictured left)* was added in 1988. Exactly 12 years after the present day Sheikh Maktoum laid the foundations for a new training facility in the remote Nad Al Sheba area of Dubai, the track was staging the world's richest horse race, an event which today stands the Dubai track alongside the greats among racecourses of the world, such as Epsom, Churchill Downs and Longchamp.

Yorkshire trainer Bill Mather *(pictured above)* was recruited to run The Royal Stables. He recalls: "There was nothing there but the camel track, a training track and my stables."

"Everyone believed that we were in at the beginning of something new, that something big was going to happen. It just took a little longer to get racing up and running than expected." says Mather, whose ability to bring back 'broken' racehorses to the track and win with them saw him nicknamed 'the Wily Yorkshireman'. A number of lowly thoroughbreds were later transformed at The Royal Stables and went on to join Godolphin.

"During the mid and late-1980s there was no more than a handful of meetings each season. The most competitive stables, such as ours and Za'abeel, got a few ex-Europe based thoroughbreds, old handicappers mostly,' recalls Mather. "But standards were rising. Stables such as Umm Al Quwain, Jebel Ali and a few others were coming up. The whole scene was becoming more competitive."

In Europe, the likes of Maktoum stars Oh So Sharp, Mtoto and Nashwan had done their thing and retired to stud before anyone had really begun to contemplate racing under rules in the UAE. This changed with the beginning of the 1991/92 winter season. The catalyst for this was the UAE Equestrian and Racing Federation, headed by Sheikh Sultan bin Khalifa Al Nahyan, the governing body of equestrian sport in the UAE, Despite the relatively late formation of a national governing body for equestrianism, in 1985 the emirates has applied for, and was granted membership to, the Federation Equestre International. This was the first significant international recognition that equestrianism was part of the Emirates, sporting scene.

In time for the 1991/92 season a handful of tracks formed a coherent, national racing programme. These included Abu Dubai Equestrian Club, which had been running private meetings for a number of years. Racing in the Capital was managed by Pat Buckley, 1963 Grand national winning jockey and, even today, one of the most respected racing administrators in the Emirates.

Also in the programme was Al Met, Sharjah

Equestrian Club, the newly-inaugurated Jebel Ali Racecourse belonging to Sheikh Ahmed *(pictured above with Dhruba Selvaratnam)*. Jebel Ali was also to be home to an increasingly powerful stable under Selvraratnam, who would go on to win the

UAE Trainers' Championship on a number of occasions. Selvaratnam was former pupil assistant to the legendary Irish maestro Dr. Vincent O'Brien and arrived in Dubai to stamp his authority on the sport.

Sheikh Ahmed remains one of the leading patrons of the sport in the emirates. His Jebel Ali track, with its long uphill run to the finish line, remains highly successful in terms of racing and attracting spectators.

And toward the close of the 1991/92 season a new track appeared on the racing calendar. Sheikh Maktoum's vision had come of age. Nad Al Sheba had benefited from an extensive refurbishment of facilities and a relaying of the racing strip (the original surface all but washed away by storms). The new racecourse was inaugurated with a soft opening on January 29, 1992, followed, one month later, by a full blown meeting boasting the participation of star jockeys Lester Piggott *(pictured)* and Willie Carson.

Comprising of 20 meetings and more than 100 races for thoroughbreds, pure Arabians and crossbreds, this season was a huge success. New stables began to appear. More horses were being imported. Crowds were growing and media interest was greater. Racing, it seemed, had the impetus behind it now.

This fledgling campaign led to the formation of the Emirates Racing Association, charged with responsibility for organising and supervising UAE flat racing. Based in Dubai, the ERA was responsible for overseeing all racing within the UAE, a period which initially saw the emirates become associate members of the Asian Racing Conference and the International Racing Conference. It also had both thoroughbred and Arabian stud books accepted internationally, gained full membership of the World Arabian Horse Organisation (WAHO), staged the world's richest horserace and become one of the leading players on the international stage. All within just four years of its formation!

The 1992/93 campaign was effectively the first 'Under Rules'. This meant many changes. Increasing standards of professionalism were required, including transparent administration of the sport. More horses and top name international jockeys joined the fray, a development which is seen by many as the catalyst for the explosion of

Double for classy Piggott

...win after that nightmarish tumble in Florida last October comes on Bonita in the day's first race

Fancy an exciting afternoon at the races

• Hereafter, J. Brown up, winning the second race at Naad Al Sheba yesterday. —KT photos by Shakil Qaiser

RUDKIN COMES GOOD THRICE OVER
Dayflower shocke[r]

By David D'Souza & Graeme Wilson

CLASSIC contender Dayflower was sensationally beaten in her prep race for the British 1000 Guineas at the Dubai Racing Club yesterday.

The three-year old filly was being given an outing as a dress rehearsal and final sharpener for the April 30 Classic and her appearance had drawn a large crowd expecting a front showing.

Initially, she had overcome the one big test which was expected to get in her way; her hesitance of the starting stalls.

Down at the one mile start, trainer Satish Seemar had coaxed the Majestic Light filly into the stalls with few problems.

As the race began, her jockey Dennis Batteate had settled her at the head of affairs, showing hot early pace and seemed to be galloping home with the greatest of ease as the majority of the field failed to stay the pace.

With three furlongs to go, Dayflower was still running the rails, moving sweetly with Joey Brown on Palm Chat, the only animal seemingly in contention to come close to the star

● Ghurrah, Peter Brette astride, wins the third race

Just over two furlongs to go and Peter Brette on Ghurrah suddenly came into contention with a driving run. With Batteate still going smoothly, Ghurrah suddenly found a kick and before Dayflower could react, burst several lengths in front.

Still a furlong and a half to go, Batteate asked her mount for more and the filly responded to pull back some ground, but the deficit under sympathetic ride, eventually finishing two and half lengths behind the winner.

The shock of the season it may have seemed on the surface, but after her efforts at the stalls, it seems Dubai's challenge may still be on for the 1000 Guineas.

"I'm genuinely happy. She behaved at the gates an[d]

race," said Satish S[eemar]
"Don't forget, it is [...]
Dayflower has had [...]
It is easy to make [...]
not need any. My [...]
she will come on [...]
to the Guineas."

He also revealed [...]
Batteate had been [...]
flower too hard, ju[...]
she enjoyed her ou[...]
intact.

"She never reall[y...]
track and was cru[...]
Batteate. "You [...]
horse on grass that [...]
ber that Michael [Roberts]
ferred her to all th[e...]
ridden. Dayflower [...]
what it takes."

The shock winne[r...]
ble for trainer P[...]
went on to take a [...]
end of the day.

He had started [...]
hacked up in supe[rb...]
Brown and then [...]
Pabouche gaining [...]
the 5.30 under Ba[tteate...]

MAESTRO DELIGHTS ON COMEBACK

● Joey Brown on Stapleton drives for the line chased by Sabei (Kevin Davis) and Woodhaunter (Dennis Batteate) and, right, Piggott jumps the field on Red Rainbow

Seemar stars in thriller

ON THE TRACK ... with Graeme Wilson

● Shaikh Ahmed bin Rashid with Lester Piggott at Naad Al Sheba yesterday.—KT photos by Hasan Bozai

Ten of the best ride today

THE world's largest collection of champion jockeys ever assembled for one meeting warmed up towards this afternoon's International Jockeys' Challenge with a gallop at the Dubai Racing Club yesterday afternoon.

Taking their first ride on the Naad Al Sheba circuit, the ten protagonists gave their mounts a gentle spin around.

British champion Michael Roberts stuck closely throughout with old

ON THE TRACK with Graeme Wilson

friend and rival Richard Hills, watching and learning. The Japanese were separated only by language, but were one of the boys as they sped along, displaying smooth styles. The rest, all looking every inch the professionals they are, took in the track.

The ten have collected over 16,000 victories between them, picking up an Arc, one Kentucky Derby, one Melbourne Cup and two Japan Cup's along the way. They are, in short, the cream of jockeys from around the world.

"It's good for racing to have international events like this challenge, to see all the different riders. International racing is what it is all about," said

● The top 10 jockeys who are competing in the International Jockeys Challenge at Naad Al Sheba

Meeting in what has been billed an "unofficial world championship", the ten will do battle over four races worth 10 points to the winning jockey, six to the second, four points to the third,

forward to riding in such good company," said Japanese national hero Yutaka Take. "The track is easy to ride and is a soft cushion for the horses. I like my chances.

"My father was the champion of Japan and it is very important for me to do well as I would like to ride elsewhere in the world," stated the 24-

Headlines and faces from the early days of racing in the UAE. (opposite page) Sheikh Mohammed with Lester Piggott, Peter Brette, the first champion jockey. (this page) Sheikh Rashid and trainer Paddy Rudkin with then WBO Middleweight World Champion Chris Eubank.

125

interest in equestrianism throughout the Gulf. The ERA set a determined course to broaden the ownership base of the sport by increasing purses, employing public trainers, subsidised training fees and promoting two bloodstock sales in November 1992.

Until this point the sport had very much been the reserve of sheikhs and senior governmental officials; from this point on, local businessmen and expatriates joined the ranks of ownership. The sales, one in Abu Dhabi and one in Dubai, proved remarkably successful. Sheikh Mohammed donated 50 ex-Europe based thoroughbreds to the Emirates Racing Association. They sold for Dhs.4.65 million ($1.27 million).

The 1992/93 racing season got underway with an impetus fueled by a new high standard of horse and big name jockeys to add to the fare on offer such as European stars John Matthias, Richard Hills and, briefly, Lester Piggott. The infrastructure was not in place at this point to support an international event encompassing foreign horses. The result was the Dubai International jockeys' Challenge, an event encompassing 10 of the UAE in one day of competition. The Dubai International Jockeys' Challenge continued as an international focal point for the UAE season for three years, until circumstances opened the way for an event of even greater importance.

Today, Nad Al Sheba hosts the world's richest race, the pinnacle of a UAE racing programme dotted with black type races, the Festival, and witnessing some of the best racing in the world. From a viewpoint of Dubai racing's massive crowds and all the drama and glamour, it seems hard to comprehend that the Maktoum family have built such an extraordinary racing center, virtually from scratch, in less than 15 years.

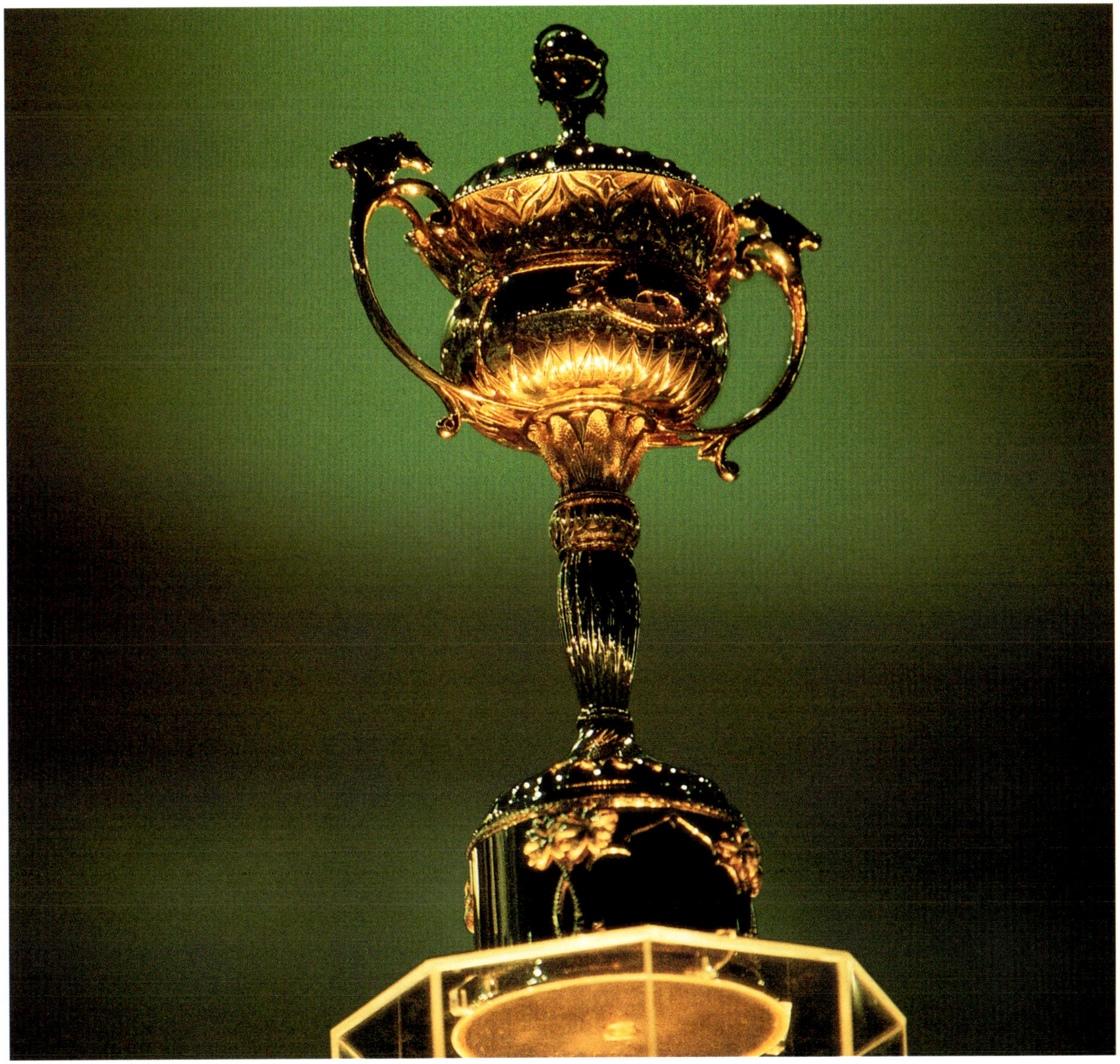

1996 - Cigar

The final two decades of the 20th Century will be remembered within racing as the years the sport went global. Cross border competition became inter-continental, encouraged by the huge purses which followed the 1981 staging of the inaugural Arlington Million.

Since then, America's Breeders' Cup, and to a lesser extent the Japan Cup, Melbourne Cup and Hong Kong Invitational Races posted prize money capable of attracting runners from around the world. However, as this most exciting genre of the sport had developed, a debate has raged around claims to be an authentic world championship.

When Sheikh Mohammed decided to bring international racing to the UAE his team set out to ensure the participation of the best thoroughbreds on earth, an event which would finally be capable of claiming such a mantle.

Carrying $4 million of prize money, the inaugural staging of the Dubai World Cup fulfilled the wildest dreams of racing lovers everywhere, bringing together champions from Europe, Oceania, Asia, the Americas and the UAE at Nad Al Sheba, for an event which was officially recognised as the strongest race ever run.

The 2,000 metre classic attracted 48 $5,000 nominations at the first entry stage in October, the depth of quality pre-ordaining Dubai's first international race as something unique. Among them were US wonderhorse and Breeders' Cup classic winner Cigar, Melbourne Cup star Jeune, Japanese dirt champion Lively Mount, Prix de l' Arc de Triomphe runner-up Freedom Cry and 2000 Guineas victor Pennekamp.

A further 19 horses joined the roster at a $10,000 second entry stage on January 2, leaving a panel of the world's leading handicappers with a list of 67 nominees from which to whittle down a field of 14 runners plus regional reserves. In late January the handicapping committee, chaired by Britain's Goeffrey Gibbs and including the UAE's Melvyn Day and US stalwart Howard Battle, met in London to nominate their preferred field.

If ongoing publicity were needed for such an event, this was more than amply provided by the undoubted star of the show, Cigar. Speculation never ended regarding his on-off trip to Dubai, with trainer Bill Mott and enigmatic owner Allen Paulson offering almost daily bulletins on the colt who had won all of his 10 starts in 1995.

"He's coming," Paulson stated in late January. "We've looked at our options and decided to go."

After returning to the racecourse to scoop the $300,000 Donn Handicap at Gulfstream at the beginning of February, the colt suffered a stone bruise on his right front foot, missed the Santa Anita Handicap and a great deal of track work. It was against the background of much rumour and pessimism that Cigar flew to Dubai, short of work in his preparation, but a definite starter according to Paulson.

However, despite these disappointments, March 27 dawned with an awesome 11 horse line up set to take to the track for the inaugural Dubai World Cup. Cigar headed the betting although his troubled build up had led to a drift in the market, the other US challengers including L'Carriere, second to Cigar in the Breeders' Cup Classic, and the Soul of the Matter, owned by songwriter Burt Bacharach.

Over 30,000 people crammed into Nad Al Sheba. Support card aside, the build up and day were about just over two minutes of thrilling action, from the moment the stalls opened until the winning horse crossed the line. Charging into the home straight, Jerry Bailey steered Cigar into the front position and instantly the wonder colt kicked on. Pentire, Halling and all his rivals were left struggling.

Under two out, Cigar suddenly had company at the front as Soul Of The Matter moved upsides and into the lead. This was the moment when Cigar could have faltered, but instead he dug deeper to find the burst which was required to retake the lead, and claim the Dubai World Cup.

It was an astonishing performance and the success of the world's greatest thoroughbred in the world's richest race set the Dubai World Cup on course to its present day status. Since then, Cigar has been joined on the Dubai World Cup Roll Of Honour by a plethora of the sports's greatest performers.

1997 - Singspiel

Sheikh Mohammed's ultra-classy globetrotting champion Singspiel gave Jerry Bailey his second successive Dubai World Cup victory in 1997 when the five-year-old horse proved too powerful for American raider Siphon.

Trained in Britain by Sir Michael Stoute, before flying to the United Arab Emirates, Singspiel had already done connections proud in claiming the Japan Cup and the Grade One Canadian International at Woodbine, as well as being narrowly beaten in the Breeders' Cup Turf. His credentials for the Dubai World Cup were clear and in front of a crowd of 35,000 he was not to dissapoint.

The son of Sheikh Mohammed's In The Wings defeated U.S. entrant Siphon by a length and a quarter, with Sandpit in third. In doing so, Singspiel became the leading earner ever among European-based horses with $5,405,495 in earnings.

Bailey solidified his grip as the world's best big-money rider with his win. Bailey had won four $3 million Breeders' Cup Classics (1991, 1993-95) and two $4 million Dubai World Cups. During those six races he had collected 10 percent of $20 million for about 12 minutes work.

After his Dubai hiroics, Singspiel would add two prestigious British Group Ones, the Coronation Cup at Epsom by five lengths and Juddmonte International at York, to cap a great career.

1998 - Silver Charm

The world's richest horse race was claimed again by an American favourite, Silver Charm. The US contender, a son of Silver Buck, was the previous year's Kentucky Derby winner. Silver Charm lived up to his illustrious billing - but only just as he scored a narrow victory at Nad Al Sheba. The Bob Baffert-trained grey broke smartly and was soon tracking the early leader US start Behrens, with Predappio close behind in third.

As the field swung into the straight, jockey Gary Stevens sent Silver Charm to the front and a comfortable victory looked assured and the horse quickened dramatically. A 50,000 strong crowd were already on their feet, hollering and applauding, seemingly recognising the winning performance of yet another outstanding champion.

But Irish star Michael Kinane and Godolphin's Swain had other ideas. Picking up from mid-division, Swain came along the home straight with the pace of a leading sprinter and put in a storming finish. Some 100 yards from the finishing line Swain was almost on terms with Silver Charm, but the Kentucky Derby was not a champion for nothing and dug deep for another gear.

The pair flashed past the post virtually stride for stride, the judge needing to split the pair in a photo-finish. French challenger Loup Sauvage kept on for third place.

1999 - Almutawakel

Almutawakel, ridden by jockey Richard Hills, won the Dubai World Cup to notch trainer Saeed bin Suroor's first success in his domestic showpiece.

The four-year-old colt, owned by Sheikh Hamdan, emerged to overtake long-time leader Central Park while holding off late challenges from Malek and Victory Gallop and keep the Cup at home for the first time.

Eight ran in a race which went at a strong pace with previous year's winner and Kentucky Derby start Silver Charm also in contention but never looking as classy as 12 months earlier.

The winner's charge for home came with two furlongs remaining of the 10-furlong race. Hill's timing was perfect. His mount quickly got the better of Central Park. Driven clear by 33-year-old Hills, who completed a double triumph after earlier taking the Group Three Dubai Duty Free, the four-year-old, who won a Group One race in France the previous summer, had to repel the challenges first of Victory Gallop and then a renewed run from the unstinting Malek.

Epsom Derby winner High-Rise entered the Nad Al Sheba blue riband under the Godolphin banner and the race was widely hailed for bringing together the winners of the Kentucky and Epsom classics, but neither was to be a major feature. The Epsom star ran a disappointing race and trailed home last.

2000 - Dubai Millennium

Dubai Millennium's phenomenal six-length victory in $6 million Dubai World Cup was the most momentous and compelling sporting triumph in recent thoroughbred racing history.

Carrying the hopes and expectations of a nation of racing fans, the four-year-old colt annihilated a world class field of champions to prove that he was every inch the greatest horse that Sheikh Mohammed has ever had. In every way, from the very beginning of his career, Sheikh Mohammed has had utter conviction that this was the horse for the new millennium, when he changed his name from Yazeer to Dubai Millennium.

Despite not being seriously challenged, Dubai Millennium shaved one tenth of his own course record, with an impressive time of 1:59.50 seconds. Piloted by the incomparable Frankie Dettori, Dubai Millennium raced with complete fluency at the head of a 14-horse field that included runners from America, Britain, Japan, Hong Kong and Saudi Arabia. His absolute class saw him quicken at the top of the three furlong home straight to coast home a clear winner.

Behrens, ridden by American champion Jorge Chavez hung on for second place, followed three other American contenders, Public Purse, Puerto Madero and Ecton Park. Japan's big hope, World Cleek, was sixth.

2001 - Captain Steve

Captain Steve gave America and jockey Jerry Bailey their third victory in the six runnings of the Dubai World Cup. The winner had been purchased by his owner for just $70,000.

It was Japanese runner To The Victory that had thrown down the gauntlet to her 11 rivals, setting a scorching pace. With Frankie Dettori and his mount Best of the Bests beginning to beat a retreat after the halfway stage it was left to Captain Steve to give chase.

The Bob Baffert trained Captain Steve, a 7-4 joint favourite, quickly matched the Japanese entry at the head of affairs and was sent to the front by Bailey — who won the race on Cigar in 1996 and Singspiel a year later — inside the final furlong.

And the combination strode clear to beat the front-running To The Victory by three lengths with Hightori finishing strongly to claim third, half-a-length away.

Before a multi-national crowd of more than 50,000, the American horse crushed his 11 rivals with a power-packed display. The hopes of the hosts were all in vain with the three Godolphin contenders unable to make an impact.

Silver-haired trainer Bob Baffert punched the air as Captain Steve passed the post to secure first prize in the $6 million contest.

2002 - Street Cry

Over 50,000 spectators congregated at Nad Al Sheba for the seventh running of the Dubai World Cup, the world's richest horse race and the world's richest day of racing.

Despite the unusually low turnout of American runners on this year, the racing was still very competitive with a few surprises such as Val Royal's sound defeat in the Duty Free and Sakhee's dismissal by stablemate Street Cry. The Dubai World Cup was expected to be a coronation for 2001 Breeders' Cup Classic runner-up and Prix de l'Arc de Triomphe winner Sakhee. However, jockey Jerry Bailey, aboard stablemate Street Cry, stole the show. Sakhee, unable to keep up with Street Cry in the stretch, faded as Sei Mi rallied from twenty lengths back to finish second. It was four and a half lengths from Street Cry to Sei Mi and another four and a half lengths back to Sakhee. American invader Western Pride, leased to a Saudi owner for the one start, finished ninth after pressing the early pace.

Jockey Jerry Bailey, having won four of the seven Dubai World Cups, said; "It's great to have a horse that has so much in front of him. This is the world's richest race, an amazing race and it will always get the headlines. The race went perfectly and he quickened brilliantly."

2003 - Moon Ballad

The eighth running of the Dubai World Cup was the feature event on a card which was richest in racing with total purses of $15.2 million. With most races run on a dirt track, American horses had traditionally done well, but in 2003 the US's finest were shut out with the best finish being Harlan's Holiday, second in the main event.

The war in Iraq put a damper on the day, as attendance was only 35,000, down sharply from the over 50,000 who attended in past years. The war was the reason top American jockeys Jerry Bailey and Gary Stevens, who had ridden on every other World Cup card, did not make the trip overseas.

Harlan's Holiday and Godolphin entrant Nayef were co-favorites at 5-2, but it was 3-1 third choice and local hope Moon Ballad who cashed in, with Frankie Dettori aboard.

Moon Ballad was in contention early and always moving sweetly. Coming out of the far turn, Dettori roused Moon Ballad and he responded, leaving the rest of the field in his wake and finishing a whopping six lengths clear of Harlan's Holiday, who was in contention the whole way. Nayef was another length back in third, with another Godolphin star, Grandera, in fourth.

Moon Ballad was the first Dubai World Cup winner to be sired by a Dubai World Cup winner, 1997 champion Singspiel.

2004 - Pleasently Perfect

Some of the world's best horses traveled all the way to Nad Al Sheba for the ninth running of the Dubai World Cup, but to be fair the sheer class of the two leading market favourites meant that the race was far less open than in previous runnings.

The headline event, the world's richest race with a purse of $6 million, evolved into a highly anticipated rematch between the top two finishers in the previous year's Breeders' Cup Classic. Classic winner Pleasantly Perfect and runner-up Medaglia d'Oro. The latter was to be ridden by Jerry Bailey, a jockey who can claim to be a Dubai World Cup specialist in a way that Leeter Piggott was considered an Epsom Derby specialist, so hopes were high in that camp that Classic placings were set to be reversed.

Twelve runners went to post. Bailey kept Medaglia d'Oro close to the pace. Turning for home, Medaglia d'Oro went to the front. However, Pleasantly Perfect, who had stalked the pace in fourth under Alex Solis, came on strong around the turn and the two horses dueled over the last two and a half furlongs. Only in the latter stages did Pleasantly Perfect poke his nose ahead of Medaglia d'Oro and inched away to win by three quarters of a length. South African-bred Victory Moon was about five lengths back in third.

Pleasantly Perfect became the second Breeders' Cup Classic winner to also win the Dubai World Cup.

2005 - Roses in May

Roses in May justified his favouritism by landing the tenth running of world's richest race, sponsored by Emirates, by a convincing three lengths.

How much had changed since Cigar's win in the inaugural running of the race in 1996. Roses in May became the 43rd international winner of the 2005 Dubai International Racing Carnival, which had begun on January 20 and culminated with the World Cup. A total of 200 horses from 20 countries and representing 79 trainers had jetted into Dubai to compete in the Carnival for a total of US$25 million in prizemoney.

Racing in Dubai had clearly come of age and, in doing so, had become the most globalised center of the sport anywhere in the world

Roses in May was in fifth place early with the field being taken along by the Mike de Kock-trained Yard-Arm. Roses in May, trained by Dale Romans and ridden by John Velazquez, came around the outside and took the lead into the straight and from that moment on there was no looking back.

Dynever, trained by Christophe Clement and ridden by Jose Santos, came with a late burst of speed to take second from the Jeff Mullins-trained Choctaw Nation, the mount of Victor Espinoza.

Gerard Butler's Jack Sullivan ran the race of his life under Darryll Holland to take fourth ahead of the Dick Mandella-trained Congrats.

2006 - Electrocutionist

Godolphin triumphed again when Sheikh Mohammed's Electrocutionist won it for the home team, defeating a strong international field and showing a great deal of class in doing so.

Held up for a long time by Frankie Dettori, Electrocutionist was in mid-division as the field headed down the straight with Brass Hat up front and seemingly staying on well. The Godolphin contender made strong progress at the quarter pole and was almost upsides the pace-setting American trio of Wilko, Magna Graduate and Super Frolic.

With an eighth of a mile to go there was a wall of three horses, Brass Hat, Wilko, and Electrocutionist battling to the line and the three were almost inseperable for half a furlong.

But Electrocutionist dug deep and began to inch forward with every stride. He passed Brass Hat with just 70 yards remaining before the line. Only then did Brass Hat begin to tire, exhausted by the task of matching Electrocutionist stride-for-stride, and the eventual winner would go on to record what was a perhaps flattering margin of victory. Electrocutionist won the world's richest race by one and three quarter lengths, with three more lengths back to Wilko in third.

Dettori said; "I didn't breathe for two minutes... I did not think I could win until I was 30 yards out as I could not shake off Brass Hat."

Electrocutionist
b. c by Red Ransom — Elbaaha (Arazi)

Nobody present at Nad Al Sheba racecourse on Saturday March 25, 2006 will forget the rousing reception given to Godolphin's Electrocutionist after his hard fought victory in the Dubai World Cup. Winning jockey Frankie Dettori performed his trademark flying dismount to the delight of the crowd as he celebrated his third World Cup win, Godolphin's fourth and Saeed bin Suroor's fifth.

Unraced as a juvenile, the son of Red Ransom made a winning racecourse debut in an event restricted to unraced three-year-olds over nine furlongs. Electrocutionist then won a Listed race, before winning a conditions event. All three of those races were at Milan's San Siro racecourse, as was his next outing when a nose second in the Group one Gran Premio Del Jockey Club to German Derby and subsequent Breeders' Cup Turf and Coronation Cup winner Shirocco.

That was over 12-furlongs, as were his first two starts of 2005 when winning a Group two race at The Capannelle and his Group one victory, back in Milan, in the Gran Premio Di Milano.

Taken to England for the Group one Juddmonte International, over 10-furlongs at York, he prevailed in a thrilling three way photo to truly announce himself on the international stage.

His final start for Valiani was a third (promoted) in the Group one Canadian International at Woodbine, after which he was purchased privately by Godolphin.

He made his debut for them in the concluding round of the Maktoum Challenge, his first race on dirt and over the same course and distance as the Dubai World Cup. Struggling in the early stages, Dettori was able to extricate him from the kickback and, entering the long straight, he started to make progress. He still looked to face a stiff task two furlongs out but ran on strongly to deny the subsequently disqualified Brass Hat.

His last start was a second to Ouija Board in the Prince of Wales's Stakes. In September 2006 Electrocutionist tragically died from a heart attack.

Red Ransom (b. 1987)	Roberto	Hail To Reason
		Bramalea
	Arabia	Damascus
		Christmas Wind
ELECTROCUTIONIST (b. 2001)		
Elbaaha (ch. 1994)	Arazi	Blushing Groom
		Danseur Fabuleux
	Gesedeh	Ela-Mana-Mou
		Le Melody

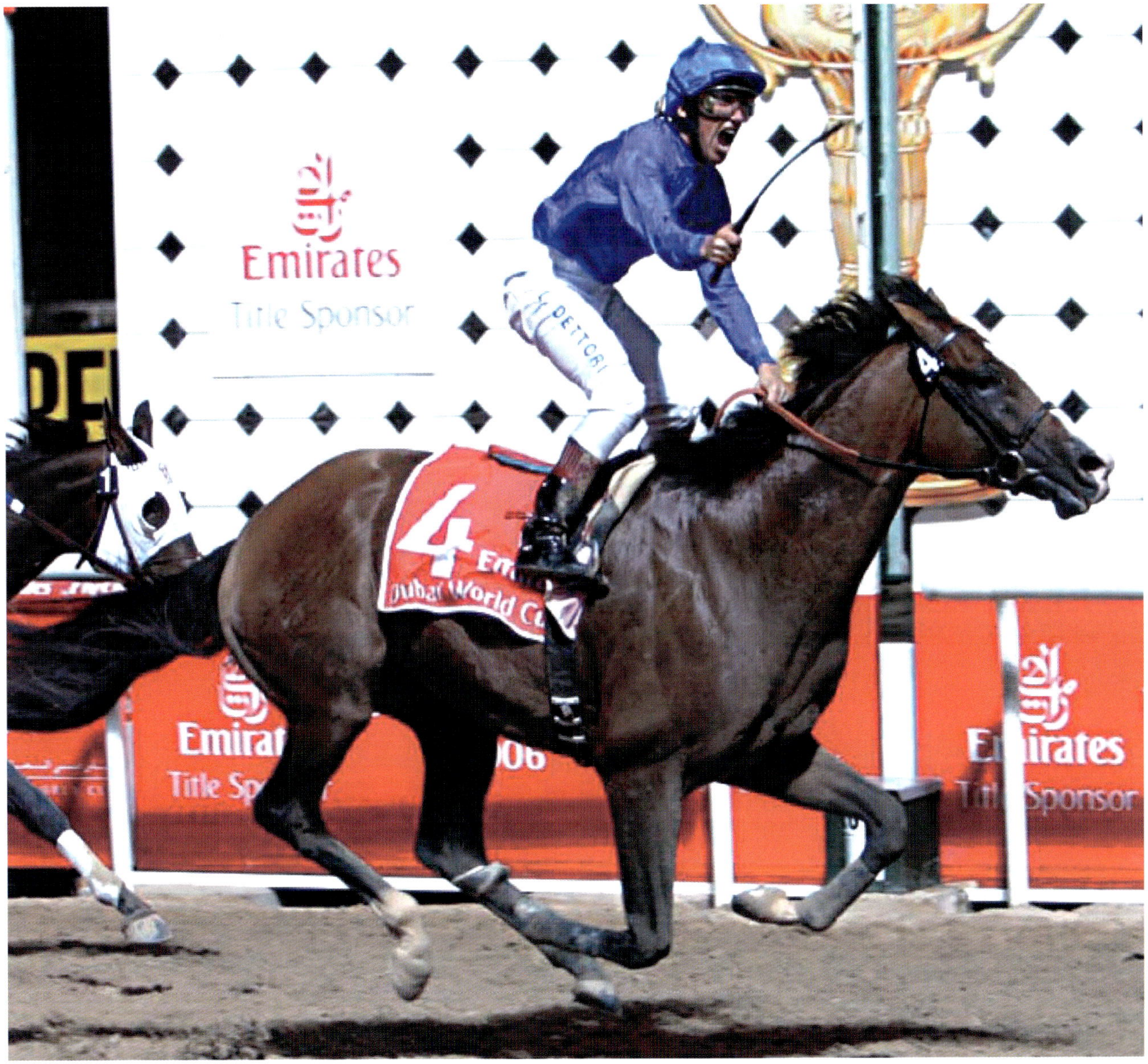
Emirates
Title Sponsor
DETTORI
4

Erhaab

br. c by Chief's Crown — Histoire (Riverman)

Well-bred, but a nervous type, Erhaab made little impact during his two-year-old season, unplaced on his first start and winning a minor Newcastle maiden on his third outing. John Dunlop's colt was clearly on a learning curve and after his success in the north of England, he began to look more settled, winning again next time out at Leicester. He finished his season with a second at Salisbury and a third in the Horris Hill Stakes at Newbury.

The colt first caught the eye as a potential Classic candidate when an unlucky second in the Fielden Stakes at Newmarket in mid-April the following season. Running as well as any, Erhaab had to be checked in the dip and recovered extremely well to finish a diminishing second to Cicerao.

If the Fielden showed potential, his next outing, the Dante Stakes at York in May, thrust Erhaab into the spotlight. Taking on a handful of Derby candidates, Willie Carson kept him mid-division but when asked for an effort he went on in emphatic style.

That performance earned him the favourite's tag at Epsom, where he faced 24 rivals, the biggest Derby field for more than a decade. The race proved dramatic. King's Theater and Colonel Collins overhauled the bold front-running Mister Baileys just before the distance. Erhaab was nowhere, having had only three behind him as they rounded Tattenham Corner. At this point Carson began to make progress up the rail and, switching to the outside as they hit the furlong marker, came with a thrilling run to collar King's Theater and Colonel Collins. In winning by a length and a quarter, Erhaab had apparently come from nowhere to snatch the world's premier Classic.

With his Derby winner not entered in the Eclipse Stakes, Dunlop supplemented Sheikh Hamdan's colt into the Sandown race for £20,000.

On the day he was hardly himself, however. Usually on his toes during the preliminaries he was surprisingly quiet and withdrawn, and considering this it was less surprising when he failed to sparkle on track. Lacking the devastating kick which won the day at Epsom, he could finish only third to Ezzoud and Bob's Return.

He reappeared in the King George VI and Queen Elizabeth Diamond Stakes and after not troubling the principals at Ascot was later found to have worrying damage to the suspensory ligaments of both knees. He never raced again.

	Danzig	Northern Dancer
		Pas de Nom
Chief's Crown (b. 1982)		
	Six Crowns	Secretariat
		Chris Evert
ERHAAB (b. 1979)		
	Riverman	Never Bend
		River Lady
Histoire (br. 1979)		
	Helvetie	Klarion
		Heiress II

Erhaab runs on strongly under Willie Carson.

Ezzoud

b. c by Last Tycoon — Royal Sister II (Claude)

The jury was out on the enigmatic Ezzoud until near the end of his career, the early part of which had been wrecked as a muscle injury ruled him out of the second half of his three-year-old season. Ezzoud had finished second to Rodrigo De Triano in the Irish 2000 Guineas, and immediately shone on his four-year-old return when winning the Earl of Sefton Stakes.

Obviously classy on his day, Ezzoud spoiled his rehabilitation when finishing second to George Augustus in the Tattersalls Gold Cup, after hanging in front, and running far below form down the field in the Prince of Wales's Stakes. By the time Michael Stoute saddled him in the International Stakes at York, he was largely ignored as a serious contender. General opinion looked correct as Ezzoud sat mid-division when the much-fancied Sabrehill pressed on alone in the last one and a half furlongs. The colt was far from beaten, however and unleashed a tremendous burst of pace, quickening again inside the last 200 metres to over haul Sabrehill.

Still the critics sniped, especially in the face of a poor performance in the Prix de l'Arc de Triomphe, but a highly credible second to Hatoof in the Dubai Champion Stakes forced a reappraisal of the colt. He followed this by a seventh to Arcangues in the Breeders' Cup Classic, in his first run on dirt.

Returning as a five-year-old, it appeared that he had reverted to the Ezzoud of old, finishing unplaced in the Prix Garnay, an unconvincing third in the Gold Cup and a neck second to Muhtarram in the Prince of Wales's Stakes, the latter coming after hanging badly.

Again his detractors were there and, again he was to silence them in the most convincing fashion, this time in the Coral Eclipse. Bowling along behind pacemaker Bob's Return early on, he swept into the lead in the closing stages and won comfortably.

On his next outing, what appeared a fine opportunity in the King George VI and Queen Elizabeth Stakes was wasted when he stumbled from the stalls and unseated Walter Swinburn. The colt was next on duty at York for a second attempt at the International Stakes. Facing a top class field, he took the lead three furlongs out and held off a late challenge to win by a head from Muhtarram.

After becoming only the second horse to win the International twice, he finished a good fourth in the Prix de l'Arc de Triomphe behind Carnegie and seventh in the Breeders' Cup Classic.

Last Tycoon (b. 1983)	Try My Best	Northern Dancer
		Sex Appeal
	Mill Princess	Mill Reef
		Irish Lass
EZZOUD (b. 1989)		
Royal Sister II (br. 1977)	Claude	Hornbeam
		Aigue-Vive
	Ribasha	Ribot
		Natasha

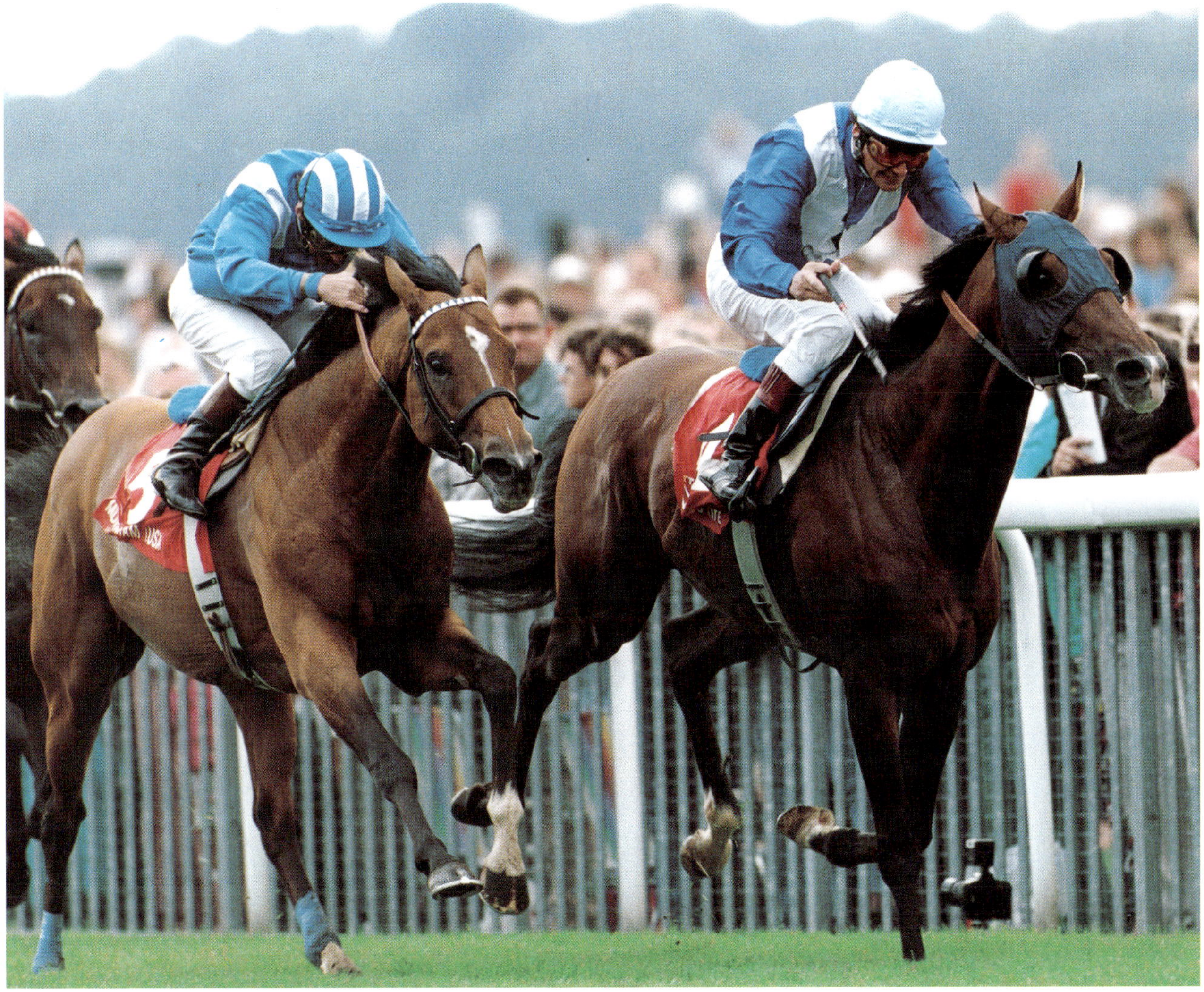

Fantastic Light
b. c by Rahy — Jood (Nijinsky)

Undoubtedly Fantastic Light can be considered one of the greatest Maktoum performers over the last 25 years. In 1988 he was trained by Sir Michael Stoute and ran in the colours of Sheikh Maktoum—who bred him—when winning two small races at Sandown and finishing third in a Godwood listed race that year.

At three, however, he matured into a classy individual. Winning the Thresher Classic Trial, he then was well beaten in the Lingfield Derby Trial. He remained near the top of his generation, however, as close up placings in the Prince of Wales's Stakes and Eclipse showed. At York in the Great Voltigeur Stakes he finally took a fighting win, and then followed this with an impressive win in the Dubai Arc Trial at Newbury. After a vague showing in the Arc, Fantastic Light wintered well and reappeared in Dubai where he made easy work of a top class field in the Dubai Sheema Classic. Soon after he was transferred into the care of Godolphin.

Running in Godolphin blue, Fantastic Light ran steady but unspectactlar races in the Coronation Cup at Epsom and the Coral-Eclipse, before a cracking second in the King George behind Montjeu.

He next appeared in the US for the Man O'War Stakes, winning this well, and was expected to show well in the Breeders' Cup Classic but was thrown off by a slow pace and trouble in running to finish fifth.

After a third in the Japan Cup, Fantastic Light now in contention for the Emirates World Racing Series and with this in mind he ran in the Hong Kong Cup. Under an excellent ride, he won race and series.

But the World Champion was not finished and continued to get better throughout 2001. After a second in the Dubai Sheema Classic, he opening his summer campaign with success in the Prince of Wales's Stakes. Next Fantastic Light met his nemesis, Galileo, in the King George, going down by two lengths. But Galileo was unable to respond to Fantastic Light's burst of speed in their eagerly awaited rematch in the Irish Champion Stakes, the shorter distance also favouring the winner.

Saeed bin Suroor opted not to run Fantastic Light in the Breeders' Cup Classic, in favour of the Turf. The colt raced off the pace for a first mile before making his move between horses, pulling into second, and going on to win by less than a length.

Rahy (ch. 1985)	**Blushing Groom**	**Red God**
		Runaway Bride
	Glorious Song	**Halo**
FANTASTIC LIGHT (b. 1996)		**Ballade**
Jood (b. 1989)	**Nijinsky**	**Northern Dancer**
		Flaming Page
	Kamar	**Key To The Mint**
		Square Angel

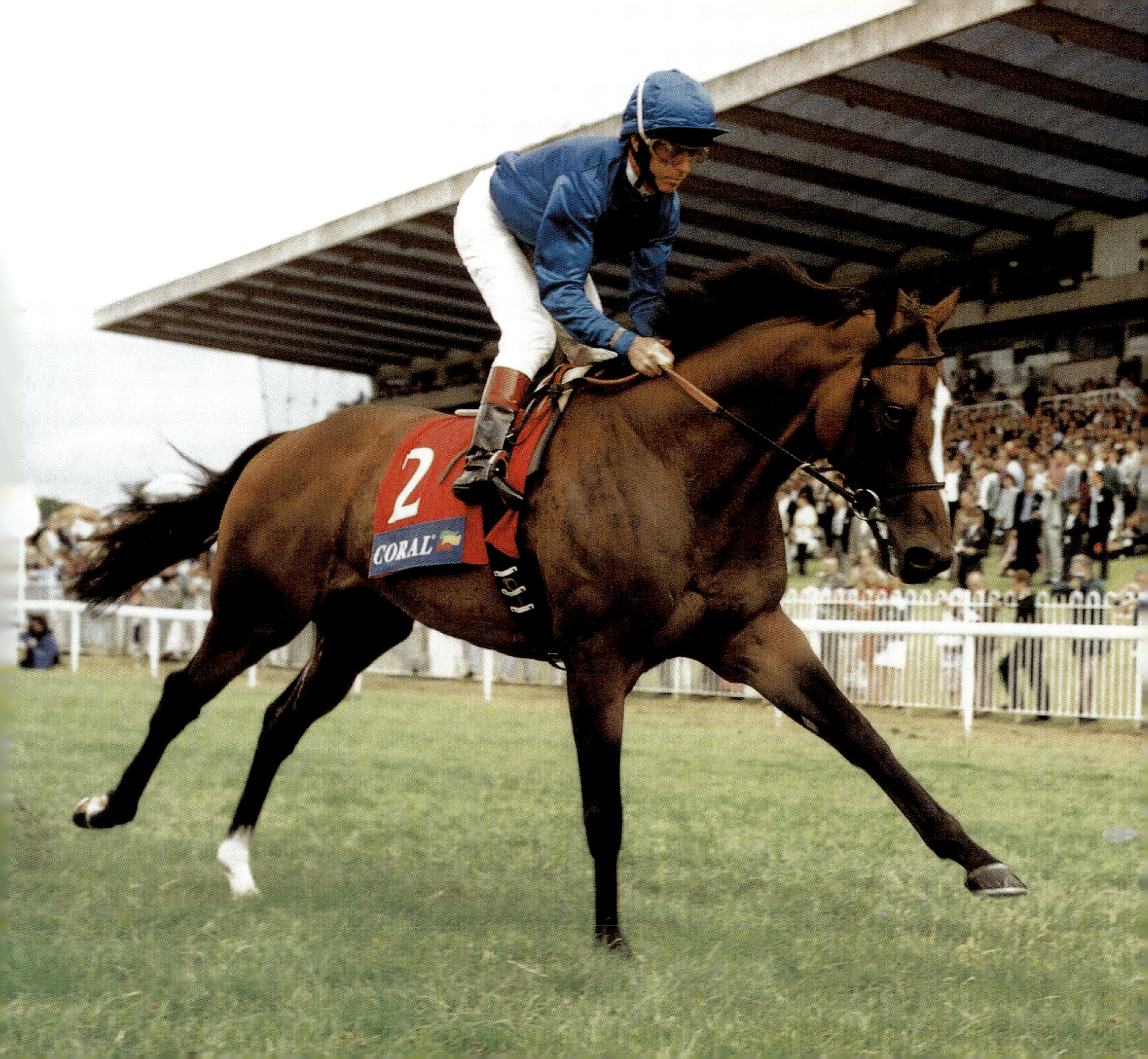
2
CORAL

Dual Time Watch
.Steel, white dial, Black Alligator strap
Automatic Movement, Dual Time, Power Reserve
Generation Calendar

Van Cleef & Arpels

damas
Les Exclusives
Toll Free: 800 4916

www.damasjewellery.com

Sheikh Hamdan bin Rashid Al Maktoum

There are many important dates in the history of horse racing but the one of May 3, 1967 is perhaps not as instantly recognisable as it should be. This was the day that brothers Sheikh Hamdan bin Rashid Al Maktoum and Sheikh Mohammed bin Rashid Al Maktoum attended their first race meeting in England. It was 2000 Guineas day and George Moore won the featured race on Royal Palace for trainer Sir Noel Murless.

As with his brothers, Sheikh Hamdan was well versed in horsemanship, shooting and hunting with falcons courtesy of his father, the late Sheikh Rashid bin Saeed Al Maktoum so his passion in horses was ingrained. His blue and white silks have become one of the most familiar sites on racecourses around the world.

Having initially been educated in the UAE, Sheikh Hamdan was sent to Cambridge to complete his schooling in the late 1960s and how he ended up at Newmarket on that Saturday afternoon.

It was 1980 that Hamdan's own silks started their rise to prominence with his first winner, Mushref, who went on to finish second in the Champion Two-Year-Old Trophy. Two years later, he registered his first Group win when Princes' Gate won the Westbury Stakes.

Racing and breeding provided Hamdan with the perfect relaxation and distraction from his government responsibilities as Minister of Finance and Industy for the UAE and Deputy Ruler of Dubai. His reputation for intelligence is well earned and amply demonstrated not just in his government work and his astute horse breeding plans, but also in electronics and he has been known to 'dabble' in inventing electronic devices – as an enthusiastic amateur.

Such distractions are great for alleviating the day to day pressure of government while his caring nature is evident in his philanthropic behaviour. He has financed orphanages, schools and hospitals in poor countries, as well as promoting education, in his own country and in others around the globe. He continues to pursue such activities.

His passion for horses is undoubted and his Shadwell breeding operation spreads around the world - both for thoroughbreds and Purebred

Arabians. In the latter, he is undoubtedly the major supporter of the industry throughout Europe and has almost single-handedly created far more interest in the sport on that continent. In the UAE his support of the Dubai International Arabian Horse Championship has created the world's most valuable such show.

However, it is his passion for breeding thoroughbred racehorses for which he is arguably best known and is, rightly, considered one of the world's foremost authorities on such breeding. Those who deal with him in his breeding operation speak of a photographic memory for pedigrees and the horses themselves, while he only sees many of his foals and yearlings on video in their early existence.

To name these animals two years later after a short sighting on video would seem impossible but something he regularly achieves by all accounts - no doubt aided by the fact he names his youngsters according to a specific trait or characteristic he notes. His Director at Shadwell in Newmarket, Richard Lancaster explains: "It is a remarkable talent that people involved in the industry as a profession, full time, could never hope to achieve. I have witnessed Sheikh Hamdan identify a horse in a field, which he has never seen in the flesh before."

His undoubted success as an owner/breeder is often attributed to the fact that he will plan the mating of his mares personally, using his encyclopaedic knowledge of pedigrees to great affect. Mirza Al Sayegh *(pictured below with Sheikh Hamdan)*, the Director of Sheikh Hamdan's Dubai office adds: "Sheikh Hamdan can reel off several generations of a pedigree, for many horses, from the top of his head. It is not just this that has made him one of the world's leading owner/breeders though. It is knowing how to apply this information."

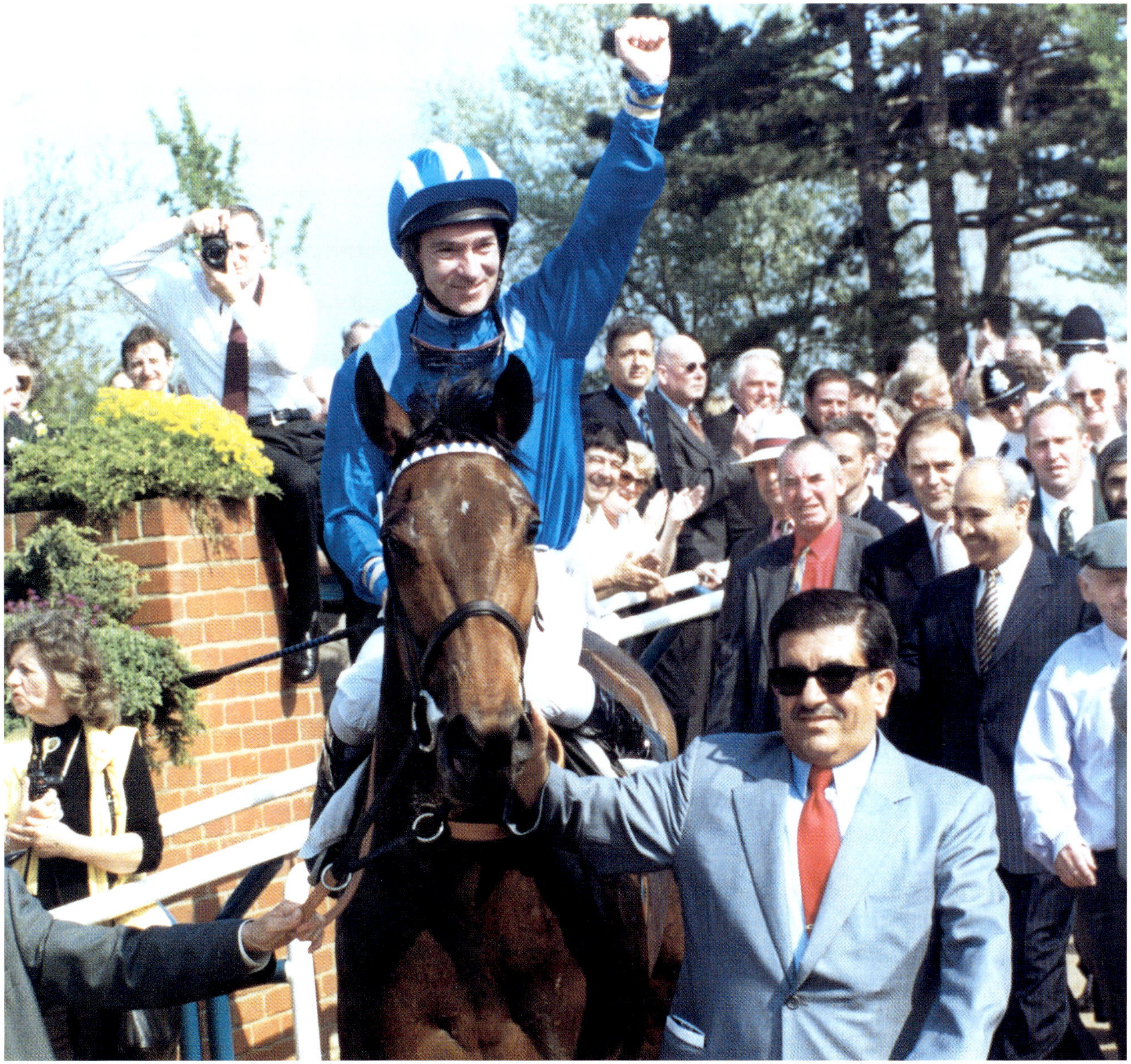

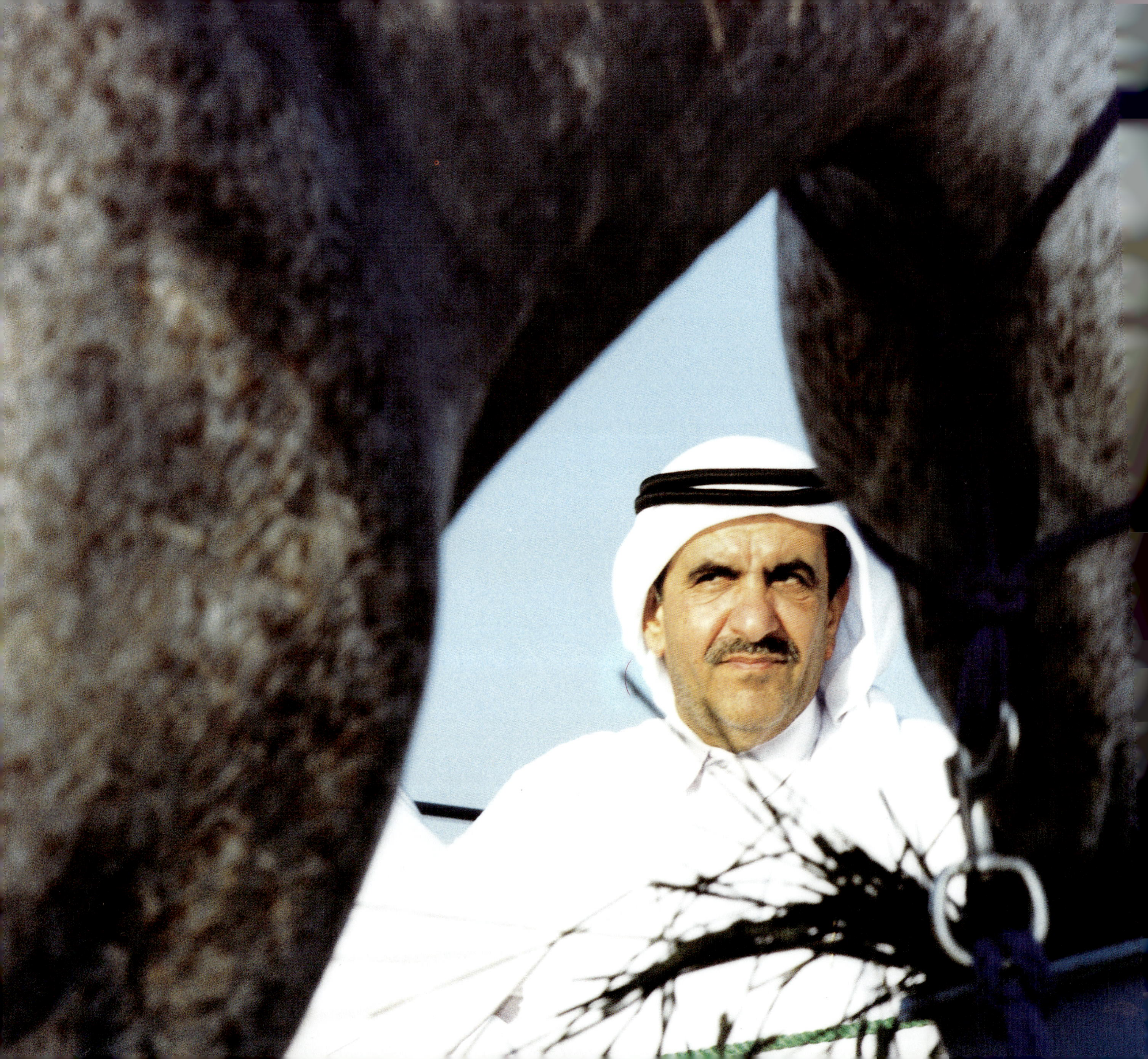

Sheikh Hamdan was the first Maktoum to win the sport's Blue Riband, the Epsom Derby, when his homebred Nashwan won the race in 1989. The horse secured his place in the history books with an unprecedented 2000 Guineas, Derby, Eclipse Stakes and King George VI and Queen Elizabeth Stakes quartet that is never likely to be repeated. Many other equine greats have carried his infamous silks, including 1999 Dubai World Cup winner Almutawakel, 2002 Sheema Classic hero Nayef, dual 1990 Classic heroine Salsabil, 1993 Derby winner Erhaab and sprint sensation Dayjur.

He has also won two Melbourne Cups courtesy of Jeune and At Talaq.

Sakhee *(pictured below)*, winner of the Prix de l'Arc de Triomphe in for Godolphin in 2001 was homebred by Sheikh Hamdan as was another Godolphin multiple Group One winning dignitary in Swain.

Shadwell are a generous sponsors of racing around the world and, like his brothers, Sheikh Hamdan puts a lot back into the sport which he loves so much. Already in 2006 he has seen the likes of Maraahel, Munsef, Etlaala and the ill-fated Mubtaker carry his silks to big race victories. The previous year Eswarah won the Epsom Oaks for him and in 2004 Haafhd won the 2000 Guineas at Newmarket.

In 2006 Sheikh Hamdan has chartered new territory by registering a first Classic win in the USA, courtesy of Jazil who won the Belmont Stakes, the concluding leg of the American Triple Crown.

In all likelihood, this most influential of owners has several more landmarks to put down before he is finished with the sport of horse racing. And the sport can be thankful to have such a sportsman-like and belevolant supporter. Certainly few, in the history of the sport, can ever have had such a profound effect on thoroughbred racing.

Favourable Terms

b. f by Selkirk - Fatefully (Private Account)

Her dam a black type winner for Godolphin, while Favourable Terms was bred by Gainsborough Stud Management and emerged a top class representative for Sheikh Maktoum.

Unraced as a juvenile she made up for lost time immediately when claiming a maiden at Goodwood on her first public outing in May. Trainer Michael Stoute was impressed and gave her every opportunity to progress next time out in Sandown's Listed Distaff Stakes. Under Kieren Fallon she won by a neck from Miss Ianhow.

A second in the Group Two Golden Daffofil Stakes at Chepstow followed, well beaten by the useful Chorist, before Stoute found an opportunity in the Matron Stakes at Leopardstown. Winning this Group Two contest, Favourable Terms showed improvement again, although an unplaced effort in the Sun Chariot Stakes at Newmarket brought a less than stellar end to her campaign.

The filly returned to the racecourse at four showing marked improvement. Fallon piloted Favourable Terms to victory in the one mile Windsor Forest Stakes at Royal Ascot. The pair passed the post two lengths in front from Monturani, an excellent performance that set her up for a crack at the highest level.

Back problems were sited as the cause of her poor run next time out, in the Falmouth Stakes, with her trainer admitting that she needed contstant attention from a physiotherapist. But the work invested paid off spectacularly near the end of July. In the Nassau Stakes, Favourable Terms claimed victory by a short head.

She remained in training the following season when her return was delayed until September and the Doncaster St Leger meeting. Despite a 14-month absence and an inadequate seven-furlong trip, she was able to win the Listed Sceptre Stakes. That was to be her final visit to the winner's enclosure. She failed to trouble the judge in her two Group 1 outings and was retired.

Selkirk (ch. 1988)	Sharpen Up	Atan
		Rocchetta
	Annie Edge	Nebbilio
		Friendly Court
FAVOURABLE TERMS (b. 2000)		
Fatefully (b. 1988)	Private Account	Damascus
		Numbered Account
	Fateful	Topsider
		Fates Reward

SEVEN MORE REASONS TO USE SHADWELL.

HAAFHD
Chestnut, 2001, by ALHAARTH - AL BAHATHRI, by BLUSHING GROOM
WINNER OF 2,000 GUINEAS & CHAMPION STAKES IN 2004.
FIRST FOALS IN 2006.

SAKHEE
Bay, 1997, by BAHRI - THAWAKIB, by SADLER'S WELLS
2001 WORLD CHAMPION.
FIRST TWO-YEAR-OLDS IN 2006.

NAYEF
Bay, 1998, by GULCH - HEIGHT OF FASHION, by BUSTINO
MULTIPLE GROUP ONE WINNER.

GREEN DESERT
Bay, 1983, by DANZIG - FOREIGN COURIER, by SIR IVOR
A SUPREME CHAMPION SIRE

STORMING HOME
Bay, 1998, by MACHIAVELLIAN - TRY TO CATCH ME, by SHAREEF DANCER
TRIPLE GROUP ONE WINNER.

ACT ONE
Grey, 1999, by IN THE WINGS - SUMMER SONNET, by BAILLAMONT
CHAMPION FRENCH TRAINED TWO-YEAR-OLD IN 2001.
FIRST TWO-YEAR-OLDS IN 2006.

MUJAHID
Bay, 1996, by DANZIG - ELRAFA AH, by STORM CAT
1998 CHAMPION TWO-YEAR-OLD.

SHADWELL
STANDING FOR SUCCESS

Contact: RICHARD LANCASTER, JOHNNY PETER-HOBLYN (Mob: 07831 261488) or LOUISE MACDONALD (Mob: 07736 019910) on +44 (0)1842 755913
e-mail: enquiries@shadwellstud.co.uk   www.shadwellstud.co.uk

Firebreak

b. c by Charnwood Forest - Breakaway (Song)

Firebreak was purchased by Godolphin for 525,000 guineas following a useful juvenile campaign. Trained by Ian Balding, the two-year-old won four of his six starts including a commanding success in the Mill Reef Stakes at Newbury. One of his defeats included a neck second in the Coventry Stakes at Royal Ascot.

Joining Godolphin, Firebreak began his three year old season in the same sort of form when beaten a nose by Essence of Dubai in the UAE 2000 Guineas. His summer was no less successful, encompassing a victory in the Supreme Stakes.

His return to Dubai that winter heralded the improvement that was expected. Firebird won the US$1,000,000 Godolphin Mile, the first of two successes in this race. His 2003 campaign ended with a trip to the Far East, where he finished a close fifth in the Hong Kong Mile.

Firebird began 2004 as he bad begun his previous season claiming the Godolphin Mile again, and he went on to prove significantly improved throughout the summer, adding the Challenge Stakesat Newmarket to his tally. This prompted Godolphin to enter him a second time in the world's richest mile race at Sha Tin. This time around the Hong Kong Mile proved somewhat luckier. Given smooth passage, Frankie Dettori moved Firebreak to the outside to deliver a challenge with 400 metres remaining. Firebird's three quarter length success gave Godolphin their eleventh Group One race of 2004.

That Group 1 victory was to be his final appearance. The winner of nine of his 22 starts and proven on both dirt and turf, he is sure to prove popular in his new career.

	Waring	Known Fact
		Slightly Dangerous
	Charnwood Forest (dkb/br. 1992)	
	Dance of Leaves	Sadler's Wells
		Fall Aspen
FIREBREAK (b. 1999)		
	Song	Sing Sing
		Intent
	Breakaway (b. 1985)	
	Catherine Howard	Tower Walk
		Righteous Girl

JEBEL ALI INTERNATIONAL
Fly Emirates
Emirates
Title Sponsor
DUBAI WORLD CUP

Grandera

ch. c by Grand Lodge – Bordighera (Alysheba)

Trained by James Fanshawe, as a three-year-old Grandera placed in three Group Ones: the Prix du Jockey-Club, the Eclipse Stakes and the Juddmonte International. He finally got his reward when claiming the Dubai Arc Trial.

In 2002 Grandera emerged with a major programme ahead of him. After a fifth in Hong Kong, second leg of the World Series, Grandera swept from the pack to take the $3 million Singapore Airlines International Cup, third leg of the World Series, at Kranji, over 2,000 metres.

Five weeks later he stamped his quality at an even higher level. In The Prince of Wales's Stakes at Royal Ascot, Grandera cruised home to a facile five-length success.

After a poor outing in the King George VI and Queen Elizabeth Diamond Stakes, Grandera reappeared in the Group One Irish Champion Stakes at Leopardstown, seventh leg of the World Series, where Grandera claimed the narrowest of wins, a short head, over Hawk Wing.

Leading the Emirates World Racing Series standings, Grandera made a trek to Australia next for the $3 million Cox Plate. The colt ran a strange race, seeming to get unbalanced round the tight turns of Moonee Valley but ran on well to finish only a length and a half behind Northerly.

His two victories and placed efforts had already virtually claimed the World Series before Grandera went for the Hong Kong Cup. His seventh there was hardly stellar, but Grandera had already stamped his class on 2002 and he crowned a fully deserving World Champion.

He was to race on the following year and started the campaign at Nad Al Sheba where he won the Group 2 Third Round of the Maktoum Challenge on his first dirt outing. That effort was sufficient to earn a start in the Dubai World Cup where he was fourth to stable companion Moon Ballad. He then disappointed on his return to Europe, albeit in the most illustrious of company, and was retired at the end of the 2003 season.

GRANDERA (ch. 1988)	Grand Lodge (ch. 1991)	Chief's Crown — Danzing / Six Crowns
		La Papagena — Habitat / Magic Flute
	Bordighera (ch. 1992)	Alysheba — Alydar / Bel Sheba
		Blue Tip — Tip Moss / As Blue

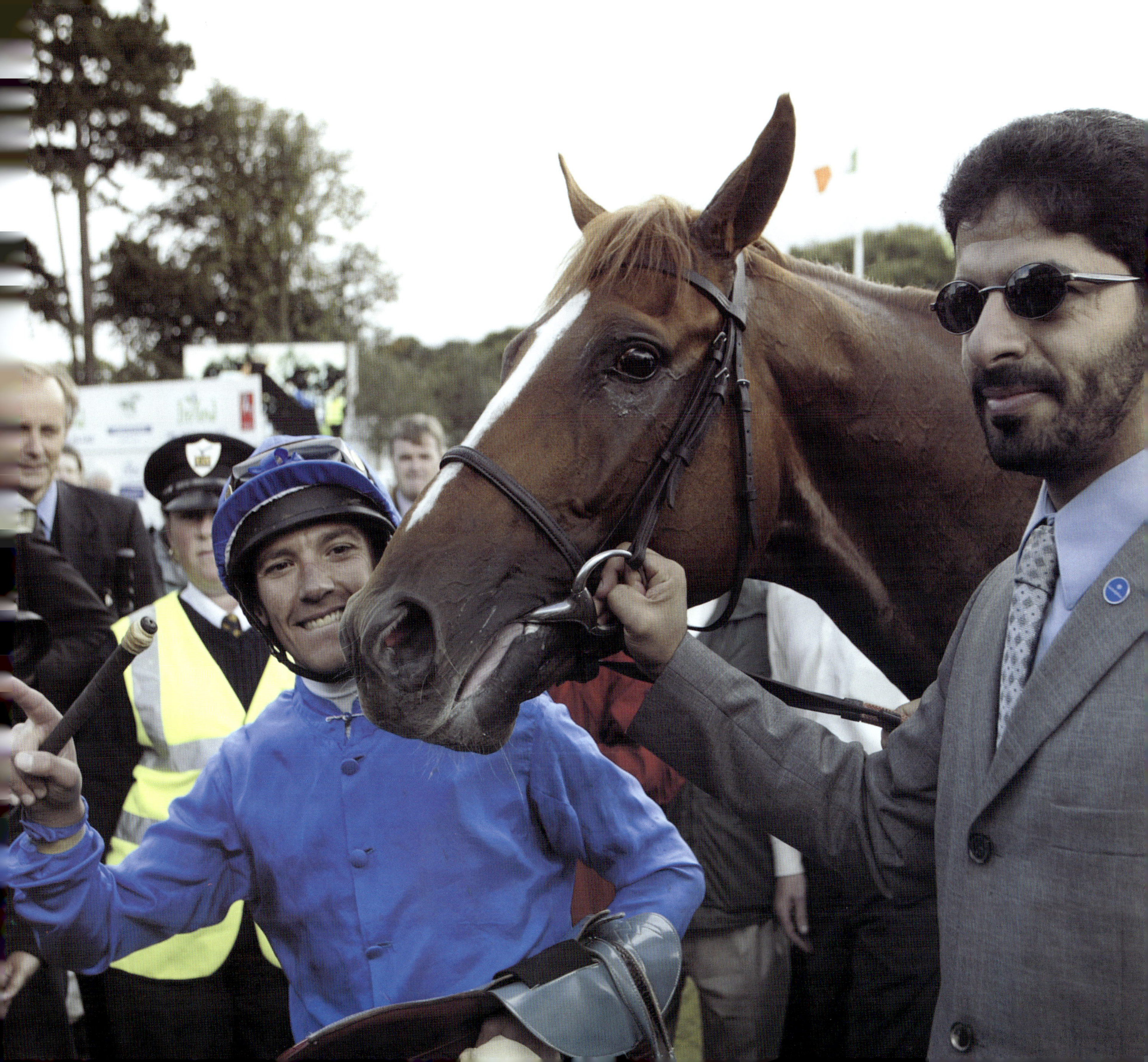

Green Desert

b. c by Danzig — Foreign Courier (Sir Ivor)

One of the finest Maktoum-owned sprinters of the last decades, Green Desert arrived on the racecourse with a big reputation. He finished second, but was sufficiently impressive to merit a step up in class for the July Stakes. The colt ran well and showed plenty of heart after being headed in the latter stages, rallying to take the race by a head.

Green Desert subsequently ran well in both the Richmond Stakes at Goodwood and Mill Reef Stakes at Newbury, before completing his juvenile campaign with a success at Doncaster in the Flying Childers Stakes. A smooth performance under Lester Piggott saw Green Desert sweep into the lead at the distance and hold a late challenge from Marouble.

After earning his kudos as a sprinter the previous year, Green Desert returned to the racecourse with trainer Michael Stoute planning a Guineas Challenge, plans which were bolstered by a fine win in the seven-furlong European Free Handicap.

He went into the Classic not unfancied and, after tracking the pacemaker, Walter Swinburn sent the colt on with two furlongs remaining. He reached front running well, but was tackled by Dancing Brave, who went on to win by three lengths.

After a fruitless outing in the Irish 2000, in soft conditions, connections were rewarded with a second place in the St. James's Palace Stakes at Royal Ascot.

The colt returned to sprinting in the July Cup at Newmarket and hit peak form in this Group One contest. Facing just four rivals, Swinburn made no mistake. He pressed on around three furlongs from home and never seriously looked like being headed.

His subsequent display over the minimum distance in the Sprint Championship at York was a further show of class over a sharp trip. Green Desert finished a close-up third to Last Tycoon and Double Schwartz.

Returned to six furlongs for the Haydock Park Sprint Cup, the colt tracked Double Schwartz during the early stages, only quickening clear at the distance. He showed a sharp turn of foot and was able to fend off a challenge from Hallgate in the closing stages, claiming the race by a neck, the pair clear.

Double Schwartz returned to the fore in the five-furlong Prix de l'Abbaye de Longchamp in October, Green Desert finishing fourth after hitting traffic problems and following a below-par performance in the Breeders' Cup Sprint he was retired.

Danzig (b. 1977)	Northern Dancer	Nearctic
		Natalma
	Pas De Nom	Admiral's Voyage
		Petitioner
GREEN DESERT (b. 1983)		
Foreign Courier (b. 1979)	Sir Ivor	Sir Gaylord
		Attica
	Courtly Dee	Never Bend
		Tulle

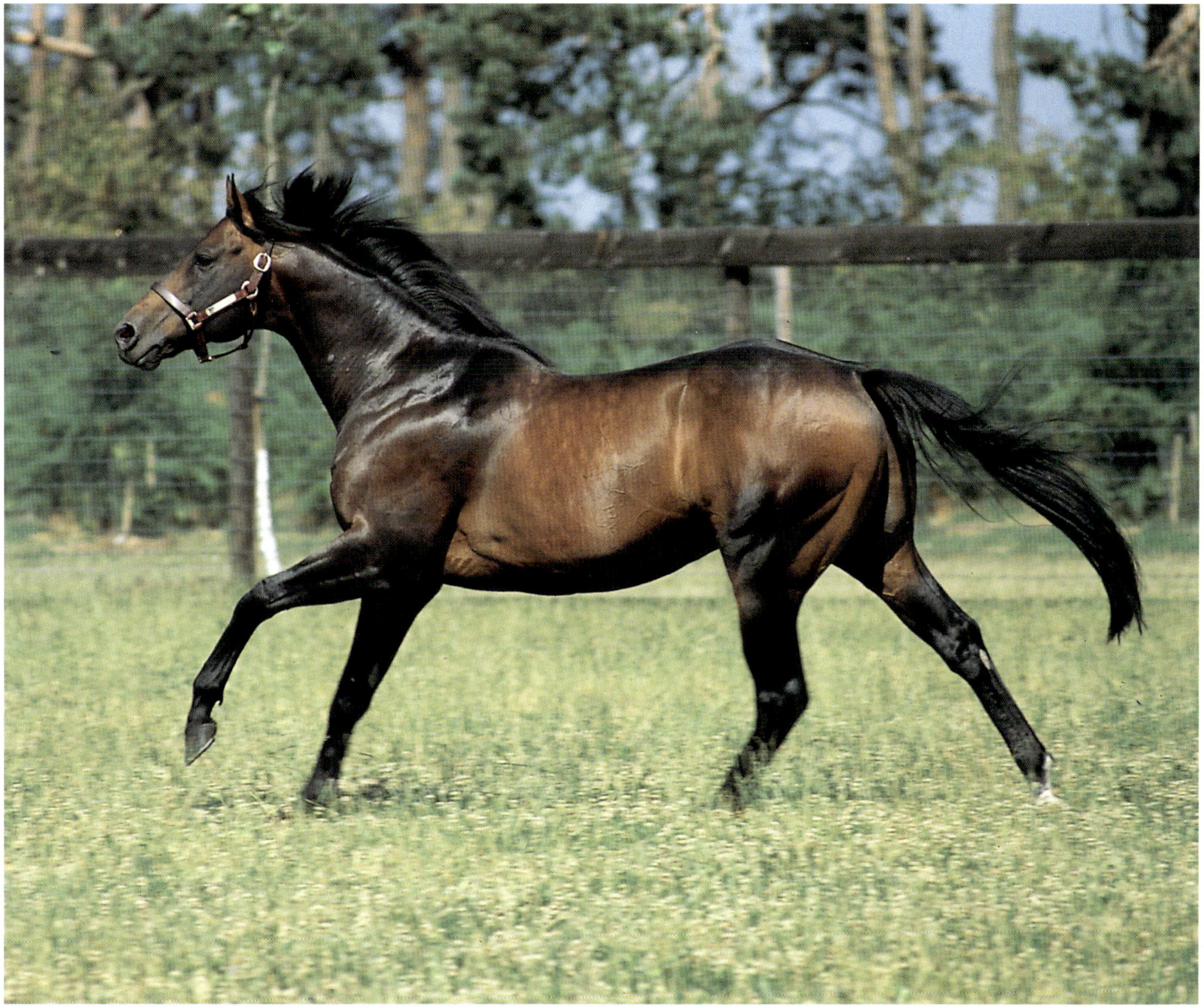

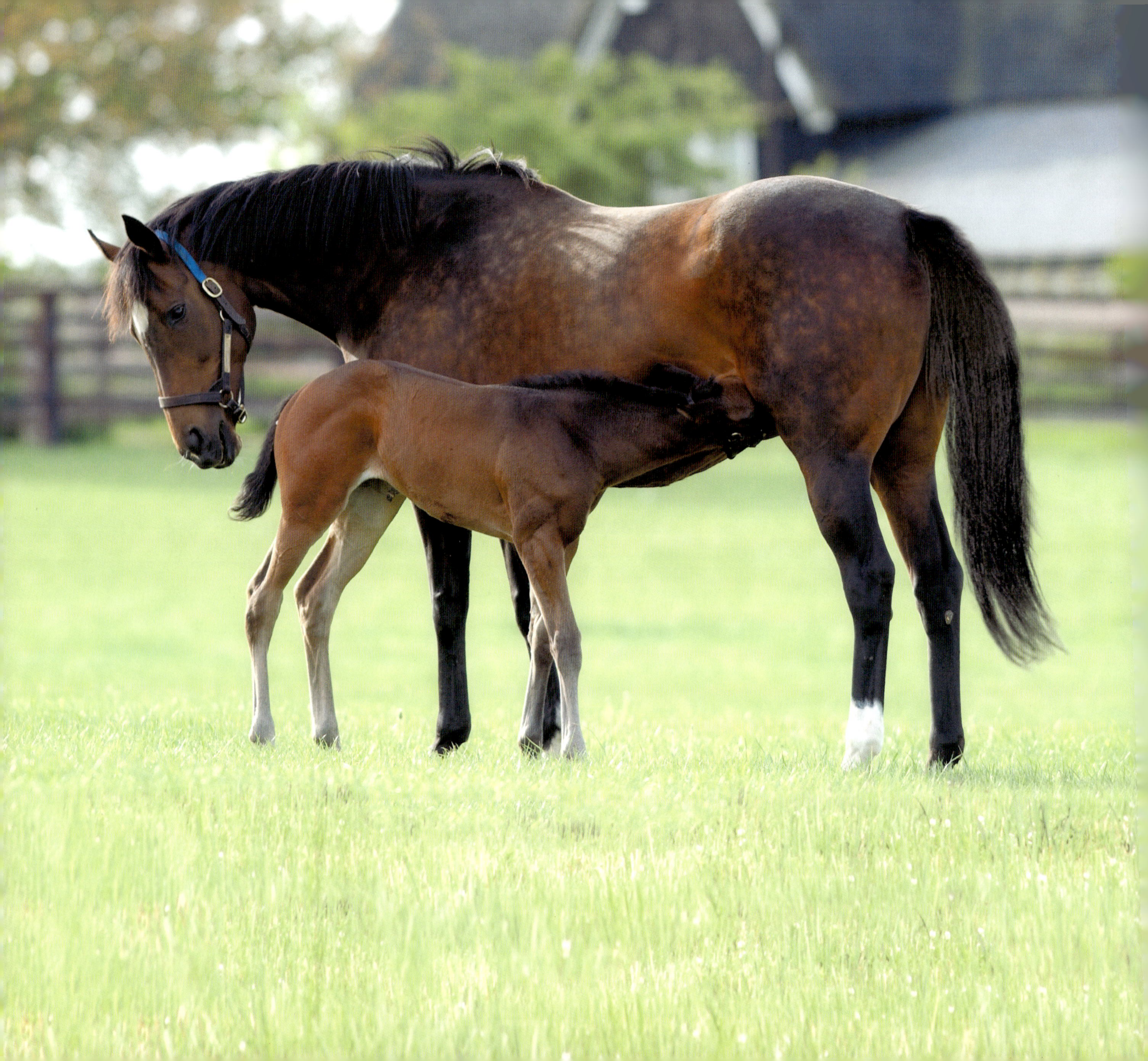

Shadwell Estates

Shadwell Estate is centerpiece to Sheikh Hamdan bin Rashid Al Maktoum's ultra successful inter-continental breeding operation. It is also one of Britain's most modern and progressive thoroughbred farms. The Norfolk estate was purchased from its founder's grandson, Sir John Musker, in 1984. Since then it has been maintained and expanded on a tradition of excellence.

From its small two-stud origin, the subsequent development of Shadwell Estates has been spectacular. A now sprawling network of five idyllic stud farms that cover some 6,000 acres in south-west Norfolk, Shadwell's progress has been inspired by home-bred Classic victories, highlighted by Nashwan's sensational summer of 1989.

It was the huge demand for stallions in England in the mid-1980's that initially persuaded Sheikh Hamdan to set up a stallion stud, and Nunnery now houses the cream of the crop, with the Nearco line, through Northern Dancer, featuring prominently in the breeding of Green Desert

Today Shadwell is one of the largest farms in the Newmarket area and certainly one of the finest. The facility is managed by Richard Lancaster, who oversees the entire Shadwell operation, coordinating activities at public and private studs. He has been working with Shadwell stallions and breeding stock since leaving the army in 1983 and is a council member of the Thoroughbred Breeders Association. Lancaster also heads Sheikh Hamdan's Arabian racing operation.

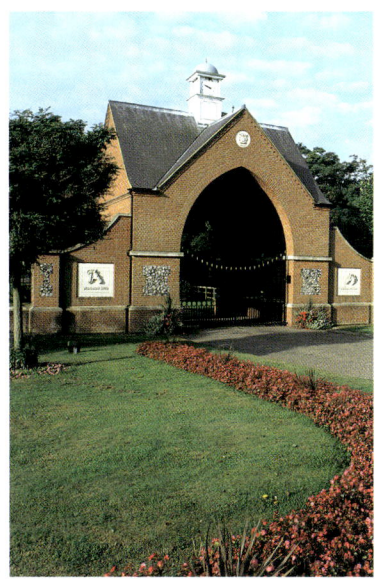

Shadwell suffered a terrible double blow in 2002 when stallion superstars Nashwan and Unfuwain both passed away. But it is a sign both of the depth of quality at Shadwell, and Sheikh Hamdan's ambitions to ensure Shadwell remains one of Europe's finest facilities, that Shadwell Estate quickly bounced back. With a number of exciting new stallion additions to their team, Shadwell remains at the zenith of European breeding.

The original studs were Melton Paddocks and Snarehill Stud. Shortly after purchase, Melton Paddocks was modernised and refurbished and is now used as an Arabian horse stud.

Snarehill Stud, meanwhile, was developed as

a rehabilitation centre for Sheikh Hamdan's growing string of racehorses in England. It is here that special care can be given to an injured or, indeed, jaded horse enabling it to return to full training and racing as quickly as possible.

The prestigious Nunnery Stud was built in 1987 to take six stallions and their visiting mares. An impressive office was also developed on site to house Sheikh Hamdan's British based breeding and racing headquarters, as well as to co-ordinate Shadwell's worldwide bloodstock operation with its links in Ireland, USA, France, South Africa and Australia.

There are currently six stallions standing at Nunnery Stud: Green Desert, the Leading First Season Sire in 1990 and the Sire with the most winners on the Flat in the UK in 1991, 1992, 1993, 1994, 1996, 1997 and 1999.

Haafhd, winner of the Classic Group 1 2000 Guineas and Group 1 Dubai Champion Stakes.

Sakhee, a brilliant winner of the Prix de l'Arc de Triomphe and Juddmonte International

Nayef, the winner of 9 races from 2-5 year olds, including the Juddmonte and Dubai Stakes.

Act One, unbeaten as a 2 year old and only beaten once in six races, won the Criterium International and Prix Lupin.

Storming Home, winner of 8 races including the Champion Stakes and Charles Whittingham Memorial Stakes from 2 – 5 year olds.

As well as the modernising and refurbishment of Melton Paddocks, Snarehill Stud and Nunnery Stud, the continued development of Shadwell has witnessed a number of new additions, including Beech House Stud in Newmarket, Elmswell Park Stud near Bury St Edmunds and Salsabil Stud outside Lavenham in Suffolk.

Beech House Stud is primarily used to stand Mujahid. Mujahid, whose progeny have commanded up to 22 times his covering fee, has enjoyed a solid couple of sales season and topped the Leading Sire of 2-y-os in Europe in 2005, by percentage of winners to runners.

The paddocks are also used to over-winter the

private Arabian young stock before they are broken in at Snarehill.

Run by Charles Walton under the guidance of Arthur Bell the Assistant Manager (Private), Elmswell Park Stud is used as a base for Shadwell's private mares. After foaling, mares

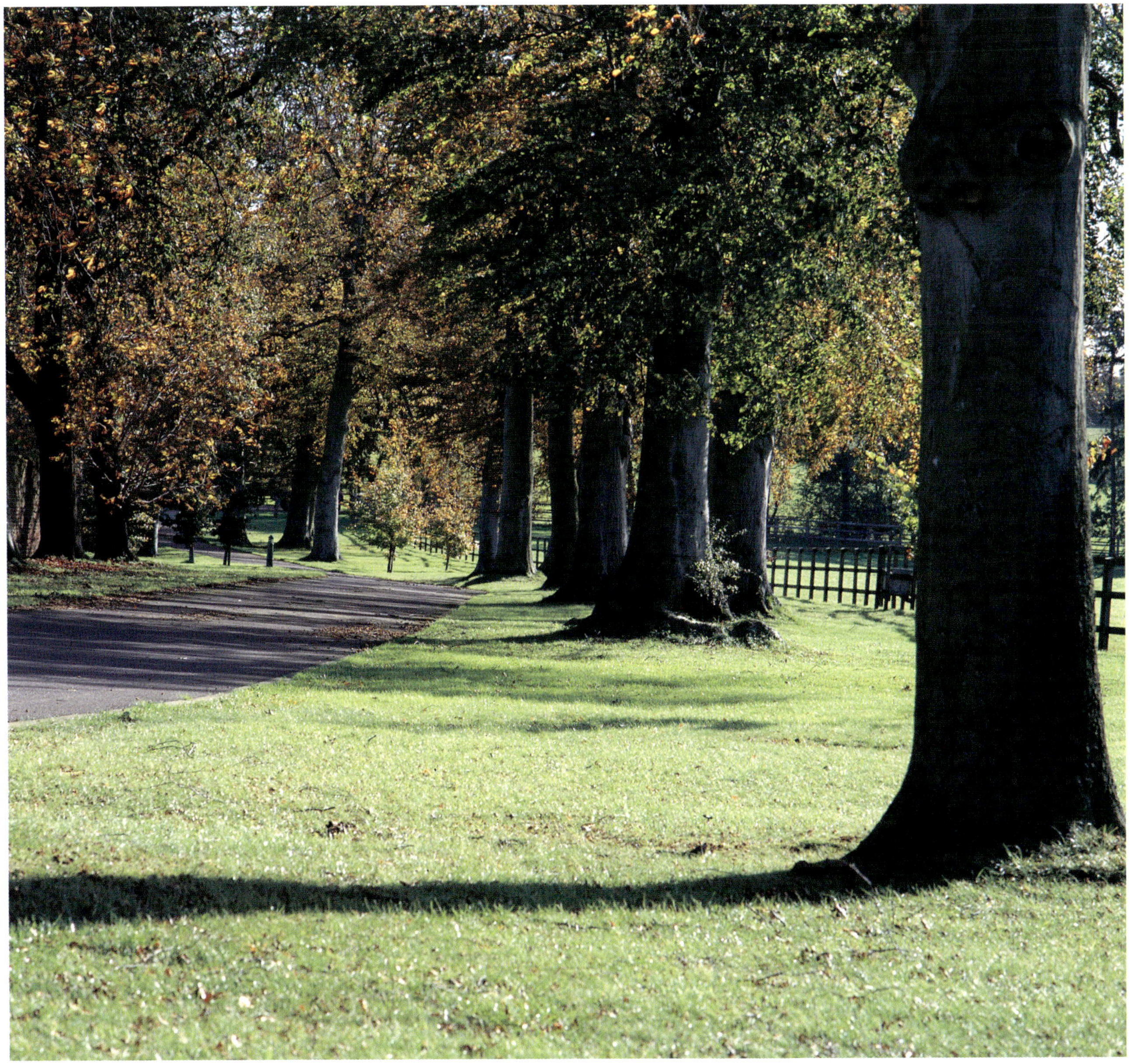

either stay at Elmswell Park, if visiting a Nunnery Stud stallion, or, if visiting a stallion in the Newmarket area, go to Beech House Stud.

Much like Elmswell Park, Salsabil is where mares are cared for prior to foaling. Once they've foaled, they can stay until they return to Ireland with their foals in the late summer. The tranquil surroundings of Salsabil are ideal for both mares and foals, particularly at the early stages of the latter's development and growth.

The truly global success enjoyed by Shadwell has only been made possible because of the dedication of Sheikh Hamdan and his highly dedicated, loyal and skilled team of professionals who all share the same dream: To produce world-class racehorses.

Shadwell has also made available some of the best Arab stallions that have won at the highest level. This has been seen to great effect with Shadwell's stallions providing a surfeit of winners in the English Arab racing season. The victory of Madjani in 2005 in the Dubai Kahayla Classic (Gr.1) was the third time in three years that Sheikh Hamdan colours have swept to victory in this prestigious prize.

The Arab centre of the Stallion operation is at Melton Paddocks but you can now also find Shadwell stallions in America, France and Germany. The progeny of these stallions are therefore performing across the globe as far a field as California and the Gulf.

Melton Paddocks was originally set up so that those top horses that had run in the colours of Sheikh Hamdan could be retired to stud there, and their breeding services could be used by international breeders through artificial insemination. The number of top performers exceeded immediate demand in Britain, so that is how these horses come to be spread around the various international locations.

Pride of place at Melton Paddocks goes to Bengali d'Albret, possibly the finest Arabian racehorse to run in Sheikh Hamdan's colours. Since retiring Bengali d'Albret has become Champion sire in Britain. Standing alongside him are Monsieur Al Maury, Eau Royal and Jiyush.

In France Shadwell is led by Champion Al Sakbe, Kairouan de Jos and Prince d'Orient. Al Sakbe and Prince d'Orient stand at Haras de

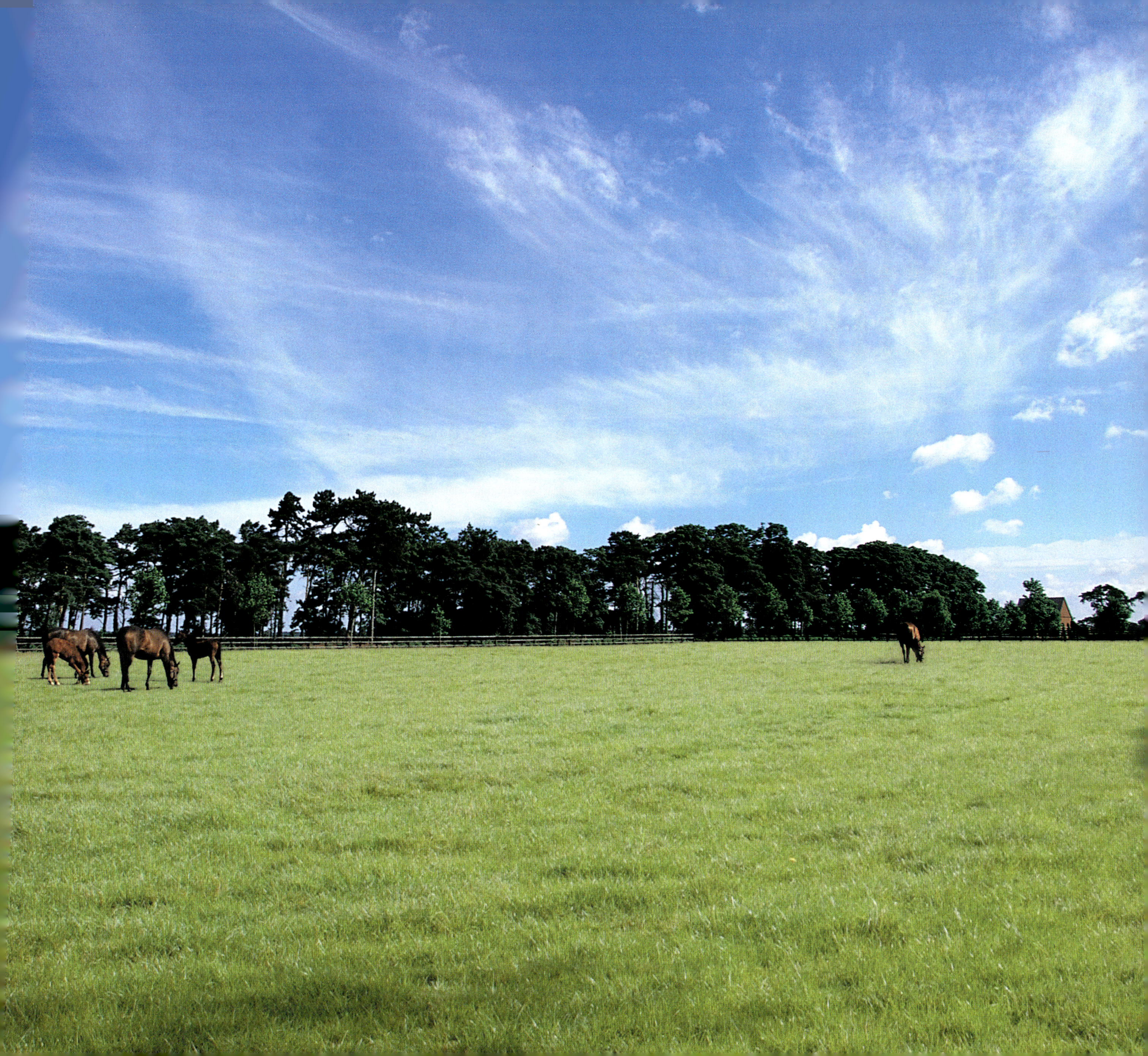

Saint-Faust, while Kairouan de Jos is based at Elevage de Thouars. In the United States, Sheikh Hamdan is also at the forefront of the industry with Chndaka at Mandolynn Hill Farm in Texas, Falina des Fabries at Trackside Farm, in Florida and Nivour de Cardonne at Cre Run in Virginia.

While Shadwell leads the Arabian industry in Europe, it is a name that will remain more closely associated with some of the world's greatest champions in the thoroughbred arena.

Long term strength in depth within their elite stallion team, coupled with the additions of brilliant Arc winner Sakhee and Champion juvenile Act One, as well as Classic winning Haafhd, means that Shadwell will continue to be at the forefront of thoroughbred breeding in general, and contribute significantly to Sheikh Hamdan's elite, multi-Classic winning racing and breeding programme.

Act One

Unbeaten as a two-year-old, only beaten once in six races and a Group 1 winner at both 2 and 3 years, winning €554,290. Act One was a Champion French trained juvenile. His first crop yearlings made up to 300,000 guineas.

Won Gr. 1	**CRITERIUM INTERNATIONAL**, 8f, Saint-Cloud, defeating LANDSEER
Won Gr. 1	**PRIX LUPIN**, 10f, Longchamp
Won Gr. 2	**PRIX GREFFULHE**, 10f, Longchamp
Won Gr. 3	**PRIX THOMAS BRYON**, 8f, Saint-Cloud
2nd Gr. 1	**PRIX DU JOCKEY CLUB**, 12f, to SULAMANI
Won	**PRIX DU VAL PROFOND**, 8f, Chantilly

Green Desert

A dual Classic winner who won five races and £222,453 from 14 starts at two and three years. Green Desert has sired over 500 winners of more than 1,480 races and over £28.5 million from his first 16 crops of racing age, including OASIS DREAM, SHEIKH ALBADOU, DESERT PRINCE, OWINGTON, ROSE GYPSY and TAMARISK

Won Gr. 1	**NORCROS JULY CUP**, 6f, Newmarket, defeating Breeders' Cup Mile Gr.1 winner LAST TYCOON.
Won Gr. 2	**VERNONS SPRINT CUP**, 6f, Haydock, defeating Prix de l'Abbaye G.1 winner DOUBLE SCHWARTZ.
Won Gr. 2	**CHILDERS STAKES**, 5f, Doncaster, defeating Royal Ascot winner MAROUBLE.
Won Gr. 3	**ANGLIA TELEVISION JULY STAKES**, 6f, Newmarket, defeating BAKHAROFF by 3 lengths.
Won LR	**LADBROKE EUROPEAN FREE HANDICAP**, 7f, Newmarket, carrying record top weight of 9st 7lb.
2nd Gr. 1	**GENERAL ACCIDENT 2000 GUINEAS**, 8f, Newmarket, to DANCING BRAVE, defeating HUNTINGDALE, SURE BLADE, TATE GALLERY.

Haafhd

Classic winner Haadhd was the winner of five races and £492,288 at two and three years, between six and 10 furlongs. First foals in 2006.

Won Gr. 1	**ULTIMATEBET.COM 2000 GUINEAS** at Newmarket, 8f, by 13/4 lengths, beating SNOW RIDGE and AZAMOUR.
Won Gr. 1	**EMIRATES AIRLINE CHAMPION STAKES** at Newmarket, 10f, by 21/2 lengths, beating CHORIST, AZAMOUR, NORSE DANCER, REFUSE TO BEND and DOYEN.
Won Gr. 1	**CRAVEN STAKES** at Newmarket, 8f, beating THREE VALLEYS.
Won LR	**WASHINGTON SINGER STAKES** at Newbury, 7f, by 5 lengths at 2 years in record time.
3rd Gr. 1	**DEWHURST STAKES** G.1 at Newmarket (7f) to MILK IT MICK and THREE VALLEYS.
3rd Gr. 2	**CHAMPAGNE STAKES** at Doncaster, 7f, to LUCKY STORY, beating MILK IT MICK.

Mujahid

Mujahid stands at Beech House Stud in Britain and Widden Stud in Australia. Boasting at Timeform rating of 125 at two, he was the winner of three races and £189,134 at two to four years. His first crop of three-year-olds achieving 44 per cent winners to runners in Europe and at the 2005 Doncaster and Tattersalls October his yearlings averaged 4 times his nomination fee.

Won Gr. 1	**SAUDI ARABIAN AIRLINES DEWHURST STAKES**, 7f, Newmarket, defeating STRAVINSKY, ENRIQUE, LUJAIN, INDIAN DANEHILL
Won	**TRINITY CONDITIONS STAKES**, 6f, Salisbury.
Won	**EBF FRANCIS GRAVES NOVICE STAKES**, 6f, Newmarket.
2nd LR	**JAMES SEYMOUR STAKES**, 10f, Newmarket.
3rd Gr. 1	**SAGITTA 2000 GUINEAS**, 8f, Newmarket.
3rd Gr. 3	**WEATHERBYS EARL OF SEFTON STAKES**, 9f, Newmarket.

Nayef

Nayef was the winner of nine races and £2,359,840 from two to five-years-old, between eight and 12 furlongs. A Timeform Champion in Europe, his first crop yearlings made up to 260,000gns.

Won Gr. 1	**DUBAI CHAMPION STAKES** at Newmarket, 10f, beating TOBOUGG and INDIAN CREEK.
Won Gr. 1	**JUDDMONTE INTERNATIONAL STAKES** at York, 10.5f, beating GOLAN and NOVERRE.
Won Gr. 1	**PRINCE OF WALES'S STAKES** at Royal Ascot 10f, by 2 1/2 lengths, beating RAKTI, ISLINGTON, FALBRAV, GRANDERA and MOON BALLAD.
Won Gr. 1	**DUBAI SHEEMA CLASSIC** at Nad Al Sheba 12f beating BOREAL and MARIENBARD.
Won Gr. 3	**CUMBERLAND LODGE STAKES** at Ascot, 12f
Won Gr. 3	**SELECT STAKES** at Goodwood, 10f, by 6l.
Won Gr. 3	**PETROS ROSE OF LANCASTER STAKES** at Haydock Park, 10.5f, by 5 lengths.

Sakhee

A brilliant winner of the Prix de l'Arc de Triomphe and Juddmonte International, Sakhee's winning distance in the former compared with that of such greats as RIBOT and SEA BIRD. He claimed eight wins and was placed three times, amassing race career earnings of £2,208,160. First crop yearlings made up to 260,000guineas

Won Gr. 1	**PRIX DE L'ARC DE TRIOMPHE**, 12f, Longchamp.
Won Gr. 1	**JUDDMONTE INTERNATIONAL STAKES**, 10.5f, York, defeating GRANDERA, MEDICEAN, BLACK MINNALOUSHE.
Won Gr. 2	**JWE TELECOM DANTE STAKES**, 10f, York.
Won Gr. 3	**THRESHER CLASSIC TRIAL**, 10f, Sandown.
Won LR	**STEVENTON STAKES**, 10f, Newbury.
2nd Gr. 1	**BREEDERS' CUP CLASSIC**, 10f, Belmont Park, finishing a nose behind TIZNOW.
2nd Gr. 1	**VODAFONE DERBY STAKES**, 12f, Epsom finishing behind SINNDAR and defeating BEAT HOLLOW and BEST OF THE BESTS.

Storming Home

Storming home has won more Group One races than any other son of the outstanding MACHIAVELLIAN. A winner of eight races and £1,001,092 from two to five years, between seven and 12 furlongs. His first yearlings will appear in 2006.

Won Gr. 1	**EMIRATES AIRLINE CHAMPION STAKES** at Newmarket, 10f, beating MOON BALLAD and NOVERRE.
Won Gr. 1	**CHARLES WHITTINGHAM MEMORIAL HANDICAP** at Hollywood, 10f, with top weight.
Won Gr. 1	**CLEMENT L. HIRSCH MEMORIAL TURF CHAMPIONSHIP** at Santa Anita, 10f, beating JOHAR.
Won Gr. 2	**KING EDWARD VII STAKES** at Royal Ascot 12f, beating MILAN.
Won LR	**FISHPOOLS GODOLPHIN STAKES** at Newmarket, 12f, by 6 lengths.
Won LR	**JIM MURRAY MEMORIAL HANDICAP** at Hollywood, 10f, beating DENON.
Won	**BLUE RIBAND TRIAL STAKES** at Epsom, 10f

Haafhd

ch. c by Alhaarth - Al Bahathri (Blushing Groom)

Sheikh Hamdan's shining star of 2004 was the result of impeccable breeding and some good judgement. Haafhd's blue blood extends through his sire and dam, both retiring following classic winning campaigns for Sheikh Hamdan. Grandsire Unfuwain also won black type for the same owner, while Unfuwain's dam, the famed Height of Fashion, needs no introduction.

This Barry Hills trained juvenile won his first two starts of 2003, beginning with a Newmarket maiden in August. This proved a hot contest, with five of the nine horses following him home winning next time out. Newmarket was followed by Newbury and the Stan James Online Stakes. There, he only served to add to a growing reputation by claiming a five length success in record time.

Subsequent third places in the Champagne Stakes at Doncaster and Dewhurst Stakes at Newmarket, while not setting the world alight, did little to diminish the fact that there was potential for all to see.

Haafhd's return to Newmarket the following spring saw him leap into the forefront of 2000 Guineas thinking. Ridden by Richard Hills, the colt led from start to finish to demolish a quality field in the Craven Stakes. Haafhd took up the running as the field sprang from the stalls in a mile-long contest, set a good pace throughout, and then put in a final burst of speed on the famous Rowley Mile course to streak home by five lengths.

Weeks later Haafhd's 2000 Guineas success provided a memorable day for the Hills family. This win gave his trainer a second Guineas success, 25 years after the first, and provided the jockey with a first in this Classic. Haafhd was always travelling best, took the lead two furlongs out and held off a challenge from Godolphin's Snow Ridge.

Haafhd went on to be found out in more mature company, finishing unplaced in a pair of Group One contests against older horses, before winning the Champion Stakes by two and a half lengths, again at Newmarket.

Haafhd was retired to stand at Sheikh Hamdan's Nunnery Stud in Norfolk, the winner of five of nine career starts.

HAAFHD (ch. 2001)	**Alhaarth (b. 1993)**	**Unfuwain** — Northern Dancer / Height of Fashion
		Irish Valley — Irish River / Green Valley
	Al Bahathri (ch. 1982)	**Blushing Groom** — Red God / Runaway Bride
		Chain Store — Nodouble / General Store

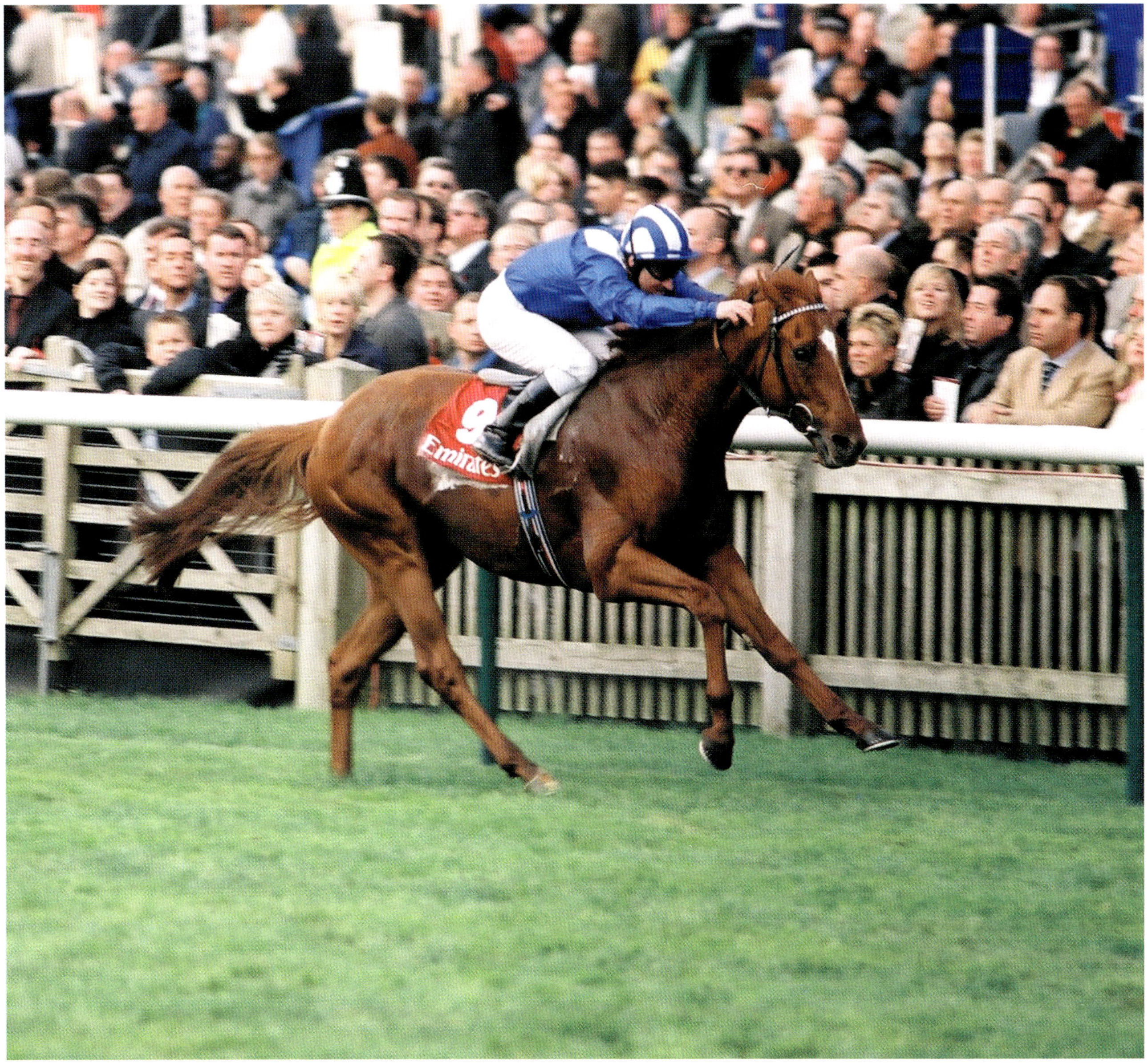

Emirates

Halling

ch. c by Diesis — Dance Machine (Green Dancer)

From handicapper to multiple Group One Winner: Arguably more than any other, Halling has underlined the strength of the Godolphin operation. Trained by John Gosden, this son of Diesis completed his three-year-old season with back-to-back handicap successes at Ripon, Doncaster and in the Cambridgeshire at Newmarket.

Certainly he was a late progressing sort, but his exploits as a four and five-year-old are unprecedented. Transferred to Dubai, Halling won all his three starts on the sand at Nad Al Sheba, including two legs of the prestigious Maktoum Challenge.

He returned to Europe under the banner of Saeed bin Suroor and despite showing great improvement according to the Dubai handicapper, was hardly among the leading fancies in the Coral-Eclipse Stakes in July. Walter Swinburn took Halling to the front from the outset, and there he stayed, running on in the latter stages to fend off a challenge from Singspiel by a neck, despite the jockey dropping his whip. That performance saw him raised 20 pounds in the ratings.

He was even more impressive next time out in August in the International Stakes at York. Tracking the leaders early, Swinburn and Halling cruised to the lead of affairs two furlongs out in the straight and when quickening in the latter stages he went on impressively by three and a half lengths, claiming his eighth consecutive victory.

His run was ended on the rain-sodden Belmont Park track in October when he trailed in last behind Cigar in the Breeders' Cup Classic.

Returning to Dubai, Halling showed up well in a prep race at Nad Al Sheba and went into the Dubai World Cup carrying high hopes, only to be soundly beaten, hardly a disaster in the strongest field ever assembled anywhere for a Thoroughbred race.

Back in Europe he made easy work of a small field in the Prix D'Ispahan at Longchamp before another front-running success to claim a second Coral-Eclipse, by a neck from Bijou D'Ilnde.

Remarkably, Halling added his fourth consecutive Group One on turf, the same two events to boot, when again making all to dominate the International Stakes.

The five year old completed his career when outpointed by Guineas heroine Bosra Sham in the Champion Stakes at Newmarket.

HALLING (ch. 1991)	**Diesis (ch. 1980)**	**Sharpen Up** — Atan / Rocchetta
		Doubly Sure — Reliance II / Green Valley
	Dance Machine (b. 1982)	**Green Dancer** — Pontifex / Soft Angels
		Never A Lady — Nijinsky / Camogie

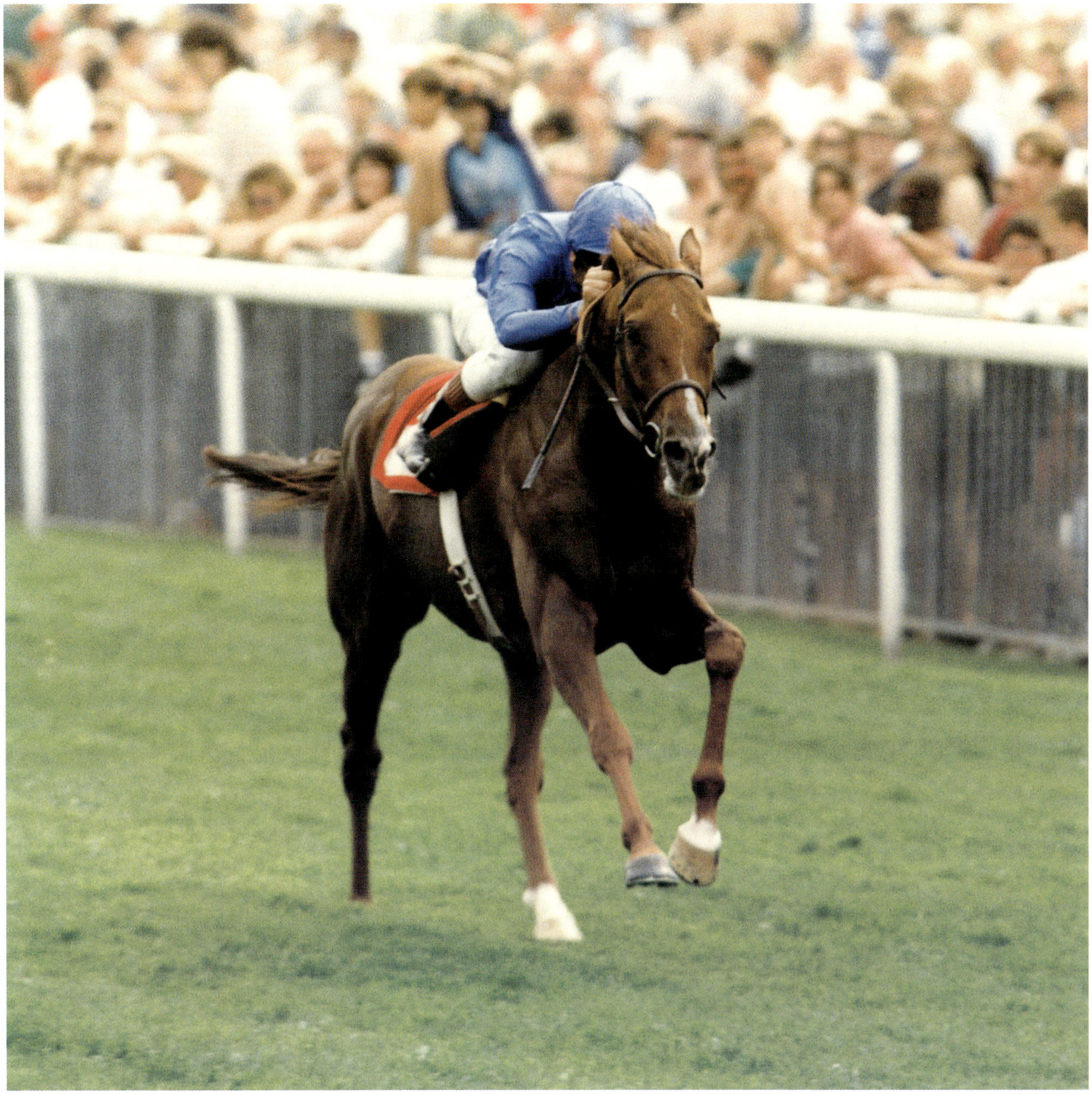

Harayir

b. f by Gulch — Saffaanh (Shareef Dancer)

Home-bred by Sheikh Hamdan, Harayir as a three-year-old was to contribute to her owner's remarkable run of three wins in six seasons in the British 1000 Guineas while establishing herself as a tremendous performer in her own right.

Even before his juvenile debut, the Dick Hern-trained filly was thought very useful, and producing an all-the-way success from a good field at Newbury confirmed her potential. The Cherry Hinton Stakes, a leading pointer to the relative merits of the cream of juvenile fillies, saw Harayir frank the form of her debut. It took a superb run from Red Carnival to deny Harayir the honours as she finished second.

Six weeks later, looking extremely well in herself, Harayir made easy work of the Lowther Stakes. Having briefly been rated highest among her generation, Harayir's final start in the Cheveley Park Stakes produced a third place.

She returned the following spring with home reports glowing and finished clear second to Diffident in the European Free Handicap, despite shouldering joint top weight.

Sheikh Hamdan was to hold an embarrassment of riches in the first classic of the season after Aquaarid's success in the Fred Darling Stakes. This pair, along with subsequent Godolphin Oaks heroine Moonshell, led the market and the race for much of the way, but from two furlongs out Harayir did seem to be travelling best. As Richard Hills made his move little more than 200 metres out, Moonshell and Aquaarid were already less than comfortable. Harayir cruised to the lead and from this point on the Classic was hers—and a first for Hills—with Aquaarid second.

Harayir failed to impress on soft ground in the Irish 1000 Guineas and then was third in the Coronation Stakes, both behind Ridgewood Pearl.

But the filly's class shone through in August in Newbury's Hungerford Stakes. The point was made even more emphatically in the Celebration Mile two weeks later. At Goodwood she looked better than ever in defeating Darnay for a second time. Under a Group One penalty in Ascot's Diadem Stakes in September, over a sharp six furlongs, she managed fourth before rounded off her track career with a final success at Newmarket, claiming the seven-furlong Challenge Stakes.

		Mr Prospector	Raise A Native
	Gulch (b. 1994)		Gold Digger
		Jameela	Rambunctious
HARAYIR (b. 1992)			Asbury Mary
		Shareef Dancer	Northern Dancer
	Saffaanh (b. 1986)		Weet Alliance
		Give Thanks	Relko
			Parthica

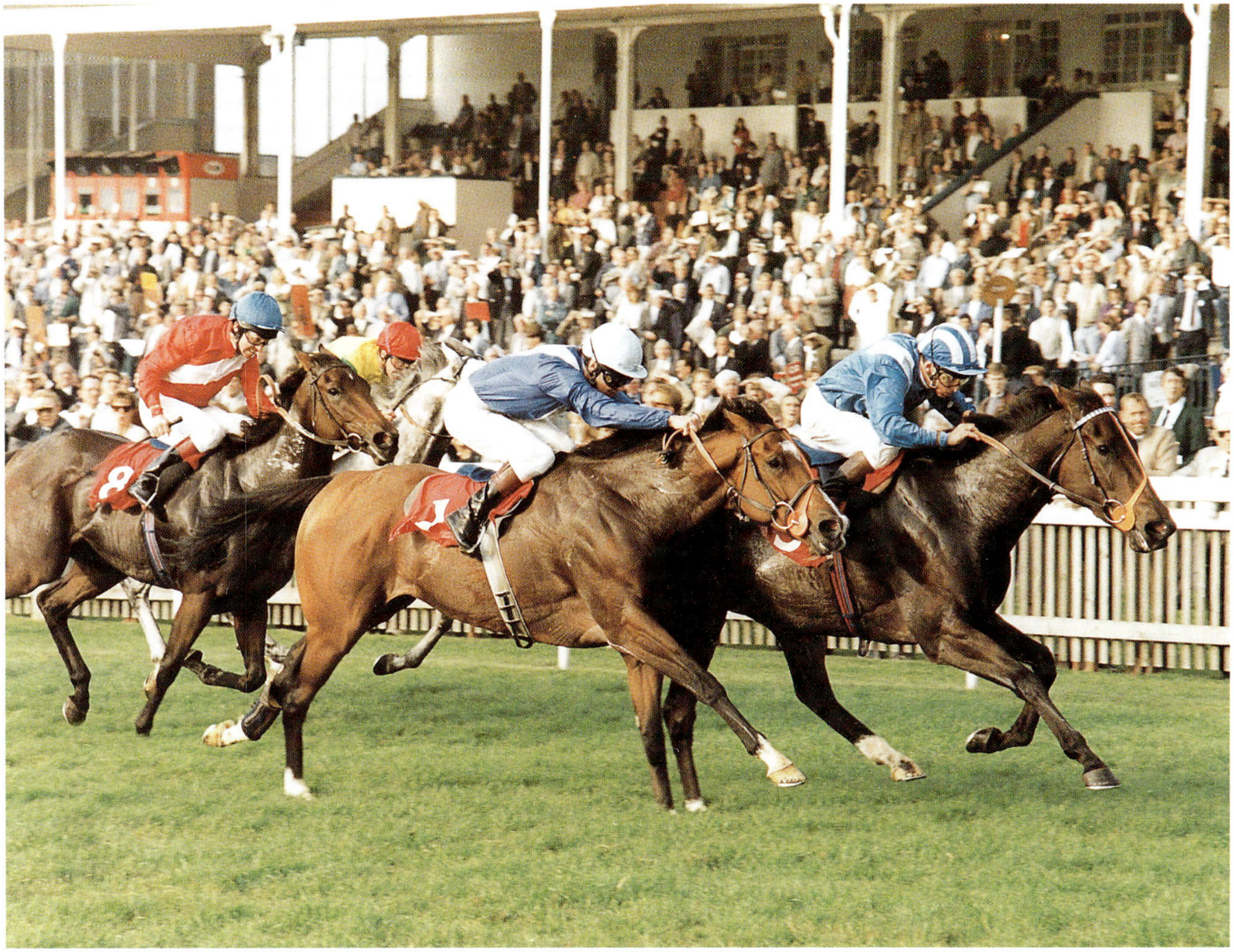

Hatoof

ch. f by Irish River – Cadeaux d'Amie (Lyphard)

Following a juvenile campaign which fully established her as a top grade filly, Criquette Head-trained Hatoof went on to become one of Sheikh Maktoum's finest performers. Two successes over a mile as a two-year-old left the impression that she would need further the following year, and her second place to Kenbu in the seven-furlong Prix Imprudence at Maisons-Laffitte in April reconfirmed that view.

As planned she crossed the Channel to contest the 1000 Guineas at Newmarket, to face a vintage field which included unbeaten juvenile Marling. Ridden by Walter Swinburn, the filly was sent off co-favourite. Swinburn rode a superb tactical race. With no stamina doubts, he kept Hatoof up with the pace and waited. She found daylight two furlongs from the line. As Hatoof overhauled Kenbu to take up the lead, Marling came with a storming run, ultimately too late as Hatoof stayed on to claim the classic.

She returned home for the French 1000 Guineas and finished an inexplicably disappointing sixth. After a three-month rest, Hatoof performed admirably but did not trouble the judge in top class mile events the Prix Jacques le Marois and Prix de Moulin de Longchamp, before claiming Longchamp's Prix de l'Opera on Arc day.

She left the dying European season behind for a trip to Woodbine, Canada, adding the 10-furlong E P Taylor Stakes to her seasonal haul.

The following spring Hatoof returned with a victory in Saint-Cloud's Prix de Muguet. After a break, she again returned to conquer in the La Coupe de Maisons-Laffitte, setting herself up for a crack at the Champion Stakes. Newmarket brought another defining moment in her career where, taking on the likes of Ezzoud and Muhtarram, she never looked in danger of losing.

Her final start of 1993 was over a mile and a half in the Breeders' Cup Turf, where she finished best of the Europeans in fifth of 14 starters.

Hatoof the five-year-old was equally successful, adding the Prix Astarte to her haul before another transatlantic sojourn. Arlington Park's valuable Beverly D Stakes, with excellent work by Swinburn, provided an emphatic success. Then in the Breeders' Cup Turf, Hatoof finished one and a half lengths second to Tikkanen.

	Riverman	Never Bend
Irish River (ch. 1976)		River Lady
	Irish Star	Klairon
HATOOF (ch. 1989)		Botany Bay
	Lyphard	Northern Dancer
Cadeaux d'Amie (ch. 1984)		Goofed
	Tananarive	Le Fabuleaux
		Ten Double

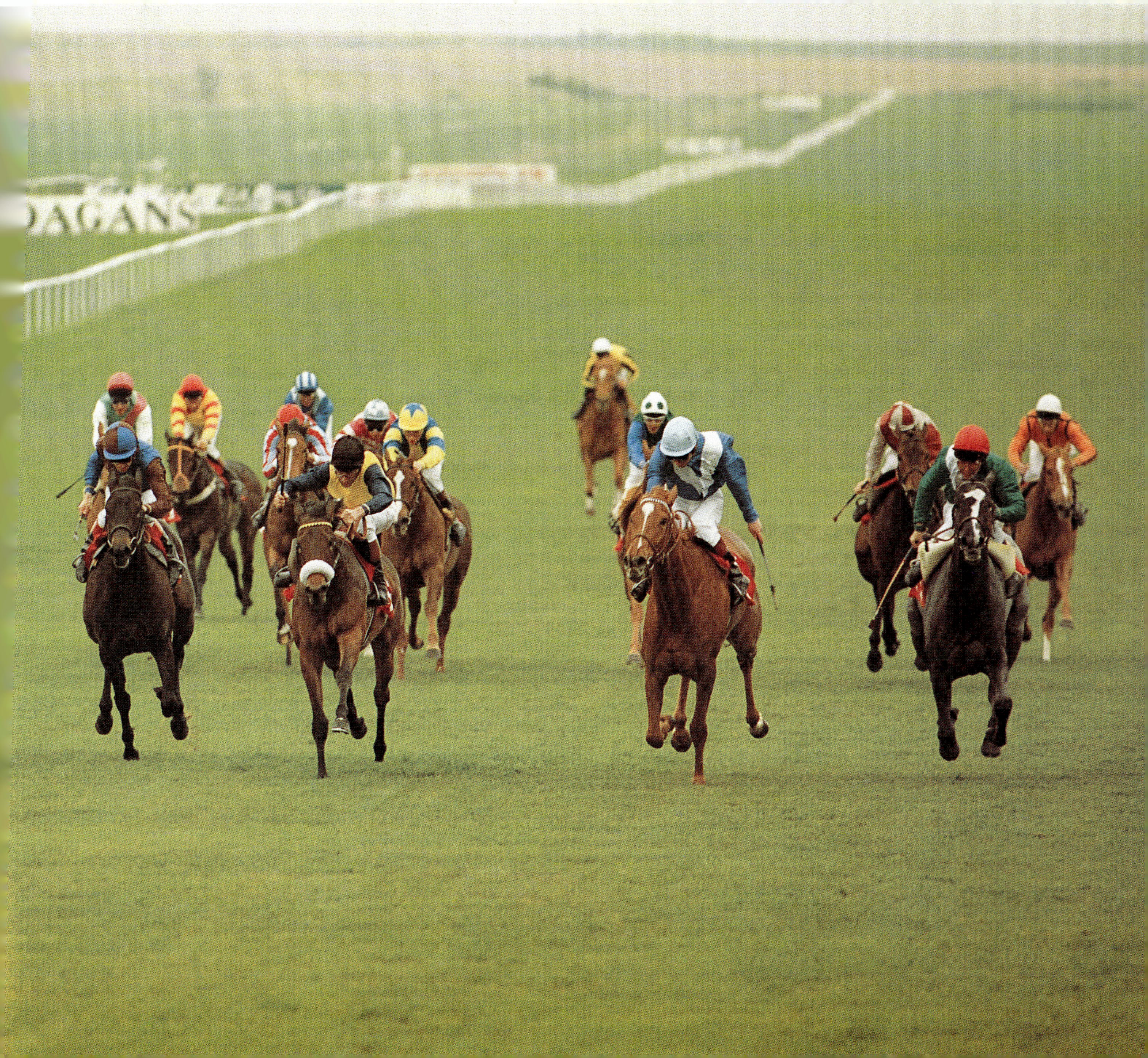

OYSTER PERPETUAL
COSMOGRAPH DAYTONA

WWW.ROLEX.COM

ROLEX

AHMED SEDDIQI & SONS

Showrooms: Dubai - Souq Murshid, Deira Tower, Twin Towers, Grosvenor House
Jumeirah Beach Hotel, Deira City Centre, Grand Hyatt Dubai, Wafi City, Mall of Emirates
Le Royal Meridien - Jumeirah, Madinat al Jumeirah, Burjuman Centre
Sharjah: Sharjah City Centre, **Fujairah:** Le Meridien Al Aqah

Sheikh Mohammed bin Rashid Al Maktoum

Now the Ruler of Dubai and Vice-President and Prime Minister of the UAE following the sad death of his brother, Sheikh Maktoum, Sheikh Mohammed bin Rashid Al Maktoum is the leader of his people as well as a forerunner in the world of horse racing. Ever a visionary, this dynamic, vibrant Royal has helped change not only the destiny of a nation, but the way in which people look at the sport of horse racing, especially international competition.

He was introduced to racing in England, as was his brother Sheikh Hamdan, at Newmarket in May 1967 when Royal Palace won the 2000 Guineas but it was almost a full decade before he became actively involved. His trip to Newmarket coincided with his completing his education at nearby Cambridge.

In 1971 he became the world's youngest ever Minister of Defence when appointed to that role by the UAE. Meanwhile, he was building his own racecourse and stables, as well as holding the post of Head of Police and Public Security in Dubai. It was a meeting with Major Dick Warden, who bought a consignment of horses to Dubai for the local police force, which persuaded Sheikh Mohammed to pursue his interest in racing in England. That was in 1975 and the following year both he and his brother Sheikh Maktoum bought yearlings at Tattersalls in Newmarket. In 1977 Sheikh Mohammed supplied the Maktoums with their first winner, a filly called Hatta, trained by John Dunlop and whose four juvenile victories culminated in the Group 3 Molecomb Stakes at Glorious Goodwood. It was the start of what has become one of the most productive terms of racehorse ownership in the world.

Sheikh Mohammed descends from one of the most notable tribes in Arabia and his family Bedouin culture and traditions explain his love of and special relationship with the horse. He was raised to be at one with nature and is equally at home on horseback, on a camel, hunting with falcons, shooting, tracking snakes and scorpions or with saluki dogs.

However, horses were his passion and he was

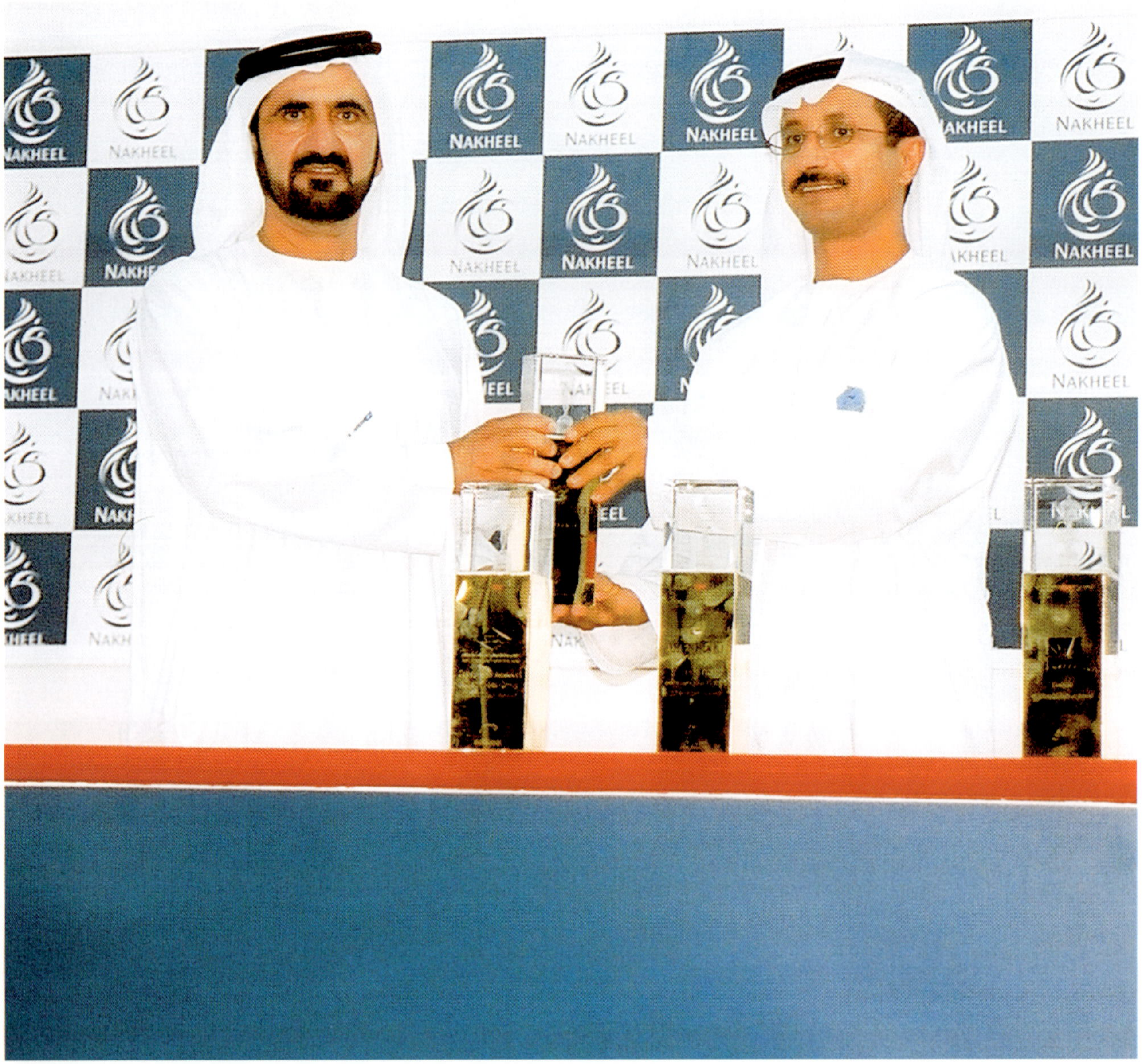
NAKHEEL

always a daily visitor to the family's stables and rode in his first race at the tender age of 12. He could always be found heading out into the desert on his horse or riding along the miles of sandy beaches along the water front. He developed a reputation for riding horses deemed 'untrainable.'

However, he was sent to Cambridge to study in 1966 and stayed with an English family in which racing was often a subject of conversation. He was proud that the most influential sire in British racing was the Godolphin Arabian - although his hosts disagreed. But that was how he ended up at Newmarket as George Moore steered Royal Palace to Classic victory.

He then went to Mons Officer Cadet School in Aldershot and graduated with the sword of honour and the highest marks of any Foreign and Commonwealth officer in his intake.

On his appointment as Minister of Defence when the UAE was created in 1971 he had to deal with the Arab/Israeli war, an attempted coup in a neighbouring state and a plane hijacking at Dubai Airport. He also set up the Union Defence Force and Dubai Dry Docks, the biggest facility of its kind in the Middle East.

Dubai oil, airport and aviation were added to his remit in 1977 - the year Hatta was cementing his horse racing passion and his maroon and white silks were to become dominant in the 1980s. Oh So Sharp, Pennekamp, Diminuendo, Indian Skimmer, Belmez, Old Vic, Opera House, Sonic Lady, Ajdal, Kings Theatre and Pebbles to name but a few triumphed all over Europe.

However, that was not enough for Sheikh Mohammed and in the early 1990's racing in the UAE was introduced under rules and Godolphin was created with global ambitions. The Dubai International Jockeys' Challenge was the first international racing event at Nad Al Sheba, closely followed by the Dubai World Cup meeting and more recently the Dubai International Racing Carnival.

The success of Godolphin is well documented and some true equine legends have carried the famous blue silks - Dubai Millennium, Daylami, Fantastic Light, Sakhee, Street Cry, Swain, Grandera, Halling, Kazzia, Mark of Esteem and Moon Ballad to name a few. Their trainer Saeed bin Suroor has also trained Lammtarra and Balanchine to Classic victories and Almutawakel to Dubai World Cup glory.

It was the advent of Godolphin which showed the world Sheikh Mohammed was a true horseman in every sense of the word, while raising the profile of Dubai to an unprecedented level.

He wanted to compete his horses around the world and to encourage others to do so the same, so he created the Dubai World Cup, the world's richest horse race.

Sheikh Mohammed's maroon silks were also carried to victory in a US Triple Crown race in 2006 when his Bernardini won the Grade 1 Preakness Stakes, the middle leg of The Triple Crown, while in 2004 Balletto's Grade 1 victory and subsequent second place in the Breeders' Cup Juvenile Fillies' race silenced those who said he could not breed top-class racehorses at his stud in Hatta.

What a lot of people may not realise is just how good a rider he actually is as his preferred field, endurance. His sons are also leading performers in this field and the UAE have enjoyed much success in recent times - mostly attributed to Sheikh Mohammed's mastery of tactics.

A pioneer, innovator and born leader, in both industry and sport, Sheikh Mohammed's vision has made Dubai the thriving, cosmopolitan place it is today.

And who knows what is next?

SARCAR
GENÈVE
Creator of dreams

SOLITAIRE COLLECTION
Rose Gold 18 carats with Diamonds.

damas
Les Exclusives
TOLL FREE 800 4916

www.damasjewellery.com

Hatta

br. f by Realm — Sayorette (Sayajiaro)

When a yearling filly by Realm passed through the sales ring at Tattersalls in Newmarket on 15 October 1976, nobody could have guessed her role in introducing to the sport the most significant individual to participate in racing during the 20th century.

Bred by Mount Coote Stud in Ireland, the youngster was sold to the Curragh Bloodstock Agency for 6,200 guineas. She later passed into the care of trainer John Dunlop, running in the colors of Sheikh Mohammed. Dunlop was reportedly pleased with his new charge, named Hatta by her owner, after a mountain enclave of Dubai.

She finished sixth on her debut and second next time out before breaking her maiden. However, she was improving in leaps and bounds and was placed to great effect by her trainer. After that first success, Hatta ran up a sequence of three wins at Brighton, Salisbury and Sandown.

After showing continual development and increasing maturity on the racecourse, Dunlop believed his filly ready for a rise in class. After her Sandown success she was pencilled in to represent the stable in the five-furlong Molecomb Stakes at Goodwood, a race that had been a stepping stone for a string of top class fillies that went on to race at the highest level. Dunlop had taken the race the previous season and in seeking a further success matched his filly against the much-touted Amaranda, who the bookmakers installed as favourite for the Goodwood event. Amaranda got her usual speedy break from the stalls, while Hatta was slow into her stride and lost a lot of ground during the early stages of the race. The leader appeared to have an unassailable advantage, but found nothing when Hatta was shaken up and came with a powerful run. Inside the last 100 yards she was in full flow, drawing away impressively to win by two and half lengths.

Despite her superb turn of foot over five furlongs, she was sent over six next time out. Dunlop dispatched her north to Scotland to contest the Firth of Clyde Stakes at Ayr. However, whether the travelling or the long season was against her, she mysteriously failed to show at Ayr and finished a disappointing fifth of six runners. Nevertheless, Hatta's place in history was assured as the first winner on a Western racecourse for a man who would go on to become one of the most influential owner-breeders in the history of the sport.

HATTA (br. 1975)	**Realm (b. 1967)**	**Princely Gift** — Nasrullah / Blue Gem
		Quita II — Lavandin / Eos
	Sayorette (b. 1965)	**Sayajirao** — Nearco / Rosy Legend
		Mlle Lorette — Lovely Night / Gallorette

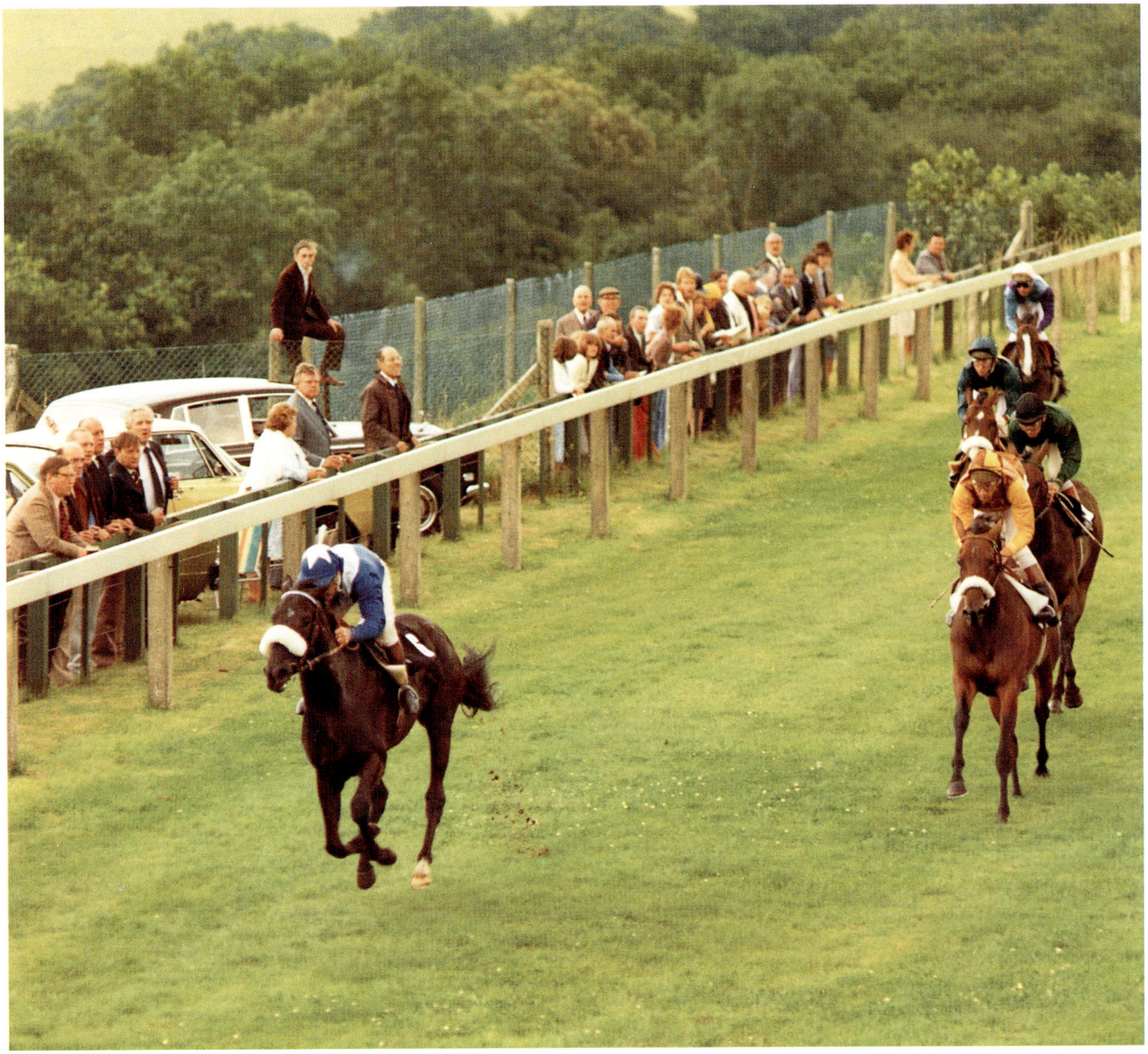

Height of Fashion

b. m by Bustino - Highclere (Queen's Hussar)

Height of Fashion is something of an anomaly within the pages of *Legends of the Turf*. The great mare, unlike all the other great horses profiled in this title, never appeared on the racecourse representing the Maktoum family. Nevertheless, so profound is her impact upon the Maktoums' racing fortunes - and indeed the sport itself - that her place among the legends of the turf is certain.

Her grandsire, Busted, won the Coronation Stakes, the Eclipse Stakes and King George at Ascot in 1967. His huge success as a stallion is shown by his Group One winning progeny, such as Bustino, Mtoto and Shernanzer who have become brilliant sires in their own right. Height of Fashion's sire, Bustino, was a Classic winner who bred Group One winners such as Terimon and was Champion Broodmare Sire on two occasions thanks to his most famed daughter.

Height of Fashion was bred by Queen Elizabeth from her mare Highclere, who she sent to Bustino. Like Nashwan later, both Bustino and Height of Fashion were trained by Dick Hern.

Height of Fashion won the May Hill Stakes and the Fillies' Mile and was then sold following her win in the Princess of Wales Stakes.

Height Of Fashion spent her entire stud career in Kentucky, and in the first two seasons she visited by Northern Dancer with both offspring from these unions proving well above average. Her first foal Alwasmi winning a Group Three, and her second foal being Unfuwain. Nashwan was her third foal, born on March 1 1986, by Blushing Groom.

Height of Fashion also produced Sarayir (Mr. Prospector), a listed winner, and Sheikh Hamdan's top class Group One winner Nayef (Gulch).

After a distinguished career, the great broodmare passed away in July 2000 at the age of 21. But her influence continued to be felt, both on the racecourse and in the breeding shed. As stallions her elite sons Nashwan and Unfuwain continued to produce top class offspring until their untimely deaths last year, Group One winners Swain and Alhaarth respectively being two prime examples.

Height of Fashion may be gone, but her influence will continue to be felt in Maktoum racing fortunes and, indeed, on the Thoroughbred breed itself.

Bustino (b. 1971)	**Busted**	**Crepello**
		Sans Le Sou
	Ship Yard	**Doutelle**
HEIGHT OF FASHION (b. 1979)		**Paving Stone**
Highclere (b. 1971)	**Queen's Hussar**	**March Past**
		Jojo
	Highlight	**Borealis**
		Hypericum

One of the world's greatest ever broodmares Height of Fashion and (above) her well tended grave on Sheikh Hamdan's Shadwell Farm in Kentucky

High Hawk

b. f by Shirley Heights – Sunbittern (Sea Hawk)

In 11 starts as a three-year-old, this little filly went from the modest surroundings of Folkestone in Southern England to Tokyo and an invitation to compete in the Japan Cup!

A 31,000 guineas yearling, High Hawk seemed only a reasonable performer as a juvenile in failing to sparkle in two starts. Indeed, John Dunlop hardly threw her in on her reappearance the following season where she finished second wearing a visor for the first time.

But from this point her remarkable development began apace, including a pair of successes at Lingfield and a second to a smart filly in another hot contest.

This improvement led Dunlop to give the filly a chance at Royal Ascot in the Ribblesdale Stakes. Seen making up a tremendous amount of ground in the final straight, she hit the front with 200 yards remaining and left her opponents behind, recording a length and a half success from Current Raiser.

This sterling performance saw High Hawk lifted in class again, to classic company for the Irish Oaks where she locked horns with one of the season's finest fillies, Give Thanks. The latter claimed her race with High Hawk well clear in second and perhaps capable of better but for a better run.

High Hawk took a break until September following the Irish Oaks, reappearing in the Park Hill Stakes to renew rivalry with Give Thanks. The classic winner hit the front with 400 metres remaining and ran on strongly. However High Hawk was revelling in the mile and three quarter trip and stayed on to take the lead and ultimately the race.

She added the mile and a half Prix de Royallieu the following month, winning by a length despite jockey Willie Carson riding out the finish at the wrong stage of the race.

In further racing on the continent she landed the Premio Roma in a tight finish several weeks later. Seemingly still on the upgrade, High Hawk was drafted into the Japan Cup after Sheikh Mohammed's Awaasif defected from the classic. She finished well down the field, though not disgraced, and was retired to the paddocks.

		Mill Reef	Never Bend
			Milan Mill
	Shirley Heights (b. 1975)		Hardicanute
		Hardiemma	Grand Cross
HIGH HAWK (b. 1980)			
		Sea Hawk II	Herbager
			Sea Nymph
	Sunbittern (gr. 1970)		Panaslipper
		Pantoufle	Etoile de France

Born in Saxony.
At home around the world.

A. LANGE & SÖHNE
GLASHÜTTE I/SA

Meticulously finished by hand, the LANGE 1 TIME ZONE is a global ambassador of the legendary perfection of Lange watchmaking artistry. Apart from the main dial, this watch features a smaller dial that can be synchronised with any of the world's 24 time zones. The position of the rotating city ring reveals the current time zone setting. Additionally, both dials have separate day/night indicators. This masterpiece is available exclusively from the world's finest jewellery and watch dealers. Ahmed Seddiqi in Dubai is one of the chosen few. www.lange-soehne.com.

––––– The LANGE 1 TIME ZONE. Exclusively at: –––––

AHMED SEDDIQI & SONS   أحمد صديقي وأولاده

Burjuman Centre, Tel. (04) 355 9090, WAFI CITY, Tel.: (04) 324 6060
www.seddiqi.com

High-Rise
b. c by High Estate – High Tern (High Line)

Owner-breeder Sheikh Mohammed Obaid Al Maktoum reached the pinnacle of the sport with High-Rise. The colt won a maiden race at Doncaster in the November of his juvenile season. Trainer Luca Cumani always liked the colt and, as he would later point out, campaigned High-Rise in similar fashion to his other Derby winner Khayasi.

High-Rise began 1998 with a win in Pontefract's Buttercross Limited Stakes. he then rose in class to the Lingfield Derby Trial. When High-Rise hit the front with two furlongs remaining the race was all but over.

Surprisingly an unbeaten High-Rise went into the stalls at Epsom rated a 20-1 chance in a field of 15. Jockey Olivier Peslier held High-Rise up for much of the way and only three were behind him as the field turned Tattenham Corner. The colt was pulled out at this point, coming with a surging run which brought him past virtually all the field within 300 metres. Only in the last few strides did it become clear that High-Rise had won a duel with City Honours to claim a remarkable victory. After a break, the colt reappeared in the King George VI and Queen Elizabeth Diamond Stakes, finishing one length second to six-year-old Swain.

The Prix de l'Arc de Triomphe was next on the High-Rise's agenda, but he failed to show. However, he did finish the season as the highest rated European middle-distance three-year-old.

After switching from Cumani to Godolphin, in March High-Rise became the first English Derby winner to compete in the $5 million Dubai World Cup, facing Kentucky Derby winner Silver Charm. In the event neither starred as Almutawakel took the honours and High-Rise finished down the field, not relishing the surface.

He subsequently returned to Britain, but a couple of niggling problems prevented Saeed bin Suroor from getting the best out of the Classic winner. In the Dubai Champion Stakes, High-Rise was putting in a good run when not finding room around one furlong out. He lost his place and, despite staying on strongly, had lost his chance. He finished sixth behind Albodora.

HIGH RISE (b. 1995)	**High Estate**	Shirley Heights	Mill Reef / Hardiemma
		Regal Beauty	Princley Native / Dennis Belle
	High Tern	High Line	High Hat / Time Call
		Sunbittern	Sea Hawk II / Pantufle

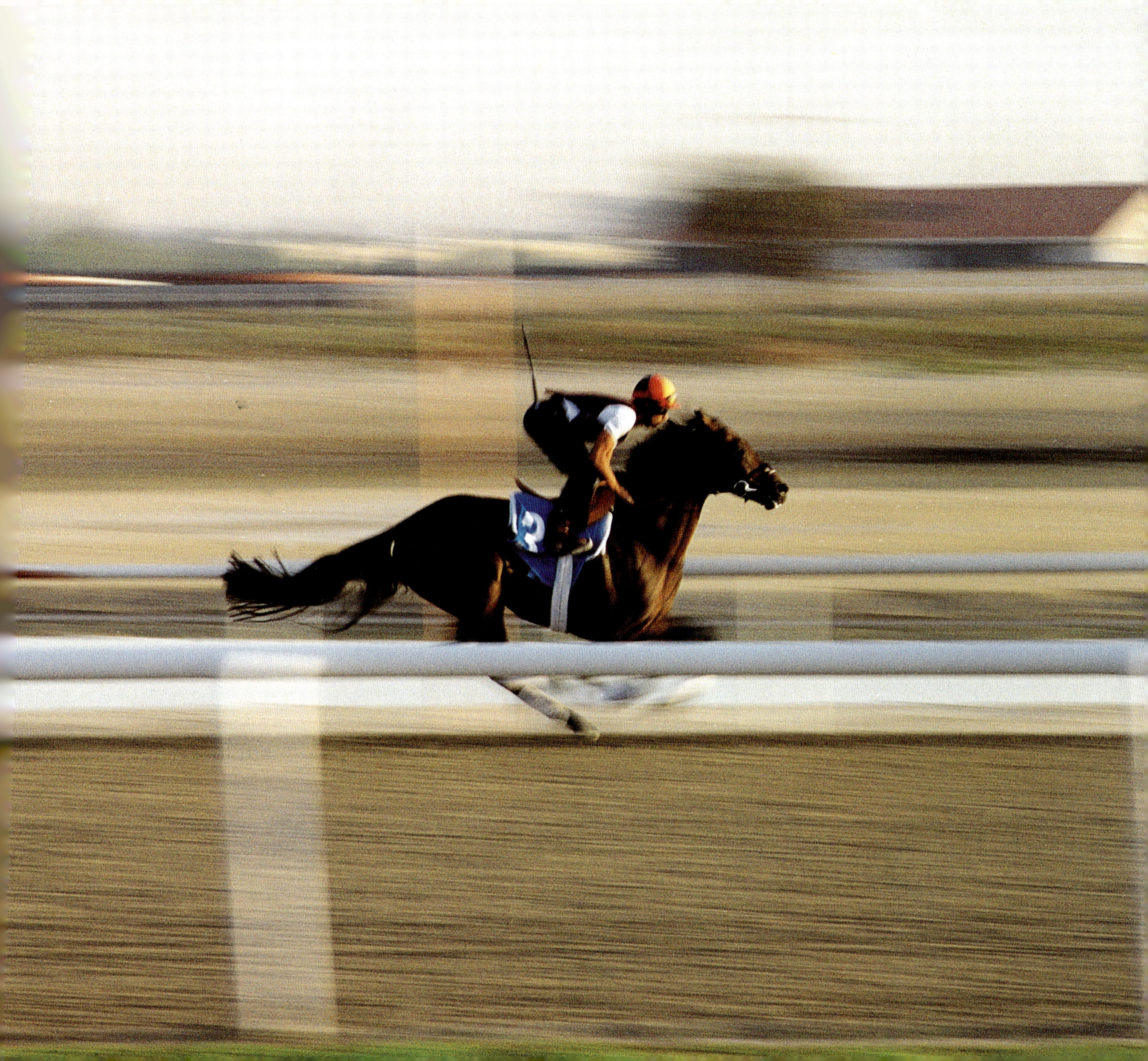

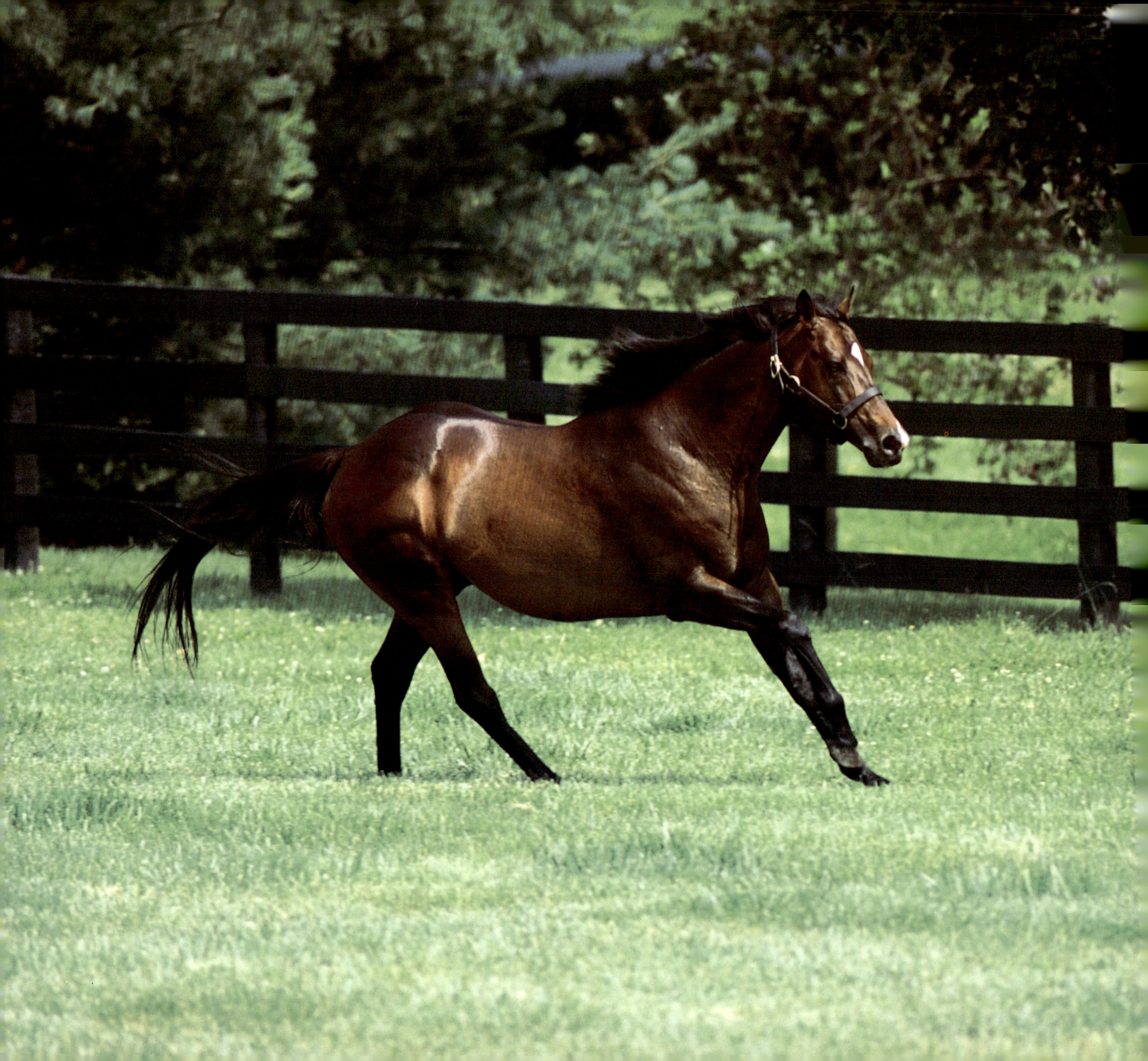

An Equine in Time

Over millions of years primitive breeds of horse migrated from their North American homeland to the Old World, across the Bering land-bridge which used to connect Alaska and Siberia where the Bering Sea is now. The last single-toed representatives of the genus Equus also took this path and, while their relatives in North America mysteriously died out about 10,000 years ago, they spread out over Asia, Europe and Africa and evolved into the familiar the present-day zebras, donkeys and horses.

Among the wild Equidae, horses had probably the largest area of distribution. During the Ice Age they were able to survive under diverse living conditions on moor and tundra, in forests, mountains, steppes and desert-like regions. Both their bodily structure and their natures were shaped by the climate, vegetation, and condition of the ground. In the course of many generations different breeds of geographical subspecies of horse evolved from having to adapt to these varying conditions, particularly where the isolated living conditions of individual populations prevented any further exchange of genes.

There were at least four main types as well as numerous hybrids. In the mountainous regions of north west Africa a comparatively large but very lightly built horse evolved. Its tapering head with swelling muzzle and the unusual distance between the eyes and the nostrils give it a very striking appearance. These Barb horses characterised by their amazing stamina and sure-footedness have been cross-bred with Arabs, but basically they trace their descent from the desert mountains breed. The Islamic conquerors took the horses with them to south-west Europe and used them as the basis for breeding.

Another basic type, a small graceful finely-boned almost gazelle-like horse evolved on the bleak expanses of the deserts of south-west Asia. As the grasses which thrived in their native habitat were not very lush, though they were nourishing, this breed of horse did not need either particularly large or long teeth or very capacious digestive organs.

There were no hiding places on that open terrain, so a quick escape was always the best protection from hostile predators. Not surprisingly, domestication of the horse did not occur for thousands of years after this, the exact dates still under scientific dispute. With a fiery temperament which guaranteed a lightning reaction to danger and a broad thorax allowing plenty of room for efficient lungs and a strong heart, more than any other breed of horse this desert type for speed. The Arabs inherited this legacy and it is an indisputable fact that the breeding of warm-blood horses throughout the world would be unthinkable without their contribution. Hybrid animals roamed over much larger areas and were highly specialised, not having adapt to such extremes of living conditions, were naturally domestic more frequently than any of main types.

The earliest recorded depictions of the modern-day horse were painted in the caves at Lascaux, in modern-day France *(pictured)*. Dating from approximately 13,000 BC, these mystical renditions seemed to celebrate the horse as a provider of food and clothing. Human society was, at this point, still in its infancy. It was only much later when humankind became 'civilised' that the horse really came into it's own as the most versatile animal. The horse was increasingly seen as a beast of burden, a means of transport, and the first, crucial, piece of light infantry when going to war.

The most ancient of all advanced civilisations originated around the year 3000 BC with the founding of the kingdoms of Upper and Lower Egypt. These were united under the Kings of the Thinite period. The 'Old Kingdom' lasted from about 2635 to 2135 BC, and was a period of tremendous cultural growth, as the Great Pyramids testify. It was, however, followed by a period of economic and cultural decline. About 2040 BC a new upsurge began with the establishment of the 'Middle Kingdom', and once again colossal monuments were constructed. These necropoli, dedicated to the gods and the dead, were decorated with magnificent paintings and relief sculptures, all of which had an underlying cult significance.

The basis of the Egyptians' wealth was their land's immense fertility. Their rich grain fields were the envy of their neighbours, but for centuries the Egyptian army was invincible—until the arrival of the horse. Then the legions of the Hyksos with their horse-drawn war chariots over-ran Syria and Palestine, driving any opposition like chaff before them. In 1650 BC they conquered Egypt, and their army leaders appointed themselves kings over the conquered territory. It was a hundred years before the

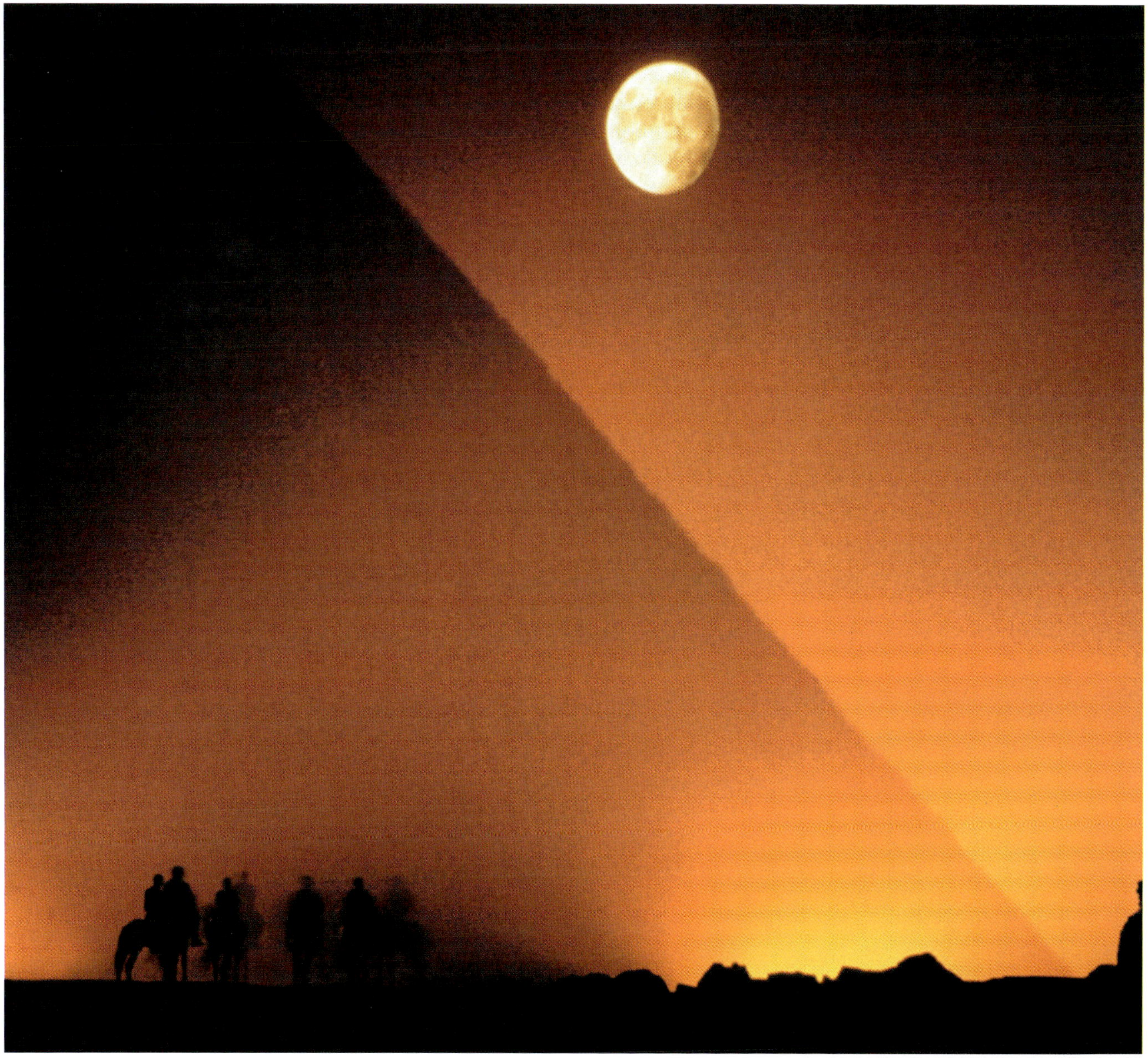

Egyptians were able to expel them, and they hit back at the usurpers with the same weapon that had been their own undoing-the horse-drawn war chariot.

From this time on, the horse was to play an increasingly important role. Soon it began to appear in reliefs and paintings, these drawings indicating that to the Egyptians the horse had become one of the noblest of animals.

During the same period, the horse has also emerged as an integral part of life on the unknown and largely unchartered Arabian peninsula. The Bedouins of the wild barren deserts bred sheep and goats, and used camels as riding and draught animals. Members of the upper classes or Royal families had long possessed horses, but little or nothing is known about these animals before the time of the Prophet Mohammed and the numerous legends passed down from generation to generation are of little help in our search for the origins of the Arab horse.

In the southwestern region of Asir and Nejran, archeologists have repeatedly found equine remains within the settlements and townships of the region.

In the territory which make-up the modern day United Arab Emirates, despite the fact that serious archeological study of the area only began relatively recently, plenty of evidence has been found to link settlers in the Lower Gulf with an equestrian ancestry.

In 1995 a German archeological team unearthed equine remains which have been carbon dated to around 230BC at a site in Meleiha, near Sharjah. Even more significantly is the way they were found. Uncharacteristically for livestock, the three skeletons were discovered buried alongside human beings. Several were wearing gold and silver ornamental head dresses, like Caesar's crown, a sure sign of the significance of the animal in Gulf society, even two thousand years ago.

Much later, by the Christian calendar some 622AD, the Prophet Mohammed was engaged in his campaign to bring Islam to the peoples of the region. He was known to have two weapons in his favour. A fervent belief in his teachings, and excellent horses. Even today, Muslims understand that their Great Prophet was endowed with a remarkable understanding of horses and horse-breeding. The religious books, and the history books, recognised that he produced the incomparable Arab pure-bred. According to legend, Mohammed ordered that a herd of horses be left without water for seven days. When their enclosure was opened the animals raced towards the watering place. But the Prophet then sounded the call to battle. Immediately five mares turned in response and raced back to him without having first quenched their thirst. All purebred Arabs are said to be descended from these five mares.

The Prophet Mohammed was stringently careful when selecting horses for breeding and demanded that the bloodlines be kept absolutely pure. He made the breeding of horses an integral part of his teachings, and in the Holy Koran, compiled after his death from his revelations, he set out rules for breeding and training horses. It states, for example, that 'no evil spirit will dare to enter a tent where there is a pure-bred horse', or, 'for every barleycorn that is given to a horse Allah will pardon one sin'.

Also in the Holy Koran, the Prophet Mohammed tells of the creation of the Arabian horses. It says; 'He told the Wind of the South to fashion a living being which will be an asset most prestigious to they who are loyal to him, a disgrace to those who are his adversaries, and a charm to they who obey him'.

Soon after the Prophet's death in 632 the Arab nation embarked on a Holy War. With horses faster, hardier, and with more stamina than all others, the Arabs were almost invincible and in an astonishingly short campaign they conquered Syria, Palestine, and Egypt, then part of the Eastern Roman Empire.

One single battle was sufficient to cause the fall of the kingdom of the Sassanides. Soon the hooves of the Arabs horses were thundering across Persia, through Afghanistan, to India, Tibet and Turkestan. They overran North Africa, overthrew the Berbers, crossed the narrow strait of Gibraltar into Europe and conquered the Isigoth Empire on the Iberian peninsula, an advance not stopped until it reached France.

At Tours, Moussais and Poitiers, a General Charles Martel was only able to stop this mobile force because of his vastly superior heavy armour. His forces were able to bring them to a halt and force them back over the Pyrenees, however, for centuries the Arabs remained as rulers in some parts of southern France and in most of Spain.

A large number of words added to the European languages give some indication of their cultural attainments: algebra, chemistry, zenith and elixir, among others. And they left the inheritance of their marvelous horses whose blood flows in almost every one of the world's breeds.

Back in the Arabian Gulf the horse which had given the Arab army it's legs was still evolving. The 20th Century Arabian horse we see on the racecourse, out performing all other breeds on the endurance circuit and in the show-ring, was defined in the Middle East. Today, the Al-Khamsa (the five) bloodlines - Kaiudani, Saglawi, Kuhailan, Hadban and Ubaiyan are still recognised as being at the bedrock of the Arabian.

Some bred the Arabian, but the equine was seen more as little more than integral part of life: "A Bedouin needed three things, his horse, his camel and his rifle," stated former Godolphin license holder Hilal Ibrahim, whose family ancestry is filled with noted horsemen. "The horse was entirely significant to the area."

Despite being coveted as possessions and regularly fought over, the Arabian horse did not have it easy. Life in the Gulf was extremely hard and among the Bedouin there were no passengers. Prized as it was, the horse was also a working animal. It was this fact which, with greater expertise of any breeder of over the subsequent two millennia, ensured that the Arabian was selectively bred. This is true both in domestic animals and those who roamed the peninsular.

For many centuries the Bedouins of Nedj in the Arabian high country were the best known masters of this marvelous breed. They placed the greatest emphasis on the animal's performance and therefore concentrated on stamina, soundness, speed, amiability and loyalty up to the point of exhaustion. To maintain the unique performance of their animals, the Bedouins were not only ruthlessly selective in their breeding programmes, but also paid fanatical attention to keeping the blood line pure. A breeder was quite prepared to ride his mare for days on end so that she could be mated with the right stallion

As early as this, Arabians, along with closely related breeds such as the Barb, are believed to have raced on a rough track laid out in Yorkshire, England. In 208AD the Roman Emperor Lucius Septimius Severus *(pictured)* led a campaign to

Quality in Concert

Alhaarth
CHAMPION 2-Y-O AND CLASSIC SIRE
Multiple **Gr.1** sire of Classic winner **HAAFHD** and multiple **Gr.1** winner **PHOENIX REACH**.

Almutawakel
A GR.1 AND CLASSIC SIRE
Sire of Classic winner **SILVER CUP** (also triple **Gr.2** winner in the USA in 2006) and of dual New Zealand **Gr.1** winner **WAHID**.

Bahri
CHAMPION MILER AND SIRE OF SAKHEE
Sire of European Champion **SAKHEE** and of leading 3-y-o filly **SECRET HISTORY** in 2005.
FIRST CROP EUROPEAN YEARLINGS 2006

Elnadim
DUAL CHAMPION SPRINTER BY DANZIG
Stakes sire of **13** European first crop winners in 2005. Also sire of Australian **Gr.2** winner and dual **Gr.1** placed **PENDRAGON**. Over **80%** of his 2-y-o's have won or placed in 2006.

Intikhab
EUROPEAN CHAMPION MILER
Classic sire of **Gr.1** winner **PAITA** and **TOUPIE**. 2006 successes include Royal Ascot Stakes winner **RED EVIE** and leading 2-y-o **HOH MIKE**.

Marju
A MULTIPLE GR.1 SIRE AGAIN IN 2006
Proven **Gr.1** sire of **SOVIET SONG**, **MARBYE**, **SIL SILA** and of **MARJU SNIP** and **VIVA PATACA** (2 x **Gr.1**) in 2006.

DERRINSTOWN STUD
Maynooth, Co Kildare, Ireland.
Enquiries to: Stephen Collins, Jimmy Lenehan or Enda Stanley.
Tel: + 353 (0)1 6286228 Fax: + 353 (0)1 6286733
e-mail: info@derrinstown-stud.ie

www.derrinstown.com

Britain. There he settled and lived out the rest of his life in Yorkshire, where he is reported to have laid out that first track and organised horse races. This imperial amusement may well have had some influence on the development of racing in England, for the Romans are said to have brought in Arabian and Barbs horses for their races, which would suggest that the indigenous ponies which later contributed to the development of the thoroughbred had some desert blood in them.

Ecclesiastical records confirm that during the centuries after the Roman occupation, horse racing, though probably not widely spread, was certainly a popular amusement, and Church dignitaries were outraged at its existence.

In 1074, William Fitzstephen published his 'Description of the City of London', in which he gave the first detailed account of racing. According to this book, horses were brought to Smithfield Market every Friday to be sold. To show off the animals' potential, professional jockeys took them at a gallop up and down a marked course in front of a grandstand which was always well filled with spectators and prospective buyers. And no doubt many of the onlookers made wagers with each other. Similar races were also held a little later on at the market in Newmarket.

The superior speed and stamina of the desert horses were obvious, and from the fourteenth century Arab, Barb, Turkish and Persian horses were imported into Britain.

Thomas Blundeville, a respected expert on horses, was one of the founders of the thoroughbred breeding industry. In a publication which appeared in 1565 and attracted a great deal of attention, he put forward a persuasive argument for the consistent breeding of noble blood-lines. In the following century the industry enjoyed considerable encouragement from the Stuart kings, and both James I and Charles I fostered racing as a sport. Under Charles in particular, Newmarket became the centre of the horse racing scene. There in 1627 the famous Spring and Autumn races were inaugurated, which always attracted the fastest horses in the country. In 1634 the King donated the first of the Gold Cups which have remained sought-after trophies.

In 1654 Oliver Cromwell *(pictured)* banned public horse racing, although, with his 'Ironsides' he had built up an outstanding cavalry force, and was personally anxious to improve the breeding industry.

The evolution of the thoroughbred could not be halted, however, and under Charles II *(pictured)* the sport of racing was soon flourishing again. Races were held regularly on 12 courses, including Epsom where the English Derby is still run, and the King provided the prizes in the form of valuable silver 'King's Plates'. These races were the precursors of what are now the classic races.

Although 103 'Oriental' stallions were registered in the General Stud Book as the founders of the thoroughbred breed, only three blood-lines have been able to maintain themselves to the present day. By 1850 traces of all others were obliterated, and only these three can be considered to be genuine founding sires: Byerley Turk, Darley Arabian and Godolphin Arabian.

Like most of the Oriental stallions of that time they bore the names of their owners. Byerley Turk fell into the hands of a Captain Byerley in 1683 at the siege of Vienna. Like so many of the Turks horses, the light bay stallion was very nobly bred, perhaps even a pure-bred Arab, and because he had an iron constitution the English officer kept him as a cavalry horse. He rode him in the Irish campaign undertaken at the instigation of King William III in 1690, and then the horse was sent to stud in England where he covered a very few mares.

Unfortunately little is known about them, though some doubtless had excellent qualities, and Byerley Turk sired outstanding progeny, the most noteworthy of his direct descendants being Jig, whose great-grandson King Herod, foaled in 1758 on the Duke of Cumberland's Stud, became one of the most prepotent of all sires.

Darley Arabian was bought by Thomas Darley, the British Consul in Aleppo, Syria, for his brother Richard (according to one story, he was exchanged for a gun).

The stallion reached England at the beginning of 1704, in good health despite the conditions of war that prevailed at the time, and the beautiful, dark bay, pure-bred Muniqi Arab became the stud stallion on the Darley estate in Aldby, Yorkshire, where he lived to the ripe old age of thirty years.

It is hard to imagine how the thoroughbred breeding industry would have developed without this stallion. Of the something like 800,000 thoroughbred horses in the world today, 90 per cent are his descendants through his great-great-grandson Eclipse.

Godolphin Arabian, the third of the founding sires, had the most remarkable history. Unlike the other two founding sires, his appearance, with tiny ears and a powerful fat neck, would not have created a very good first impression, although if contemporary drawings can be believed he was otherwise splendidly built. Originally taken to France as a present for Louis XV from the Bey of Tunis, because Baroque parade horses of Andalusian and Neapolitan descent were currently in fashion there, the stallion was not considered suitable for the Royal Stables.

One story is that he then pulled a water-cart through the streets of Paris, but that is probably only an embellishment to his Cinderella-like tale. What is certain is that in 1729 he was discovered by an Englishman named Coke, who took him to England. When Edward Coke died in 1733 the stallion, which was originally called Sham, is said to have been bequeathed to one Roger Williams, a coffee-house owner who, as a sideline, also dealt in racehorses. He in turn sold the horse to Lord Godolphin who took him to Cambridgeshire where he is reputed to have served as a teaser, until a mare named Roxana obstinately refused to receive the stud stallion Hobgoblin, and for want of a better alternative Sham was allowed to cover her. The facts, however, are that by 1731 Sham had already covered Roxana at Coke's stud, and it is unlikely that the stallion ever had to endure the humiliating role of a teaser. The result of the mating was Lath, one of the greatest racehorses of his time. Sham remained on Lord Godolphin's stud and continued to cover numerous mares until his death on Christmas Day 1753, aged 29.

His most noteworthy descendant was Cade who sired Matchem. Like King Herod and Eclipse, the descendants of Byerley Turk and Darley Arabian respectively, Matchem was the only descendant of Godolphin Arabian able to perpetuate his great qualities.

William Augustus, Duke of Cumberland *(pictured)* and son of George II, might have been an unlucky commander, but he was an outstanding horse-breeder. King Herod was among many fine horses bred in his stables, and a horse which was born on 1 April 1764 on his stud at Windsor Great Park deserves at least as much recognition as the three founding sires. He was called Eclipse because he was said to have been born during an eclipse of the sun. There was a problem, however, in that the colt's mother, Spiletta, had been covered by two stallions, Shakespeare and Marske. Although the Duke's equerry declared publicly that Marske had been the sire of Eclipse, and this was recorded in the General Stud Book, lingering doubt remains.

In 1765 the Duke died of a stroke at the early age of 44, and did not live to enjoy the unprecedented success of this most outstanding of all his horses, Eclipse, later sold at an auction. A livestock dealer named William Wildman, who bought the horse, almost decided to have the young stallion gelded.

Fortunately a man was found who was able to cope with the animal's unruly temperament. Wildman did not allow Eclipse on the racetrack until he was five-years-old, but even before the stallion had run a race the touts at training had noticed that they were dealing with an unusually fast horse. In his first race, at Epsom on 3 May 1769, the odds were already four to one in his favour. One of the spectators, an Irishman named Colonel O'Kelly who owned a stud and racing stable close by, was so impressed by this first run that he made the now famous comment, 'Eclipse first-and the rest nowhere'.

Although many writers describe Flying Childers, the son of Darley Arabian *(pictured)*, as the first English thoroughbred, Eclipse was certainly the greatest representative of this breed, and therefore possibly the most outstanding horse of all. Eclipse's unique prepotencey was even more important, and 344 of his foals won a total of 862 races. His most notable descendants were King Fergus and Pot-8-Os, horses whose blood-lines have been maintained to the present day. When Eclipse died on 27 February 1789 he was dissected and measured by the French anatomist Charles Vial de St Bel. The skeleton of this wonder horse was much sought-after by collectors. In fact, no one knows for certain where the genuine one is, for there are at least six, all said to be Eclipse.

The first races for three-year-olds were held in 1756 and only from 1776 onwards were there races for two-year-olds. So that these young horses should not be overtaxed, distances were reduced, and it was in these races that the so-called 'Classics' had their origins.

They have remained the supreme tests. The St Leger, inaugurated in 1776, and named after its founder, is one and three-quarter miles long. Three years later the Oaks was run for the first time. This one-mile race is named after the country house of the twelfth Earl of Derby near Epsom. Lastly, in 1780 came the Derby, which has remained the most prestigious of all horse races.

Lord Bunbury, the first president of the Jockey Club, and Lord Derby, tossed a coin to see who should name the race. Derby won, but it was some consolation to Bunbury that his horse Diomed was the winner of the first Derby at Epsom on 4 May 1780.

Over the next 150 years, the thoroughbred and the sport racing went global, establishing in Europe, North America and Australia as part of a billion dollar industry. And what of the lands from whence the breed had originated?

In the Arab world, the culture of the horse remained largely on the backburner during the second half of the millennium. Of course the Arabian remained a cultural centerpiece, but the daily grind of eking out a living meant that the Arabs had better things to think about. The Arabian horse remained, and in the traditional setting of the Royal Court, ruling families across the Middle East maintained an Al Khamsa so entrenched in their pasts.

That is not to say that the horse was cosseted. While horses were being raced around rough oval tracks throughout the West, the Arabs continued the age old tradition of desert racing. At festivals and religious holidays, the best of the breed were matched over grueling distances, a forerunner of today's endurance.

In the west, Arab influence on the sport was minimal.

The name of the Aga Khan continued to be well known and several holders of the title, held by the Spiritual Leader of the Ismailis, a Muslim sect, have been regarded as among Europe's finest owner-breeders. But, aside from the Aga Khan, to all intense and purposes, thoroughbred racing belonged to the West.

Back in the Middle East, the equestrian

.mirates.com

One continent.

The world's continents were once all joined together as one. And there's no reason why they shouldn't be again. Which is why Emirates now serves more than eighty destinations across the world with crew from over one hundred nations.

Geologists call it Pangea. We call it Emirates.   Fly Emirates. Keep discovering.

Emirates

traditions continued into the present century, with it being the done thing in Royal circles for Rulers and their sons to be competent in the historical traditional sports, such as hunting and horse riding. This was true in Dubai where the ruling Maktoum family always maintained a small stable, according to the recently published book *Rashid's Legacy*.

In 1903 the Viceroy of India, Lord Curzon, visited the Lower Arabian Gulf and his Royal Navy Sloop anchored off Sharjah for a meeting with the rulers of the area. The Ruler of Dubai was Sheikh Maktoum bin Hasher Al Maktoum (great-grandfather of the present Ruler of Dubai), who is recorded as arriving with his party in Sharjah on horseback.

A decade later, Sheikh Saeed bin Maktoum, his son, was in charge of the sheikhdom. According to *Rashid's Legacy*, the Ruler maintained a large family plot of date gardens in Ras Al Khaimah. It was here that the Ruler's youthful son, Sheikh Rashid bin Saeed, was taught the finer skills of horsemanship, providing the most intriguing historical connections in the unwritten world of racing.

In the late 1920's and early 1930s English racing was being dominated by the likes of Derby winners Gainsborough, his son Hyperion, and Mahmoud. In America the likes of Gallant Fox and Omaha were achieving their own immortality by winning the Triple Crown. Half a world away, a young Crown Prince of Dubai, Sheikh Rashid bin Saeed Al Maktoum *(pictured)* was developing into a horseman of some repute locally. He loved riding and was seen in the saddle nearly every day, taking his beloved Arabian, named Al Sqalawi, on a punctual mid-afternoon tour of public works and construction sites round the city-state.

Childhood friend and lifelong friend Hamad bin Sukat recalls Sheikh Rashid's fondness for horses. According to Bin Sukat, Al Sqalawi would follow at his owner's shoulder if Sheikh Rashid dismounted. Even after buying his first car, in 1934, Sheikh Rashid still preferred to ride Al Sqalawi. No surprise then, that the keen rider found time away from his relentless task of building Dubai, to tutor his sons, Sheikh Maktoum, Sheikh Hamdan, Sheikh Mohammed and Sheikh Ahmed, in this noblest of Arab pursuits.

In 1969 Sheikh Maktoum was the first to open

what could be called a Western style racecourse, when he developed a small training yard, a grandstand and tight oval racecourse, complete with wooden running rail, at a site in Al Ghusais, now overrun by Dubai International Airport. For his part, Sheikh Mohammed had Za'abeel Stables, situated on the site of the present day Trainers' Championship winning yard of Satish Seemar. Indeed, inside Seemar's training track, one can still see the sandy oval on which Sheikh Mohammed himself rode in competitive races among friends.

During the early years of the 1970s, the four brothers—Sheikh Maktoum, Sheikh Hamdan, Sheikh Mohammed and Sheikh Ahmed—were playing an increasingly important role in the fortunes of Dubai and the fledgling United Arab Emirates. It was in his capacity as head of the Dubai Police Force that Sheikh Mohammed came into contact with the man who is identified as having laid the foundations of the Maktoums' entry into the sport in Britain.

"I've met this charming Arab who would like to buy a few horses. I think that one day he could be a very big owner."

That was how the late Colonel Dick Warden *(pictured)* recounted to colleagues a meeting with Sheikh Mohammed. Warden had just completed a commission on behalf of the Curragh Bloodstock Agency to supply horses for the Dubai Police force. His trip was subsequently to change the course of racing history, and the demographics of the sport. The young Arab sheikh and the veteran horseman struck up a friendship which was to last until Warden's untimely death in 1991, it was he who suggested to Sheikh Mohammed that ownership in Britain would be a natural extension of his growing attraction to the sport. By the time of the Tattersalls October Yearling Sales of 1976, Sheikh Mohammed and Sheikh Maktoum were convinced, allowing Warden and the Curragh Bloodstock Agency to buy on their behalf. The result was three purchases, two of which came during a 10-minute period, both from a consignment of seven from Mount Coote Stud. All three horses went into training with John Dunlop, another person who was to play a major role in the Maktoums first 25 years in the sport, particularly on the fortunes of Sheikh Hamdan. The horses were named Hatta and Haddfan, registered as owned by Sheikh Mohammed, and Shaab, registered to Sheikh Maktoum.

In 1977, for the first time as an owner, Sheikh Mohammed enjoyed a taste of the colour and tradition surrounding the noble sport of thoroughbred racing. The Realm filly Hatta proved a wise investment when claiming four wins, most notably the Group Three Molecomb Stakes at Goodwood. While Shaab would make Sheikh Maktoum wait patiently for his first winner until reeling off four successes in 1979 headlined by the Gordon Carter Handicap, Hatta provided an almost immediate pay-off for her 6,200 guinea investment.

Sheikh Mohammed's first star took a while to find her form after debuting at Sandown on 27 May 1977, but having reached the winners' enclosure at Brighton on her third start, she ran up a sequence of four.

Sheikh Hamdan entered the winners' enclosure as an owner for the first time in 1980 with Mushref, who also finished third in the Champion Two-Year-Old Trophy, while Sheikh Ahmed's remarkable first season, in 1983, was dominated by Irish 2000 Guineas winner Wassl.

After a gradual period of growth during the early years, Sheikh Mohammed's burgeoning team burst onto the scene in 1982, with 20 individual winners in Britain, among them Yorkshire Oaks heroine Awaasif, Jalmood and Khaizaraan. The following summer he enjoyed 54. But if Sheikh Mohammed had arrived in the spotlight, Sheikh Maktoum was hitting the very heights in 1982 through tough colt Touching Wood, a double St Leger winner and second in the Epsom Derby. Ma Biche *(pictured)* and Shareef Dancer continued the classic run in 1983.

By this time the Maktoums' string ran to around 250 in training, while they had also purchased Dalham Hall, Aston Upthorpe and Gainsborough Studs to cater for a growing interest in the breeding side of the industry.

The search for success was not just concentrated in Britain or Europe, however, with the Maktoums becoming familiar personalities, and major players, at the world's leading bloodstock sales. Their participation in the yearling market particularly fueled a period of growth which polarised the industry as never before.

While few understood the enigma they were

witnessing, there was no denying that the Maktoum family's bulk purchasing of well-bred and top-performing thoroughbreds included, as one would expect, some tremendous animals. Champions such as Touching Wood, Guineas heroine Ma Biche, Irish Guineas hero Wassl, Jalmood and Irish Derby winner Shareef Dancer all brought the now-famous Maktoum silks to the fore during the early 1980s.

But while it was, and is, the European racing theater which holds most sway on the family's interests. Big events, top prize-money and improvements in the international transportation of horses were opening the doors for global racing, a concept which in years to come the Maktoums were to master like no other.

In 1984 Sheikh Mohammed added the Breeders' Cup Turf to his credits through Clive Brittain-trained Pebbles, the second season of racing's first World Championship meeting.

That same year Sheikh Maktoum had the first US-based Maktoum winner when his Vice Regent filly Deceit Dancer took five races, including the Grade Two My Dear Stakes.

Sheikh Hamdan was part of the international arena too, having had his first winner in Australia through Nouvelle Star during the 1994/95 season. He registered the first of two successes in the Southern Hemisphere's biggest event, the Melbourne Cup, through Colin Hayes-trained At Talaq in 1986.

As top performers retired from the track, the true benefits of the Maktoum involvement in European racing became clear. For years the best in European horses had been snapped up by North America's bloodstock moguls, largely to stand in the bluegrass country of Kentucky. The superior financing of American Stud owners ensured a drain of top bloodlines across the Atlantic.

As the bloodstock markets of the US continued to enjoy a balmy state of inflation, the early greats of the Maktoum era were retiring to stallion and broodmare duties in Europe, among them some of the decade's greatest stars such as Nashwan, Mtoto, Salsabil, Oh So Sharp, Diminuendo, and Green Desert.

With a continuing hemorrhage of top breeding prospects to America, the policies of the Maktoum family not only ended a confirmed rot within the European bloodstock industry, but reversed the trend altogether. For the first time, Europe now had breeders whose approach to the sport was able to sustain top stallions on the continent in which they raced to prominence. By the second half of the decade, the first Maktoum homebred horses began to reach the track.

Over the past few years, a growing percentage of the annual draft of Maktoum yearlings has been home-bred, including subsequent stars such as Lammtarra, Alhaarth, Mark Of Esteem and Erhaab. Indeed, the family's racing interests have been so successful that many of the finest stallion prospects, such as Derby winners Lammtarra and Erhaab, have been surplus to requirements within the Shadwell, Darley and Gainsborough operations and sold on.

With the breeding operation now mature and producing a constant flow of winners, a new cutting edge side of the empire has altered the demographics of the sport.

It had long been the desire of the Maktoums to share their interest in the sport with their fellow countrymen. As early as 1969, Sheikh Maktoum had built the first racecourse in what was to become the UAE. And far from being a venue for various ex-European Maktoum horses in their dotage, the UAE, with Dubai as its epicenter, is today one of the world's most vibrant racing nations. With an attention to detail which has been apparent throughout his years in the sport, Sheikh Mohammed introduced professional racing to the emirate.

It is recorded that Sheikh Mohammed viewed his first Derby from the Epsom grandstands in 1970, the year Sir Ivor was saddled to success by the great Vincent O'Brien. Sir Ivor had wintered by enjoying the sunshine of Piza, Italy, before his double classic winning season. Perhaps as early as this, the germ of an idea, one which later matured into the Godolphin operation, was already dawning on Sheikh Mohammed.

Nearly a quarter of a century after witnessing his first Derby, he shipped two juveniles to Dubai following promising starts in Britain. One, the filly Dayflower, progressed so well that by the time her peers back in Britain were just emerging from winter quarters to go back into training, she was feeling the benefits of the Gulf sunshine and in full work on Sheikh Mohammed's private training track.

Dayflower returned to Britain with confidence high and not only achieved the distinction of becoming the first Dubai-wintered horse to compete in a classic, the 1000 Guineas, but finished a prominent fifth.

Dayflower was followed by Balanchine, Moonshell, Lammtarra Halling and Swain, a few names among what became a multitude of top animals molded in the desert sunshine of Dubai. With the breathtaking success of his Dubai satellite, Sheikh Mohammed has transformed world racing, just as the Maktoums have put their stamp on world racing by turning Dubai itself into an international standard racing and training centre.

Racing has never before seen anything like the Maktoum family. And while the sheer size of the Maktoums' investment in the sport invariably carries considerable influence, the only arena in which we have witnessed it has been the modernisation of racing at competition level, ultimately the most enduring feature which the Maktoum family will be remembered as having brought to the sport, on a global level.

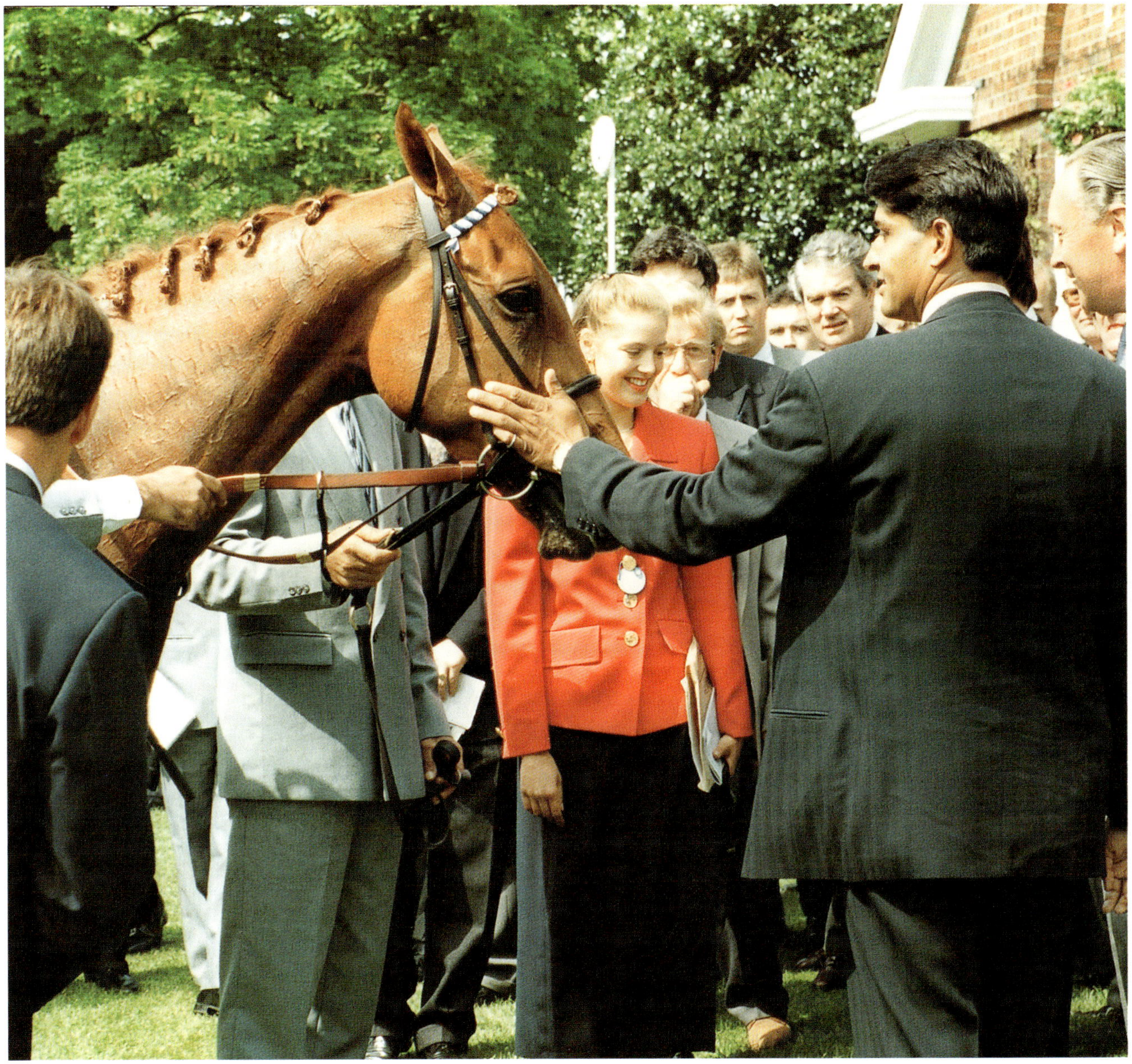

In The Wings
b. c by Sadler's Wells — High Hawk (Shirley Heights)

In The Wings won a Chantilly maiden as a juvenile and went on to score in a listed race at Deauville. The Andrew Fabre charge wintered with hopes that he might prove top class, but a chipped knee bone intervened to hold up his season.

He returned in the Group Three Prix du Prince d'Orange where he recorded a half-length success, enough to persuade connections that he merited a crack at the Prix de l'Arc de Triomphe despite a lack of experience. At Longchamp, despite running credibly, he never landed a blow, finishing six lengths off the winner, Carroll House.

He reappeared the following year in France's first big race of the season for older horses, the Prix Garnay at Longchamp, where he finished second to Creator. Fabre then sent his charge across the Channel for the Coronation Cup, a race in which he started favourite. He not only justified the mantle, but landed his first first Group One contest with considerable flair. In The Wings reached Tattenham Corner giving his closest market rival, Ibn Bey, an advantage of eight lengths. Early in the straight he was involved in barging with another runner but recovered well and set off after the leaders. Striding out impressively, the colt showed pure class, overhauling both Ibn Bey and Observation Post with more than a furlong remaining, going on to record a three-length success.

Having established himself firmly in the top class bracket, the colt returned to France, adding a further Group One with the Grand Prix de Saint-Cloud, a performance which gained him a place in the King George VI and Queen Elizabeth Stakes. The Ascot race was run on unsuitable firm ground, however and this undoubtfully contributed to a below par fifth.

Returning to the winner's enclosure on his next outing in the Prix Foy, he again made Longchamp for a second Prix de l'Arc de Triomphe challenge. Utilizing his turn of foot, the colt came with a charging run late to finish three lengths fourth to Sumarez.

Encouraged, connections headed him for America and Breeders' Cup Turf. When Gray Stevens asked his mount to pick up, early in the back straight, In The Wings immediately began picking off his opponents. On the far turn he balked momentary when finding no room, but soon found a gap and was in contention rounding the final bend. Running with the leaders, In The Wings went on in the last hundred yards to record a half-length success.

```
                                      Nearctic
                      Northern Dancer
                                      Natalma
       Sadler's Wells (b. 1981)
                                      Bold Reason
                      Fairy Bridge
                                      Special
IN THE WINGS (b. 1986)
                                      Mill Reef
                      Shirley Heights
                                      Hardiemma
       High Hawk (b. 1980)
                                      Sea Hawk II
                      Sunbittern
                                      Pantoufle
```

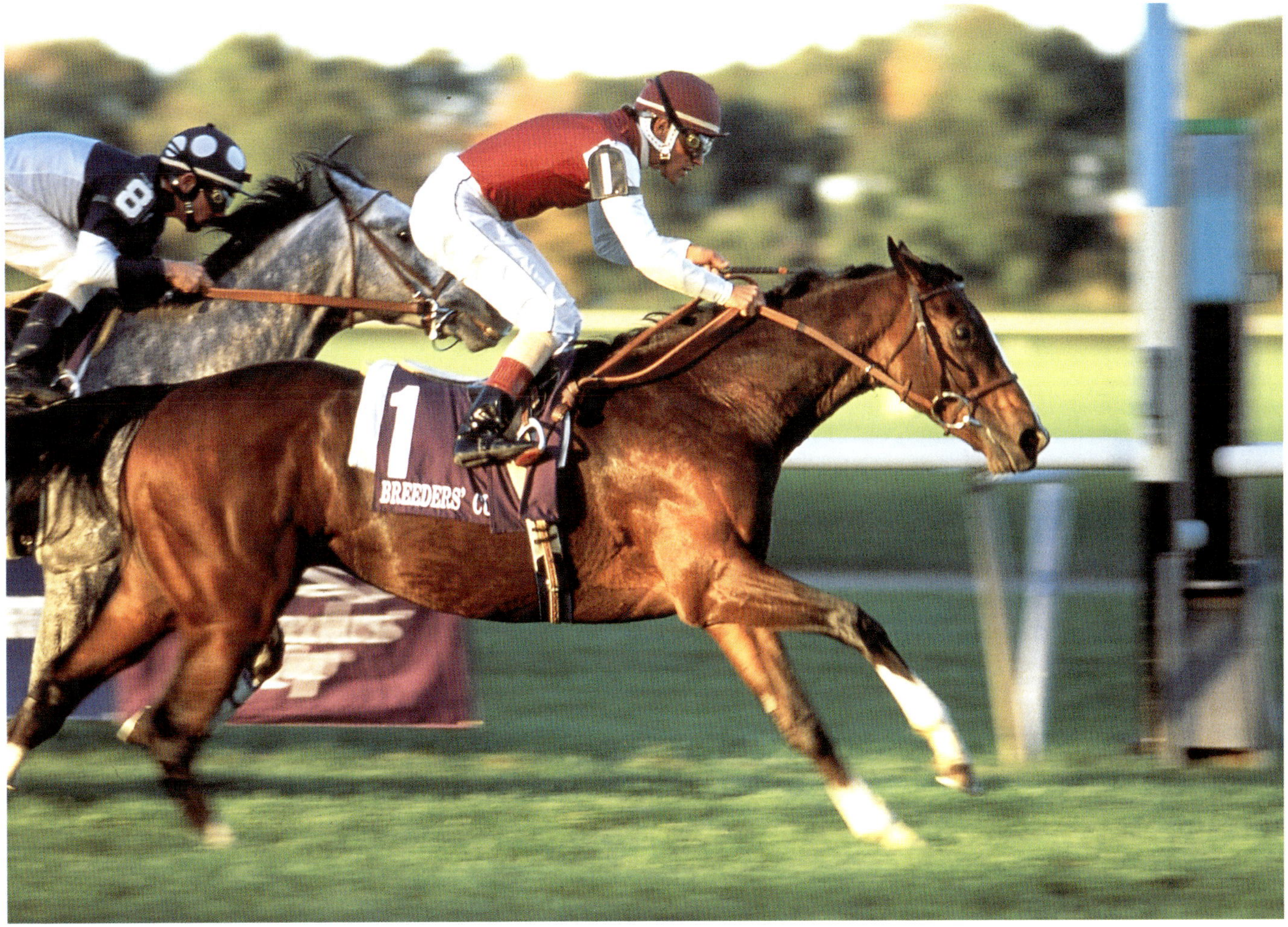
8
1
BREEDERS' CU

Indian Skimmer

gr. f by Storm Bird – Nobiliare (Vaguely Noble)

The Sheikh Mohammed and Henry Cecil combination was again at the fore with this $350,000 yearling, whose injury-interrupted career begged comparisons with no less than Petite Etoile.

Indian Skimmer made her racecourse debut in a juvenile maiden at Newmarket, finishing a gently-handled fourth in a big field.

The following year she reappeared via the unusual route of a £1,000 graduation race at Wolverhampton, but showed sufficient style in a 10-length success to warrant moving up significantly in class, despite reportedly not having wintered well.

Her next outing was in the Pretty Polly Stakes, where she received the favourite's mantle on the strength of favourable gallop reports. In the event, the work watchers were proved right as Indian Skimmer trounced a field containing 11 horses holding Oaks entries. Only two rivals faced Cecil's charge on her next appearance, the Musidora Stakes at York, where she again won with plenty in hand. The filly put in another commanding run several weeks later in the Prix Saint-Alary.

After four successes in as many outings, Indian Skimmer had her first taste of Classic action in the Prix de Diane Hermes at Chantilly in June where she met Miesque, the only member of her generation and gender thought to be remotely in her class. The result was a relatively easy four-length success.

Re-occurring back problems put an end to her season after the Classic and she was not seen on the racecourse for nearly a year, reappearing in the Brigadier Gerard Stakes at Sandown.

The filly rediscovered a winning thread in the Phoenix Stakes in September and one month later Indian Skimmer was certainly back to her best in the Sun Chariot Stakes. Giving away weight, she put matters beyond doubt when she found top gear one furlong from home, a performance which booked her a trip to the Breeders' Cup, where she finished a close-up third.

The five-year-old returned at Sandown in April in the Gordon Richards EBF Stakes, where despite carrying condition and facing fitter rivals, she just got up on the line.

After claiming the Prix d'Ispahan at Longchamp and then missing much of the summer due to hard ground, the filly made her last racecourse appearance when third to Nashwan in the Eclipse Stakes.

Storm Bird (b. 1978)	**Northern Dancer**	**Nearctic**
		Natalama
	South Ocean	**New Providence**
INDIAN SKIMMER (gr. 1984)		
Nobiliare (gr. 1976)	**Vaguely Noble**	**Shining Son**
		Noble Lassie
	Gray Mirage	**Bold Bidder**
		Home By Dark

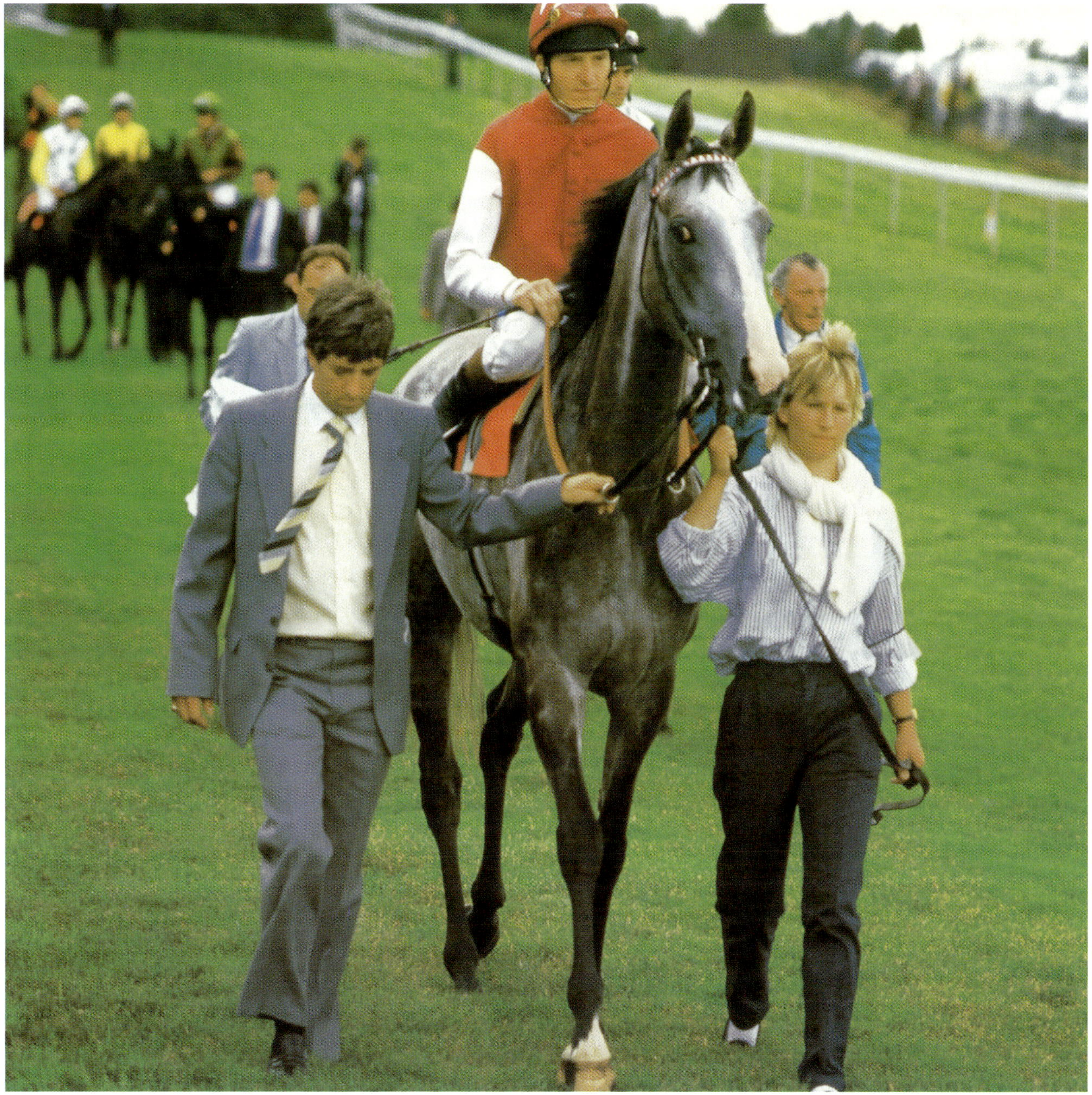

Intrepidity

ch. f by Sadler's Wells — Intrepid Lady (Bold Ruler)

Intrepidity, although a Classic winner, may not be one of the greatest Maktoum horses off all time, but few could find fault with the complete class of her success in the Epsom Oaks.

Andre Fabre unveiled the filly as a juvenile in a minor event, Maisons-Laffitte, which she duly won well. The following April she was stepped up in class for a nine furlong listed race at Longchamp, in which she obliged again, for the first time catching the eye as an Oaks hope.

In her third outing she was truly tested for the first time, taking on a Group One field for the Prix Saint Alari at Longchamp. Partnered by Michael Roberts, the filly responded by beating Dacienne by length.

Fabre routed the filly to Epsom where, as the only Group One winner in the field, she appeared to enjoy an outstanding chance. As so often is the case at Epsom, the undulating course proved a stern test, causing Intrepidity great difficulty. Roberts was lucky to recover as she stumbled across a path less than two furlongs from the stalls. After that Intrepidity seemed uncomfortable and unwilling to go on. At the halfway point only two of her 13 opponents were behind.

Entering the straight she was tenth and a long way off the leader, when Robert began to make ground. As she stretched, the filly reeled in beaten horses and made ground on the leaders, but even with two furlongs remaining looked to have no chance. Only at the distance did she look a threat. Drawing alongside the leaders with 50 yards remaining, she went on by three parts of a length at the line to record a remarkable win.

After a flat performance in the Irish Oaks, Intrepidity claimed the Prix Vermeille at Longchamp.

Routed to the Prix de l'Arc de Triomphe, she made a brave late run to claim fourth behind Urban Sea, but then disappointed in the Breeders' Cup Turf, finishing well down the field.

The following season, Intrepidity was not quite the same force, although she did finish second in the Prix Garnay and Prix Foy, and was retired to the paddocks.

INTREPIDITY (b. 1990)	**Sadler's Wells (b. 1981)**	**Northern Dancer** — Nearctic / Natalma
		Fairy Bridge — Bold Reason / Special
	Intrepid Lady (b/br. 1970)	**Bold Ruler** — Nasrullah / Miss Disco
		Stepping Stone — Princequillo / Step Across

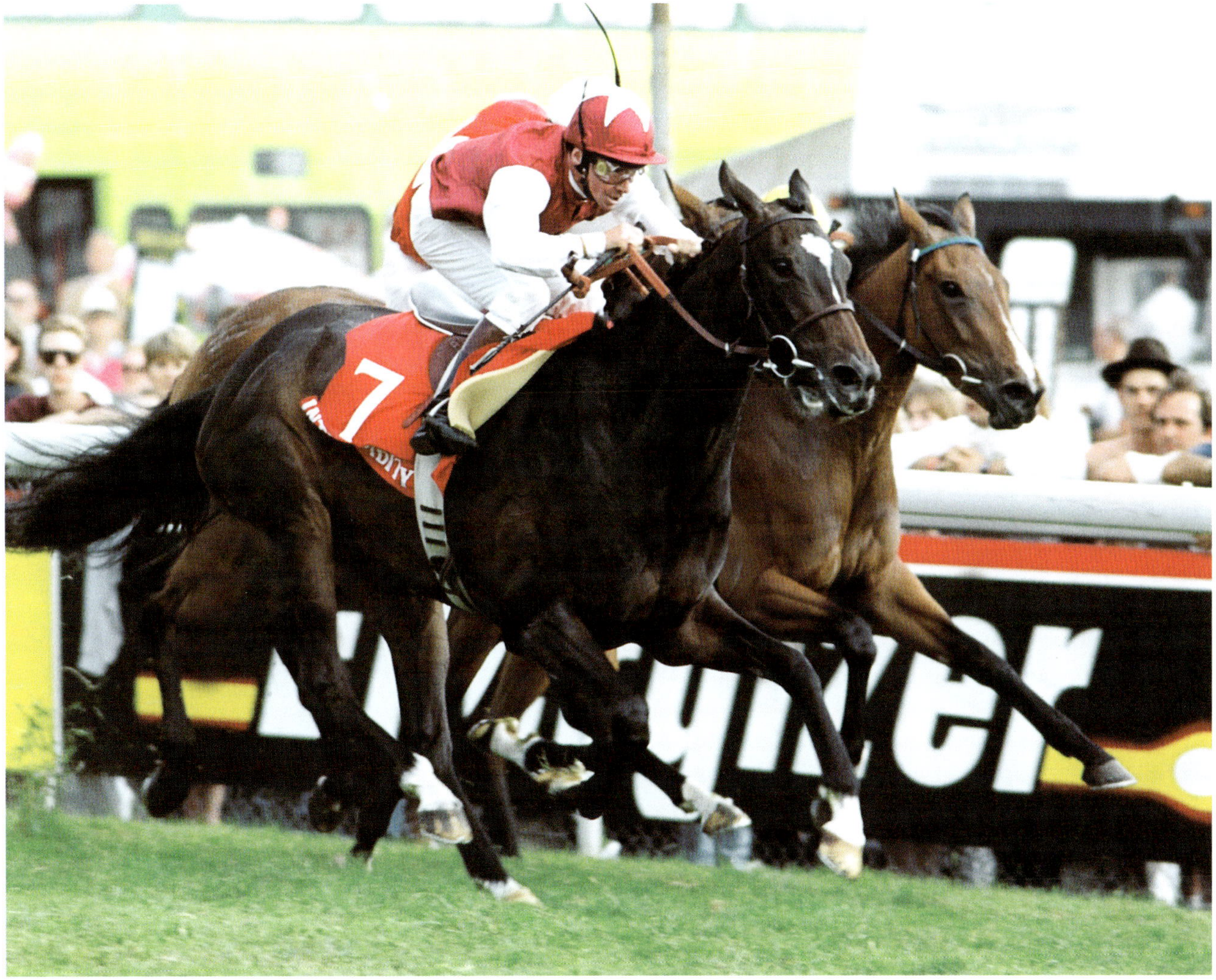
7

Island Sands

b. or br. c by Turtle Island — Tiavanita (J O Tobin)

As an 18,000 Guineas yearling, out of a half-sister to Corrupt, Island Sands began his career in training with David Elsworth and looked to be a useful prospect when making a smooth winning debut on firm ground in a Salisbury maiden. Island Sands returned to Salisbury two months later, entered in a good class conditions race. Despite the ground being heavy, Island Sands was sent off as odds-on favourite and finished an unhurried two lengths winner. It was indeed an impressive performance and one which attracted the attention of Godolphin. Island Sands was purchased privately and wintered in Dubai.

The colt first came to the attention of media in April following a trial race staged at Nad Al Sheba Racecourse in Dubai. Winter Guineas betting had been dominated by Dubai Millennium, but it was Island Sands who showed off his well being with a dominating performance. His odds were immediately cut, as events were to prove that Godolphin's trials were one of the most reliable Classic pointers.

Island Sands arrived in Newmarket with a major shipment of horses from Dubai just five days before the 2000 Guineas. On the day of the colts' classic he looked tremendous in the paddock, but despite strong reports from the Middle East he remained a second string in the betting.

Throughout the early stages of the 2000 Guineas he was near the head of affairs. With 400 metres remaining Island Sands was leading the field and running on very strongly. From the rear, Enrique was coming with a strong run, and over the final furlong these two top class colts fought out a tremendous battle. Island Sands was the stronger of the pair, however, and lengthened under pressure, crossing the line with a neck to spare.

In May his reappearance in the Irish Guineas was a troublesome affair. Not right in his coat and heavily bandaged behind, he finished well down the field and was not seen again that season.

As a four year old he finished second in the Prix Quincey.

	Fairy King	Northern Dancer
		Fairy Bridge
Turtle Island (b. 1991)		High Top
	Sisania	Targo's Delight
ISLAND SANDS (b. or br. 1996)		
	J O Tobbin	Never Bend
		Hill Shade
Tiavanita (b. or br. 1986)		Right Royal V
	Nirvanita	Nuclea

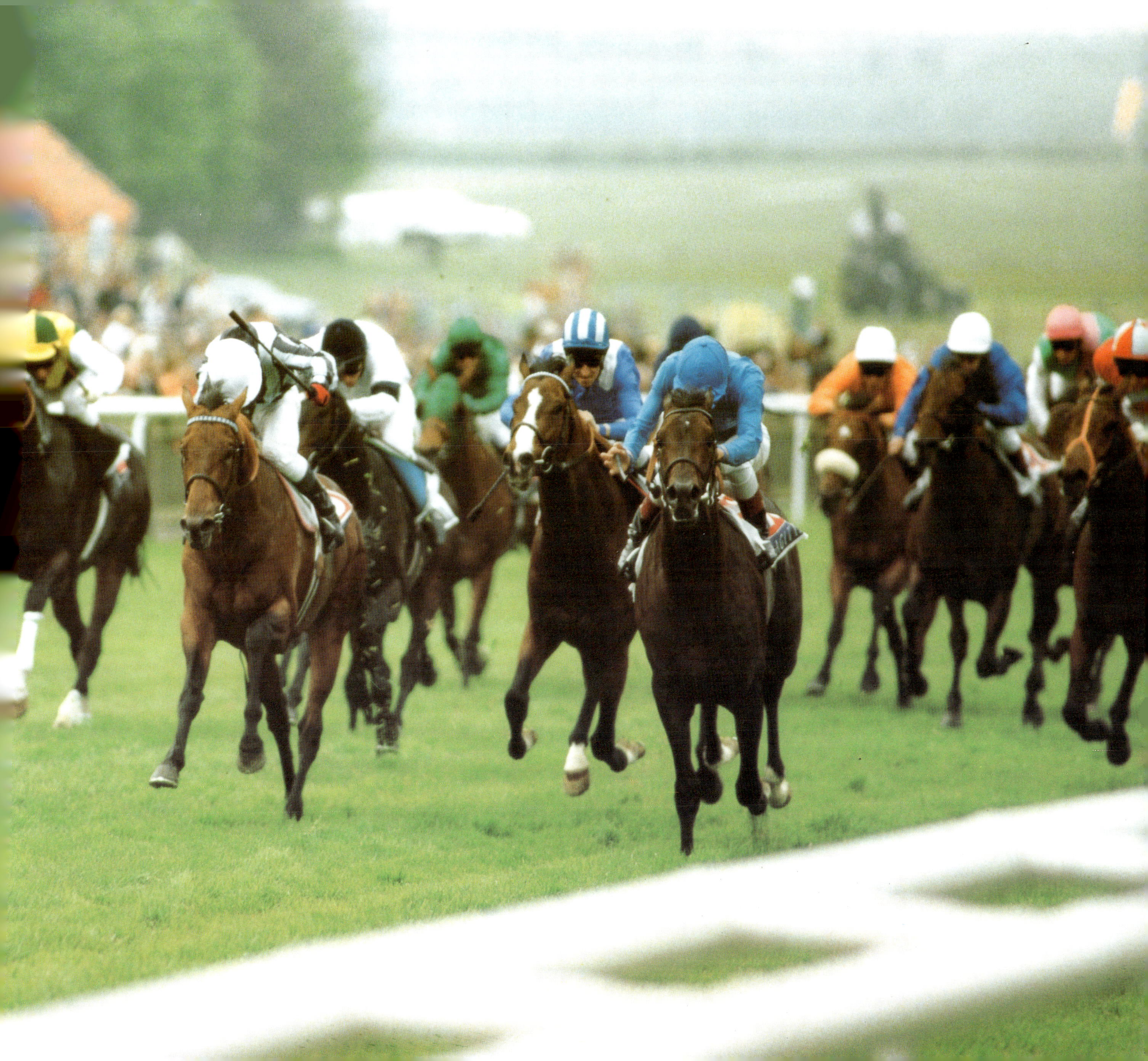

CHRONOSWISS

Faszination der Mechanik

First skeletonized tourbillon wrist watch with regulator dial tourbillon cage turnable by all bearing with app. 72 hours power

Reserve blued steel hands pear (Poire CH 3120 S) massive platinum 950
Louisiana-Crocodile-Leath

damas
Les Exclusives

TOLL FREE 800 4916

Sheikh Ahmed bin Rashid Al Maktoum

Sheikh Ahmed bin Rashid Al Maktoum's famed colours, his distinctive yellow with black epulates, burst onto the European scene in spectacular fashion in 1983 when his classy Wassl claimed the Irish 2000 Guineas and Greenham Stakes. The last of the four Maktoum brothers to enjoy racecourse success in Europe, Sheikh Ahmed's arrival as a classic-winning owner capped a lifetime of devotion to equestrianism.

Like his three elder brothers, Sheikh Ahmed could ride almost as soon as he could walk. Taught the skills of horsemanship by his father, late Dubai Ruler Sheikh Rashid bin Saeed Al Maktoum, he took to the saddle with a passion. Former retainers with Sheikh Rashid state that the young prince rode nearly every day during his formative years and one of his loves was to go hacking in the desert.

During his teens, Sheikh Ahmed was a devotee to the sport, maintained stables and he continued to ride most days. During school holidays his habit was to go hunting on horseback, a falcon on his arm, in search of the elusive houbara.

After 1969, when Dubai had its first Western-style race tracks at Al Ghusais and Za'abeel, Sheikh Ahmed emerged as a major owner, supporting several trainers and encouraging Nationals to participate in the sport that he viewed as a birth.

Courtesy of Wassl, in 1983 Sheikh Ahmed joined his brothers in reaching the sort of heights that some owners work a lifetime to achieve, or may never taste. And more was to come, as he enjoyed a remarkable period of success almost unheard of for a new owner. One year after Wassl's Irish 2000 Guineas success, the Mill Reef colt added the Juddmonte Lockinge Stakes to his tally.

After several seasons of continual black type success, Sheikh Ahmed then emerged as one of Europe's leading owners with his Busted colt Mtoto. In 1987 Mtoto took the Coral Eclipse, Prince of Wales's Stakes and

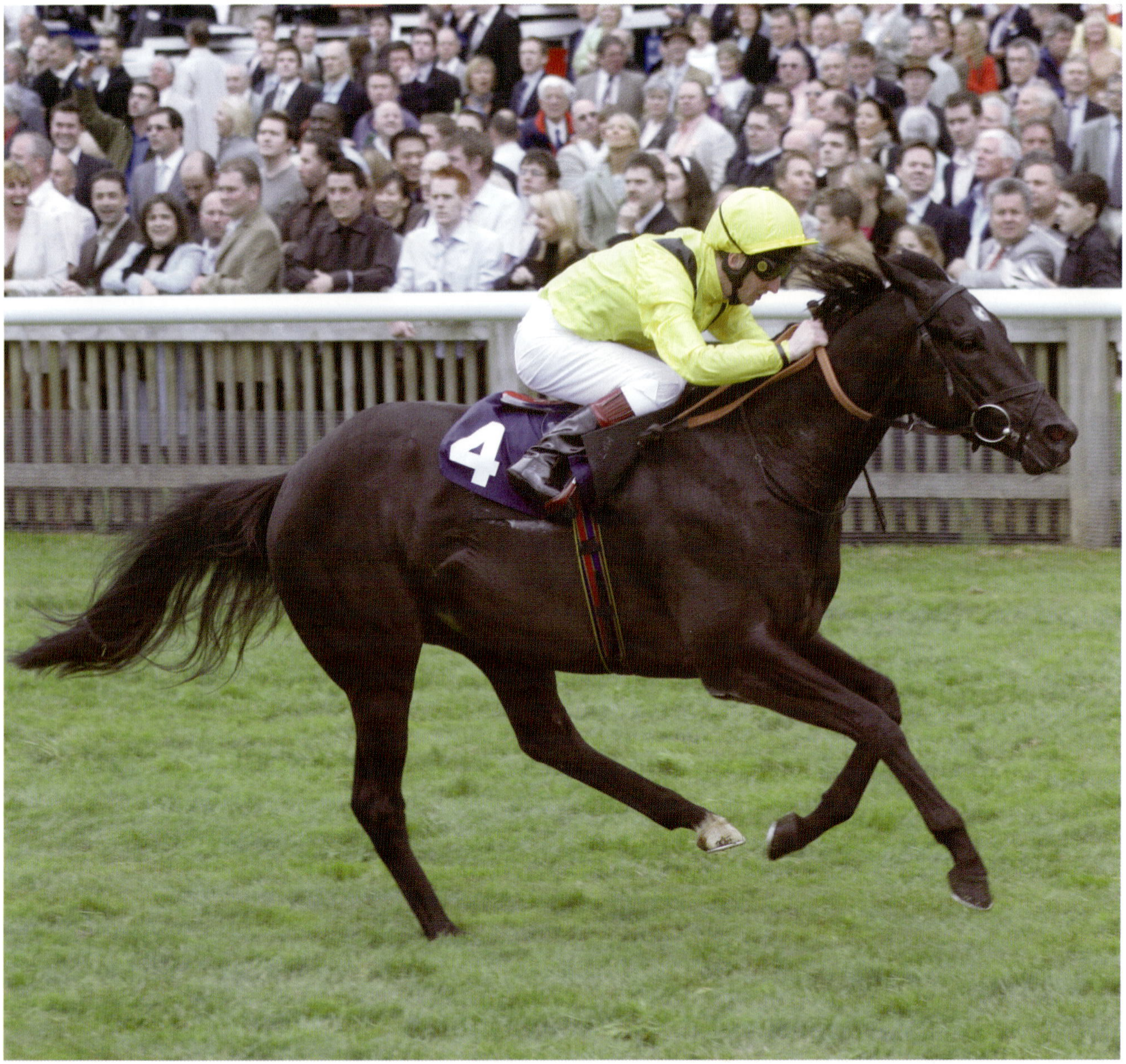
4

Brigadier Gerard Stakes, before finishing fourth in the Prix de l'Arc de Triomphe. The following year, Mtoto added a second Prince of Wales's Stakes, before going on to claim a rare Coral Eclipse and King George VI and Queen Elizabeth Stakes double. It was truly a golden summer of success.

"Mtoto was a wonderful representative and gave me some of my greatest moments in the sport," said Sheikh Ahmed. "He was a courageous horse, a great champion. It is the privilege of only a few owners to have such a great animal run in their colours. I am grateful for that privilege."

Since that time Sheikh Ahmed's yellow and black silks have continued to maintain an eye-catching presence at the highest level in Britain and abroad. Among his prime contenders for Group race honours have been the likes of Alnasr Alwasheek, Del Deya, Keefah, Maylane, Mashallah, Possessive Dancer, Raah Alghab, Tobougg and Wassl Merbayeh. All kept Sheikh Ahmed well represented in Black Type events and punching far above his weight for an owner with a relatively small team in training.

Sheikh Ahmed was one of the central supporters of horse racing as it began to establish itself as a professional sport in the United Arab Emirates. During the early 1990s he constructed Jebel Ali Racecourse on the outskirts of Dubai. This has gone on to be a highly successful venue, on occasion attracting up to 20,000 people to its meetings. He installed at the track trainer Dhruba Selvaratnam, former pupil assistant to Dr. Vincent O'Brien, one of the greatest trainers ever to grace the sport. Sri Lankan Selvaratnam has maintained one of the most successful stables in Dubai and has twice

Bachir Cape Cross Carnegie Comeonmom
Dubai Millennium Elusive Quality Fly To The
Daylami Diktat
The Wings Josr Algarhoud Kabool Kayf
High-Rise
Lion Cavern Lord Of Men
Darley
Lujain
Best Lend A Hand
Medaaly Mtoto Pennekamp Polish
Mark Of Esteem
Saratoga Springs Singspiel
Sagamix
Worldly Manner Xaar Bachir
Cross
Carnegie Comeonmom Chief
Elusive Quality Fly To The
High-Rise
Josr Algarhoud Kabool
Lord Of Men Lujain
Pennekamp Polish
Springs Singspiel
Manner Xaar Bachir
Daylami Diktat Dubai
Halling High-Rise In The
King's Best Lend A Hand
Mark Of Esteem Medaaly
Quiet American Sagamix
Timber Country Torrential
Darley

been the champion trainer of the UAE. Selvaratnam and his Jebel Ali Stables had the honour of sending out the Emirates' first ever black type winner when Wafayt claimed the National Day Cup (Listed) in December 1996, one of dozens of top class winners.

Sheikh Ahmed's affection for his horses remains at the core of his racing interests, and partly as a result of this he remains a keen supporter of racing in less evolved nations. For example, he was the first owner to send thoroughbreds to Lebanon, where racing authorities have been struggling to boost the sport in the wake of the Civil War.

"Sheikh Ahmed was very supportive and patient as we attempted to develop racing in this country. The sport suffered a great deal in the troubles," said Deeb Sefudeen, a Lebanese trainer who later handled a string in the UAE for the Ruler of Umm Al Quwain. "It gave us a great boost locally when people found out that one of the world's biggest owners was ready to support racing here."

On a different level, Sheikh Ahmed has also played a role in the development of Godolphin, some of his better performers joining Saeed bin Suroor. He remains a leading proponent of the sport's increasing internationalism and as such assimilates his breeding and racing interests fully into bin Suroor's operation.

Sheikh Ahmed success in the sport is based upon his passion for the traditions on which racing is based and an affection for the animals which represent him. It is a basis upon which we are sure to see the black and gold competing at the highest level for years to come.

227

Jalmood

b. c by Blushing Groom – Fast Ride (Sicambre)

One of the first top performers under the Maktoum banner, over three seasons Sheikh Mohammed's Jalmood proved both thrilling at his best and frustrating when not. Trained by John Dunlop, the colt took three attempts to break his maiden as a two-year-old, but rewarded connections by then going on to record a treble of successes, the latter pair over a mile.

After improving during the winter, Jalmood's preparation was interrupted by an injury, one of several which were to plague his campaign, causing him to miss a programmed start in the 2,000 Guineas. He returned to the racecourse in Sandown's Derby Trial and put in a tremendous performance. Running on in the last furlong, Jalmood finished third to Peacetime, showing improvement which had many shortlisting him for the Epsom classic itself.

Next seen out in Lingfield's Derby Trial, Jalmood confirmed the good impression over the classic distance with an encouraging run. Moving well throughout, he took up the running two furlongs from the line and stayed on impressively to defeat the fancied Mr Fluorocarbon.

On Derby day the colt looked a picture in the paddock and left for the start with connections seemingly confident. However, as so often at Epsom, the best laid plans came to nothing as Jalmood put in perhaps the worst run of his three-year-old campaign. Back in the Dunlop yard he was diagnosed as having a muscle injury in his quarters.

His subsequent start brought an excellent success in the 11-furlong Scottish Derby, coming with a strong run close to home to power past Epsom fifth-placed Norwick to win.

Unfortunately his niggling injury reappeared on his next outing when finishing third as odds-on for the Gordon Stakes at Goodwood and was again reported to be feeling the problem on his final start of the campaign, the St Leger at Doncaster, when Jalmood did put in a fine run. Boxed in for a great deal of the home straight, Jalmood ran on into a respectable position.

Staying in training as a four-year-old, Jalmood added the Premio Presidente della Republica in Rome to his tally before being retired to stud.

JALMOOD (b. 1979)	**Blushing Groom (ch. 1974)**	Red God — Nasrullah / Spring Run
		Runaway Bride — Wild Risk / Aimee
	Fast Ride (br. 1966)	Sicambre — Prince Bio / Sif
		Fast Lady II — Fastnet / Charbonniere

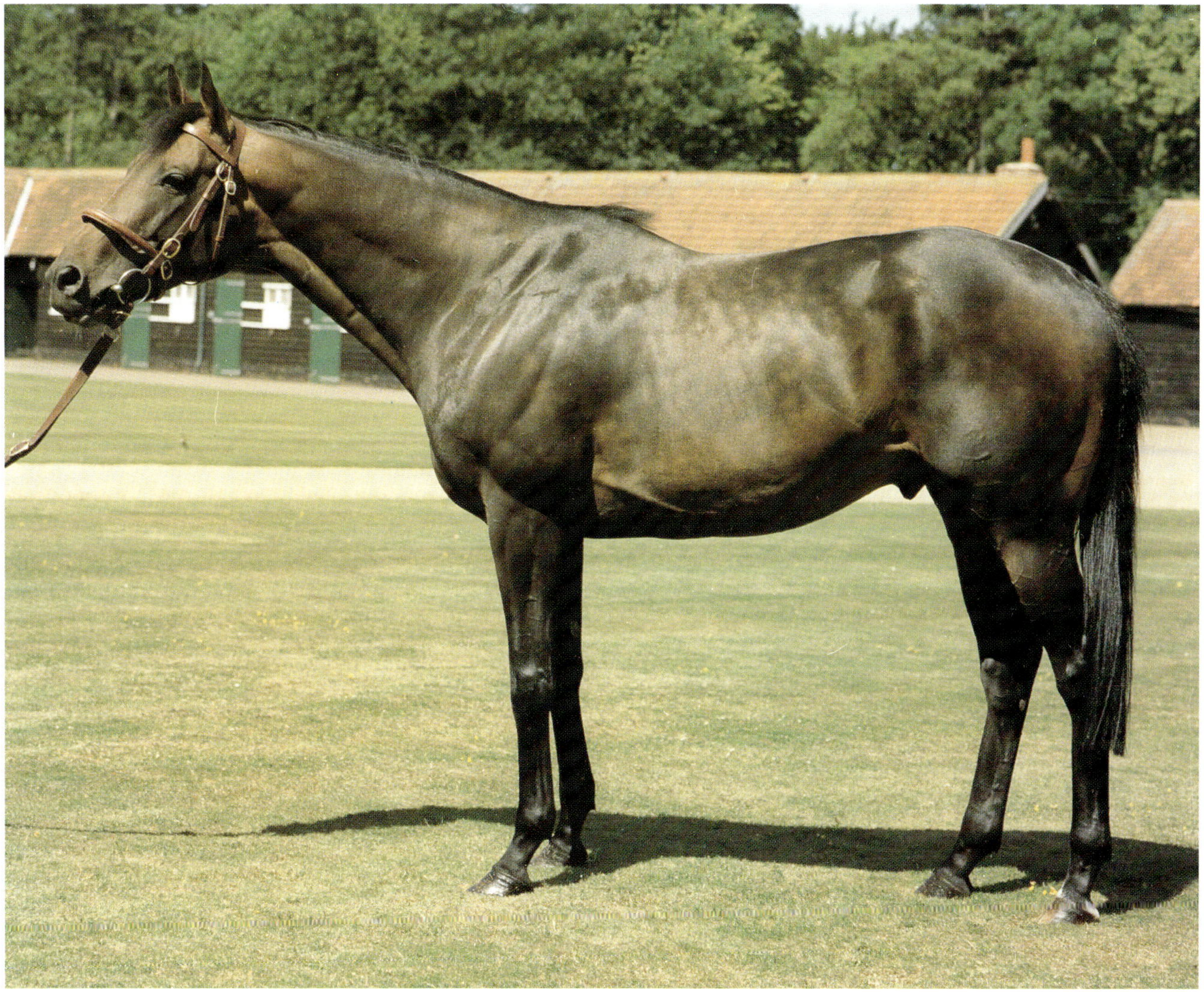

Jazil

b. c by Seeking The Gold — Better Than Honour (Deputy Minister)

It was not until December 2005 that Sheikh Hamdan's Jazil was able to shed his maiden tag, his sole win among his first seven career starts a juvenile maiden at Aqueduct.

Even in this initial stage of his fledgling career it was clear that stamina was his forte. His first start was over 1,100 metres; his second over seven furlongs and his maiden win achieved over 1,700 metres. For a two-year-old, even in December, that is still a fair test of stamina.

His three-year-old campaign started in allowance company with a decent second over nine furlongs at Gulfstream Park, before a seventh over the same course and distance in the Grade Two Fountain of Youth Stakes.

It was a return to Aqueduct which suggested there was more to come, in the Grade One Wood Memorial Stakes. He was second to Bob and John but had shown connections enough to earn a tilt at the Kentucky Derby, America's most famous race and the first leg of The Triple Crown.

He was far from disgraced; dead-heating for fourth and he missed the Preakness Stakes, the middle leg of The Triple Crown, to be readied for the concluding leg, the Belmont Stakes. The Belmont is a 12-furlong contest, as opposed to the 10-furlongs of the first two races and this was paramount in the mind of Sheikh Hamdan's team.

Ridden by 18-year-old Fernando Jara, Jazil outstayed Bluegrass Cat in the straight to secure a first Triple Crown win for trainer, jockey and owner. Perhaps more remarkably, it was a first US Classic winner for his sire, Seeking The Gold.

The effort was all the more commendable when you realise that Jara lost an iron at the start after the horse jumped awkwardly. He was happy to hold his mount up in rear along the back straight, before closing out wide on the bend and challenging the leaders. Finally he had justified the $725,000 price tag attributed to him at Keeneland in September 2004 and he looks the type to improve with age.

JAZIL (b. 2003)	**Seeking The Gold (b. 1985)**	Mr Prospector — Raise A Native / Gold Digger
		Con Game — Buckpasser / Broadway
	Better Than Honour (b. 1996)	Deputy Minister — Vice Regent / Mint Copy
		Blush With Pride — Blushing Groom / Best In Show

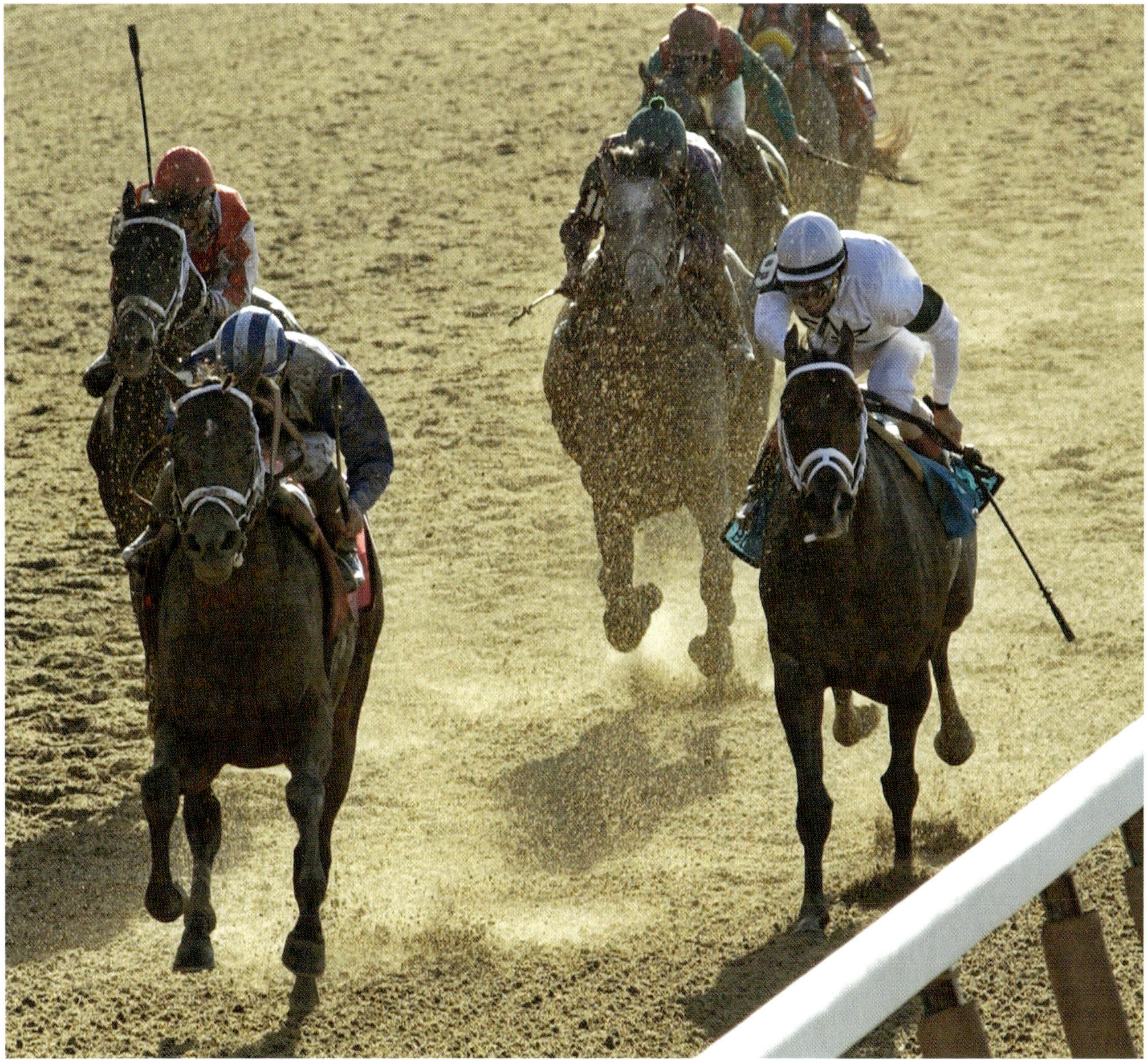

Jet Ski Lady

ch. f by Vaguely Noble – Bemissed (Nijinski)

Rarely have the five British classics thrown up such a commanding winner and, certainly in the post-war era, one which created such surprise. Sheikh Maktoum's Irish-trained filly won a maiden and a Leopardstown nursery in the Emerald Isle, before being entered in Longchamp's Group One Prix Marcel Boussac, Europe's leading test for two-year-old fillies. She went into the winter having finished a respectable five lengths seventh behind Shadayid.

Trainer Jim Bolger brought his charge back to win a listed race at The Curragh, before she was chanced in the Derby Trial at Leopardstown. Enjoying little luck in running, Jet Ski Lady took a hard knock in the final straight but stayed on well to finish fourth behind three colts.

Lining up for the Epsom Oaks, Jet Ski Lady was sent off an unconsidered outsider at odds of 50-1. Jockey Christy Roach kept Jet Ski Lady at the head of affairs almost from the off, the remaining field of nine close-up. She maintained the lead as the field rounded Tattenham Corner, her powerful stride giving the impression that of all the field, she was set to stay every yard of the trip.

In the straight she lengthened away, chased by race favourite Shadayid who briefly looked as thought she was capable of catching the leader but was soon seen to be labouring. Jet Ski Lady was still in full flight, though, and as the rest struggled she pulled way from record an emphatic 10-length success.

Jet Ski Lady's margin of victory in the Oaks was only once matched, by Sun Princess in 1983, and the race has never been won by one adjudged to be such an outsider.

Her next engagement was the Irish Oaks which, run on unsuitable ground, brought another courageous display. Entering the latter stages Jet Ski Lady had a fight on her hands. Joined at the head of affairs by Italian Oaks heroine Possessive Dancer, the two fought out a superb finish. Only in the last 100 metres did Possessive Dancer go on, with Jet Ski Lady claiming second.

After a second place in the Yorkshire Oaks she was routed to the Prix de l'Arc De Triomphe. At Longchamp, however, she looked uncomfortable on the soft surface, never landing a blow, and was subsequently retired to the paddocks.

Vaguely Noble (b. 1965)	Vienna	Aureole
		Turkish Blood
	Noble Lassie	Nearco
JET SKI LADY (ch. 1988)		Belle Sauvage
Bemissed (b. 1980)	Nijinsky	Northern Dancer
		Flaming Page
	Bemis Heights	Herbager
		Orissa

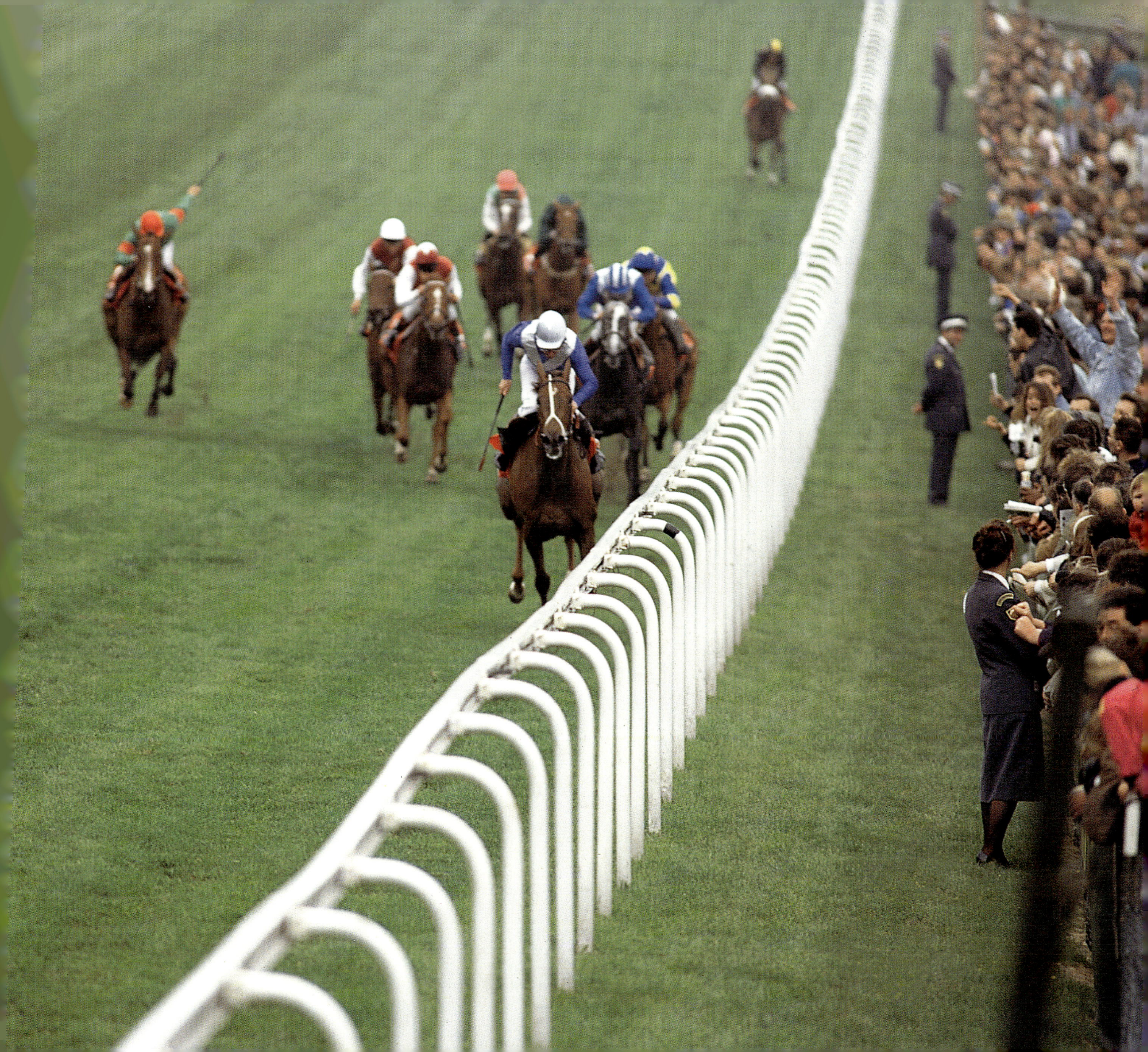

Jeune

ch. c by Kalaglow — Youthful (Green Dancer)

Jeune, perhaps one of the best horses ever to run in Australia, began his career with Geoff Wragg in Britain, winning two Classic trials as a three-year-old, despite not holding a Classic entry. He followed that up by winning the September Stakes and Hardwicke Stakes the same summer

The colt appeared heading for a career in America, but the deal fell through. Instead, he was shipped to Australia after Sheikh Hamdan purchased him.

After a gentle pipe opener, a placed run at Cheltenham, he came to prominence at Flemington in the Craiglee Stakes, finishing one length off Mahogany and State Taj.

Trainer David Hayes had his charge firmly on course for the Cups. Jeune underlined his status next time out in the Underwood Stakes at Caulfield, winning the Group One contest from the dogged Paris Line.

After a second in the Caulfield Stakes to New Zealand gelding Rough Habit, Jeune disappointed in the WS Cox Plate at Moonee Valley, before a second to Paris Lane in the LKS Mackinnon Stakes, his Melbourne Cup prep race.

The A$2 million Cup itself unfolded perfectly for Jeune, but only after a terrible start in which he seemed to have ruined any chance. The latter stages proved the tenacity of the horse: as openings appeared Jeune slotted through and suddenly, with just a furlong remaining, he was in contention. Below the distance Jeune collared Paris Lane to collect the biggest race on the continent.

Jeune's connections accepted a late invitation to participate in the Japan Cup. Having obviously been trained to peak four weeks earlier, he finished a credible sixth.

The following February, Hayes brought back the Cup winner for a win on his appearance, the CF Orr Stakes, before a frustrating, and unbelievable run of four consecutive seconds in Group One company.

He broke that sequence in April with a sterling victory from Danewin in the Queen Elizabeth Stakes at Randwick.

JEUNE (ch. 1989)	**Kalaglow (1978)**	Kalamoun	Zeddaan
			Khairunissa
		Rossitor	Pall Mall
			Sonia
	Youthful (1980)	Green Dancer	Nijinsky II
			Green Valley
		First Bloom	Primera
			Flower Dance

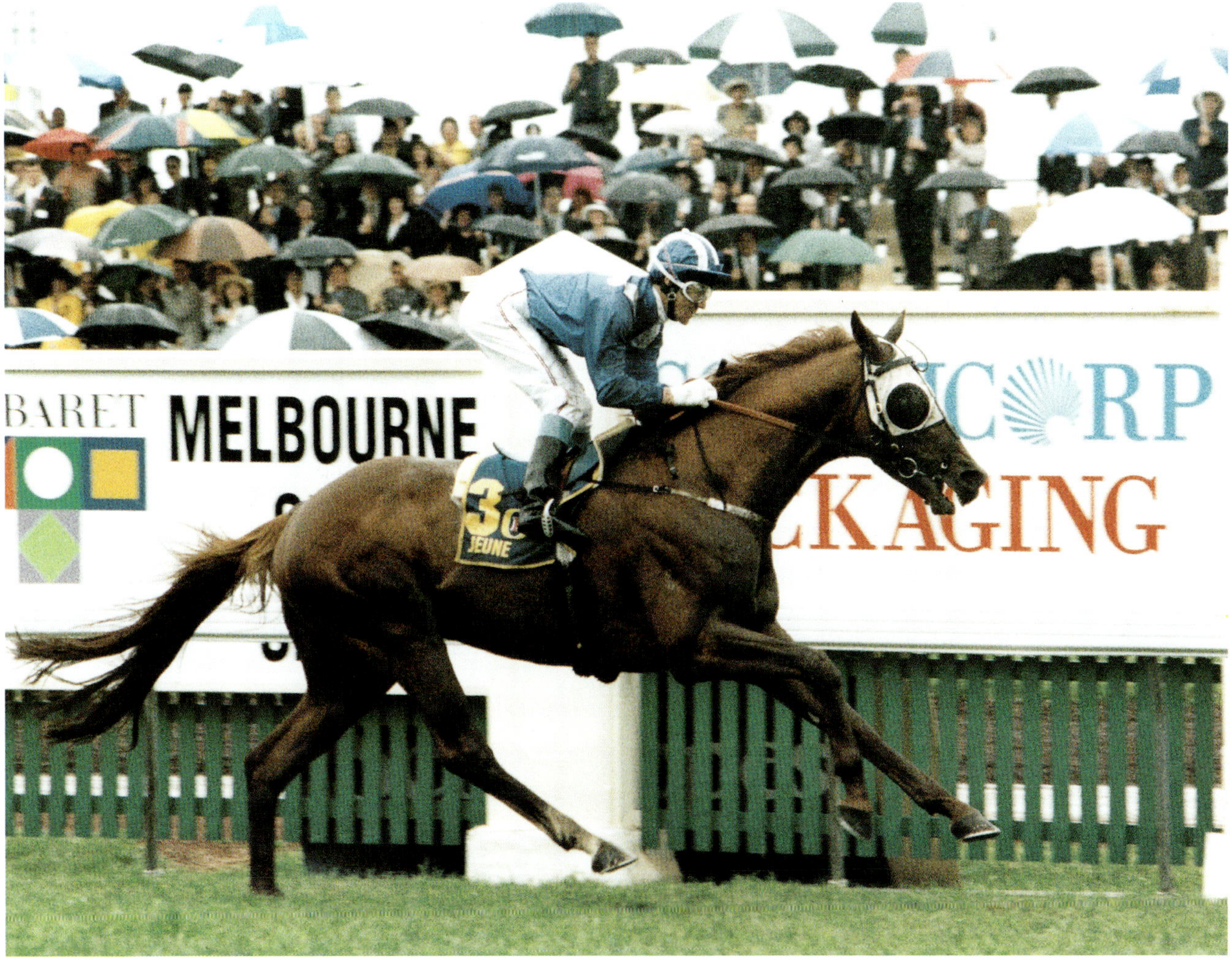
BARET
MELBOURNE
JEUNE
CKAGING

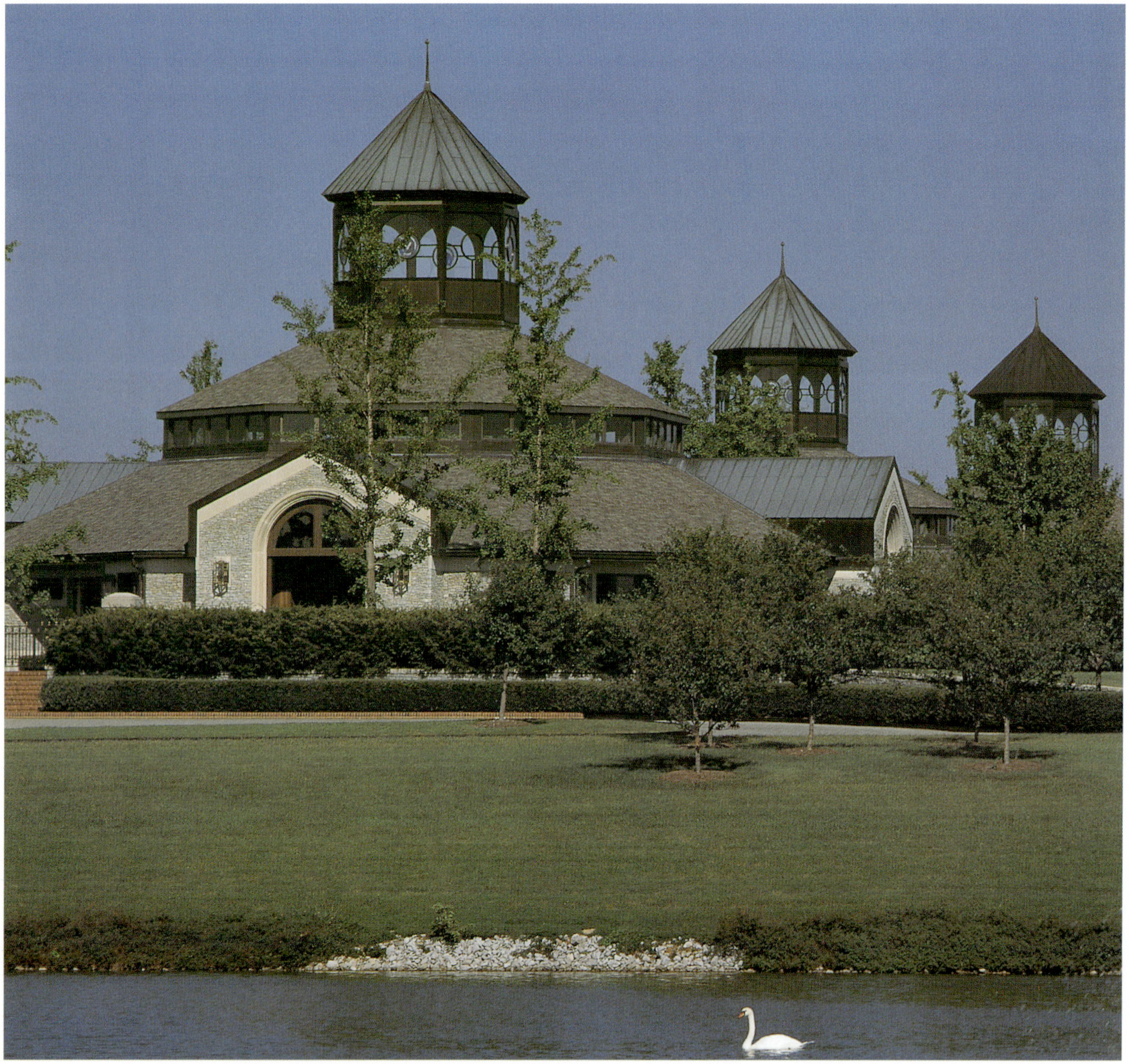

Gainsborough

Thomas Gainsborough was one of the most famous portrait and landscape painters of the 18th Century. He was one of the originators of the 18th Century British landscape school and was one of the dominant British portraitists of the second half of the century. He is still considered one of the great Royal portraitists and counted King George III as one of his most ardent palace patrons.

The name Gainsborough is associated with a different field of excellence today. But nonetheless it is an attention to detail and a passion for beauty that has seen Gainsborough the thoroughbred breeding operation match the painter when it comes to wining worldwide acclaim.

Gainsborough is a name which carries a great deal of history within racing and thoroughbred breeding industry. The stud is named after the Triple Crown hero of 1918, homebred by Lady James Douglas who became the first lady to own a winner of the Derby, albeit a substitute affair staged at Newmarket due to the First World War. He won five of his nine starts, including the Ascot Gold Cup.

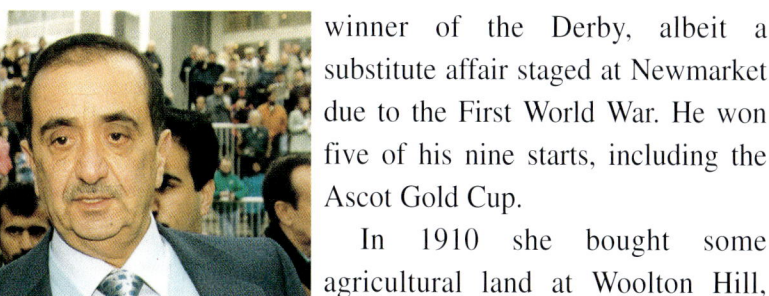

In 1910 she bought some agricultural land at Woolton Hill, south of Newbury, which she converted into a stud with the assistance of John Porter of Kingsclere. Lady Douglas died in 1941 when Harwood Stud, as the place was then called, was sold to Herbert Blagrave

Gainsborough, who died aged 30 in 1945, is buried there. He was twice champion sire during a long and distinguished career, and gained immortality as the sire of Hyperion, one of the truly great progenitors of the twentieth century and champion sire on six occasions.

Herbert Blagrave, an all-round sportsman, who owned considerable property in Reading, was unique amongst his contemporaries as an owner-trainer-breeder. A license holder from 1928 until his death in 1981, he ran a strictly private stable at Beckhampton Grange, opposite the more famous Beckhampton House establishment.

Among the stallions during Blagraves' years at Harwood were, Atout Maitre, taking up residence in 1941. He was succeeded in turn by Roi de Navarre, Tudor Minstrel, Match III and Reliance. In 1980 Herbert Blagrave sold the property to James McCaughey, who changed the name of the stud to Gainsborough.

In October 1981 the stud was purchased by Sheikh Maktoum as the centerpiece of what would quickly become one of the most successful breeding and racing operations in the world. Sheikh Maktoum was a horseman in his own right, and drew around him some of the industry's most effective individuals. Within just a few years Sheikh Maktoum's vision of a trans-Atlantic breeding operation was realised and over the subsequent years Gansborough became a by-word for excellence.

Sheikh Maktoum not only preserved this historic farm, but since 1981 extensively refurbished the site and made it the administrative centre of his thoroughbred operations. Today, the facility is a testimonial to the love the late Dubai Ruler had for the sport, visitors encountering one of the most stunning stud farms to be seen anywhere in the world. The Gainsborough was not just for show and was functional as well as beautiful, being responsible for administering a racing and breeding operation that spanned the globe.

In Britain Gainsborough maintains five stallions: Cadeaux Genereux, Fantastic Light, Green Desert, Royal Applause and Zilzal. On site Sheikh Maktoum's blue-blooded broodmare band,

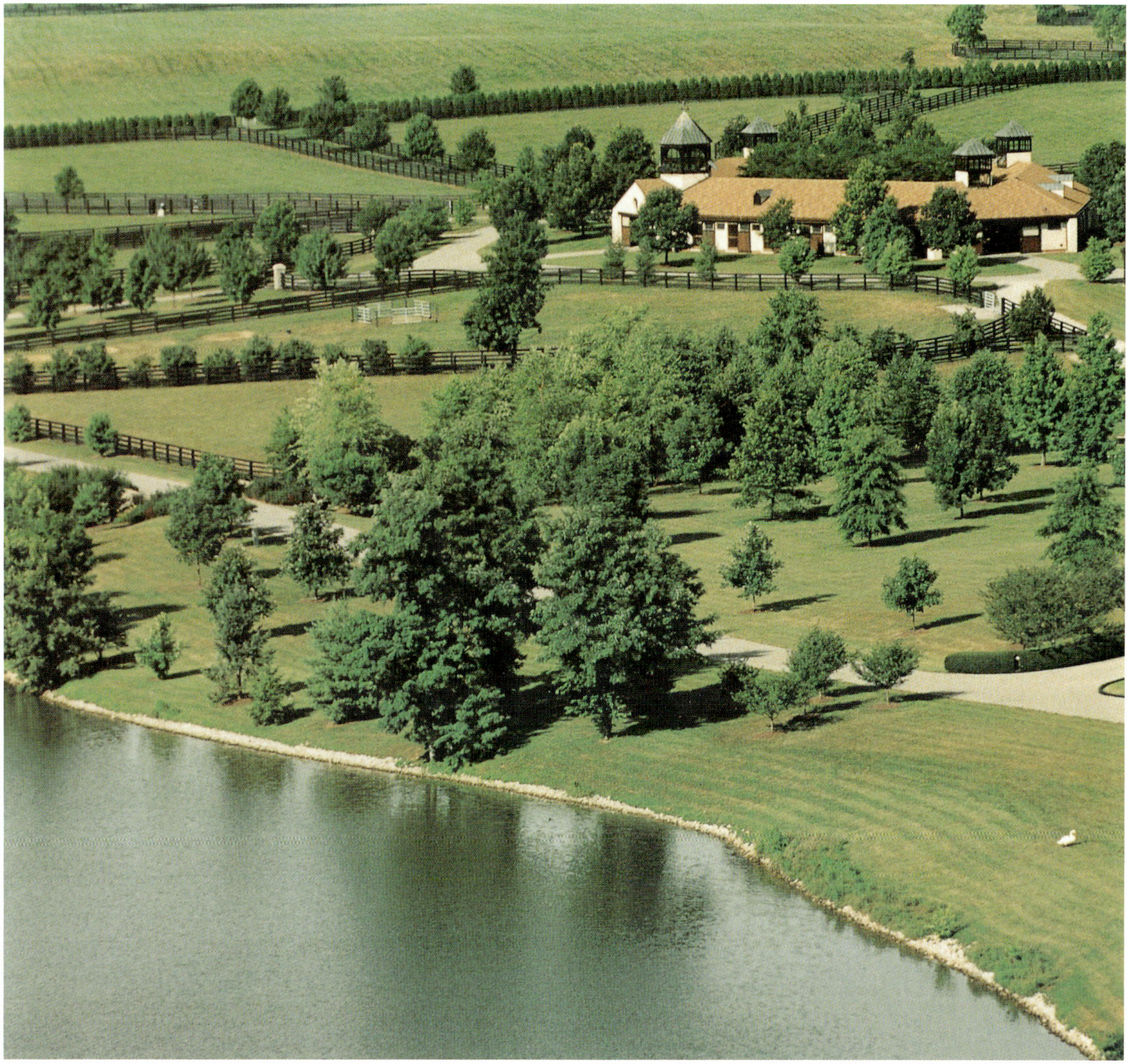

numbering around 100, boasts astonishing quality, highlighted by the likes of Blue Duster, Criquette, Fatefully, Jet Ski Lady, Moonshell, Serengeti Bride, Snow Bride and Youm Jadeed.

The lead satellite of Gainsborough in Britain is Gainsborough Farm USA, in the Central Kentucky area and originally a tobacco and cattle farm. Founded by Sheikh Maktoum in 1984 the facility comprises of 1,800 acres of prime bluegrass.

Gainsborough breeds and raises some of the best thoroughbreds in the world. In addition to being a highly successful business, boasting stallions of the quality of Elusive Quality, Labeeb, Quiet American, Shadeed, Gainesborough produced some 70 homebred foals for Sheikh Maktoum every year, with a resident broodmare band boasting champions such as Balanchine, Cape Verdi, Hatoof, Pricket and Sayyedati. A few of the stars bred at Gainsborough Farm include familiar names such as Fantastic Light, Hatoof, Sayyedati, Key of Luck and Rock Hopper

In addition to the two Gainsborough facilities, Sheikh Maktoum's breeding Empire can truly said to be a global affair. Other offshoots include Woodpark Stud and Ballysheehan Stud in Ireland, while Sheikh Maktoum stands stallions in Canada, Ireland and South Africa. In Australia, Sheikh Maktoum maintains a broodmare band at Arrowfield Stud, where around 30 mares foal between August and October.

The tragic passing of Sheikh Maktoum will not dim his achievements. He will be remembered in racing's history books with the same reverence as Thomas Gainsborough is recalled in art circles — as a master of his field.

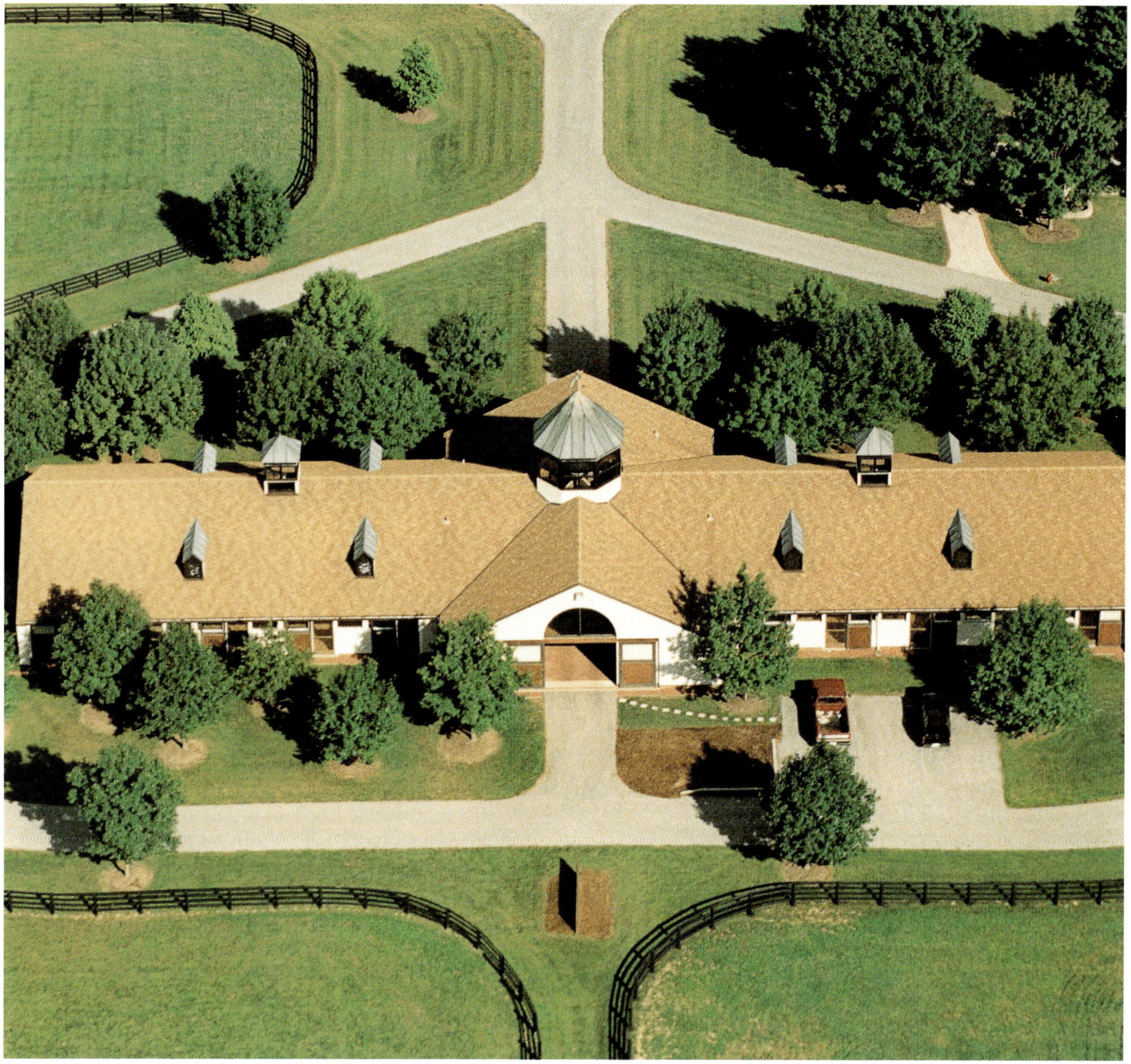

Kayf Tara

b. c by Sadler's Wells — Colourspin (High Top)

Kayf Tara almost arrived from nowhere to win the 1988 Gold Cup for Godolphin, and then went on to become one of the leading stayers of the 1990s. The son of Sadler's Wells had raced just four times before Ascot, winning once as a three-year-old, and in 1988, running in Godolphin blue, showed considerable improvement to finish third in the Henry II Stakes at Sandown.

He reappeared, relatively unfancied, in the Ascot Gold Cup and ran a superb race in testing conditions, staying on at the finish to outgun Double Trigger. It was a sterling performance, but one that would carry with it a tough Group One penalty. This extra weight would contribute to two game defeats on his next two starts—in the Goodwood Cup and Prix Kergorlay—before a return to level weights allowed him back to the winners' enclosure. In a top notch running of the Jefferson Smurfit Memorial St Leger, Kayf Tara was always comfortable and stayed on from Silver Patriarch over the last 400 metres to win by two lengths. The following summer was planned with Australia's premier race, the Melbourne Cup, in mind for Kayf Tara. He returned to score a facile success in the Prix Vicomtesse at Longchamp and then the Prix de Barbeville.

Seeking a repeat in the Gold Cup, the colt's chance dimmed as the ground at Ascot firmed and in the event he finished a dogged third. However, he reappeared in the Goodwood Cup and ran a splendid race, easing down well before the line and recording a winning margin of four lengths.

Between this and the Jefferson Smurfit Memorial St Leger, Kayf Tara won the Prix Kergorlay with ease, and then headed to Ireland where there was never any doubts that he was destined to take the laurels. The winning margin was eight lengths.

He was an outstanding chance for the Melbourne Cup when, during a piece of work in Australia, he injured a ligament in his near-fore and was withdrawn. The same injury would see him scratched from the King George the following summer, but 2000 remained a year to remember for his supporters. Kayf Tara won the Yorkshire Cup and amazingly become the first horse since 1819 to regain the Ascot Gold Cup crown.

KAYF TARA (b. 1994)	**Sadler's Wells (b. 1981)**	**Northern Dancer** — Nearctic / Natalma
		Fairy Bridge — Bold Reason / Special
	Colourspin (b. 1983)	**High Top** — Derring-Do / Camenae
		Reprocolour — Jimmy Reppin / Blue Queen

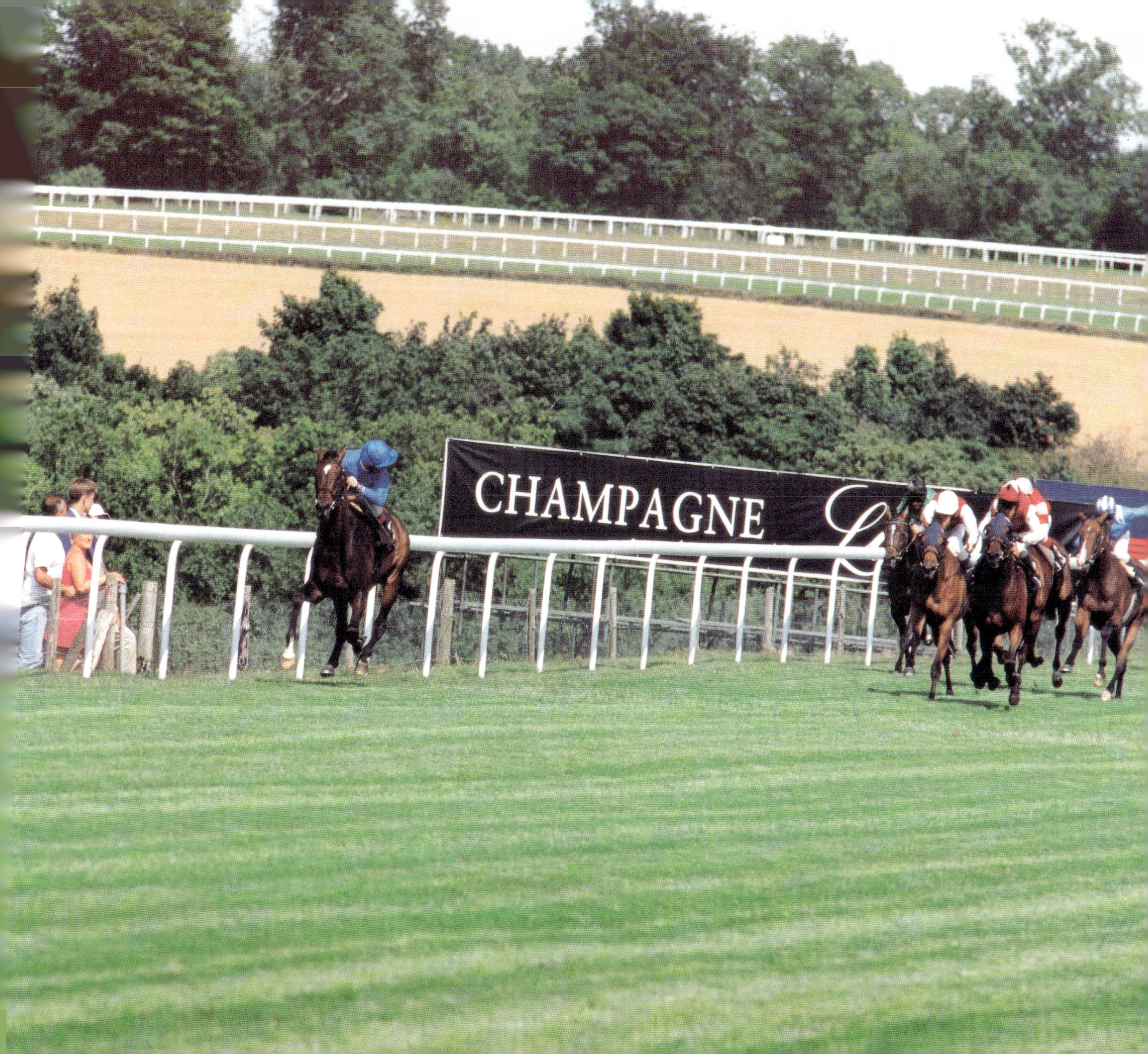
CHAMPAGNE

Kazzia

b. f by Zinaad - Khoruna (Lagunas)

Godolphin's filly Kazzia was purchased from Germany as a twice-winning juvenile and would prove an inspired acquisition in 2002, claiming a rare Guineas-Oaks double.

She went into the fillies classic at Newmarket with little confidence. Godolphin's management wanted to route her to the Italian Oaks, with Sheikh Mohammed insisting that she was good enough for Newmarket. That decision proved spot-on. Kazzia was always prominent in a less than strongly run race. Frankie Dettori asked her to quicken and she surged ahead in the final furlong, battling clear of Snowfire to win by a neck.

With a pedigree that showed plenty of stamina, connections now believed that she could go on to become the first filly since Salsabil in 1990 to complete a Guineas-Oaks double. Between Newmarket and Epsom she improved markedly and confidence was high as she strode onto the Epsom track looking by far the most impressive of the fillies on parade. In the race itself this impression continued as she dazzled in an all-the-way success. She gamely led throughout on rain-softened ground, shrugging off a late challenge from Quarter Moon for a half-length win, with Shadow Dancing 14 lengths back in third.

After the Oaks it was mooted that Kazzia would make a bid for the fillies' Triple Crown by running in the St Leger. Only two horses since the war, Sheikh Mohammed's Oh So Sharp (1985) and Meld (1955) had achieved that treble. But this was not to be. After a fourth in the Yorkshire Oaks, a foot abscess sidelined her during the early part of September. Instead a programme was mapped that would take her to the Breeders' Cup.

She shipped to the United States early in order to get acclimatised early, and put in a big performance in her prep race. Under Senor Chavez, identical forcing tactics as Epsom were employed to dominate a top class field in the Grade One Flower Bowl. Kazzia went to the lead and stayed there, defeating Turtle Bow by a neck.

Sadly an abscess in her left front foot was to interrupt Kazzia's final days of work ahead of the Breeders' Cup. Despite missing several days training she still showed, leading for the first mile of the Fillies and Mares Turf, but was caught as the field turned for home.

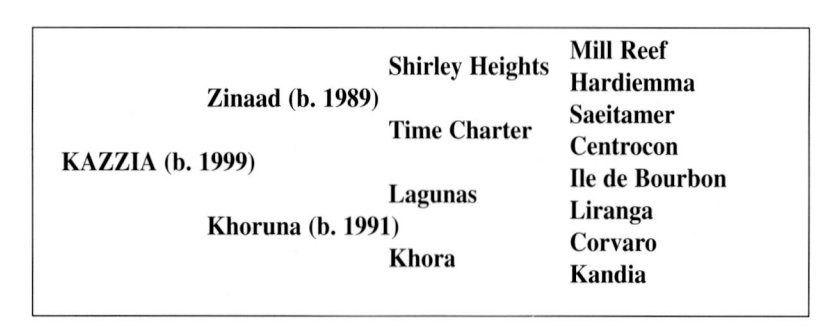

KAZZIA (b. 1999)	Zinaad (b. 1989)	Shirley Heights	Mill Reef
			Hardiemma
		Time Charter	Saeitamer
			Centrocon
	Khoruna (b. 1991)	Lagunas	Ile de Bourbon
			Liranga
		Khora	Corvaro
			Kandia

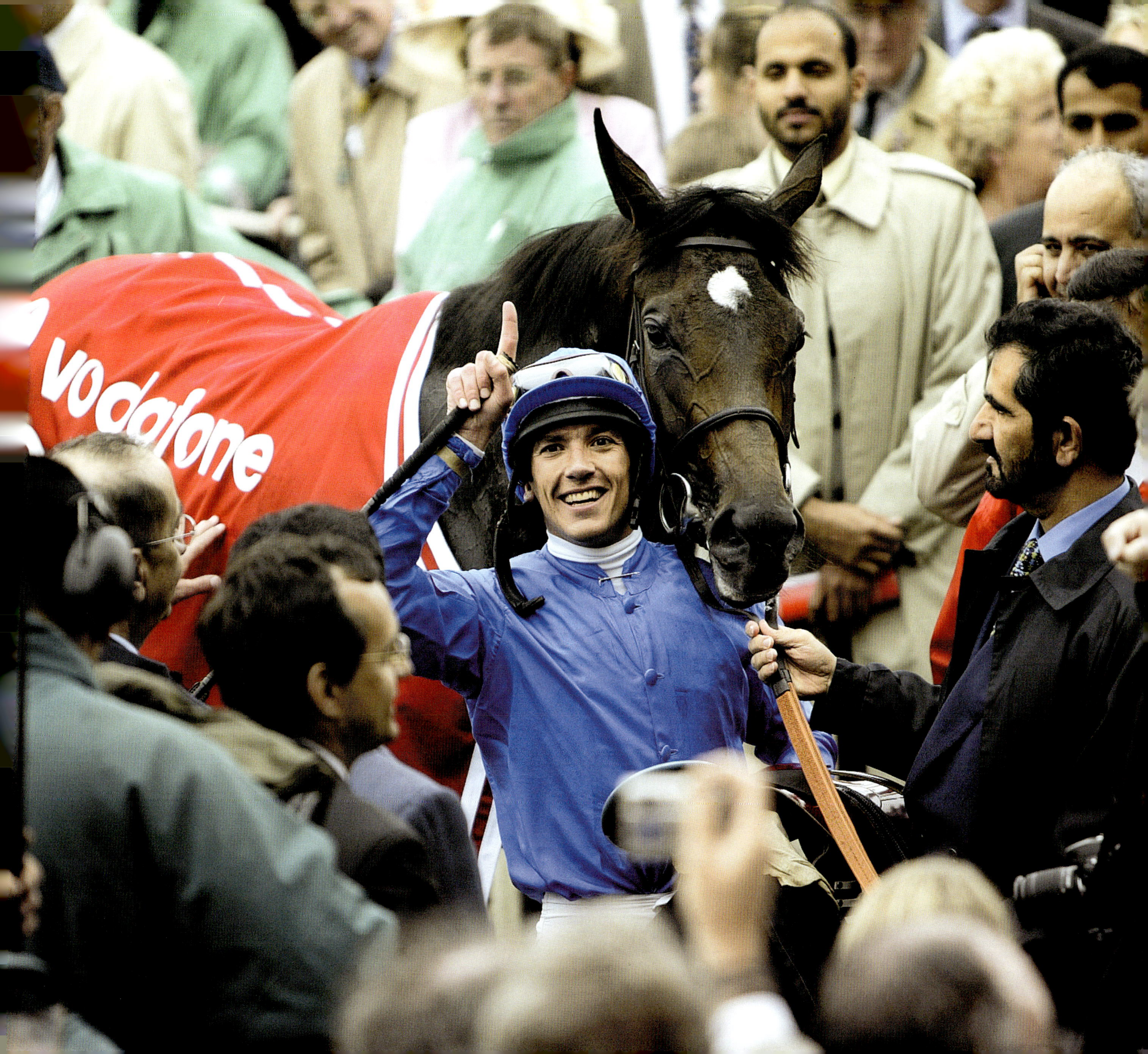
vodafone

Lahan

b. f by Unfuwain – Amanah (Mr. Prospector)

Sheikh Hamdan's home-bred filly enjoyed a tragically short career that stamped her as top class. A daughter of Shadwell Stud's Unfuwain, she was placed in training in Newmarket with John Gosden.

Lahan first appeared in the unromantic surrounds of Redcar in the north-east of England. Taking on seven furlongs and a mediocre field she won easily and then graduated to the Owen Brown Rockfel Stakes in October. At Newmarket she was sent off favourite and put in a superb effort for only her second career outing. A big, lengthy filly for her age, when asked for an effort she picked up and took the lead with two furlongs remaining, staying on strongly from a late challenge by Clog Dancer. This performance put her firmly in the 1000 Guineas picture

Lahan moved with her trainer to the Manton training complex that winter—and suffered alongside her stablemates as Manton had one of the coldest and wettest winters in its history. In order to have her ready for a spring campaign, Gosden boxed her near the stable's boiler room to stay warm.

After an unsuitable preparation, her seasonal debut came in the Dubai Duty Free Fred Darling Stakes at Newbury. Clearly in need of a run given her shortness of home work, she nevertheless put in a superb race, running well throughout, leading for a time on the bridle and tiring into fourth behind Iftiraas on deep ground.

It was an excellent performance for a filly still short on work, yet despite this she was a relative unfancied contender for the 1000 Guineas. Lining up against hot favourite Petrushka and Godolphin's impressive Bintalreef, Lahan even looked less than ready in her coat, such was her limited preparation.

Richard Hills kept Lahan well covered up behind horses early in the Classic, and looked to be heading nowhere even during the second part of the race. But quickly the complexion of the race changed. Inside the final furlong Hills asked Lahan for her effort and she responded magnificently, bursting to the front to claim the 1000 Guineas by a length and a quarter.

With a better preparation over the summer, observers believed she would turn out to be another of her owner's great fillies, in the mould perhaps of Salsabil and Shadayid. Sadly it was not to be. After missing the Coronation Stakes at Royal Ascot she was found cast in her box and was forced into retirement through injury.

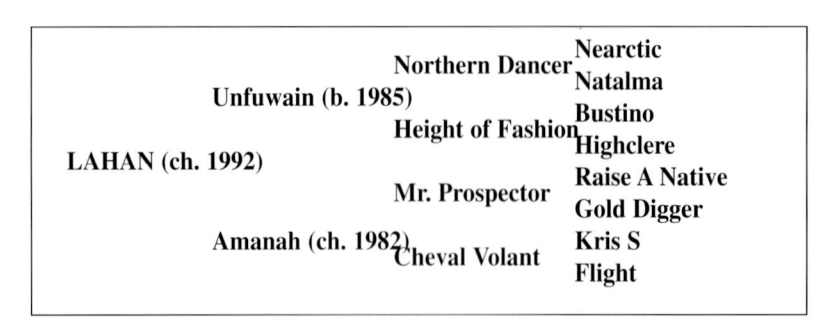

LAHAN (ch. 1992)	Unfuwain (b. 1985)	Northern Dancer	Nearctic
			Natalma
		Height of Fashion	Bustino
			Highclere
	Amanah (ch. 1982)	Mr. Prospector	Raise A Native
			Gold Digger
		Cheval Volant	Kris S
			Flight

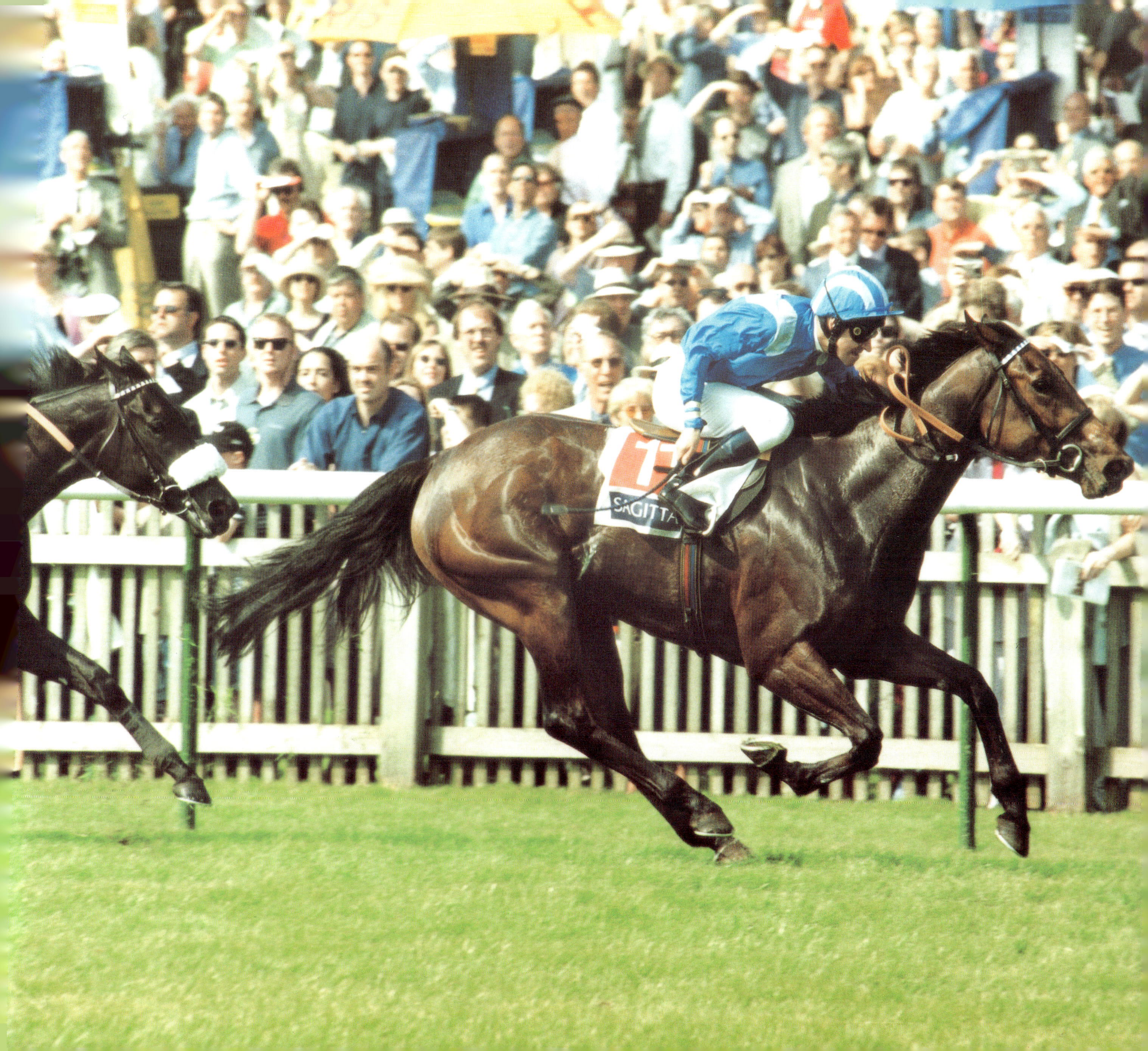
SAGITTA

Lammtarra

ch. c by Nijinsky — Snow Bride (Blushing Groom)

Out of the tragedy of the death of his trainer, Lammtarra rose like a Phoenix to become the leading three-year-old in Europe of 1995. Alex Scott had thought the well-bred colt to be something special as a juvenile. His one run that year confirmed this view. Carrying condition and slightly outpaced at times, he scored well in a Newbury maiden.

After Scott's death, Lammtarra was transferred to the care of the Godolphin team in Dubai. Connections plotted a campaign that might have led to Epsom and the Derby. However, Lammtarra's chances of returning to the track were not certain after a life-threatening abscess to his lung saw him transferred to Dubai Veterinary Hospital.

The handsome chestnut recovered well and showed himself progressing nicely. In May, he was still reported as behind in training, but began to make startling progress and was allowed to take his place in the Epsom showpiece despite having a far from ideal preparation.

In the Classic, jockey Walter Swinburn kept him prominently early, but Lammtarra dropped back slightly after encountering traffic problems and was well off the pace entering the home straight. With two furlongs remaining, Lammtarra was still seven lengths behind the leader lying fifth at the distance. But when asked for a final surge, the colt unleashed a tremendous kick. Inside the last hundred yards, the colours of Sheikh Saeed bin Maktoum Al Maktoum hit the front and Lammtarra went on to claim a success by one length in a record time.

After missing the Irish Derby due to an injury, Lammtarra returned in the King George VI and Queen Elizabeth Diamond Stakes. In the race itself Frankie Dettori was working the colt some way out. Pentire looked the winner, but Lammtarra made a sustained late challenge and wore down the leader, edging home by a neck.

Lammtarra next travelled to Paris for the Prix de l'Arc de Triomphe. Only four horses had ever achieved a King George-Prix de l'Arc de Triomphe double, and of those only Mill Reef had also claimed the Derby. At Longchamp he travelled the early part of the race behind pacemaker Luso, and when Dettori asked for an effort rounding the home turn, only Freedom Cry was able to mount a challenge, edging into the lead late. Again Lammtarra showed his courage to win back an advantage at the finish.

LAMMTARRA (ch. 1992)	Nijunsky (b. 1967)	Northern Dancer — Nearctic / Natalma
		Flaming Page — Bull Page / Flaring Top
	Snow Bride (ch. 1986)	Blushing Groom — Red God / Runaway Bride
		Awaasif — Snow Knight / Royal Statue

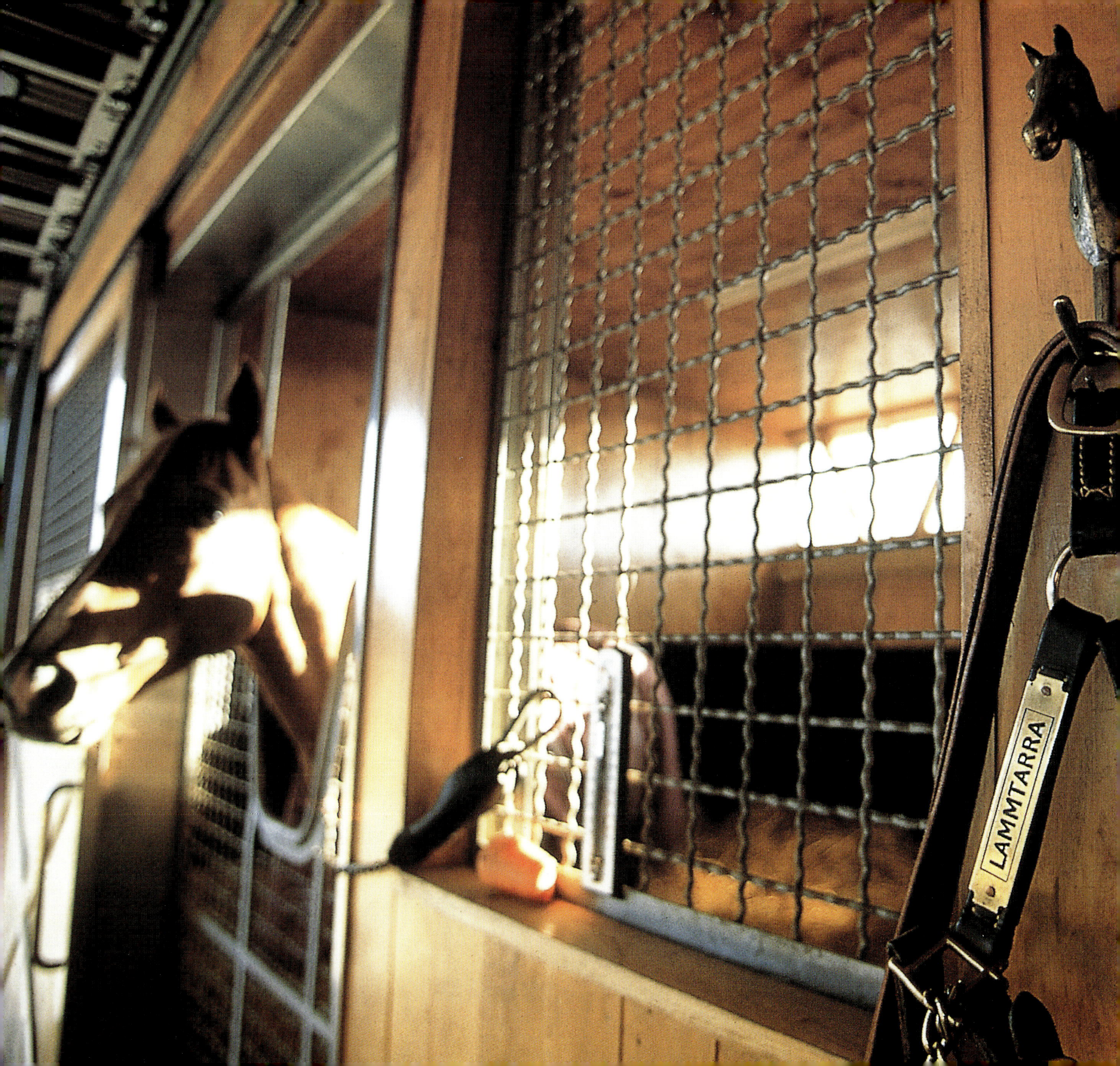
LAMMTARRA

PERRELET
1777
INVENTOR OF THE AUTOMATIC WATCH
POWER RESERVE
Functional and easy-to-read
Automatic movement with Perrelet decoration
Exclusive Perrelet rotor with glass
Alligator strap, deployment buckle
damas
Les Exclusives
Toll Free: 800 4916
www.damasjewellery.com

Sheikh Ahmed bin Saeed Al Maktoum

The unassuming and softspoken Sheikh Ahmed bin Saeed Al Maktoum is perhaps the least known member of the Maktoum family within racing in terms of ownership, having enjoyed just a handful of winners in the UAE and in Europe. Yet as chairman and chief executive of Emirates, Sheikh Ahmed has become arguably the biggest supporter of horseracing around the world today.

On the track, Sheikh Ahmed's green and white colours are a rare sight nowerdays. Never owning more than a handful of horses in training at any one time, his finest moments as an owner came courtesy of Wizard King, a son of Shaadi, who was skillfully placed by trainer Sir Mark Prescott. The tough and game Wizard King ran a phenomenal 24 races in three seasons, 13 outside Britain, and as far afield as Hong Kong, where he finished fourth in the International Bowl. Wizard King's many success included the Concorde Stakes at Leopardstown in Ireland, twice, and the Beeswing Stakes at Newcastle, this Sheikh Ahmed's first British black type victory. Before retirement, Wizard King won nine group races,

Sheikh Ahmed also patronised racing in his native Dubai, especially during the sport's fledgling seasons under rules in the mid-1990s. For several seasons he was represented in many leading Arabian races by tough multiple winner Saham.

Sheikh Ahmed is still found in the paddocks of some of the world's biggest racecourses today, but it is in his role as a benefactor and major sponsor for which he is best known.

"Emirates' sponsorship of race meetings and from a broader perspective our sponsorship of other major sports and non-sport event – is part of our contribution to the promotion of Dubai and the destinations that we serve," he says. "Being associated with such events is beneficial for our image and commercially strategic in reaching target audiences."

In hardly over two decades, Emirates has gone from start-up carrier with two wet-leased aircraft to one of the world's most successful airlines. The company is a brand, as recognisable in some parts of the world as the Pepsis, McDonalds and Fords, the great established corporate identities. This has been achieved, in no short measure, through sport. Football has been key to this strategy, and Sheikh Ahmed has taken his 20 year old organisation into profile tie ups with leading European sides such as Arsenal *(he is pictured above with Gunners star Thierry Henry)* in England's Premiership. This agreement is the largest sponsorship agreement in the history of English football, including naming rights for Arsenal's new 67,000 seat stadium, the Emirates Stadium.

Elsewhere in the continent Emirates has shirt deals with Hamburg in Germany and Paris St Germain in France. The company's backing of the 2006 FIFA World Cup and all FIFA events until 2014 has linked Emirates corporate identity firmly with the world's most popular sport.

Emirates has committed itself to Emirates' Team New Zealand in the America's Cup yacht race, the Emirates Rugby Sevens in Dubai, London, South Africa and France, and the Dubai Cricket Council, among others. Emirates is also the official carrier for golf's Dubai Desert Classic, the BMW International Open in Munich, the BMW Asian Open in Shanghai, the Holden New Zealand Open and the Dubai Tennis Open, in addition to sponsoring all international cricket umpires through the International Cricket Council and all referees in the English Premiership.

But arguably most effectively of all at developing brand awareness, barring football, is Sheikh Ahmed's policy of supporting racing. Today, Emirates counts among its stable of events the world's richest horse race, the Dubai World Cup. After just 11 runnings of the race, Emirates has backed a winner, as the event has grown in stature, recognition, status and publicity to become one of the leading racedays anywhere in the world,

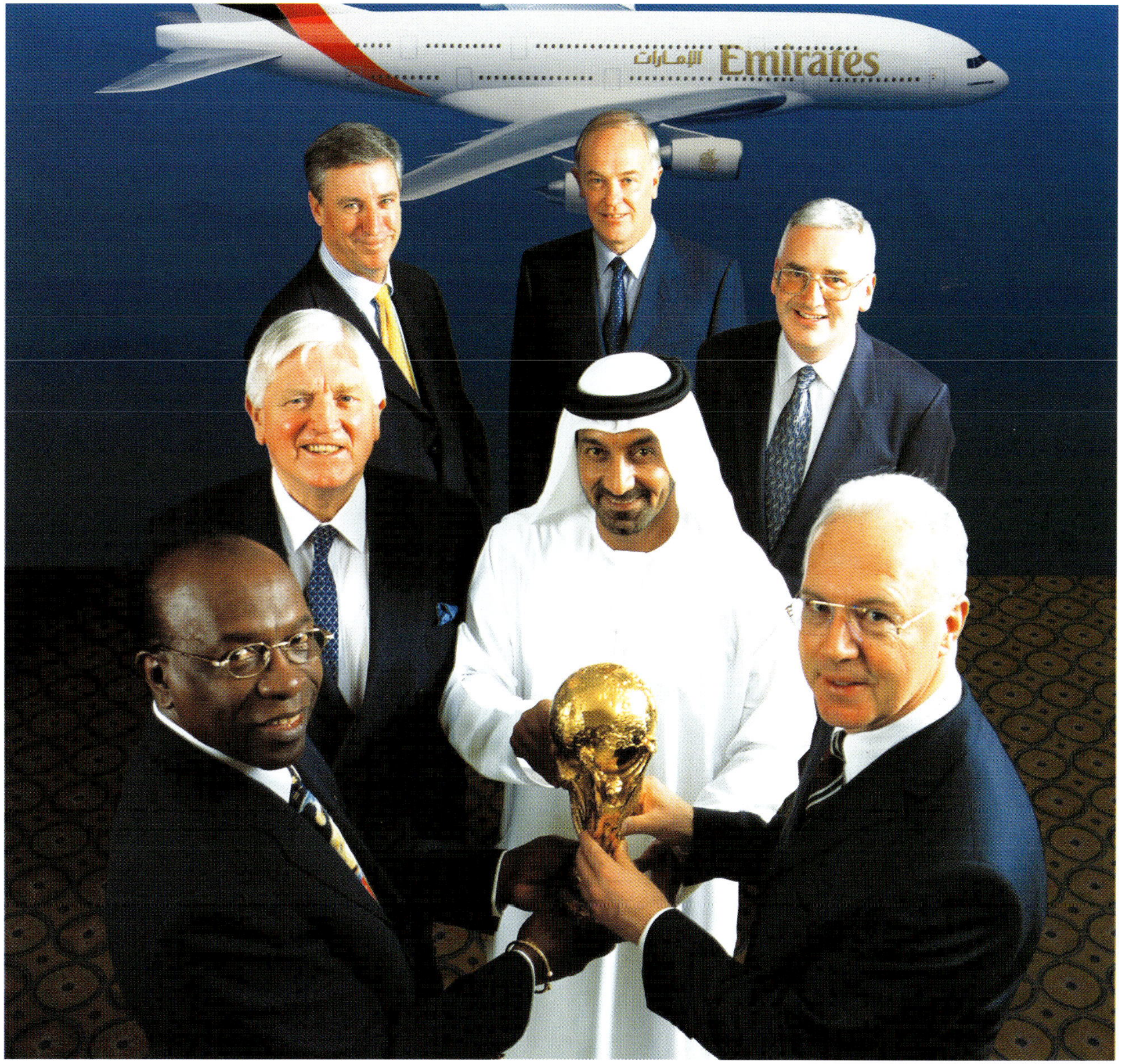
الإمارات Emirates

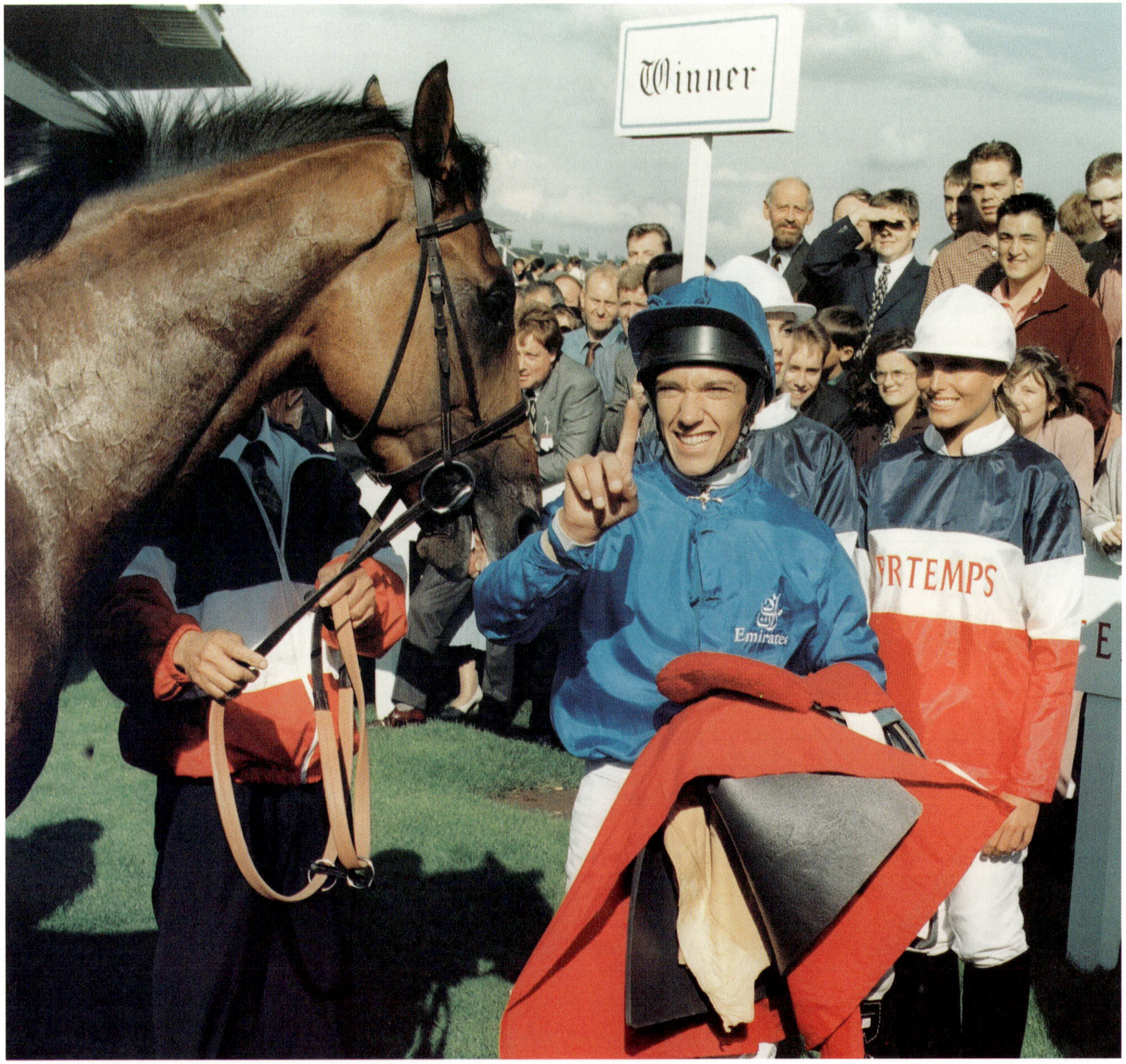
Winner
Emirates
RTEMPS

on a par with the Breeders' Cup and Royal Ascot as 'the' racing event on the calendar.

But racing in Emirates' home nation is just the tip of a very large iceburg. At Sheikh Ahmed's direction, the carrier has invested in premium races all over the world.

In July 2004 Emirates announced a seven-year partnership deal with the Victoria Racing Club to become the main sponsor of Australia's top horse race, now named the Emirates Melbourne Cup. The continent of Australia grinds to a halt for this event, arguably the biggest horse race in the Southern Hemisphere, and made this an ideal vehicle for Emirates as it continues to capitalise on already excellent penetration into the Australia, one of the airline's biggest markets.

Entering the United States with a non-stop flight to New York, Emirates took the same tack. In April 2005 the company unveiled a multi-year sponsorship agreement, becoming the title sponsor of the $2 million Emirates Airline Breeders' Cup Distaff and the $1 million Emirates Airline Breeders' Cup Filly and Mare Turf races at the Breeders' Cup.

Add to this elite portfolio races in other nations, such as the S$1 million Emirates Singapore Derby, the Group 3 Emirates Airline Minstrel Stakes held at the historic Curragh Racecourse in Ireland and pattern events at some of Britain's premier racecourses, including Newmarket and York, along with others in France and Ireland, Emirates can boast a roll call not matched by any other sponsor. Emirates and its chairman have also committed to Dubai's Godolphin in recent years and the airline's corporate image appears on Godolphin's silks.

Sheikh Ahmed is not visible in the winners' enclosure anymore. Yet his massive support for the sport makes him one of the racing's great patrons.

Ma Biche

b. f by Key To The Kingdom — Madge (Roi Dagobert)

In 1983, Sheikh Maktoum enjoyed Classic success in Britain for the second successive season when Ma Biche claimed the 1000 Guineas at Newmarket.

The filly looked a top-class prospect throughout her two-year-old season, her four victories in six starts including the Group One Cheveley Park Stakes at Newmarket in September, where she beat the classy Favouridge by three-quarters of length. She also won the Group Three Prix Robert Papin, a top French sprint for juveniles.

Looking highly impressive on her three-year-old reappearance, in the Prix Imprudence at Maisons-Laffitte in April, she won easing up on testing ground, finishing one and a half lengths to the good of Dancing Display, a top-class animal the previous summer himself.

That performance showed that she was clearly suited to a mile, and on the strength of this the filly was promoted to clear favourite for the first British Classic of the season, the 1000 Guineas.

During the early stages of the race at Newmarket, Ma Biche was held tight to the pack, just off the pace, with Favouridge tracking her closely. Royal Heroine who had gone to the front with the early pacesetters dropped away. A long way from home, however, Ma Biche appeared to be moving easiest and as they hit the rising ground she picked up extremely well, took the lead, and easily held off a renewed challenge from the eventual runner-up.

In winning the 1000 Guineas for Sheikh Maktoum, Ma Biche also created history in becoming the first British Classic winner trained by a woman, Criquette Head.

After Newmarket the filly encountered problems. She was beaten in the Prix Marois and was then forced to miss the Prix Moulin.

In fact, Ma Biche did not return to the racecourse until August and even then looked below her best. Giving weight to all her rivals in the Prix d'Astarte at Deauville, she looked to be moving well at the halfway stage but faded into fourth.

Dropped to seven furlongs, she made her final start of the campaign in the Prix de la Foret at Longchamp, looking superb in her coat despite a long, troubled season. Ma Biche won by half a length from Pampabird the claim the fourth Group One of her career.

Ma Biche (b. 1980)	Key To The Kingdom (b. 1970)	Bold Ruler — Nasrullah / Miss Disco
		Key Bridge — Princequillo / Blue Banner
	Madge (br. 1975)	Roi Dagobert — Sicambre / Dame d'Atour
		Midget — Djebe / Mimi

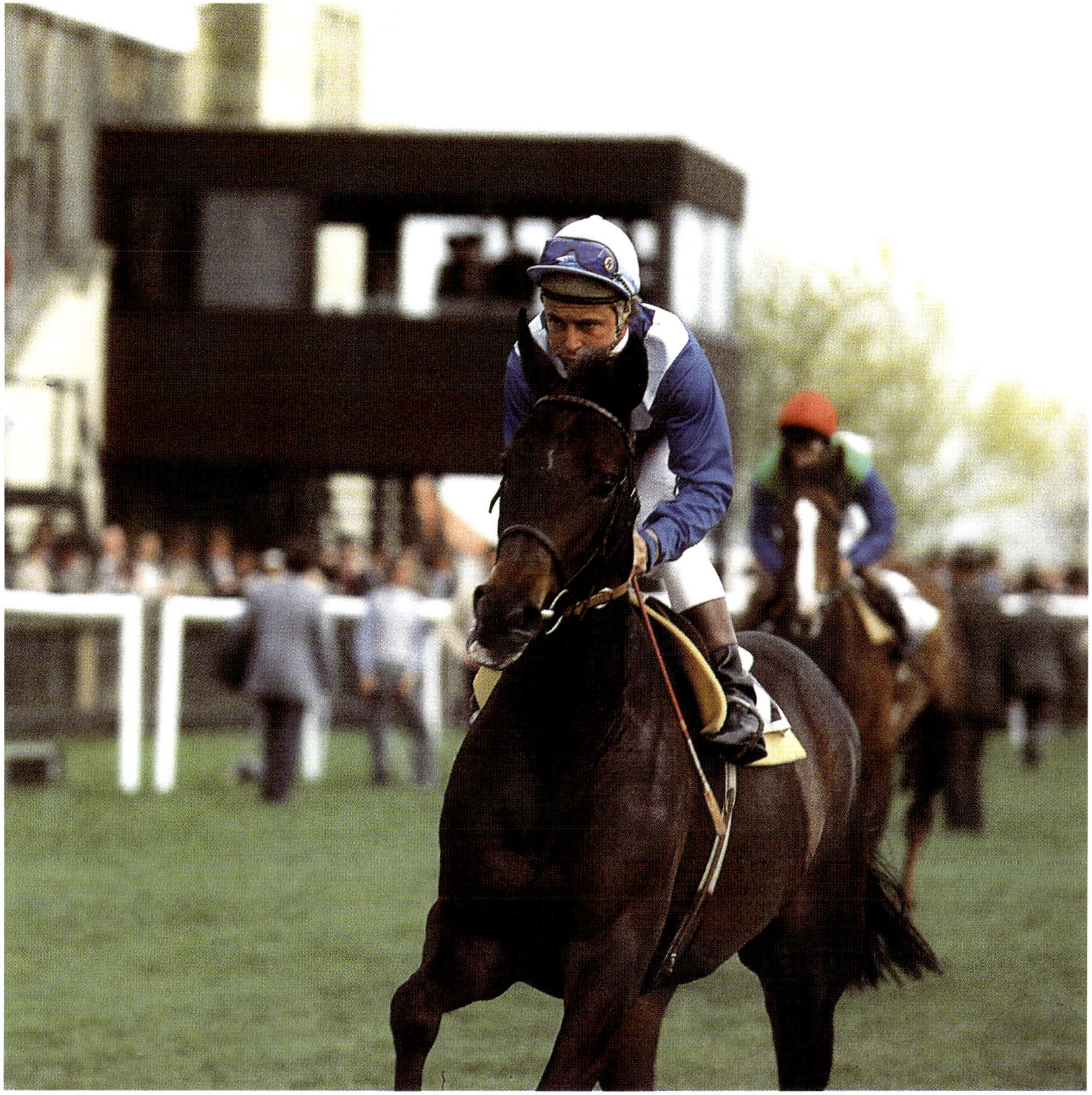

Marienbard

b. c by Caerleon - Marienbad (Darshaan)

Marienbard was perhaps a typical Godolphin performer. Having begun his career with Michael Jarvis in Britain, he joined Godolphin after his three-year-old campaign. Only did then did he realise his full potential.

The following season he returned from wintering in Dubai to claim the Group Two Yorkshire Cup. Marienbard was then favourite for the Ascot Gold Cup, but finished a disappointing fifth. Later he contested the Irish St Leger where he finished third. That was good enough to book Marienbard a place in the Melbourne Cup, where he ran handily and stuck on well, but slipped back when running wide, finishing seventh.

He finished the campaign with a Timeform rating of 119 and hopes high that more improvement was set to come. After again wintering in Dubai, Marienbard returned as a five-year-old with something to prove. After being campaigned as a stayer the previous season, Godolphin boasting a plethora of top class middle-distance horses during that particular season, he was now to be tried over shorter trips. This was to prove his making.

His racecourse return came in the Jockey Club Stakes in Newmarket's Guineas meeting. Considered Godolphin's second string with Frankie Dettori opting for Kutub, Marienbard hit the front of the pack late under Jamie Spencer and got up by a neck to pip Millenary.

After a pair of Group One success in Germany: the WGZ Bank-Deutschlandpreis and the Grosser Preis von Baden, in which he recorded a smooth victory over Salve Regina, Marienbard was given his chance in the highest company.

Frankie Dettori partnered the five-year-old in the Prix de l'Arc de Triomphe Lucien Barriere. With a £557,000 first prize it was the 81st running of Europe's richest middle-distance event, a year on from Godolphin's success with Sakee in the race.

Pre-race favourites Sulamani and High Chaparral were both in contention but it was Marienbard who came through to take up the running. Sulamani found a second wind but Dettori drove Marienbard home for a famous victory.

Soon after it was announced that the son of Caerleon was retired. Marienbard had won eight of his 17 starts for £1,181,425 in prizemoney.

MARIENBARD (b. 1997)	Caerleon (ch. 1988) — Nijinsky II	Northern Dancer / Flaming Page
	Caerleon (ch. 1988) — Foreseer	Round Table / Regal Gleam
	Marienbad (b. 1991) — Darshaan	Shirley Heights / Delsey
	Marienbad (b. 1991) — Marie de F'noy	Lightening / Primula

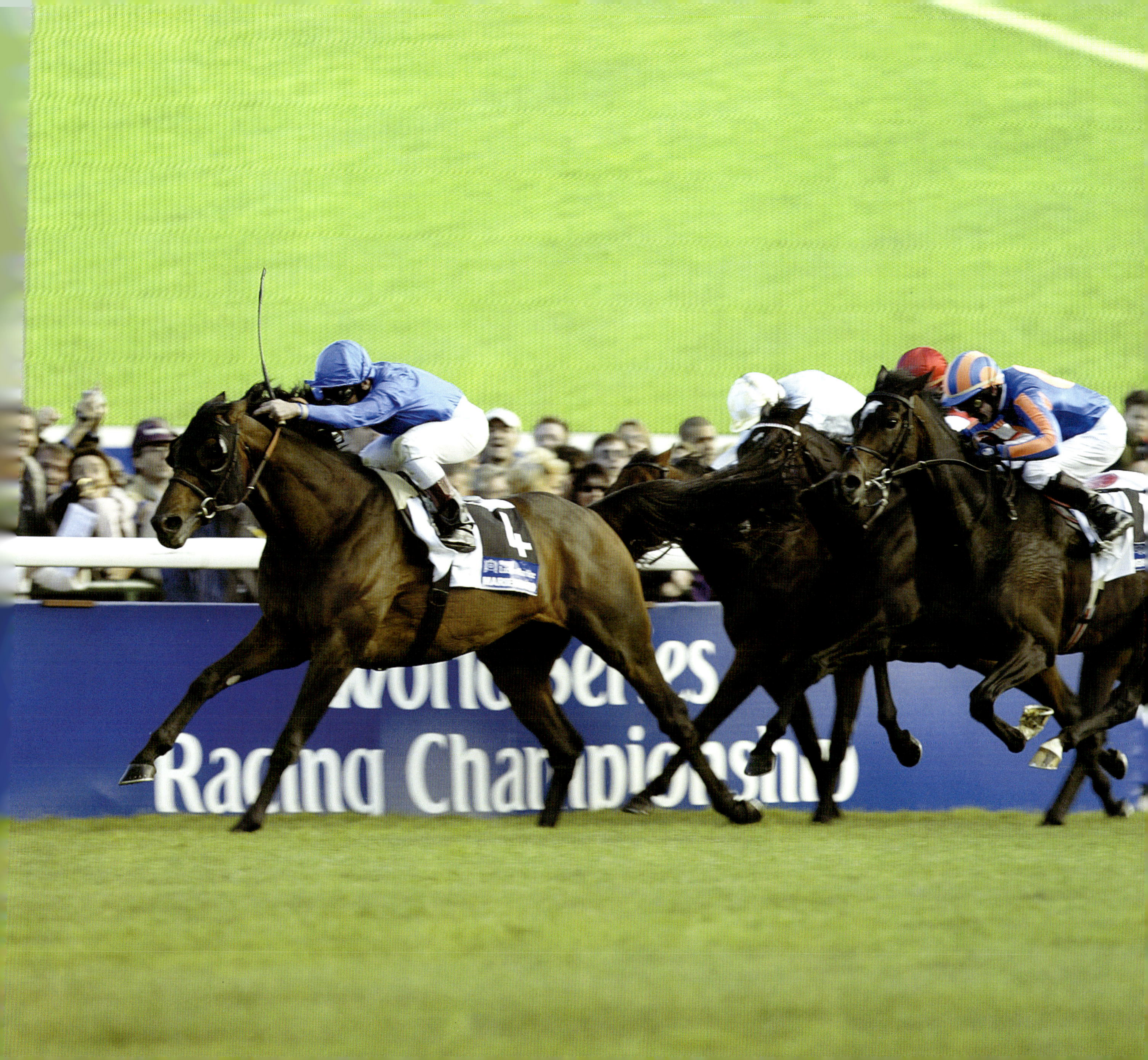
4

Mark of Esteem

b. c by Darshaan – Homage (Ajdal)

On his debut Mark of Esteem finished a neck second at Newmarket to Alhaarth, the latter a leading juvenile of his generation. Controversy notwithstanding, it was Mark of Esteem who shone at three, while his conqueror at headquarters struggled.

Following his close-up second, trainer Henry Cecil saddled his charge in a Goodwood maiden. On his second outing, Mark of Esteem showed himself a talent, lengthening in a striking manner when asked for an effort two furlongs out, and going on to claim the race by an unhurried three lengths.

Noted as a bright prospect for the following season, he was entered in the Royal Lodge Stakes.

The following spring, the colt returned in the 2000 Guineas as one of Godolphin's leading hopes. Looking extremely fit, Mark of Esteem was always moving sweetly and after hitting the front under Frankie Dettori more than a furlong out, held off late challenges from Even Top and Bijou D'Inde in an extremely tight finish.

Running a temperature, he missed the Epsom Derby and when reappearing in the St James's Palace Stakes where he ran well below his best form in eighth place, hardly registering for much of the race.

It was a different animal who travelled to Goodwood for the Celebration Mile in late August. Dettori held him up early behind leader Alhaarth, but when he began a run, Mark of Esteem found himself boxed in.

The Classic winner was switched to the right where he found daylight and picked up dramatically, hitting the front just before the distance and going on to take the race by three and a half lengths from Bishop of Cashel.

Dettori was back in the plate in the Queen Elizabeth II Stakes at Ascot in September, using much the same tactics to see off a very strong field, including, 1000 Guineas heroine Bosra Sham who found herself unable to fend off Mark of Esteem's speedy late challenge. In winning by one and three-quarter lengths, Mark of Esteem provided the third leg of Dettori's 'Magnificent Seven.'

He shipped to Canada for the Breeders' Cup Mile at the end of October, where despite being in touch for most of the way found little in the straight and finished seventh to Da Hoss.

	Shirley Heights	Mill Reef
Darshaan (br. 1981)		Nardiemma
	Delsy	Abdos
MARK OF ESTEEM (b. 1993)		Kelty
	Ajdal	Northern Dancer
Homage (b. 1989)		Native Partner
	Home Love	Vaguely Noble
		Homespun

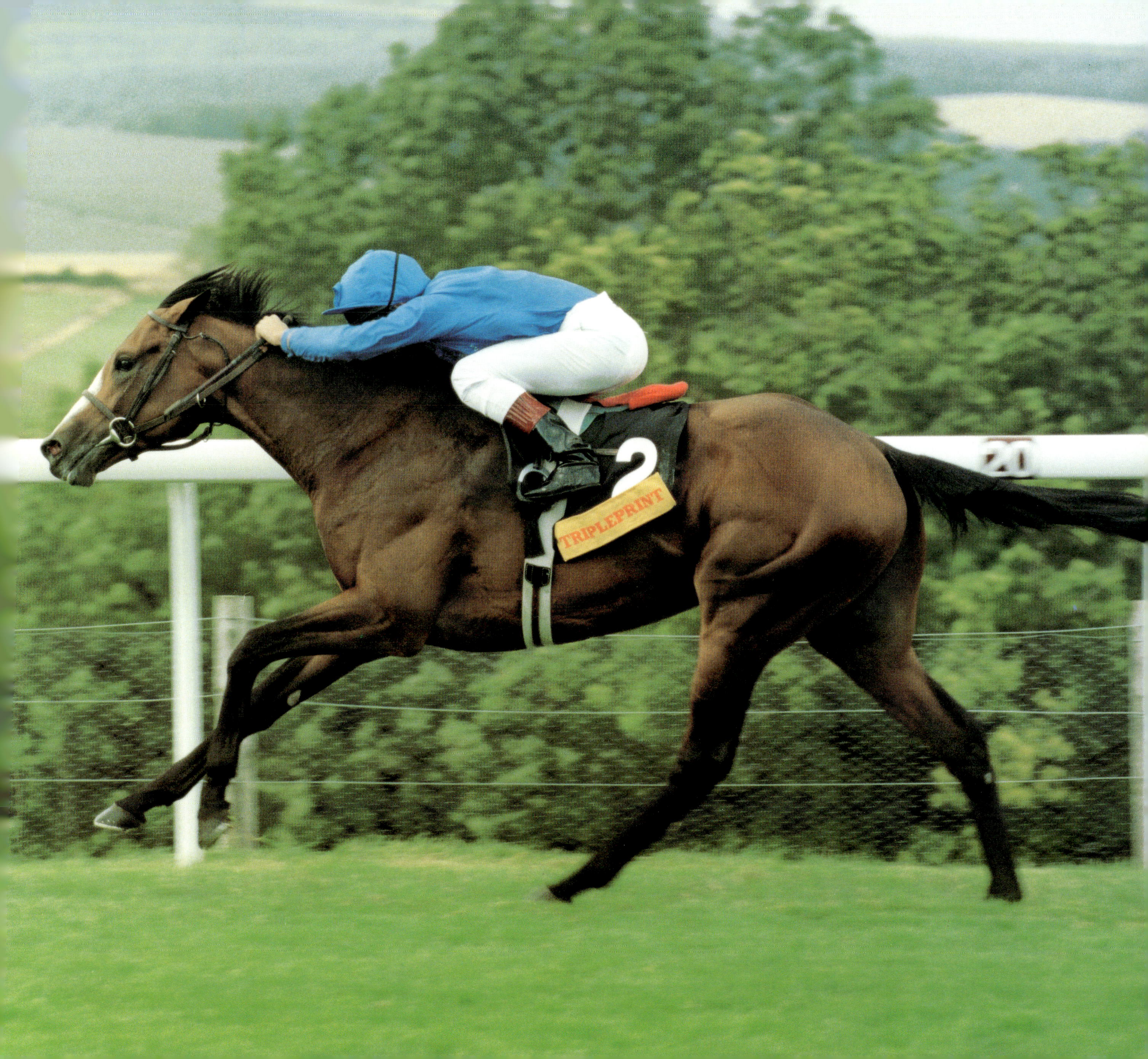
2
TRIPLEPRINT

Moon Ballad

ch. c by Singspiel - Velvet Moon (Shaadi)

Sold for 350,000 Guineas at the Tattersalls October Yearling Sale, this progressive son of Singspiel went from strength to strength as a three-year-old and began 2003 by emulating his sire in winning the Dubai World Cup.

Despite his Northern Dancer sireline, Moon Ballad was plagued by snipers who raised stamina doubts, pointing out that his dam was a six furlong Lowther Stakes winner. But the plucky colt went on to prove himself to have the ability, the stamina, and to be a tough, robust performer.

This epic story began in March 2002 with a little race at Nad Al Sheba. His European bow came in the Pearl and Coutts Newmarket Stakes, a Listed race over one mile two furlongs, where Moon Ballad was caught close to home by Highdown.

This was proof enough for Godolphin, who raised the stakes further by entering him in the Dante, a key Derby trial, against the likes of Queen Elizabeth's well touted hope Right Approach. Right Approach flopped, but Moon Ballad showed off his genuine class. Fully two furlongs from home the colt had the Dante won.

Next came the Derby itself, where Moon Ballad ran a superb race. Moon Ballad set them fair pace through the first half mile. Under ordinary circumstances, they may have been successful, but were unlucky that 2002 threw up to superb Aidan O'Brien runners in High Chaparral and Hawk Wing. Moon Ballad kept on well for third.

The colt would return to the winners' enclosure through an emphatic victory in the Group Three Select Stakes at Goodwood, making all and breaking the track record. This led him to the Emirates Airline Champion Stakes, which was won by Storming Home while Moon Ballad settled for second. It was a loss on the books, but showed that he was continuing to progress. He was now short listed for the Dubai World Cup. This was confirmed on his seasonal debut in Dubai where a powerful victory in the Sheikh Maktoum Challenge Round II, won him a place in the classic.

Frankie Dettori and Moon Ballad were in contention early in the Dubai World Cup. Coming out of the far turn, Dettori roused Moon Ballad and he responded, leaving the rest of the field in his wake and finishing a whopping six lengths clear of Harlan's Holiday.

Singspiel (b. 1992)	In The Wings	Sadler's Wells
		High Hawk
	Glorious Song	Halo
MOON BALLAD (ch. 1999)		Ballade
Velvet Moon (b. 1991)	Shaadi	Danzig
		Unfurled
	Park Special	Relkino
		Balilla

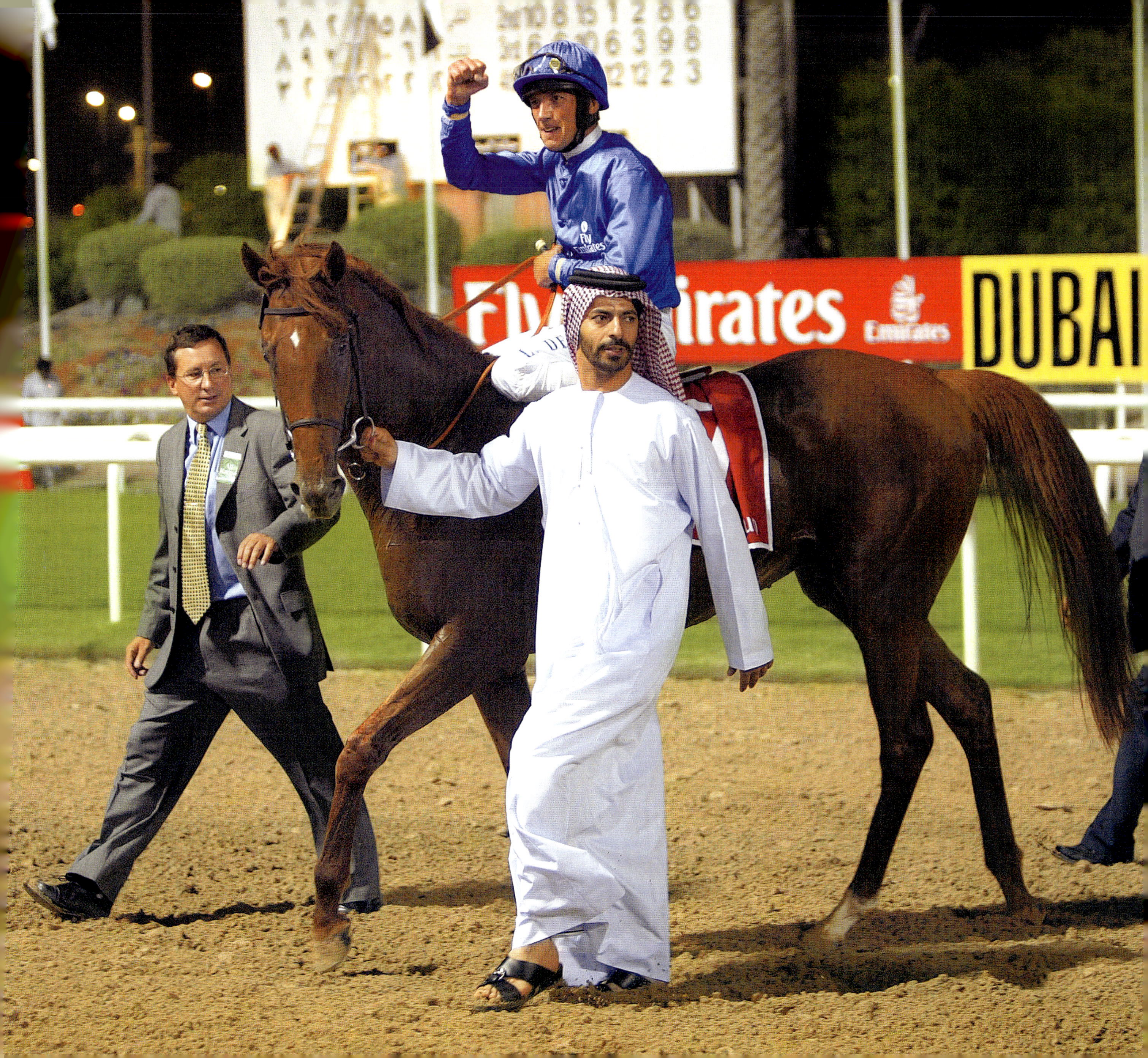
Fly Emirates
Emirates
DUBAI

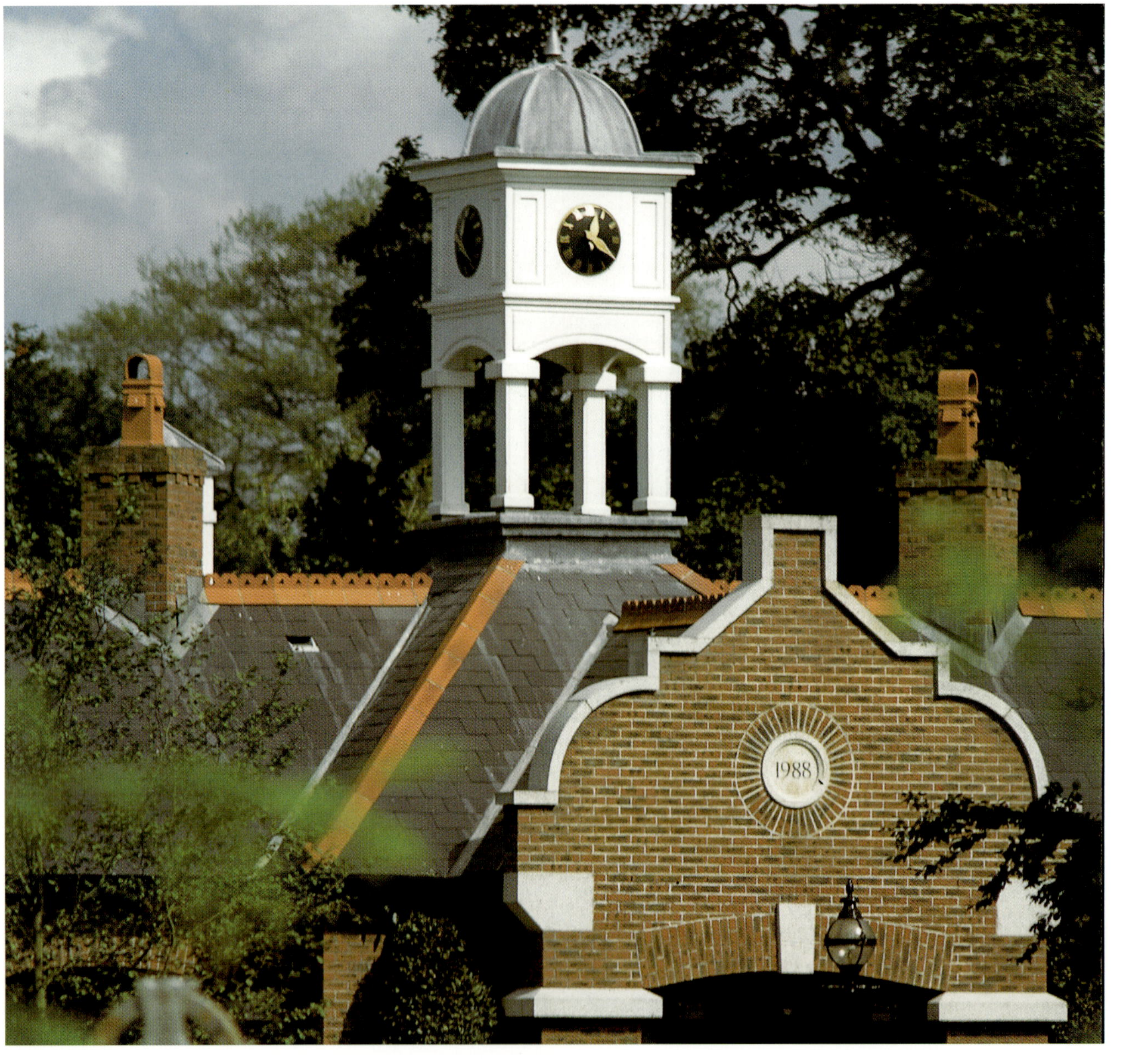
1988

Darley

Darley is an umbrella organisation encompassing one of the most vast and much accomplished breeding operations in the world. The sheer size of Sheikh Mohammed's top class breeding arm has made him one of world's most successful owner breeders and the largest in Europe in terms of acreage.

But it is in terms of quality that Darley stands out. Sheikh Mohammed has shaken up the breeding industry in a way reminiscent of the way he has shaped and modernised racing through Godolphin. This year it will stand dozens of stallions worldwide, a majority in Europe. The use of shuttle stallions (standing stallions in the Southern Hemisphere during the Northern Hemisphere off-season) has helped offset, in terms of profitability, the altruistic handicap placed upon Darley by Sheikh Mohammed in preventing his stallions seeing oversized books of mares. This is a phenomenon that, according to experts, will have a negative effect on the thoroughbred gene pool, concentrating it in too few bloodlines. To counter this, Sheikh Mohammed has deliberately prevented his stallions being over utilised. He restricts the number of mares booked to each stallion and also donates one nomination in aid of the European Breeders' Fund.

The centre of the operation, Dalham Hall Stud, was purchased by Sheikh Mohammed in 1981. Known as Derisley Stud until November 1970, its present name was actually taken from another stud situated four miles south-east of Newmarket. Derisley Stud had a long history of standing top class stallions, including sprint champion Honeyway and Great Nephew. The latter produced two Epsom Derby winners with Grundy and Shergar. Great Nephew was buried at Dalham Hall when he died in 1996.

The stud remains the centrepiece of the Darley organisation and brought almost immediate success for Sheikh Mohammed upon its purchase: Among the broodmare band which was part of the deal was Oh So Far, in foal to Kris with the champion filly Oh So Sharp.

Machiavellian has been the star of Dalham's operation, consistently producing crops with calibre performers such as Godolphin-owned classic winner Vettori and Best of the Bests,

From the initial purchase of Dalham Hall in 1981, a succession of additional studs have been added to the overall operation, including the 285-acre Rutland Stud in 1984, 190-acre Hadrian Stud in 1986, and in 1998, the 161-acre Warren Stud, 43-acre White Lodge Stud and 210-acre Church Hall Farm Stud. More recently Sheikh Mohammed has acquired the Someries Stud, in 1991, and Rockingham Yard in 1993.

Each is a vital cog in the smooth-running machine, from Rutland which is used privately, to Church Hall Farm Stud which has a world-class foaling unit, largely utilised by mares from Europe. Someries Stud is a base for fillies out of training, while Rockingham Yard fills an important role as a centre for horses before they go into training and a rehabilitation centre. It is also used for sales preparation.

In Britain alone, leaving aside an extensive Irish operation centred around Kildangan Stud, Dalham Hall and its satellites encompass some 2,125 acres, 230 paddocks and around 600 boxes.

At the centre of Sheikh Mohammed's breeding operation is Kildangan Stud in County Kildare, Ireland. This pristine facility, covering some 1,500 acres, also encompasses one of the best-known collection of trees in the Northern Hemisphere. Kildangan was purchased by Sheikh Mohammed in

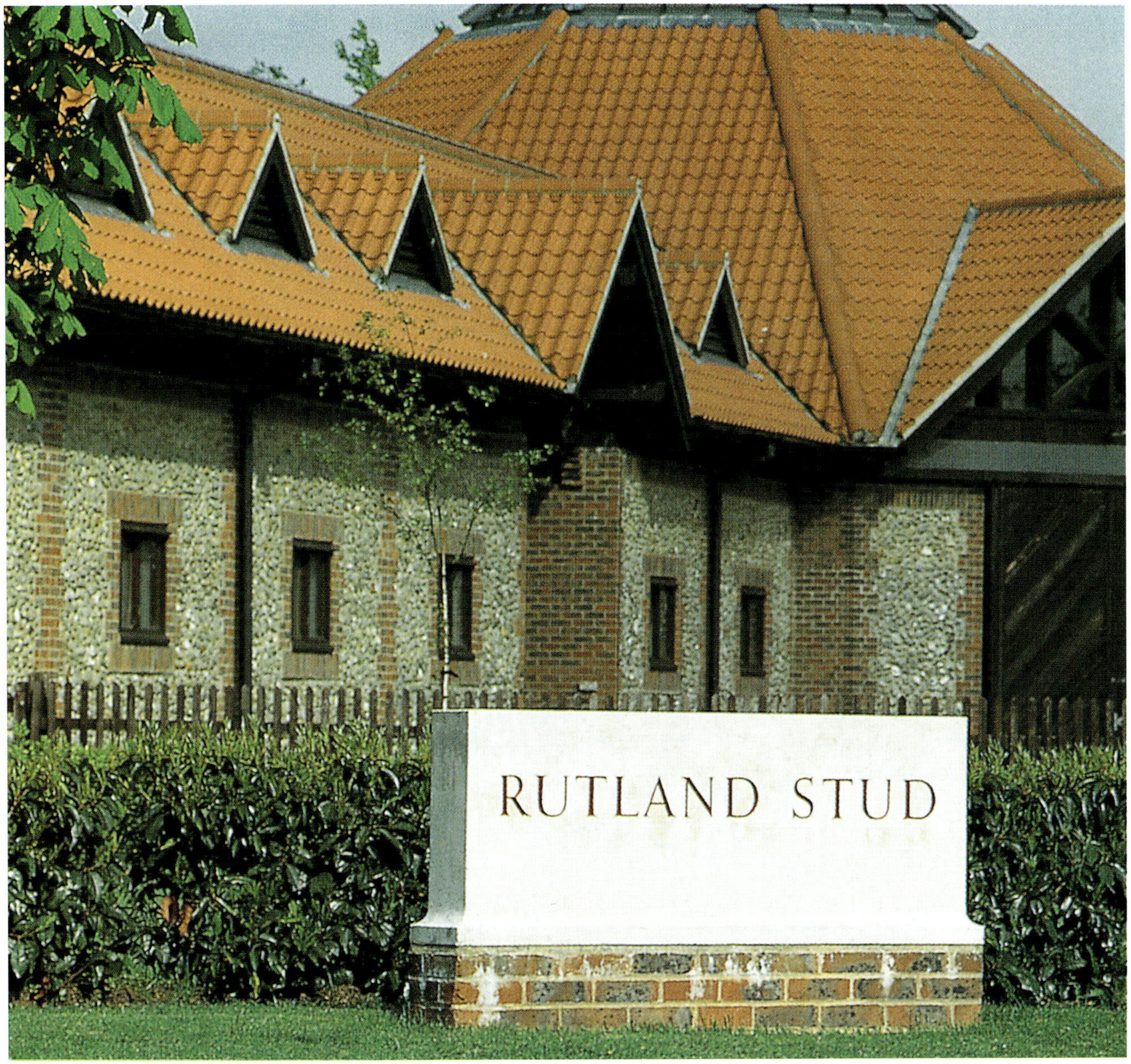
RUTLAND STUD

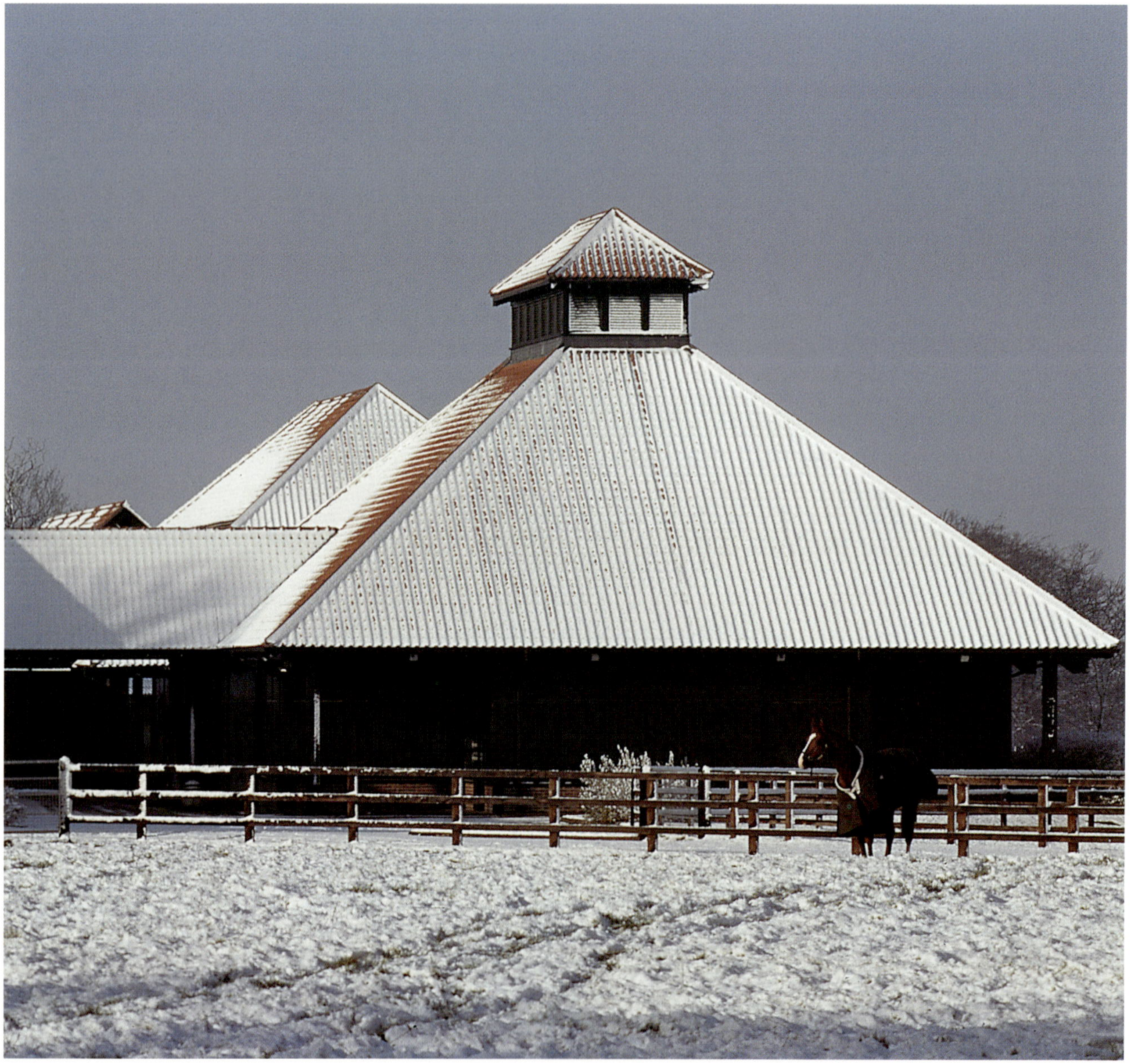

1986 from famous Irish breeder Roderick More O'Farrell, who bred classic winners such as Ambergris, Parnell and Rosanati.

Since then, Kildangan has playing a pivotal role as a nursery for the majority of Sheikh Mohammed's annual crop of yearlings from Europe and North America, in addition to housing around 100 mares each year which visit stallions in Ireland.

Across the English Channel and the Atlantic, Darley also exerts a heavy influence in France and United States, where the organisation stands a number of leading stallions, with considerable commercial success. In recent times Darley has emerged as a major player in the Bluegrass State of Kentucky

The emergence of Japanese breeding and racing has also attracted Darley, which has made a significant impact into a nation which has seen its breeding burst onto the world stage in recent years, while further south in Australia, a number of Darley stallions spend the Southern Hemisphere breeding season.

Darley's modernist approach will continue to have a major impact on the industry, while Sheikh Mohammed's commitment to quality looks certain to ensure that the Maktoums continue to enjoy the same level of success during their second quarter century patronising the sport.

Moonshell

b. f by Sadler's Wells — Moon Cactus (Kris)

Supremely well bred and always highly thought of, Sheikh Mohammed's Moonshell arrived on the racecourse as a juvenile with a growing reputation at home. If anything she showed even more potential than expected.

Entered in a hot Doncaster maiden where she was sent off favourite, the filly travelled strongly behind the leaders, slipped into the lead with little more than 200 yards remaining and quickly sprinted clear to finish three lengths ahead of the runner-up with the third a further four lengths adrift.

Going into the winter, Moonshell was not set for the traditional preparation but was selected as part of the growing band of animals based with the Godolphin operation in Dubai.

Joining Saeed bin Suroor, Moonshell thrived in the Gulf sunshine and progressed to rank among Godolphin's leading classic prospects.

Moonshell was to make her seasonal reappearance in the 1000 Guineas at Newmarket and showed herself well forward, looking outstanding in the paddock beforehand. In what was only her second racecourse appearance, Moonshell belied her experience over a distance which would appear too sharp, to finish third behind Harayir and Aqaarid.

The post-race view was that Moonshell would, as her breeding suggested, improve for a longer distance and the filly was much fancied for the mile and a half Epsom Oaks thereafter.

Moonshell was sent off second favourite at Epsom. In testing conditions, the Godolphin runner was always moving well throughout the race and as the also-rans dropped away, along with a below-par Aqaarid, Moonshell hit the front with two furlongs remaining, holding off a sustained late run from both Pure Grain and Dance A Dream by a length and a half and three quarters of a length.

The filly was being prepared for the Irish Oaks a few weeks later when she picked up a training injury which curtailed her three-year-old season.

Extremely lightly raced, Moonshell returned to Dubai for the winter and on her reappearance in Europe the following season ran credibly in several events.

	Northern Dancer	Nearctic
		Natalama
Sadler's Wells (b. 1981)		
	Fairy Bridge	Bold Reason
		Special
MOONSHELL (b. 1992)		
	Kris	Sharpen Up
		Doubly Sure
Moon Cactus (b. 1987)		
	Lady Moon	Mill Reef
		Moonlight Night

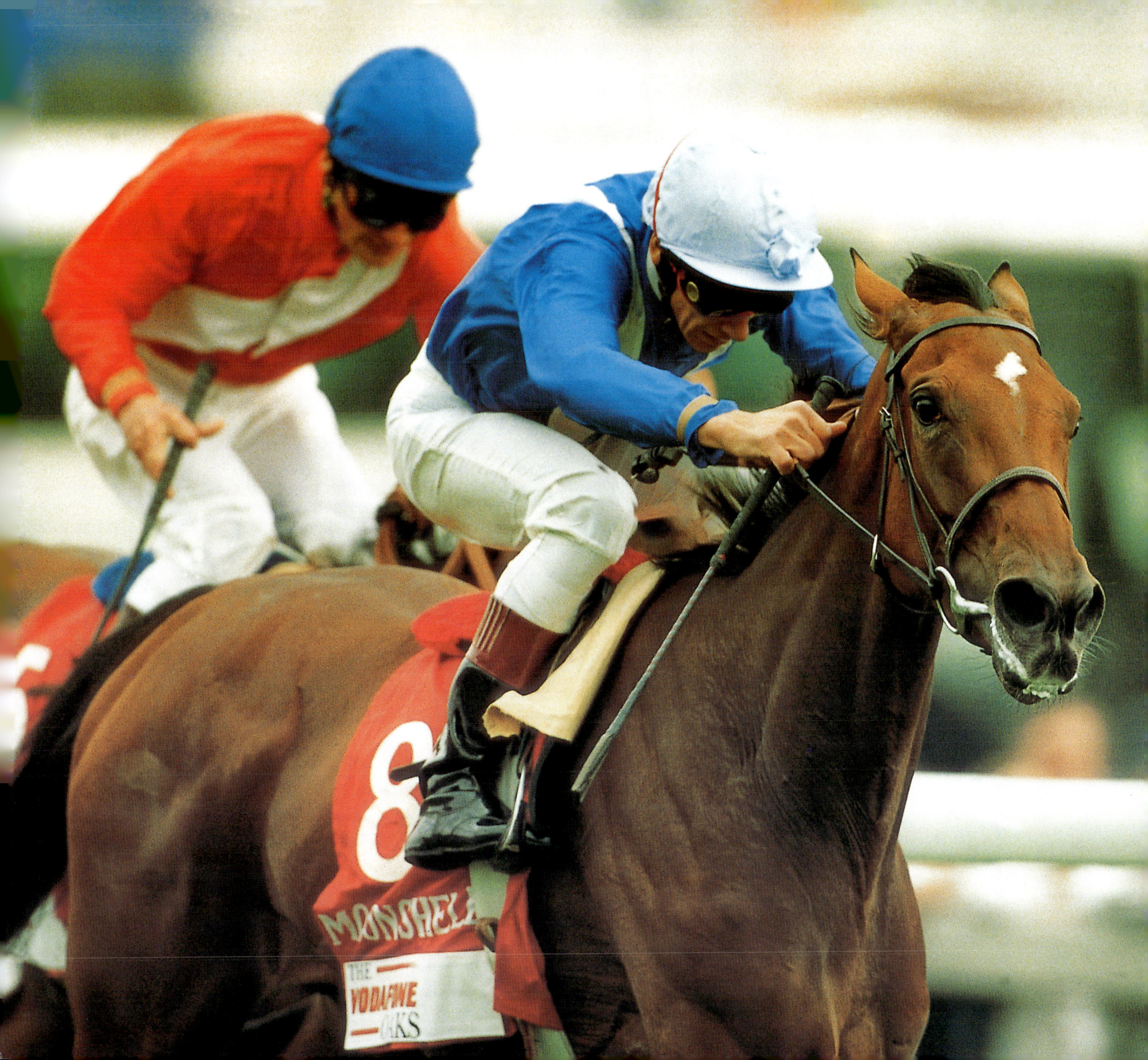
8
MOONSHEL
THE
VODAFONE
OAKS

Mtoto

b. c by Busted — Amazer (Mincio)

Mtoto was always a horse which connections thought would improve as he matured, and this certainly proved to be the case. He was campaigned in pattern company throughout his three-year-old season, finishing in the frame in the Queen Elizabeth II Stakes and fifth in the King Edward VII Stakes, his only success being a maiden at Haydock.

The 110,000 Guinea yearling made his four-year-old reappeance in the Brigadier Gerard Stakes at Sandown, where, carrying condition, he was among the outsiders of an eight-horse field. Held up far off the pace much of the way, last as they entered the final turn, the colt produced a spectacular turn of foot which took him to the front in just two furlongs.

A similar success followed in the Prince of Wales's Stakes before Mtoto returned to Sandown for the Coral-Eclipse. Derby winner Reference Point set a strong gallop and proved extremely hard to overhaul. The duo fought a head-to-head battle in the last 400 metres, which the older horse only going on the last furlong.

Despite a lack of race fitness Mtoto subsequently ran a credible fourth behind Trempolino in the Prix de l'Arc de Triomphe.

The following summer it was an even more complete looking animal who paraded at Goodwood prior to his winning reappearance in the voided Festival Stakes in May. This false start was soon forgotten when, as odds-on favourite, Mtoto accounted for three rivals in the Prince of Wales's Stakes at Royal Ascot, his second success in that event, again his final stepping stone toward the Coral-Eclipse.

At Sandown, Mtoto overcome a poor start and, in usual fashion, came with a sustained late run to claim the honours by a neck.

It takes a top-class animal to complete a Coral-Eclipse-King George double, the likes of Brigadier Gerard, Mill Reef and Mtoto's sire, Busted. Given a perfect ride by Michael Roberts, Sheikh Ahmed's champion unleashed his devastating turn of foot to take up the running one furlong out.

After success in the Select Stakes at Goodwood in September, Mtoto returned to Longchamp for the Prix de l'Arc de Triomphe. Again the colt was held up, but as the time came to launch his run the colt was momentarily boxed in. When he did find room, he kicked on and made ground with every stride on the leader, Tony Bin, going down by just a neck.

MTOTO (b. 1983)	Busted (b. 1983)	Crepello	Donatello II
			Crepascule
		Sans Le Sou	Vimy
			Martial Loan
	Amazer (b. 1967)	Mincio	Relic
			Merise
		Alzara	Alycidon
			Zabara

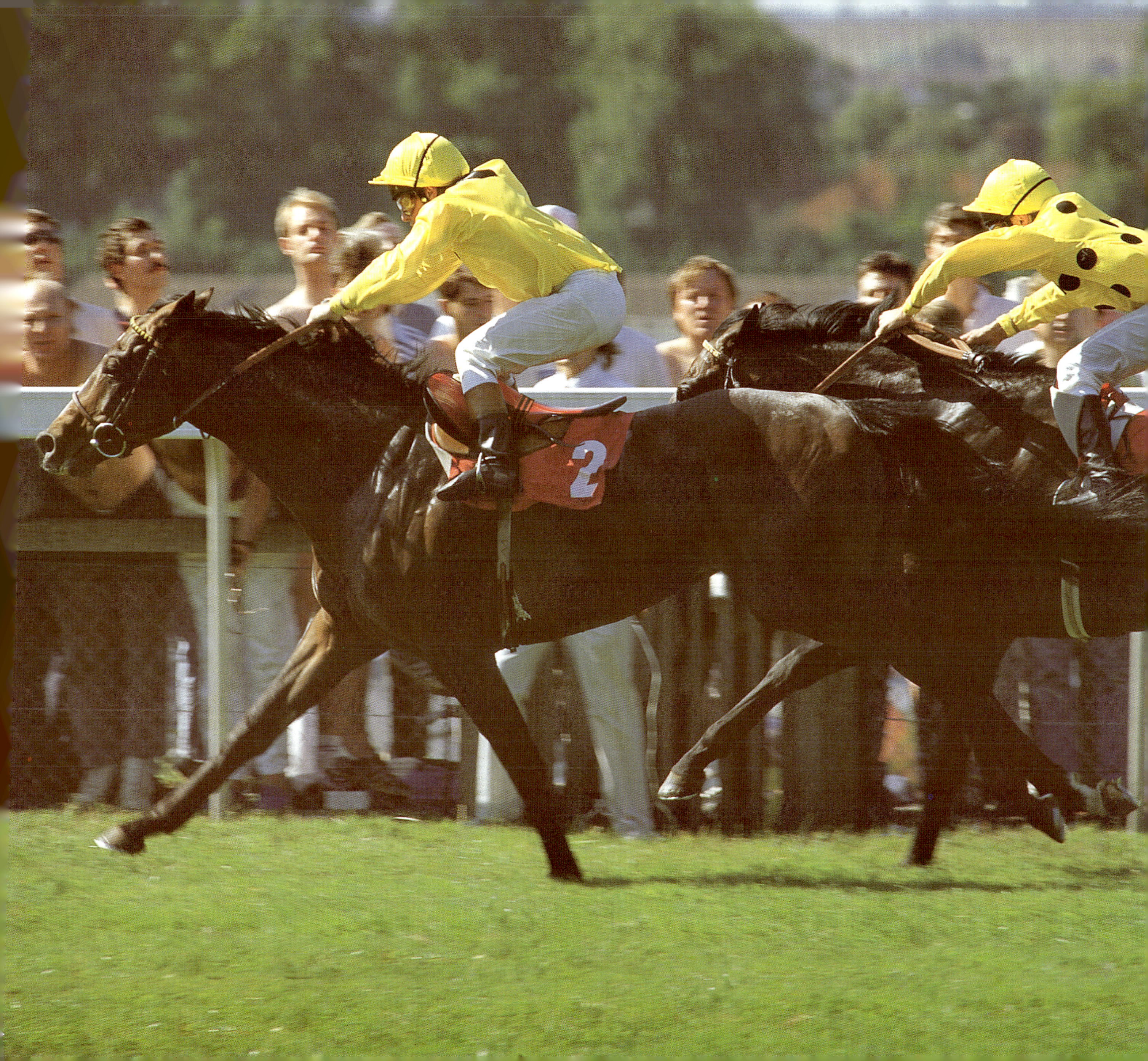
2

Mubtaker

ch. c by Silver Hawk — Gazayil (Irish River)

At two, Mubtaker was second in a small race at Deauville, while he won his first start as a three-year-old, in a maiden, by eight lengths. This was followed by a third in a Doncaster listed race.

It was as a four-year-old that Mubtaker began to bloom under trainer Marcus Tregoning, winning three races from eight starts, including the Festival Stakes and two Newmarket listed events.

After wintering in Dubai Mubtaker ran just twice that season, winning the Geoffrey Freer Stakes at Newbury, a race that was to become his.

The six-year-old repaid his connections decision to keep him in training in style. After picking up injury in Dubai over the winter, he returned to the track to claim the Stevenson Stakes and then collect a second Geoffrey Freer. After an commanding five length success in the September Stakes at Kempton, Sheikh Hamdan passed on lesser targets and decided on a bold entry in the Prix de l'Arc de Triomphe. The French Blue Riband went to Dalakhani, but the colt had to dig very deep to fight off a brave challenge by Mubtaker. It was a top drawer performance by a horse who was still progressing.

Mubtaker did not have the best 2004, but still achieved the remarkable feat of winning the Geoffrey Freer for the third time. He completed his seven-year-old campaign with a fourth place in the Group 1 Canadian International.

He returned to action early the following season but took a while to find his form. He was a gallant second when seeking a fourth victory in the Geoffrey Freer and it was not until his fourth start of the campaign, the March Stakes at Goodwood in August, that he won again. He followed that up with another Listed win before adding the Group 3 Cumberland Lodge Stakes.

In 2006, he made a winning return at his beloved Newbury in the John Porter but disaster was to strike and he was euthanised after a gallops accident.

	Roberto	Hail To Reason
Silver Hawk (b. 1979)		Bramalea
	Gris Vitesse	Amerigo
MUBTAKER (CH. 1997)		Matchiche II
	Irish River	Riverman
Gazayil (ch. 1985)		Irish Star
	Close Comfort	Far North
		Caterina

Mubtaker (right) works on the Nad Al Sheba track with stablemate Nayef

Sheikh Rashid bin Mohammed Al Maktoum

Five successive times Champion Owner in his homeland and increased success in Britain in recent years have seen Sheikh Rashid bin Mohammed Al Maktoum rise quickly to prominence as a racehorse owner. His all black and all gold colours were well recognised in the UAE until replaced last year by all burgundy red silks.

In Europe it is the gold silks which in 2006 were carried to Royal Ascot victory for the first time by Hellvelyn who won the Group 2 Coventry Stakes, the opening race of the meeting. The horse has won all three of his starts to date and is prominent in the market for the 2000 Guineas of 2007 - all a far cry from Sheikh Rashid's first UK winner in 2001, Nobelist in a Lingfield seller!

Everyone who deals with Sheikh Rashid in racing, be it trainer, jockey or fellow owners, all agree that his knowledge and passion for racing is remarkable. His retained jockey, Ted Durcan once said: "I am sure Sheikh Rashid knows the pedigree, rating and form of all of his horses - of not every horse in training in the UAE. His knowledge and memory are amazing."

He has enjoyed tremendous success in the UAE with both Satish Seemar and Mazin Al Kurdi and it is Seemar who now has the reins at Sheikh Rashid's Millennium Stables.

He saw his colours carried to Dubai Duty Free victory in 2000 by the Saeed bin Suroor-trained Rhythm Band and in 2005 Mike De Kock's Grand Emporium won the Godolphin Mile in Sheikh Rashid's black colours. Parole Board, Estimraar and Cherry Pickings have been three of his other standard bearers in recent seasons with Big Easy and Velte among his Arabian leading lights. He has seen his colours carried to victory well over 200 times in the UAE over the last five seasons.

An accomplished horseman, he has ridden six winners in amateur races in the UAE, he is better known as a leading Endurance rider. On the Endurance circuit he has won races in the UAE, as well as Spain, Switzerland, Ireland, Italy, France, Syria, Australia, Jordan, Egypt and Kuwait.

With such determination and such affinity with the horse, there is no telling just how far he will progress - either as an owner or on horseback.

PARMIGIANI
SWISS WATCHES PAR EXCELLENCE

Kalpa XL Tourbillon Platinum
Hand winding. One week power reserve
18ct gold base, Javelot - shaped hands

damas
Les Exclusives
Toll Free: 800 4916

www.damasjewellery.com

Mutafaweq
b. c by Silver Hawk — The Caretaker (Caerleon)

Staying star Mutafaweq would prove a top-notch representative for Godolphin, winning one Classic and in three different countries. But more than that, he was proven to have a level of determination that is rare even in the mighty Thoroughbred.

He began as a juvenile for Saeed bin Suroor, finishing second in a small race at Yarmouth and then winning a 23-runner Newmarket maiden well.

After wintering in Dubai the colt continued his winning ways in a Doncaster race, going on to show class form with a two length success in the King Edward VII Stakes. A staying-on fourth in the Great Voltigeur behind Fantastic Light was no disgrace, and bin Suroor was persuaded to try him in the St Leger. In the final English Classic of the season Mutafaweq would emerge not only as victor, but put in perhaps the bravest performance by a Thoroughbred ever witnessed on British television.

On an unseasonally warm day, Mutafaweq took on an above average St Leger field. With three furlongs remaining Ramruma had made her move and Godolphin's Adair was also thereabouts. The trio were abreast for a moment, while Mutafaweq began to edge on. With a furlong remaining Mutafaweq was in the lead and still edging forward, but Ramruma continued to press on. The Godolphin runner had to dig very deep indeed and was one length to the good as they passed the post. The drama was not over, however, and for a time television cameras and the crowd held their breath. Mutafaweq was distressed and seemingly in trouble, and only some sharply administered veterinary care prevented a possible tragedy. Mutafaweq had put so much heart into winning his race that there was simply nothing left. By all standards, his performance was extraordinary.

He was not seen on a racecourse for eight months after Doncaster, reappearing with a third in the Tattersalls Rogers Gold Cup and a below-par seventh in the Hardwicke Stakes. Two subsequent outings in Germany brought one success, before a third in the Irish St Leger. Mutafaweq's 2000 was rounded off with victory in the Canadian International Stakes.

The following season much was expected. After a dissapointment in the Dubai Sheema Classic, he made all to claim the Coronation Cup, a race previously won by the likes of Daylami, Swain and Singspiel.

	Roberto	Hail To Reason
Silver Hawk (b. 1979)		Bramalea
	Gris Vitesse	Amerigo
MUTAWAFEQ (b. 1996)		Matchiche II
	Caerleon	Nijinsky
The Caretaker (b. 1987)		Foreseer
	Go Feather Go	Go Marching
		Feather Bed

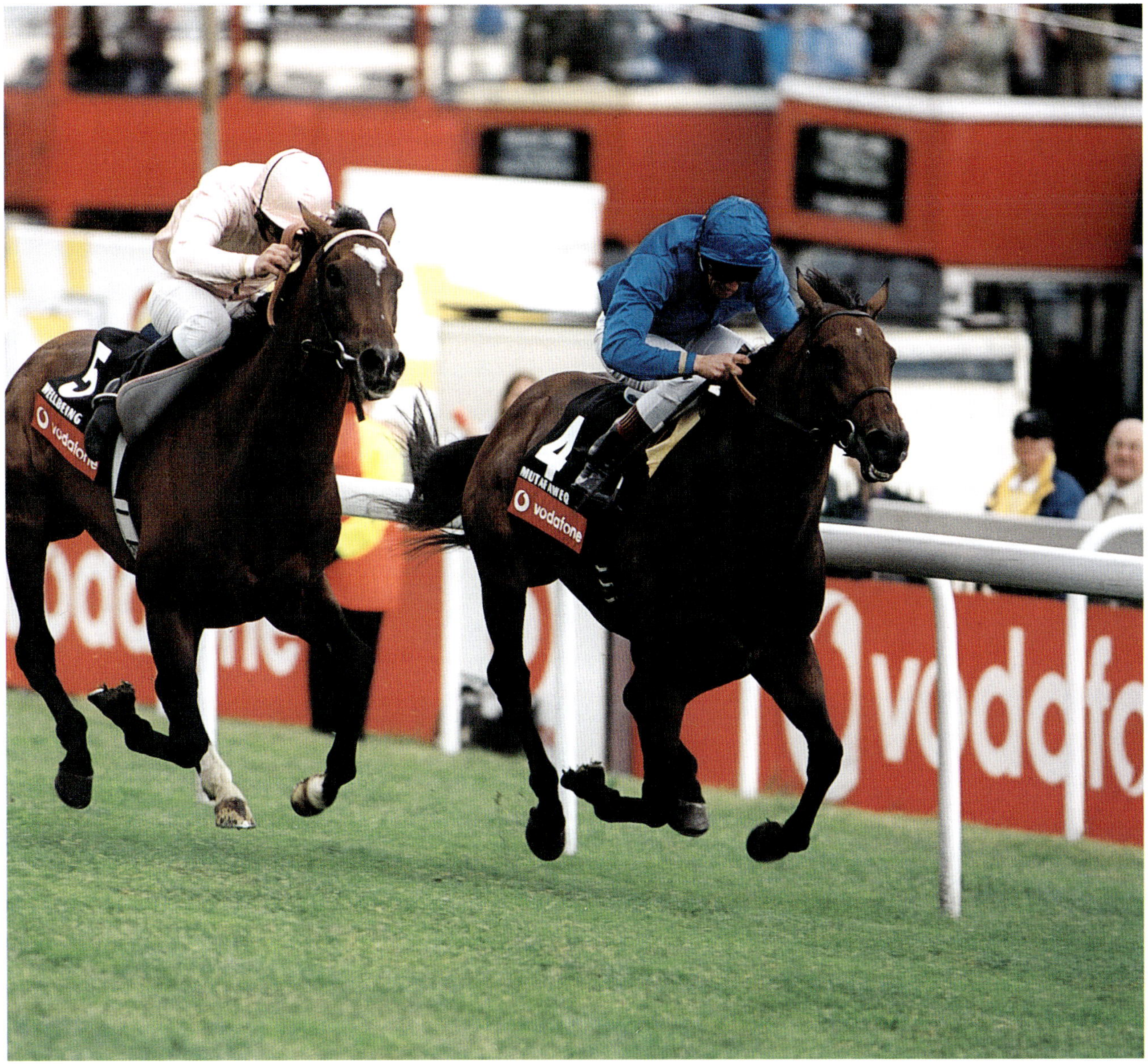
5
WELLBEING
vodafone
4
MUTAFAWEQ
vodafone

Mutamam

b. c by Darshaan — Petal Girl (Caerleon)

Mutamam was a late bloomer who was campaigned cleverly during his early years on the racecourse. Winning two of his three starts as a juvenile, the colt came into his own during the second half of his three-year-old season. After an excellent second in the Predominate Stakes and a fully anticipated poor performance in the Epsom Derby, a mid-summer break of nearly two months helped Mutamam mature. .

His comeback race saw him make short work of a small field in a minor Sandown race, before trainer Alec Steward raised him in class to claim the Rose of Lancaster Stakes from the useful Teapot Row. Next time out he completed a treble in fine fashion, trouncing his opponents in the Select Stakes at Goodwood. Connections were suitably impressed with this to raise him in class again for the Dubai Champion Stakes, where he finished three lengths off the winner in fourth.

Such was Mutamam's apparent progress and potential that he was transferred to Dubai and the care of Godolphin. However, he failed to blossom as expected and raced only once in 1999, when showing little in the Dubai Turf Classic at Nad Al Sheba. By the spring of 2000, the colt was back with his former trainer, Alec Stewart, and at this point he began to emerge in no uncertain fashion as a top-class animal.

After a year off the track, he re-emerged with a second in a small allowance race at Newmarket and went on to claim a weak contest at Goodwood. These outings readied him for the Hardwicke Stakes, and at Royal Ascot Mutamam revealed that he was still a force to be reckoned with, producing a fine third behind Fruits of Love. Mutamam went on to record back-to-back successes in the Group Two September Stakes and Group Three Cumberland Stakes, before shipping to the US for the Breeders' Cup Turf.

Churchill Downs was to prove him the genuine article, and Mutamam finished fourth, less than one length behind the winner after a game late run. His astonishing improvement led Sheikh Hamdan to keep his star in training as a six-year-old and the decision was more than rewarded. Following success in the Prince of Wales's Stakes at Royal Ascot he was unplaced in the King George on unsuitably firm ground, before again winning the September Stakes. As a finale for the season, he returned to North America to win the Group One Canadian International at Woodbine.

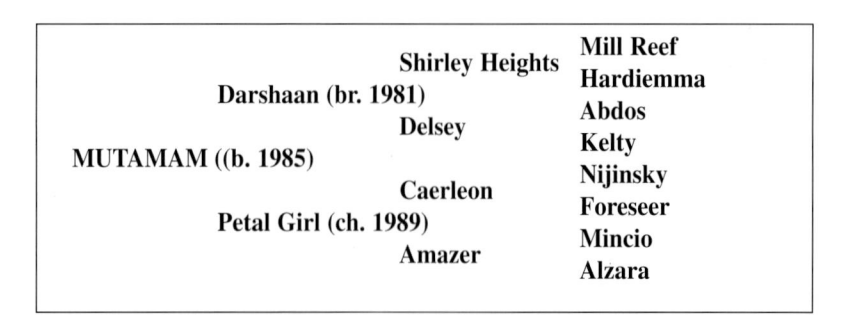

MUTAMAM ((b. 1985)	Darshaan (br. 1981)	Shirley Heights — Mill Reef / Hardiemma
		Delsey — Abdos / Kelty
	Petal Girl (ch. 1989)	Caerleon — Nijinsky / Foreseer
		Amazer — Mincio / Alzara

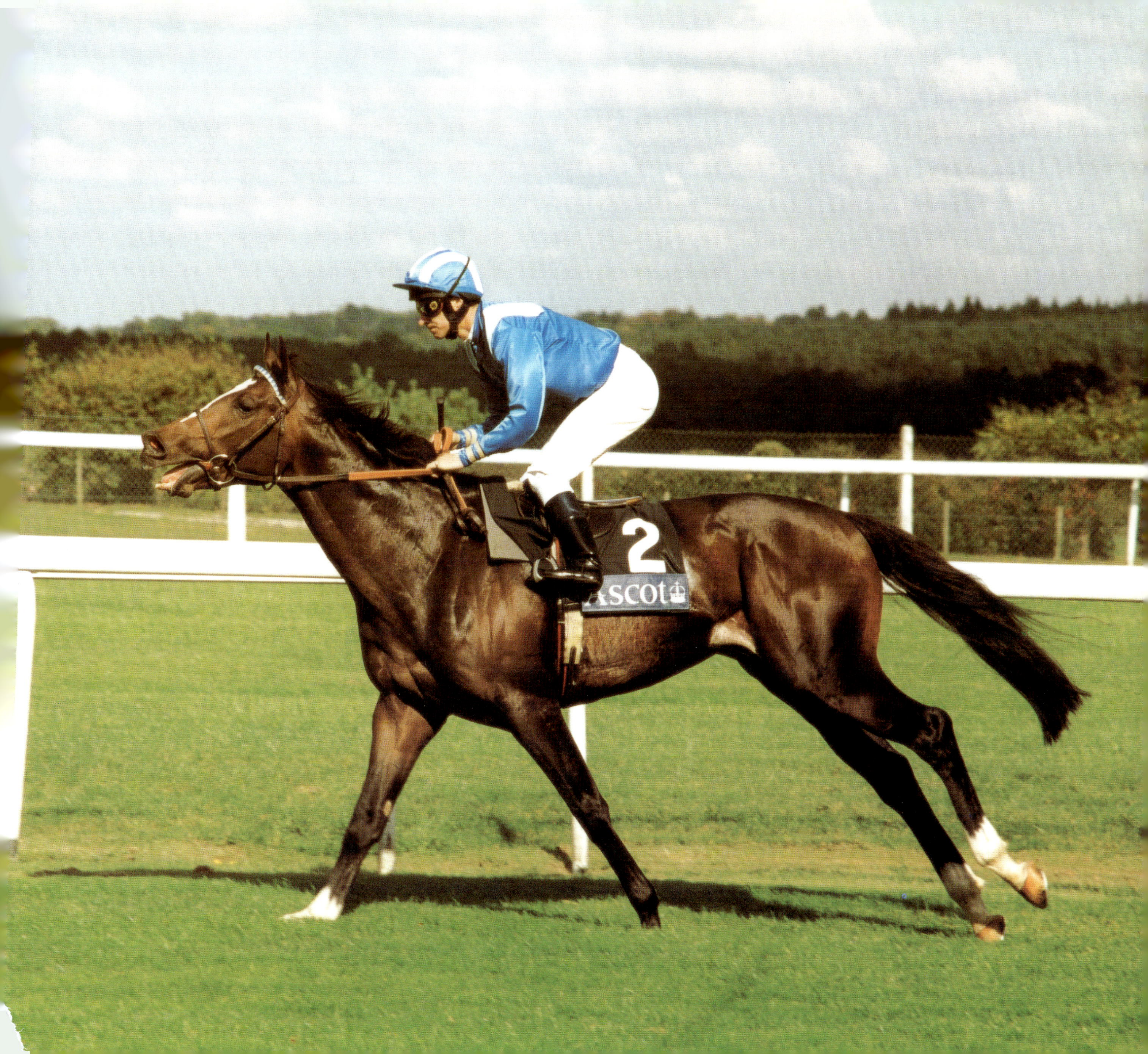
2
Ascot

Nashwan

ch. c by Blushing Groom — Height Of Fashion (Bustino)

Coming from a decidedly black type family, Nashwan appeared twice as a juvenile, in a Newbury maiden in August and two months later in the Autumn Stakes at Ascot, both outings resulting in a win.

Possessing a long, fluent stride, the colt was thought to be something special—as well he proved to be as a three-year-old—but not before a January training setback had ruled him out of a Guineas prep race. Having been all but written off, Nashwan came back into contention purely on his sparkling home work. At Newmarket the colt was positioned close up on the pace by Willie Carson and with two furlongs remaining went on to record a length and a half success. The winning time was the fastest recorded since the introduction of electronic timing in the 1950s.

Not since Nijinsky had a horse won the Guineas-Derby double, but such precedents failed to intimidate connections who saddled their star as favourite at Epsom. Settled mid-division, Nashwan was placed fourth as they rounded Tattenham Corner. Two out Nashwan was challenging the leader and he cruised into the lead, going on to win by five lengths. Nashwan's win also marked a first Epsom Derby success for Sheikh Hamdan.

The colt reappeared in the Eclipse Stakes at Sandown and such was the class of the field that the press billed this as the 'race of the century.' But Nashwan put paid to any thoughts of a memorable finish however, when, in the space of one furlong, he wiped out a six-length deficit to the front-runner and went on two furlongs from home to notch another rousing success.

The extent of Nashwan's exertions at Sandown became apparent at Ascot two weeks later in the King George VI and Queen Elizabeth Diamond Stakes, when the colt was joined at the head of affairs by Cacoethes, 400 metres out. The Derby winner was actually headed briefly before going on by a neck at the line.

Nashwan was then routed toward the Prix de l'Arc de Triomphe, via the Prix Niel, but an unexplained poor third in his prep race proved to be his final outing. In winning all but his last start as a three-year-old, Nashwan entered the record books with an unprecedented Guineas, Derby, Eclipse and King George four-timer.

NASHWAN (ch. 1986)	**Blushing Groom (ch. 1974)**	Red God → Nasrullah / Spring Run
		Runaway Bride → Wild Risk / Aimee
	Height of Fashion (b. 1979)	Bustino → Busted / Ship Yard
		Highclere → Queen's Hussar / Highligh

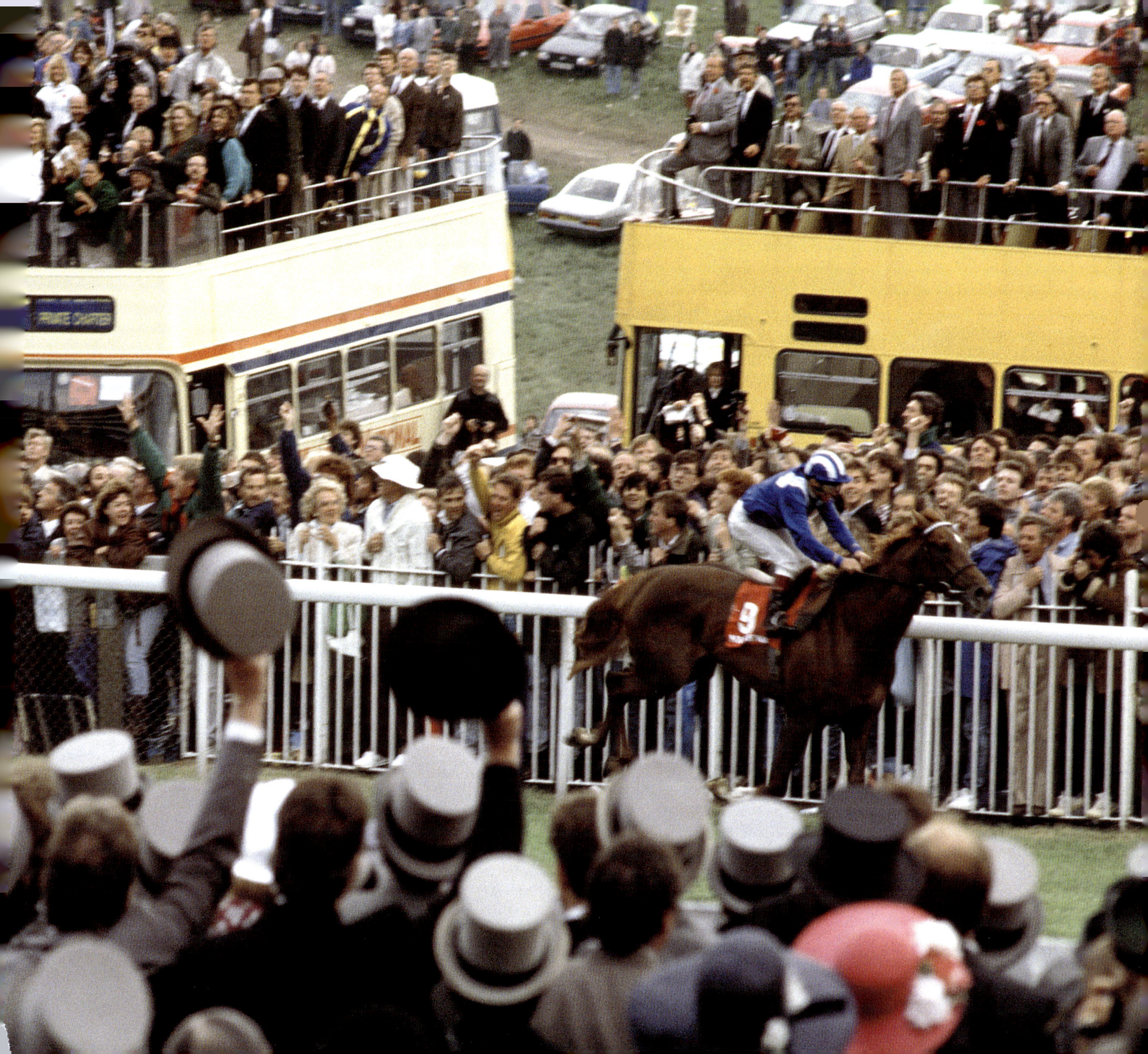
9

Nayef
b. c by Gulch - Height of Fashion (Bustino)

The Nayef story is a sentimental one. He was the last colt produced by Height of Fashion, Shadwell Farm-based mare of legend who also produced the great Nashwan and Unfuwain. Height of Fashion passed away in 2000, while 2002 saw both Nashwan and Unfuwain die relatively young.

Nayef was a late foal, born in May 1998. When his dam died, Nayef was an unraced juvenile with a big reputation. He remained unbeaten as a two-year-old, winning at Newbury and Ascot.

Nayef returned next season for the Craven Stakes with a third, followed by a disappointing eighth in the 2000 Guineas and a third in the Gordon Stakes.

Finally he got off the mark in the Lancaster Stakes. Winning by five lengths. A fascicle six length success in the Select Stakes was followed by a win in the Cumberland Lodge Stakes. He completed a smart four- timer with a smooth win in the Dubai Champion Stakes.

Sheikh Hamdan then entered his star in the Dubai World Cup. Switched late to the Dubai Sheema Classic, Nayef was held off the pace early by Richard Hills and glided to victory from an international cast.

After his slow start as a three-year-old, big things were expected in 2003. In rain softened conditions he finished fourth in the Tattersalls Gold Cup, followed by fourth in the Prince of Wales's Stakes. He finally returned to his best in the King George VI and Queen Elizabeth Diamond Stakes, finishing second to Golan.

Connections believed that Nayef was almost there and took on Golan again in the Juddmonte, hitting the front early. Golan challenged over the final two furlongs, but Sheikh Hamdan's colt stayed on to his task and claimed revenge.

He began 2003 with a good third in the Dubai World Cup behind Moon Ballad, despite the fact that his action at Nad Al Sheba suggested that he was not best suited by a sand surface.

The highlight of his final campaign on track was a commanding two and a half lengths success in the Prince of Wales's Stakes at Royal Ascot, beating the likes of Rakta, Islington, Fabrav, Grandera and Dubai World Cup winner Moon Ballad

Gulch (b. 1984))	Mr Prospector	Raise A Native
		Gold Digger
	Jameela	Rambunctious
NAYEF (B. 1998)		Asbury Mary
Height of Fashion (b. 1979)	Bustino	Busted
		Ship Yard
	Highclere	Queen's Hussar
		Highlight

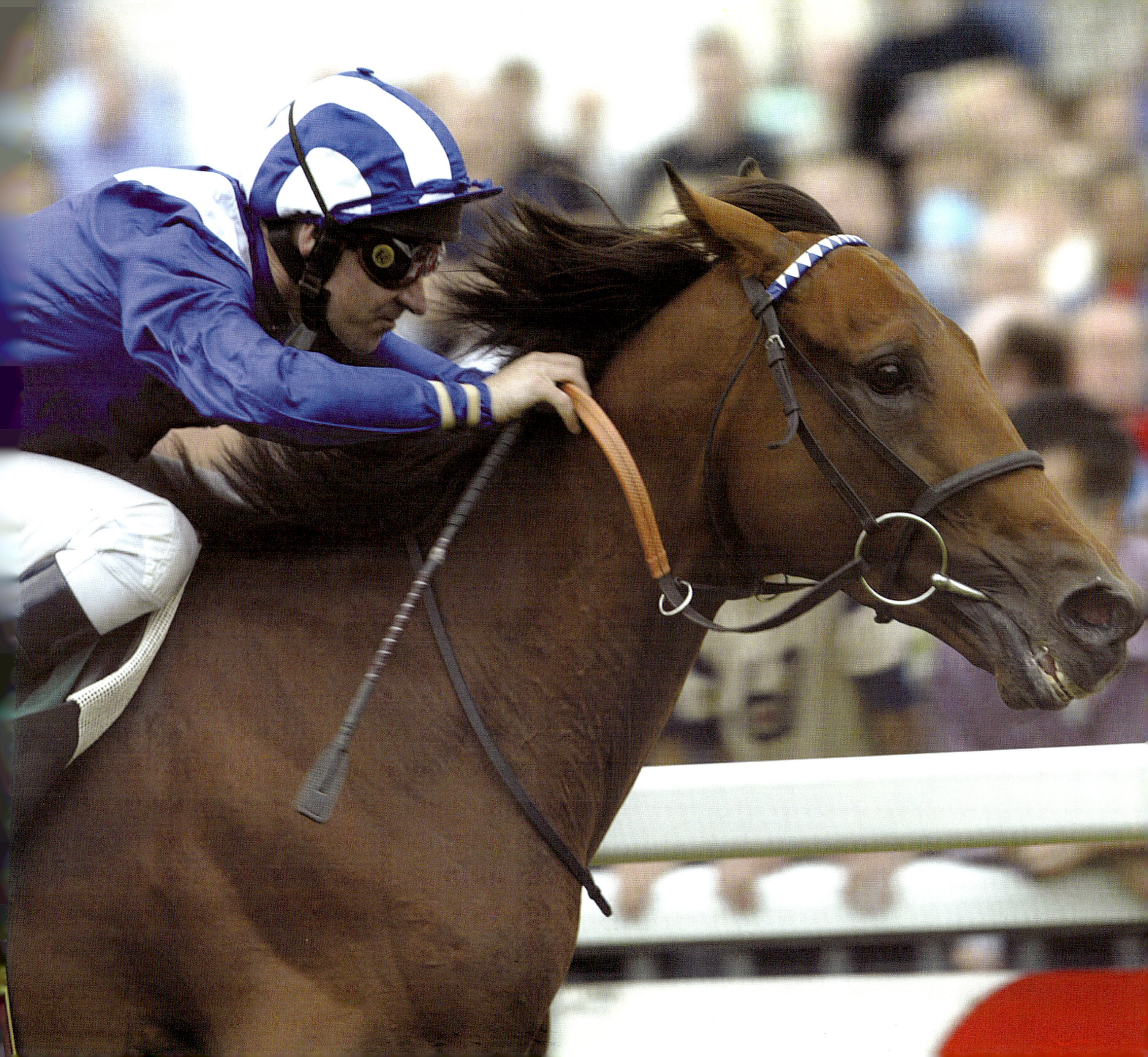

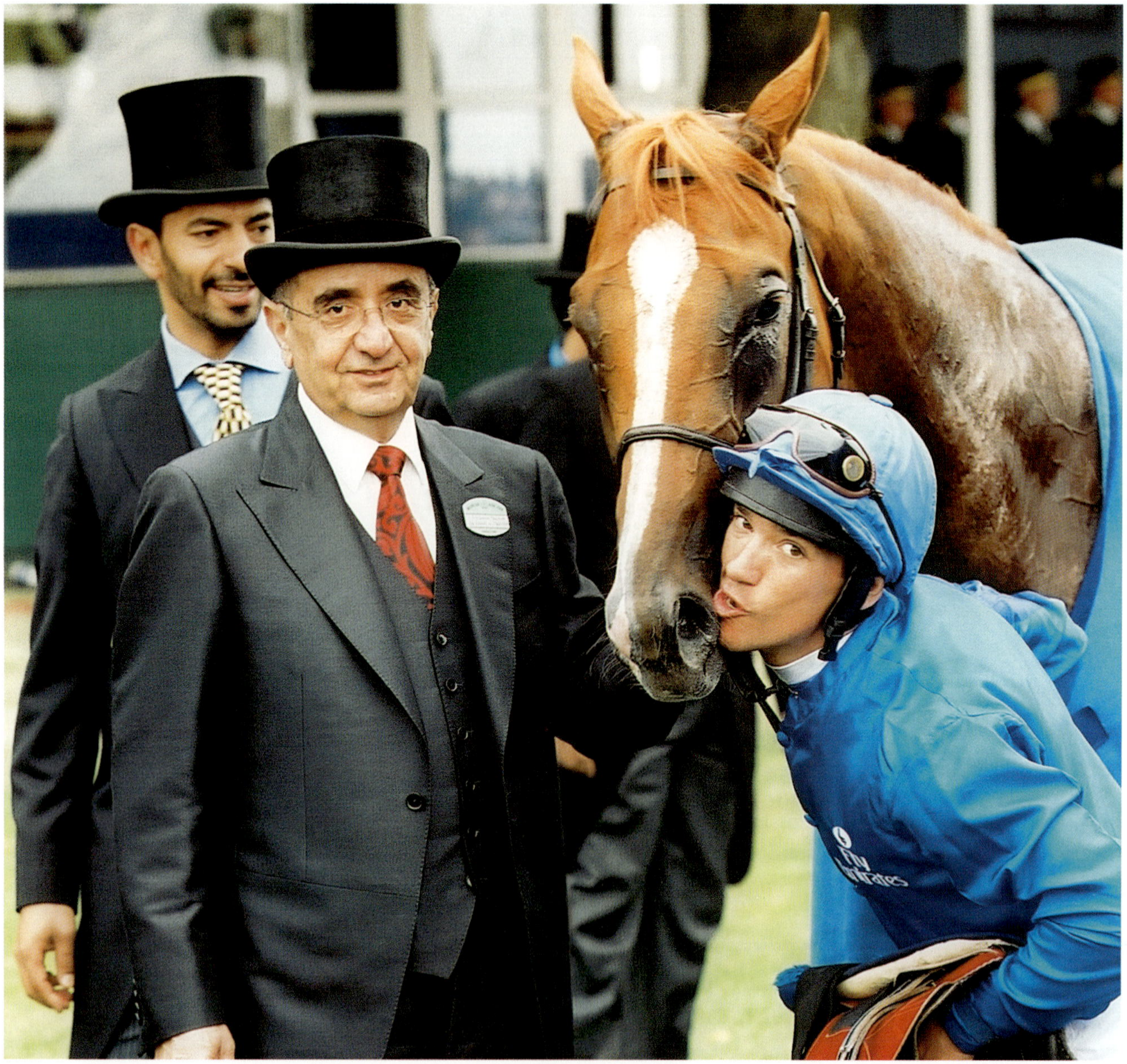

The Godolphin Enigma

Balanchine led the way. She was the first horse to capture a Group One victory for Godolphin. In 1994, she triumphed in the Epsom Oaks and subsequently recorded an epic victory against the colts in the Irish Derby.

Suitably inspired, Godolphin enjoyed a spectacular year in 1995, winning Group One races in five countries. The unbeaten Lammtarra won the Derby at Epsom, although history was against him. The colt suffered from illness in the prologue to England's pre-eminent Classic, yet he fought to a majestic victory, breaking the track record in the process. Lammtarra went on to record further impressive triumphs in the King George VI and Queen Elizabeth Diamond Stakes and the Prix de l'Arc de Triomphe.

In May 1995, Godolphin enjoyed an unprecedented weekend of Group One wins around the globe with Flagbird (Italy), Heart Lake (Japan) and Vettori (France).

In 1996, Mark of Esteem added the English 2000 Guineas and Queen Elizabeth II Stakes to Godolphin's ever-growing Group One haul. Halling, simply outstanding, won three Group One races, including the Coral-Eclipse and the Juddmonte International for a second successive year. Medaaly's victory in the Racing Post Trophy secured Saeed bin Suroor's first Trainers' Championship in the United Kingdom.

In 1997 and 1998, Swain posted consecutive victories in the King George VI and Queen Elizabeth Diamond Stakes, and Cape Verdi opened 1998 for Godolphin by winning the English, 1000 Guineas. Also in that year, Cape Cross won the Juddmonte Lockinge Stakes and Central Park triumphed in the Italian Derby – another first.

Kayf Tara landed his first Group One success in 1998 but went on to dominate for two more seasons before he retired in 2000. A specialist at long distance events, he won the Irish St Leger in 1998 and 1999 and the Gold Cup at Royal Ascot in 1998 and 2000.

A remarkable season, 1999 opened with Almutawakel winning the Dubai World Cup, sponsored by Emirates, in March. The year continued victoriously through to November, when Daylami crowned an exemplary campaign by winning the Breeders' Cup Turf at Gulfstream Park.

A perfect example of Godolphin's global ambitions, Daylami scored four Group One victories that year, including another win for Godolphin in the King George VI and Queen Elizabeth Diamond Stakes at Ascot. He was honoured with the prestigious American Eclipse Award as Champion Male Turf Horse. When the year closed, Godolphin had amassed 18 Group/Grade One races with 13 individual horses.

The year 2000 ushered forward a horse that had been named for the moment. Godolphin's founder, Sheikh Mohammed, was convinced that Dubai Millennium would be a horse like no other. And having won two Group Ones the previous year, that faith was vindicated in the most spectacular fashion in March 2000. Dubai Millennium put one of the great performances of recent decades when he romped to victory in the Dubai World Cup. He went on to demolish a high-class field in the Prince of Wales's Stakes at Royal Ascot by eight lengths.

Meanwhile, Mutafaweq traveled from Europe to Canada to record his second Group One triumph in 2000. He followed up his win in the WGZ Bank Deutschland Preis with success in the Canadian International at Woodbine.

Fantastic Light posted two Group One wins in 2000, but that was just a prelude to a brilliant season for Godolphin in 2001. He began by winning the Tattersalls Gold Cup at the Curragh and went on to win three further Group One races: the Prince of Wales's Stakes, the Irish Champion Stakes and the Breeders' Cup Turf at Belmont Park. He was decorated as Cartier Horse of the Year and, for the second successive year, his international exploits won him the Emirates World Series.

Other notable performances in 2001 came from Noverre in the Sussex Stakes at Goodwood, and Sakhee in the Juddmonte International at York ahead of his six-length victory in the Prix de l'Arc de Triomphe at Longchamp. On a memorable Breeders' Cup Day in America, Godolphin sent out Tempera to win the Breeders' Cup Juvenile Fillies

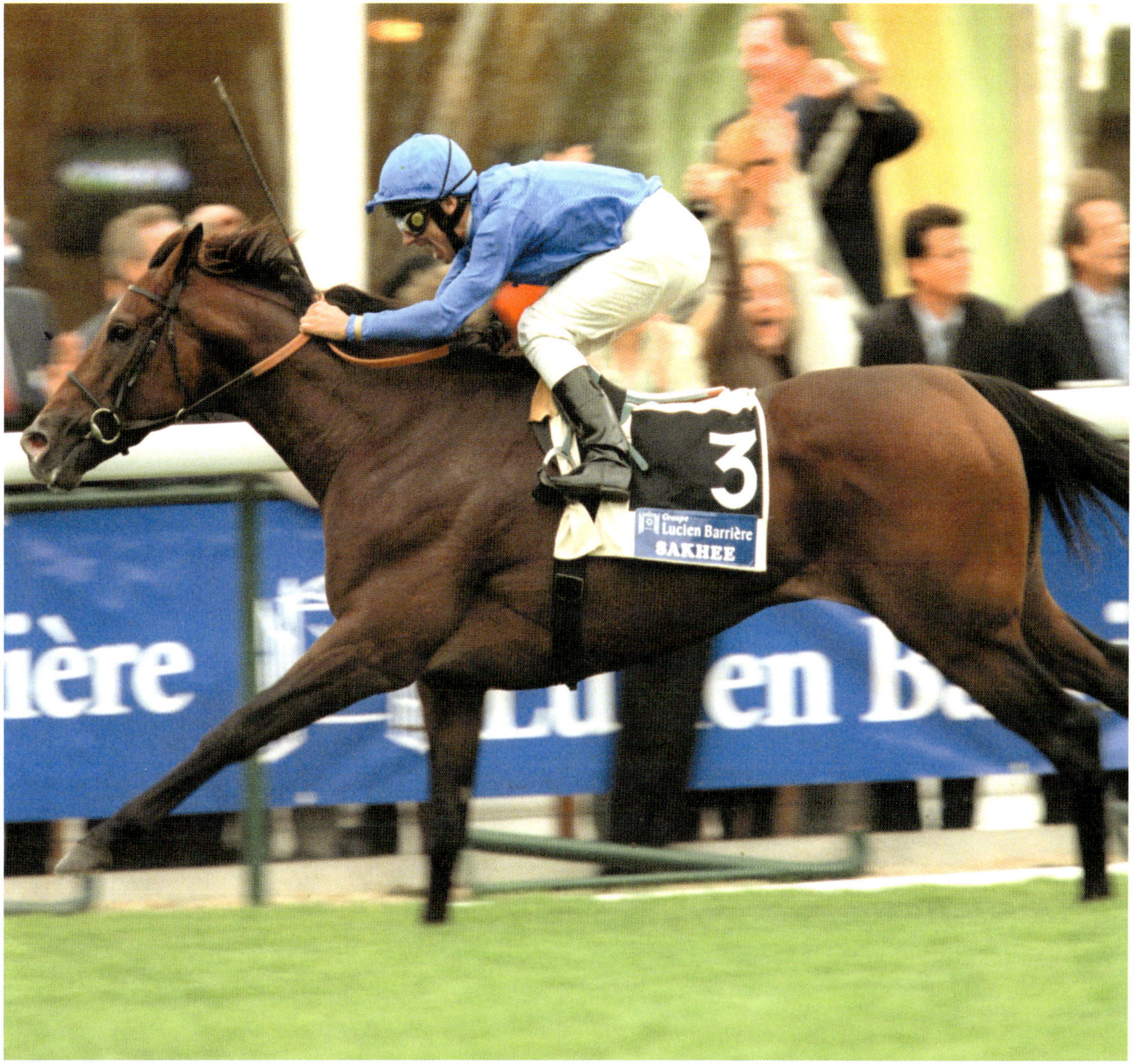
3
Groupe
Lucien Barrière
SAKHEE
ière
en B

before Sakhee came within inches of completing the Prix l'Arc de Triomphe/Breeders' Cup Classic double. The feat had never previously been attempted. Also that year, Kutub won Group One races in Germany and Italy; Slickly in France and Italy.

The scale of Godolphin's global adventure was the abiding memory of 2002. The stable embarked on a worldwide campaign that would culminate in Group or Grade One triumphs in eight different countries. As ever, it all started in Dubai, where Street Cry, Marienbard, Grandera and Imperial Gesture all reappeared at Nad Al Sheba. In the $6 million Dubai World Cup, Street Cry powered clear of a cosmopolitan field while Marienbard evolved into a destructive galloper who closed his career by winning the Prix de l'Arc de Triomphe.

Meanwhile, Grandera traversed the globe, running in Dubai, Hong Kong, Singapore, England, Ireland and Australia in a campaign that bore eloquent testimony to Godolphin's global outlook.

His best performance came in winning the Irish Champion Stakes. And Kazzia, a dual Classic heroine in 2002, went on to a win at the highest level in America, where Godolphin enjoyed other high-profile triumphs with Jilbab, Imperial Gesture, E Dubai and Essence of Dubai.

The milestone of 100 Group/Grade One wins was achieved during the 2003 campaign, which included Moon Ballad's barnstorming win in the Dubai World Cup. It was a memorable night for Godolphin at Nad Al Sheba with Sulamani also winning the Group One Dubai Sheema Classic. He went on to notch further victories in the Arlington Million – the stable's 100th Group/Grade One win – and the Turf Classic Invitational. In the meantime, Dubai Destination's breathtaking triumph in the Group One Queen Anne Stakes at Royal Ascot represented the definite performance at Europe's most prestigious racing occasion.

Saeed bin Suroor would be champion trainer in the United Kingdom for the fourth time in 2004, when Godolphin captured 11 Group One races. Refuse To Bend and Sulamani netted a brace apiece, while Papineau's victory in the Group One Gold Cup at Royal Ascot was one of six for Godolphin at the five-day extravaganza. Doyen later ran away with the King George VI and Queen Elizabeth Diamond Stakes and subsequently received multiple awards for his achievements.

However, pride of place belonged to Dubawi, a two-year-old colt from the only crop sired by Dubai Millennium. Dubawi's unbeaten streak in 2004 included the Group One National Stakes at the Curragh. Dubawi would advance to the rank of a Classic winner in 2005 with an authorative victory in the Irish 2000 Guineas at the Curragh. It was a delicious moment for Godolphin, who had always maintained that Dubawi belonged in the highest class. However Dubawi would exceed that achievement when saddled for the Group One Prix Jacques le Marios at Deauville.

He was asked a big question, aligned, as he was, against Europe's top milers. The two pacemakers aside, the four remaining runners had collectively amassed 12 Group One races, yet Dubawi left them standing after a brilliantly executed tactical plan involving his pacemaker, Council Member in what was a particularly satisfying triumph for the Godolphin team.

Another miler of exalted ability was Shamardal, who racked up three Group One victories in a season that would yield nine in all for Godolphin. In an unprecedented month-long blitz, Shamardal landed the French 2000 Guineas, the French Derby and the St James's Palace Stakes at Royal Ascot. It was a tour de force unmatched by any other colt in 2005.

England was also the venue for a notable landmark. On October 19, at Nottingham, Highlander became Godolphin's 1,000th worldwide winner. And the stable gains extended to America once more, where Stellar Jayne confirmed her reputation as a top-flight older filly with a resounding score in the Grade One Ruffian Handicap at Belmont Park.

All told in 2005, Godolphin saddled more than 100 winners for prize-money earnings in excess of US$9.3 million. Beyond doubt, however, the headline horse was Dubawi, who proved himself a chip off the old block.

Like father, like son.

Godolphin statistics: Facts and Figures from 1992 to 2005:

• Godolphin's first runner was Cutwater at Nad Al Sheba on December 24, 1992. Godolphin's international operation started in 1994.

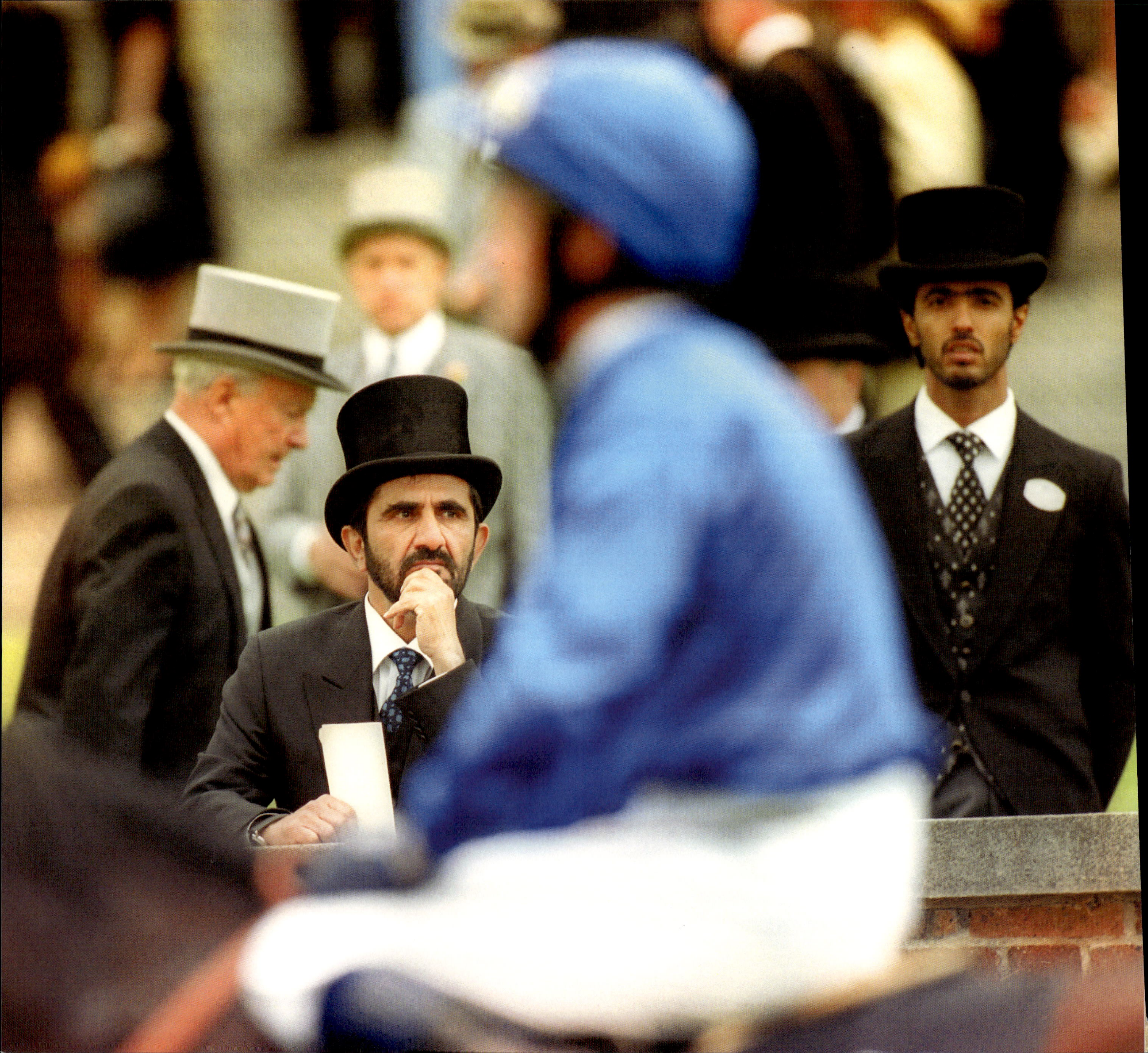

- Dubai Millennium, Halling and Kayf Tara have been the most successful Godolphin horses by number of wins, each winning nine races.

- Daylami and Fantastic Light have been the most successful Godolphin horses in Group or Grade One races, each winning six times at this level.

- Street Cry has been the most successful Godolphin horse with regard to prize money, earning approximately £3,500,000 or $5,150,000.

- In Dubai, Godolphin's home country, 380 individual horses have run on 863 occasions, resulting in 220 victories.

- The most successful racecourse for Godolphin has been at home at Nad Al Sheba in Dubai, with 200 wins coming from 795 runners.

- A total of 998 individual Godolphin horses have run on 4,093 occasions.

- The ratio of winners to runners is 55 per cent. Out of every 100 horses running for Godolphin, 55 have won at least once.

- The Godolphin Strike Rate (wins to runs) is 24.64 per cent

- Godolphin has had runners in 14 countries.

- Godolphin horses have run 115 racecourses.

- Godolphin horses have been ridden by 163 jockeys.

- Fankie Dettori is the most successful rider gaining 509 successes from 1,648 rides.

- Godolphin has run 264 horses in 544 Group or Grade One races.

- These Group or Grade One races have been staged in 12 different countries.

- Godolphin has won 124 Group or Grade One races with 64 individual horses.

- Godolphin's most successful year numerically was 2001 during which 133 races were won.

- The Godolphin horses who have run around the world are the progeny of 265 individual stallions.

Oh So Sharp
ch. f by Kris — Oh So Fair (Graustark)

Although a Triple Crown success of Guineas, Derby or Oaks and St Leger has become increasingly unlikely in recent years as priorities have changed, a trio of British Classic successes was considered the ultimate for any Thoroughbred for nearly two centuries. Up to 1985, only 15 colts and nine fillies, including greats such as Nijinsky and Meld, had managed this ultimate test.

In Oh So Sharp's juvenile season, Henry Cecil saddled her to win a minor maiden at Nottingham in August before routing her to the Solario Stakes at Sandown at the beginning of September. Lining up against several well-thought-of colts, Oh So Sharp justified confidence and showed herself a truly gifted racehorse. Settled just off the pace in the seven furlong contest, she was given her head in the straight, immediately opening up a smooth striding action which carried her into the lead in the final furlong.

Later the same month, Cecil entered her in the Hoover Fillies Mile where she again was favourite. Running just off the leader early in the race, Oh So Sharp hit the front as she entered the straight and looked every inch the winner.

Opening her three-year-old campaign with success in the Nell Gwyn Stakes, Oh So Sharp went off at 2:1 in the 1000 Guineas, but there were momentary doubts as she failed to pick up when asked for an effort in the dip. When she did respond just as they hit the rising ground, she was three lengths off the pace. Stretching toward the line she came with a tremendous burst of speed to win in the final stride.

Returning to the Newmarket gallops, she was reported to be working so well that speculation was rife. Connections were said to be looking seriously at taking on the colts in the Derby. In the event, however, the Oaks was selected. Running over a much more suitable trip, there was little doubt as to the outcome as soon as Oh So Sharp quickened two out and she drew away to record a superb six-length success.

She then went to Ascot for the King George VI and Queen Elizabeth Diamond Stakes, where she accounted for a top-class field including Irish Derby winner Law Society and Rainbow Quest, only to be caught in the final stages by Petoski. The mighty filly completed her remarkable season with success at Doncaster in the St Leger where, her stamina thoroughly tested, she finished three-quarters of a length to the good of Phardante.

OH SO SHARP (ch. 1982)	Kris (ch 1979)	Sharpen Up — Atan, Rocchetta
		Doubly Sure — Reliance II, Soft Angels
	Oh So Fair (b. 1967)	Graustark — Ribot, Flower Bowl
		Chandelle — Swaps, Malindi

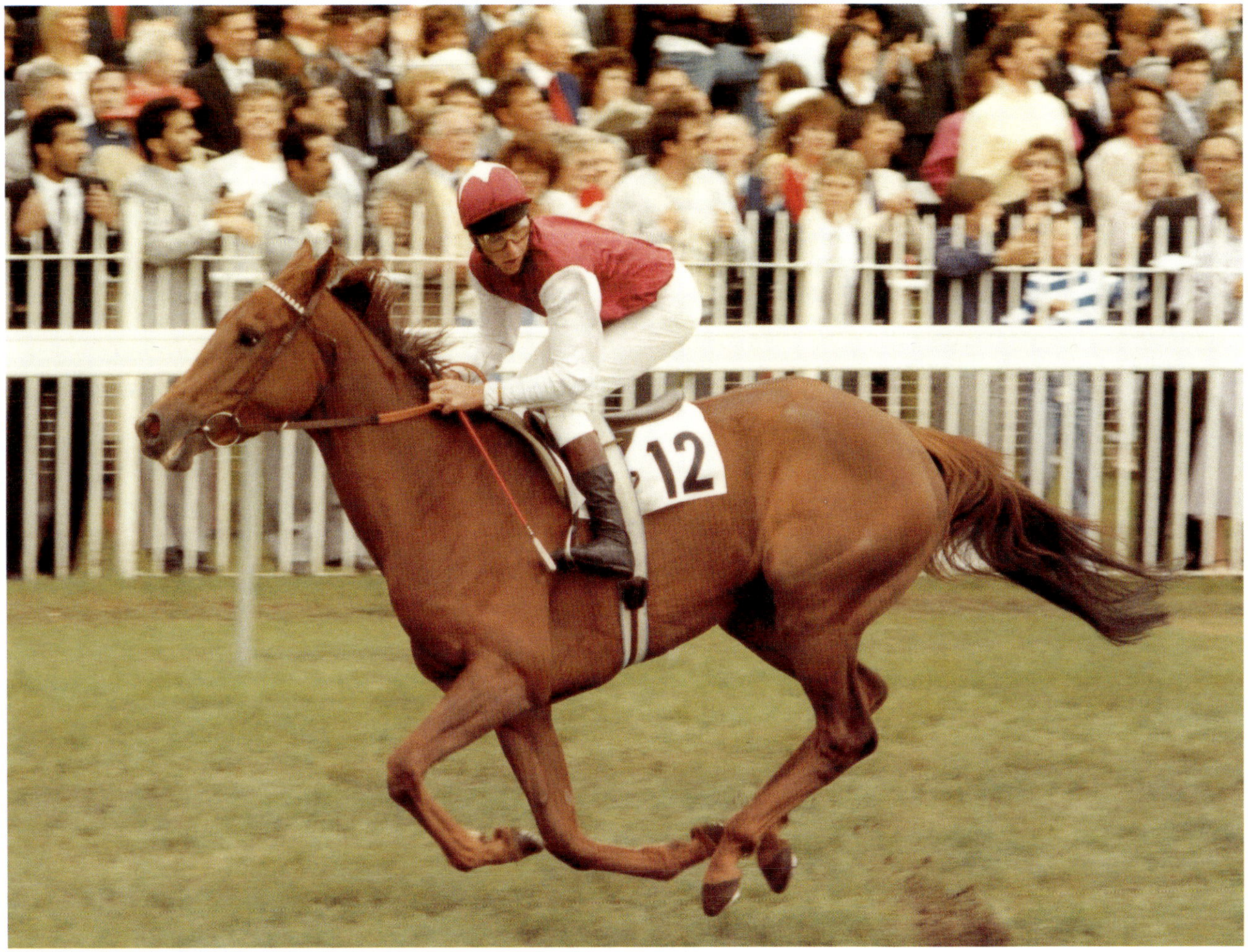
12

Old Vic
b. c by Sadler's Wells – Cockade (Derring-Do)

A 230,000 Guinea yearling from the first crop of Sadler's Wells, Old Vic ran once as a two-year-old, taking a Haydock maiden. Having developed well over the winter months, he returned to trounce his opponents in a Newbury race and on the basis of that commanding performance, was routed to the Classic Trial at Sandown.

Soft ground in Surrey saw the field cut up badly. Old Vic duly disposed of a poor field with comparitive ease. With connections pondering the Italian Derby as a likely target, trainer Henry Cecil sent Old Vic for the Chester Vase. After smashing the course record in winning at Chester, an appearance at Epsom was firmly on the agenda instead of a trip to Italy.

However, the colt clearly preferred give in the ground and with a lack of rain likely to ensure that the Derby at Epsom was run on a firm surface, Old Vic was supplemented in the French Classic at Chantilly.

No English challenger had won the Derby at Chantlly during the 20th Century, but this statistic did not seem to cross jockey Steve Cauthen's mind as he jumped into an early lead and attempted to make all from the front. Always at the head of affairs, the leader pulled away fluently and never troubled the judge with a superb seven-length success.

This authorative success stamped Old Vic as one of the best colts of his generation in Europe that year. With this in mind, Cecil sent his charge to Ireland seeking a second Derby.

At the Curragh, Old Vic showed that he had improved again since France. If anything, Sheikh Mohammed's colt was even more in command and dealt with his opponents in almost dismissinve fashion to record a four and a half length success.

The dual Derby winner was highly rated now and expected to campaign in some of the top European championship races through what remained of the summer. Unfortunately, however, a muscle injury and coughing kept him off track for the reminder of the year.

The following summer he reappeared in the Hardwicke Stakes at Royal Ascot, finishing third, before being routed to the King George VI and Queen Elizabeth Diamond Stakes. Old Vic fought out a Classic struggle with stablemate Belmez over the final furlong, going down by just a neck in one of the races of the year.

```
                              Northern Dancer   Nearctic
              Sadler's Wells (b. 1981)           Natalma
                              Fairy Bridge      Bold Reason
OLD VIC (b. 1986)                                Special
                              Derring-Do        Darius
              Cockade (b. 1973)                  Sipsey Bridge
                              Camenae           Vimy
                                                 Madrilene
```

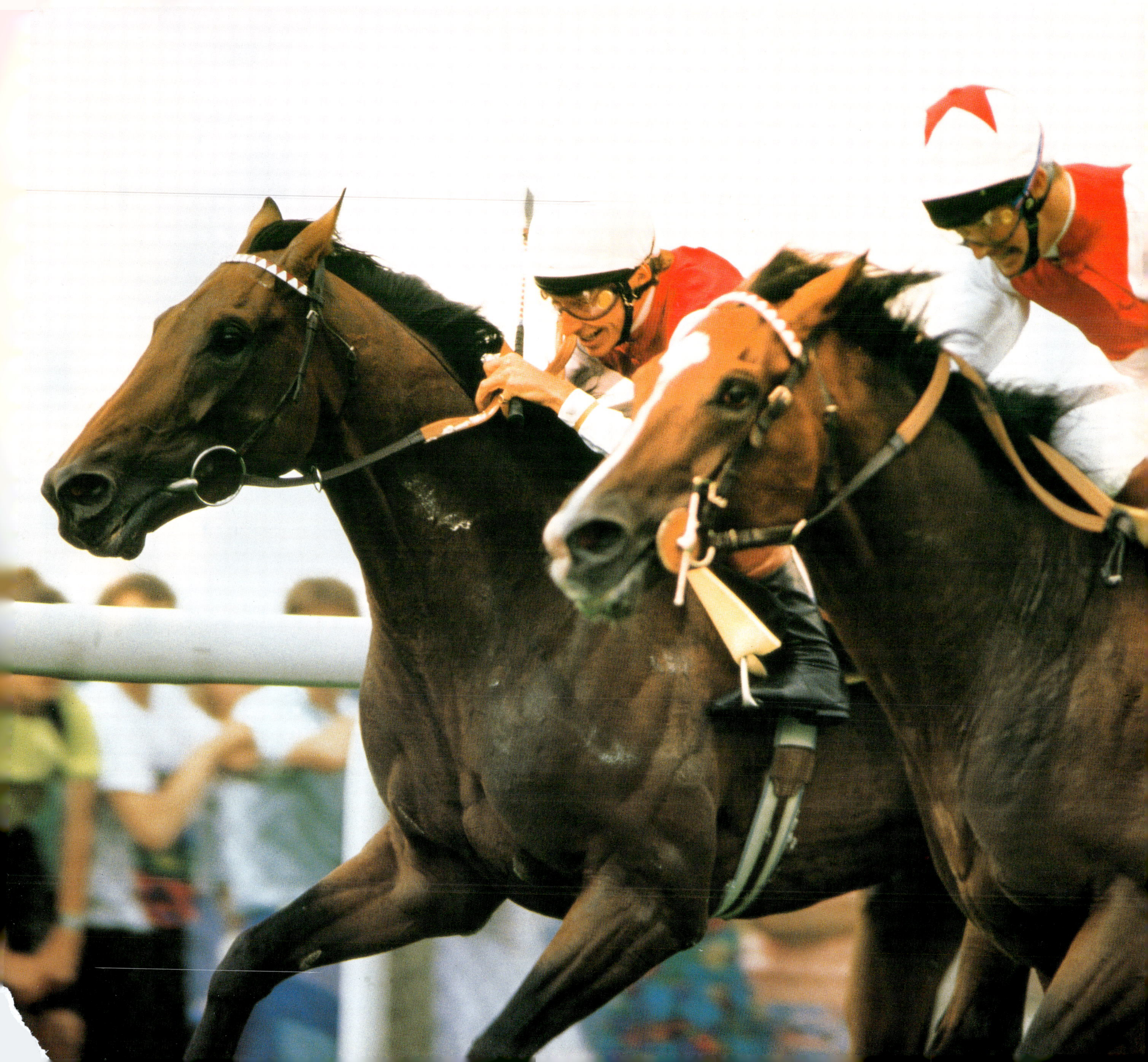

Opera House
b. c by Saddler's Wells — Colourspin (High Top)

Much touted following a juvenile success, Opera House had a restricted three-year-old campaign due to injury, but finally lived up to expectations at four. He returned to the track fully fit in 1992 with a third place in the Gordon Richards Stakes, followed by a first pattern triumph in the Tattersalls Rogers Gold Cup.

The Brigadier Gerard Stakes also went the way of Opera House, persuading trainer Michael Stoute that he was worthy of an outing in the highest company. This came in the Group One Eclipse Stakes at Royal Ascot, where he finished a credible length and a half second to Kooyonga.

Raised to a mile and a half for the first time in the campaign, for the King George VI and Queen Elizabeth Diamond Stakes, he again reached the frame behind odds-on favourite St Jovite.

Eased in class for the Cumberland Lodge Stakes, over course and distance, he took his final race of the season with an improved performance. Going into the winter it was clear that Opera House woul return an even better five-year-old.

Following a second in the Prix Garnay, he produced a strong finish to win the Group One Coronation Cup at Epsom after meeting with trouble, adding another success in the Eclipse Stakes in July.

His next start came in the King George VI and Queen Elizabeth Diamond Stakes, probably the highest class middle distance field of the entire summer, taking on, among others, unbeaten Derby winner Commander In Chief, Italian Derby hero White Muzzle, the much-hyped Tenby and User Friendly. Kept in touch with the pace by Michael Roberts, Opera House, White Muzzle and Commander In Chief drew away from the rest of the field off the turn, with Sheikh Mohammed's star pulling ahead of the two three-year-olds to record a one and a half length success from White Muzzle. Opera House became the first horse since Royal Palace to win the Coronation Cup, Eclipse and King George in the same season.

Looking for a rare King George-Prix de l'Arc de Triomphe double in the same season, Opera House made good account of himself in Paris by finishing third. He also made it to the starting line-up for the Breeders' Cup Turf several weeks later, acquitting himself well to finish sixth.

OPERA HOUSE (b. 1988)	Sadler's Wells (b. 1981)	Northern Dancer — Nearctic, Natalma
		Fairy Bridge — Bold Reason, Special
	Colourspin (b. 1983)	High Top — Derring-Do, Camenae
		Reprocolour — Jimmy Reppin, Blue Queen

Opera House strides away from Misil to take the 1993 Coral-Eclipse at Sandown.

Pebbles

ch. f by Sharpen Up — La Dolce (Connaught)

A fast-improving juvenile in 1983, Pebbles gave her best performance of the season in the autumn, showing her true capability when a fast-finishing second in the six-furlong Cheveley Park Stakes at Newmarket. That strong showing followed successes in the Kingsclere Stakes at Newbury and the Childwick Stakes at Newmarket, although before the Cheveley Park she had disappointed with a weak performance in the seven-furlong Waterford Candelabra Stakes.

The following spring she lined up in the Nell Gwyn Stakes and handed a one-length beating to Leipzig, with Meis El-Reem a further half-length away in third. On that performance, the Clive Britain-trained filly went into the 1000 Guineas as joint second favourite behind the unbeaten Mahogany. Nervous during the preliminaries, she was the consummate professional during the race, showing class to finish three lengths clear of runner-up Meis El-Reem.

Routed to the Coronation Stakes, Pebbles ran well but was beaten one and a half lengths by Irish 1000 Guineas heroine Katies, the pair finishing well clear.

Pebbles missed much of the remainder of the season due to a chipped hoof, returning to the racecourse for the Dubai Champion Stakes, where she reminded the world of her status. In a top-class field she was held up early, but came with a late rattle and caught all but Palace Music before the line.

Having a restricted campaign, but clearly still improving, the filly stayed in training at four and played a significant role in a vintage summer for Sheikh Mohammed. At the end of 1985, Pebbles was overwhelmingly voted Horse of the Year, ahead of the likes of Oh So Sharp, Never So Bold and Slip Anchor, coming on the back of successes in the Eclipse Stakes and Champion Stakes among others.

The fillip of her season, however, was an ambitious trip to America for the second Breeders' Cup meeting, staged at Aqueduct.

In the Breeders' Cup Turf she was kept mid-division early, but rounding toward the final straight was in a pocket. As they cleared the final turn, she was presented with an opening and came with a storming run to take the lead, finding a little more under pressure when challenged late, to take the race by a neck. Her victory broke the track record and netted connections £629,371, the highest figure ever won by a British-trained horse in a single race, anywhere in the world.

PEBBLES (ch. 1981)	**Sharpen Up (ch. 1969)**	Atan — Native Dancer / Mixed Marriage
		Rocchetta — Rockefella / Chambiges
	La Dolce (ch. 1976)	Connaught — St Paddy / Nagaika
		Guiding Light — Crepello / Arbitrate

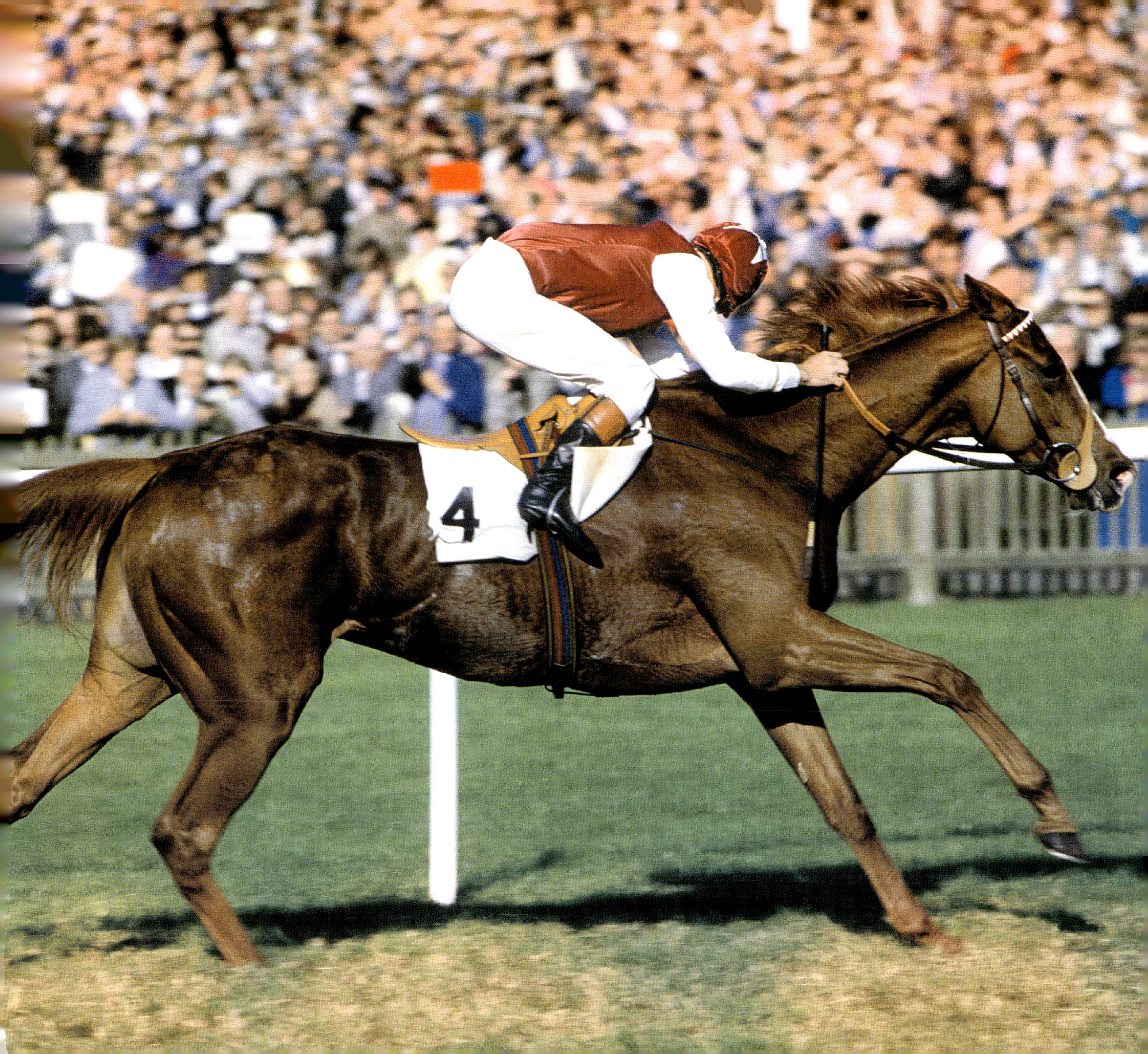
4

Sheikh Hamdan bin Mohammed Al Maktoum

Sheikh Hamdan bin Mohammed Al Maktoum has clearly inherited the ambition, drive and vision of his father whom he is regularly seen alongside. His determination to succeed has borne fruit as an owner and in the saddle, as well in the Endurance arena.

His maroon silks have been present on the UAE's racecourses ever since the inception of racing under rules and were first carried to victory in January 1993. He enjoyed his most prolific season in 2001/02 with 15 winners. His string has been somewhat reduced since then and the 2005/06 season produced three winners. However, he was represented in three of the seven races on Dubai World Cup night - albeit without joy.

He has had three winners in the early part of the 2006 British season with the very useful Akona Matata having won twice and run with credit in both the Royal Hunt Cup and Bunbury Cup more recently. In 2003 his Satchem, like Akona Matata trained by Clive Brittain, won the Group 3 Sirenia Stakes and is now with Godolphin.

Like his brother Sheikh Rashid his interest is far more than just the ownership and he won three amateur races in the UAE to add to his impressive achievements in the endurance field. Blessed with an athletic build and having inherited his father's prowess for equestrianism he has continued from strength to strength in the saddle. In August 2005 he celebrated another major endurance championship victory when winning the European Open in Compiegne, France, with the UAE team also winning the team medal. He topped the world rankings in 2000 and in 2001, as a junior, he was part of the team who won the World Endurance Championship. He has won over 20 Endurance races around the globe, including in the UAE, Jordan, Syria, France, England, Ireland, Belgium, Spain and has become an integral component of the national team.

What has endeared Sheikh Hamdan to those around him is his willingness to listen and learn. He welcomes advice, assimilates it and uses it. Like us all, he admits to making the odd mistake. Pointedly, he says he does not make the same mistake twice!

Live your passion

FREDERIQUE CONSTANT
GENEVE

Live your passion

damas
Les Exclusives
Toll Free: 800 4916

FC-910MC3H9
Heart Beat Manufacture
18ct Or Rose

www.damasjewellery.com

Pennekamp

b. h by Berring – Coral Dance (Green Dancer)

From early in his career it was clear that Pennekamp was top drawer. Andre Fabre first saddled him to dominate a small Evry race and a Deauville listed event—and from this beginning the juvenile was to confirm his status with every appearance.

In September the colt took on a class field in one of France's premier juvenile contests, the Prix de la Salamandre at Longchamp. Tracking the leaders early, Pennekamp unleashed a smart turn of foot just before the furlong pole and hit the front close to home to defeat Mountjoy and Bin Nashwan.

His debut summer ended with a cross-channel raid on the Dewhurst Stakes when, looking superbly well developed in the paddock, he confirmed that impression on the track.

Over the seven-furlong straight course, Pennekamp looked to be travelling the best almost from the outset and when Thierry Jarnet began a move he was making smooth headway from over a furlong out. Pennekamp looked good value for a one-length success

Next spring, Fabre unveiled the colt in the Prix Djebel for a success that confirmed his credentials as a prime contender for the English 2000 Guineas. At Newmarket he faced Celtic Swing, runway Racing Post winner who was being spoken as a wonder horse. In the event, Pennekamp looked closer to that mantle. Celtic Swing looked very much the winner when sweeping into the lead two furlongs out, but soon found himself with company as Pennekamp picked up well. Celtic Swing battled back, but the French colt had just too much fire power.

Immediately following his Newmarket success, Pennekamp was promoted to favourite for the Epsom Derby and connections were full of confidence on the day of the race.

Something clearly was amiss, however, as Pennekamp laboured to an 11th spot behind Lammtarra, Jarnet reporting the colt's performance untoward from rounding Tattenham Corner. One week later the news was worse, as x-rays revealed a serious hairline fracture to his off-fore.

Missing the remainder of his Classic season, Pennekamp was confined to his box for several months and seemed to be making a striking recovery towards a Dubai World Cup bid. He was ensconced in Dubai and reportedly working well when a reoccurrence of the Epsom injury forced his retirement.

Bering (1968)	Arctic Tern	Sea Bird II
		Bubbling Beauty
	Beaune	Lyphard
		Barbra
PENNEKAMP (b. 1992)		
Coral Dance (1978)	Green Dancer	Nijinsky
		Green Valley
	Carvinia	Diatome
		Coraline

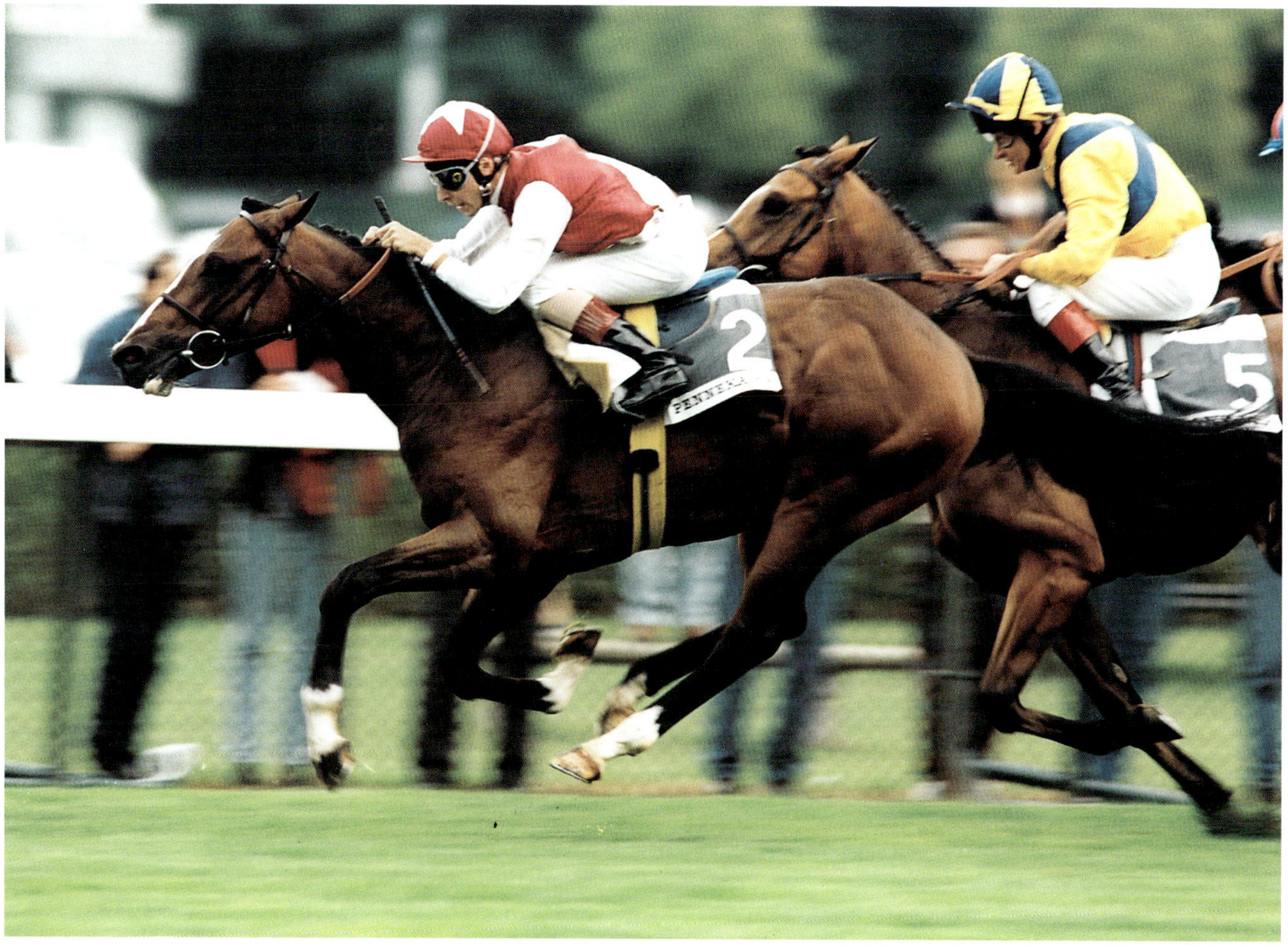
2
5

Refuse To Bend

Sadler's Wells - Market Slide (Gulch)

Veteran Irish training maestro Dermot Weld brought this classy colt to win a classic for Moyglare Stud Farm, before Godolphin continued his progress at four-years-old.

A half-brother to Weld's Melbourne Cup winner, Media Puzzle, the Naas-based trainer prepared this son of Sadler's Wells to win both starts as a juvelline, opening his account in a Gowran maiden, then on to win the Group One National Stakes at the Curragh. Refuse To Bend claimed two notable scalps here, beating Van Nistelrooy and Dublin, the former the world's most expensive yearling in 2001 and one of the favourites for the Guineas in 2003.

After a successful return in the Leopardstown 2000 Guineas Trial, Refuse To Bend shipped across the Irish Sea to Newmarket.

Ridden by Pat Smullen, Refuse To Bend held off outsiders Zafeen and Norse Dancer to win a tightly-fought contest.

In a very open race, the field came stands side of the course from the stalls and remained closely bunched until well into the final stages. Refuse To Bend got his nose in front two furlongs out and held off Zafeen's late challenge.

After a failure in the Espom Derby when sent off favourite, Refuse to Bend was rested for ten weeks, before returing to give weight all round and win the Desmond Stakes at Leopardstown. Despite a loss in the Prix Du Moulin, Sheikh Mohammed subsequentally purchased Refuse To Bend, leasing him back to Moyglare Stud Farm for his last run in their colours, when he ran below par in the Breeders' Cup Mile.

Under Godolphin in 2004, Refuse To Bend returned to his very best to claim the Group One Queen Anne Stakes at Royal Ascot in June. Later he showed he had courage to match genuine ability when winning the Group One Coral-Eclipse Stakes at Sandown in July. Stepping up in trip to ten furlongs and running on ground on the soft side of good, Refuse To Bend answered all calls from Frankie Dettori to hold Warrsan by a head.

Refuse To Bend had joined an elite group of horses to have won at Group One level at two, three and four years. He went on to finish third in the Queen Elizabeth ll Stakes and was later retired to take up stallion duties at Kildangan Stud.

```
                                    Northern Dancer    Nearctic
                                                       Natalama
              Sadler's Wells (b. 1981)
                                    Fairy Bridge       Bold Reason
                                                       Special
REFUSE TO BEND (b. 2000)
                                    Gulch              Mr Prospector
                                                       Jameela
              Market Slide (ch. 1991)
                                    Grenzen            Grenfall
                                                       My Poly
```

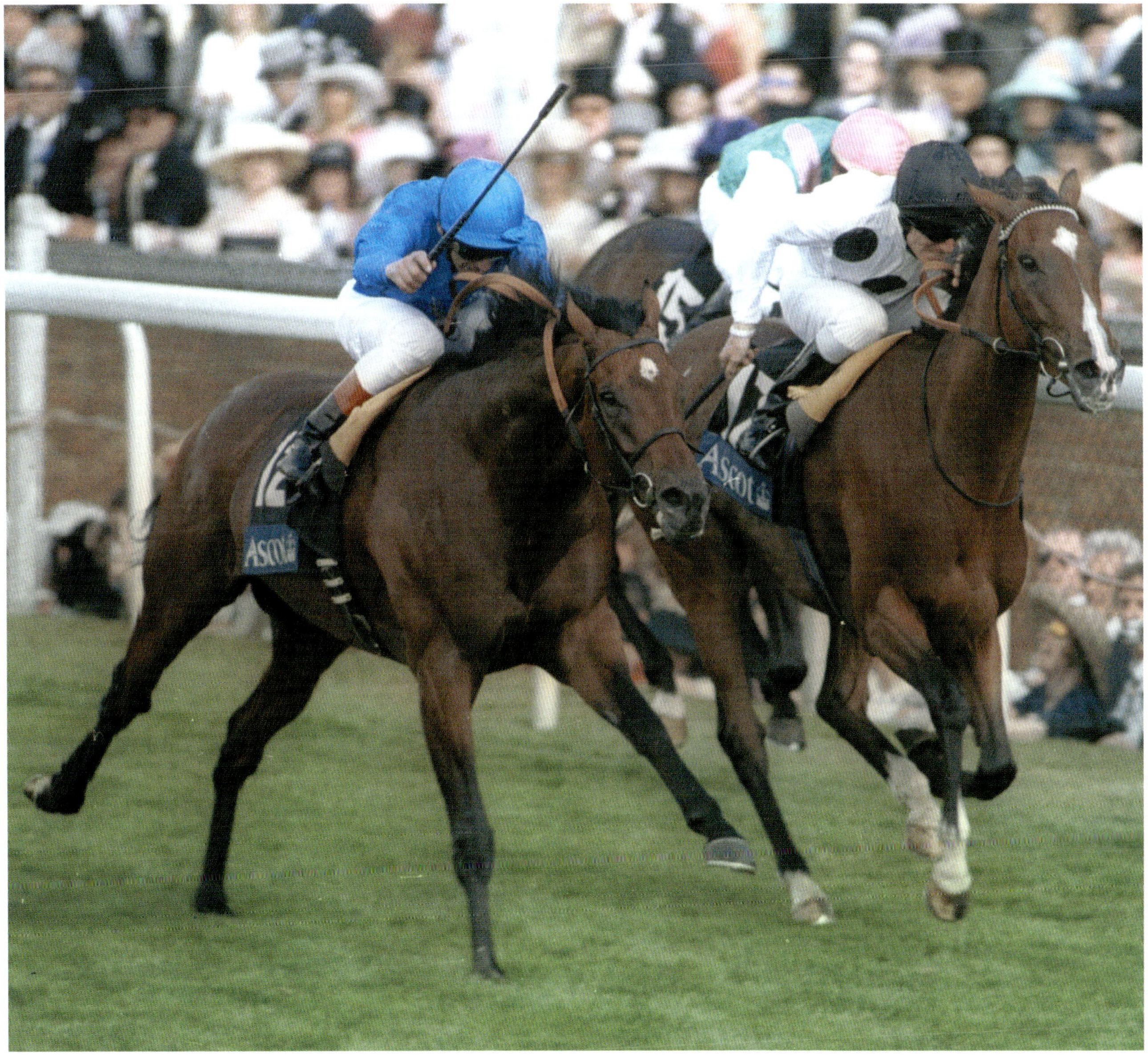
Ascot

Rule of Law

b. c by Kingmambo - Crystal Crossing (Royal Academy)

Trainer David Loder made his mark as a top handler when employed to train two-year-olds for Godolphin. His talent for producing winning juveniles brought him much success and his nurturing ability brought on dozens of horses that would go on to represent Godolphin at the highest level. Rule of Law is a typical example.

As a juvenile the colt won a York maiden by seven lengths and progressed to win a listed race at the same Yorkshire track. Targeted at the Royal Lodge Stakes he completed his campaign by finishing three quarters of a length third to Snow Ridge. Transferring to Dubai, Rule of Law continued to progress.

Second in the Vodafone Derby at Epsom, having missed the King Edward VII Stakes at Ascot because of a slight infection, and then finishing fourth in the Irish Derby, the son of Kingmambo ran the perfect trial for his long term target, the St Leger at Doncaster, when claiming the the Group Two Great Voltigeur Stakes at York.

Frankie Dettori set a moderate pace out of the stalls but quickened it up five furlongs out and finished strongly to triumph by two-and-a-half lengths from Let the Lion Roar.

Finally Rule of Law delivered what he had always promised when winning the St Leger. Sent off joint favourite with Quiff, Rule of Law did things the hard way, setting the pace from the onset. He displayed great courage and determination and held off a sustained challenge from Quiff to win by a head under Kerrin McEvoy.

He missed the whole of the following season having suffered a foot injury and was returned to training for the 2006 season.

	Mr Prospector	**Raise A Native**
		Gold Digger
Kingmambo (b. 1990)		
	Miesque	**Nureyev**
		Pasadoble
RULE OF LAW (b. 2001)		
	Royal Academy	**Nijinsky**
		Crimson Saint
Crystal Crossing (b. 1987)		
	Never So Fair	**Never So Bold**
		Favoletta

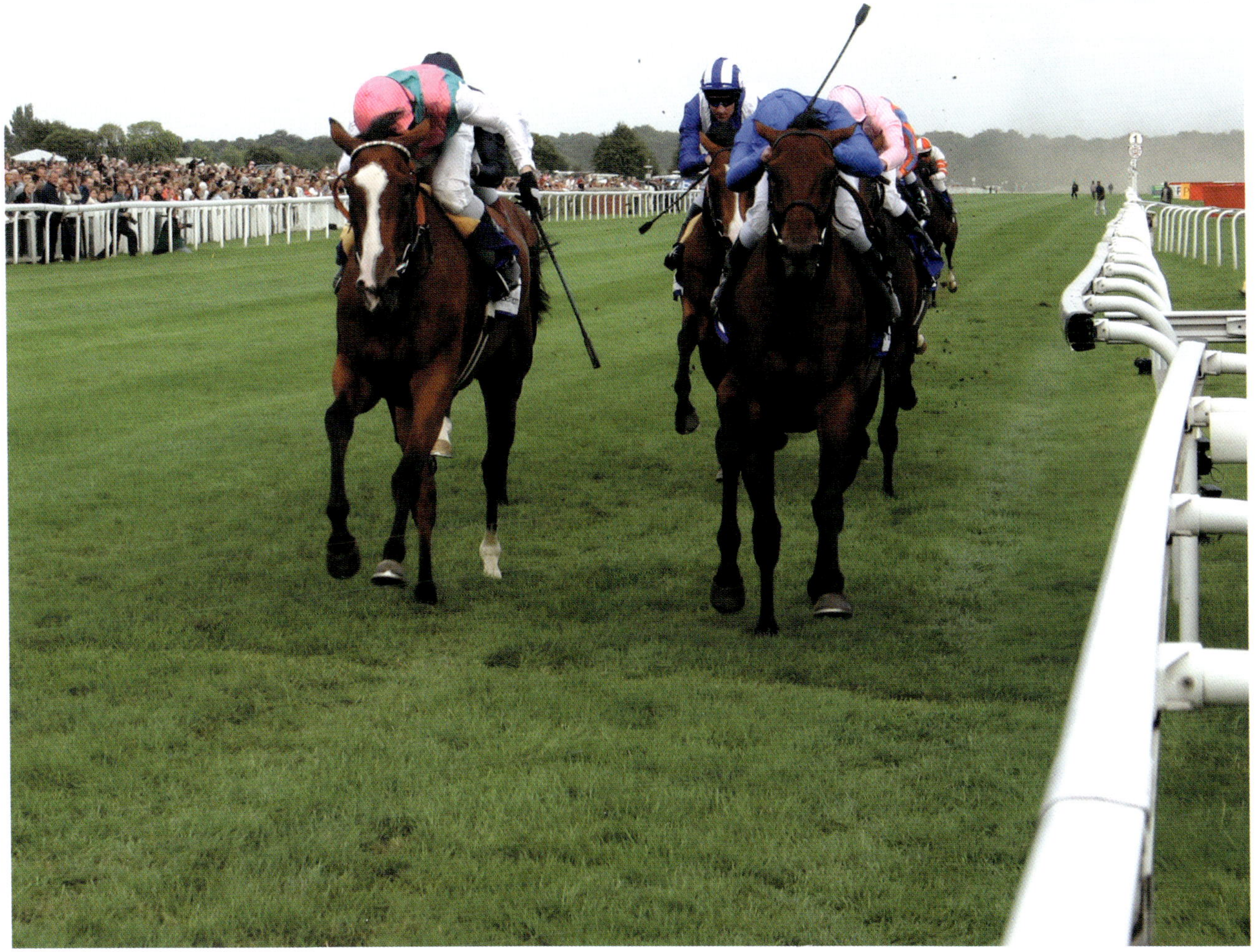

Sakhee

b. c by Bahri – Thawakib (Sadler's Wells)

Once again Sheikh Hamdan's elite racing and breeding programme threw up a champion, and in 2002 Sakhee could still materialise to be one of the best Thoroughbreds anywhere in the world for many seasons.

As a juvenile, the son of Bahri was based with John Dunlop, who trained him to win races at Nottingham and Sandown. It was at three, however, that Sakhee first shone, with two glittering wins in The Thresher Classic Trial and Dante Stakes, both of which set him up to follow the likes of Nashwan and Erhaab as winners of the premier Classic for Sheikh Hamdan.

At Epsom, Sakhee let no-one down. In the closing stages of the race he drew clear of the field with Sinndar, and the two fought out a battle royale in which the latter only got up in the last 100 yards. Sinndar would later prove to be an above average Derby winner—and Sakhee would go on to become an even brighter champion.

Before the end of the summer of 2000 he ran a slightly below par fourth in the Coral-Eclipse, and was subsequently transferred to Godolphin.

It was under Saeed bin Suroor that Sakhee materialised into a special horse, even by Godolphin's heady standards. Reappearing in Britain in the Juddmonte International Stakes, Sakhee unleashed one of the performances of the summer at York in trouncing a Group One field by a remarkable seven lengths. But even this would pale against his end-of-season exploits.

Routed to the Prix de l'Arc de Triomphe at Longchamp, Sakhee produced one of the finest displays in a top middle-distance race for many years in claiming the French showpiece. In finishing six lengths clear of his nearest pursuer, Aquarelliste, he equalled the record for the longest winning margin, a benchmark of greatness set by two of racing's all-time superstars, Ribot in 1956 and Sea Bird II in 1965.

Sakhee ended 2001 with another class performance in the Breeders' Cup Classic, where Tiznow—the 2000 Horse of the Year and first horse to win back-to-back Classics—nosed him out at the finish after a thrilling duel at Belmont Park.

SAKHEE (b. 1997)	**Bahri (b. 1992)**	Riverman	Never Bend
			River Lady
		Wasnah	Nijinsky
			Highest Trump
	Thawakib (b. 1990)	Sadler's Wells	Northern Dancer
			Fairy Bridge
		Tobira Celeste	Ribot
			Heavenly Body

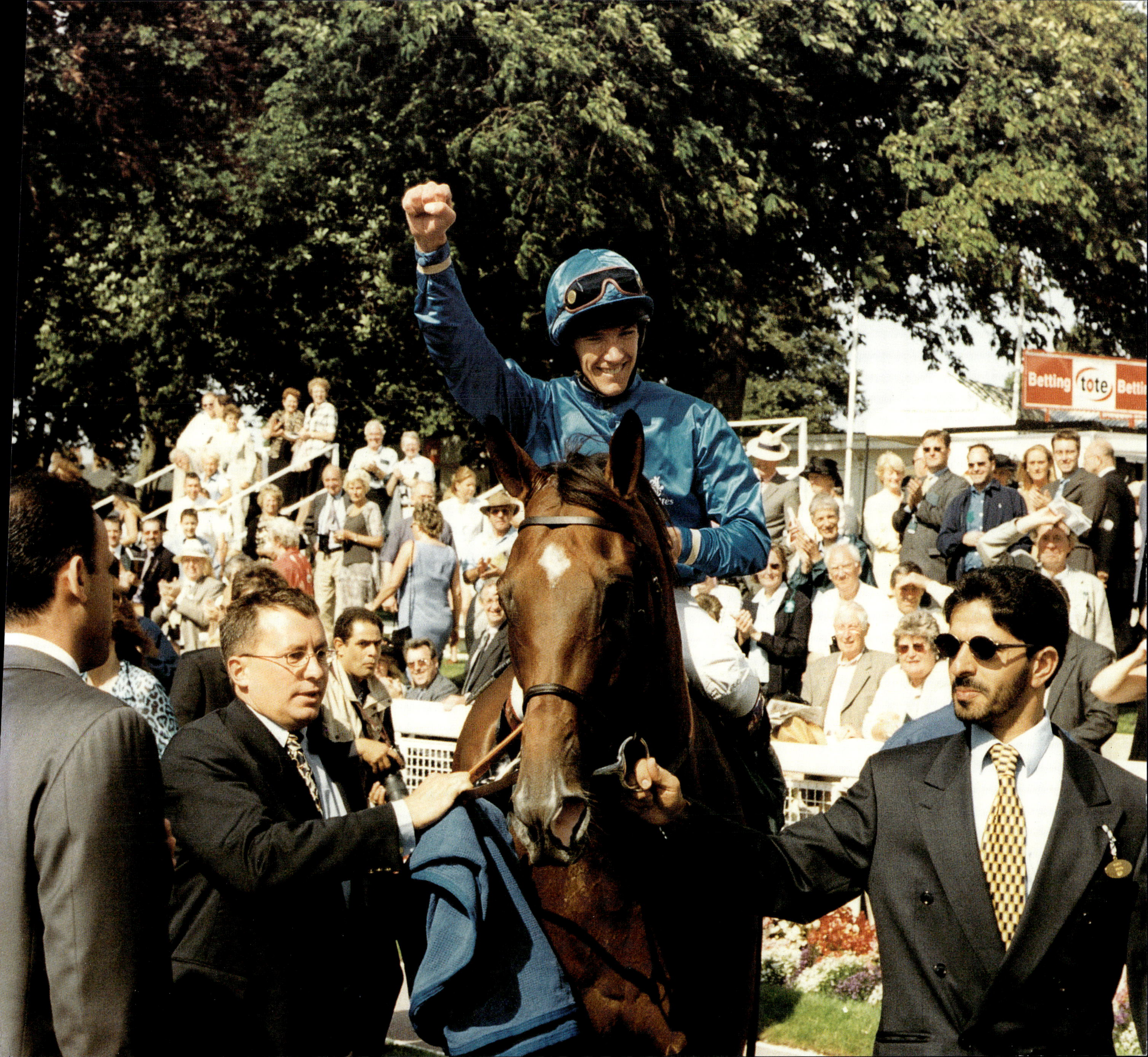
Betting tote

Kingwood House Stables

Sheikh Hamdan's Kingwood House Stables is, without doubt, set in one of the most picturesque estates in England. The 230 acre estate is set among the lush, rolling chalk downs of Lambourn and provides the perfect setting for training racehorses. As such, it has been home to many equine champions whose careers have been crafted from their time as a yearling, through to their date with destiny on the racecourse.

Nashwan, one of the all time equine greats, is an obvious example but just one of a host of big race and classic winners associated with the yard. Most recently, 2006 Derby winner Sir Percy has been added to the illustrious roll call of equine inmates who have plied their trade from the yard. Sir Percy is not a Maktoum horse but one of those the current master of Kingwood House, Marcus Tregoning, trains for outside owners.

It was noticeable how, after Sir Percy's magnificent and heart-stopping victory on the Epsom Downs, Tregoning was so quick to thank Sheikh Hamdan for allowing him to train such horses who all benefit from the state of the art facilities developed by Sheikh Hamdan.

Today, Kingwood House comprises of four purpose built yards housing over 100 horses in well ventilated stabling - so important to a horse's health. All stables have rubber flooring, solar heating panels and infra red lamps and there is also a separate row of eight isolation boxes at the trainer's disposal.

The private gallops, both at Kingwood itself and also at Farncombe Down provide Tregoning with a wide variety of both gradients and surfaces on which to train. It also helps prevent the horses going 'stale' and getting bored of the same old routine.

As well as the existing and recently refurbished grass gallops, there is also a straight six-furlong Polytrack gallop with a gentle uphill gradient. Another Polytrack gallop, over a mile, offers a steady uphill gradient. Such artificial surfaces allow the trainer to keep his horses on the go throughout the winter if frost or heavy rain means the grass is unusable.

Tregoning has vast experience of the gallops at

his disposal, having served as assistant to Major Dick Hern for six years (having worked for him 14 years in total having started as a Pupil Assistant) before eventually replacing him as the licence holder in 1997 on the Major's retirement. During that time, Tregoning was involved with such equine luminaries as Nashwan, Dayjur, Elmaamul and Harayir who all carried the Sheikh Hamdan silks with distinction.

Tregoning, like his mentor Hern, is a great belief in the teamwork ethic and much of the yard's success he attributes to the close knit team that has been developed in the yard. Providing the perfect combination of professional experience with enthusiasm, loyalty and dedication, the Kingwood Stables success story promises to continue for a very long time.

Tregoning, the Master of the stables or Captain of the ship, has a varied and broad experience of the racing industry to put to good use. He studied stud management in Newmarket, at the National Stud, before spending four years abroad, in New Zealand and America to be precise, furthering his experience and broadening his horizons. It was then that he returned to the UK and to Major Hern as Pupil Assistant - the rest, as they say, is history.

A successful amateur rider on the Point to Point circuit, Tregoning remained loyal to Hern for the next 14 years, spending the last six as assistant and it was he who took the helm in 1997 when Hern retired. It was Sheikh Hamdan's Nayef with whom he made his name in his early years. A victory in the 2001 Group One Champion Stakes at

Newmarket was followed by victory in the Group One Sheema Classic on Dubai World Cup night. The trainer, yet alone the horse, had proved he had the temperament for the big, international, stage and had justified the faith shown in him by Sheikh Hamdan.

Much had been expected of Nayef at the start of that 2001 season but he disappointed in the Craven Stakes, 2000 Guineas and then Gordon Stakes at Goodwood. The trainer never lost faith though and was rewarded with four straight wins that year - culminating in that Champion Stakes victory at the expense of Sheikh Ahmed's Tobougg.

His Sheema Classic win was supplemented by further Group One success in 2002, in the Juddmonte International at York after which he was a gallant third to Godolphin's Moon Ballad in the Dubai World Cup of 2003. That year's Group One Prince of Wales's Stakes was to be the horse's final victory and he was retired to stud at the end of that season - the winner of nine of his 19 starts and four times in Group One company.

Perhaps more important was the way his trainer handled his career. For Sheikh Hamdan to send a 'rookie trainer' a half-brother to both Nashwan and Unfuwain was a huge vote of confidence. Tregoning repaid that faith by winning a Group One race with the horse three years running.

It is easy to see why, other than the trainer's undoubted skill, why owners wish to have horses in training at Kingwood House. The facilities are second to none. As well as the stabling and gallops mentioned, the infrastructure supporting the running the yard is state of the art.

Two covered walking machines, an equine treadmill and a covered ride with an all-weather surface offer a wide range of exercise alternatives. The weighing machine is a vital tool of the trade and the equine solarium a very beneficial treatment tool, as is the equine spa.

There is a very large team striving for the success the yard craves - from Sheikh Hamdan's jockeys Richard Hills and Martin Dwyer, through the secretaries, other administration staff, the assistants, head lads, travelling staff, work riders and grooms. Teamwork is the key and no detail is left to chance. From the initial race planning stage to the horse returning safely after its race - all is planned in detail and nothing left to chance.

Obviously Hills and Dwyer are particularly valuable assessing the unraced horses and the well being and fitness of the established ones.

The year 2006 is one that the yard will never forget. Winning the Epsom Derby is the pinnacle for any trainer and to do it within 10 years of taking out a licence no mean achievement. To train a horse like Sir Percy, a bargain buy, is normally a once in a lifetime experience. Unbeaten as a juvenile when his four wins were highlighted by victory in the Group One Dewhurst Stakes, the son of Mark of Esteem has long been the apple of his trainer's eye.

He suffered his sole defeat to date in the 2000 Guineas when beaten only by an awesome display from George Washington but Tregoning's faith never diminished and he was rewarded in the best possible way at Epsom on the first Saturday in June. And typical of the trainer, he was busy emphasising that it was a team effort and only possible because of Sheikh Hamdan's support.

Such is racing that, less than a month later, Tregoning, his staff, Sheikh Hamdan and the racing world as a whole were mourning the death of stable stalwart Mubtaker who won 13 times for the yard in six season's racing - and only once out of stakes company.

It was the likes of Mubtaker and Alkaadhem who kept the trainer's name in lights since the same owner's Nayef's heyday. Combined with horses such as Dominica, High Accolade and now Sir Percy, Tregoning has been able to prove his worth ands establish himself as one of the foremost training takents in Britain and Europe. The future of Kingwood House Stables looks in very safe hands.

Salsabil

b. f by Sadler's Wells – Flame of Tara (Artaius)

The highest priced filly of the 1988 Houghton Sale at 440,000 Guineas, Salsabil arrived on the racecourse with a Nottinghsm maiden win in September of her two-year-old season. Trainer John Dunlop then took his charge to Newbury for a graduation race a fortnight later where a similar performance was expected. After making the early running, however, the filly struggled to suppress a challenge by Free At Last, going down by a short head.

Hopes were initially dashed, but her trainer persevered with his plans. Salsabil routed to the Group One Prix Marcel Boussac, the premier two-year-old contest for fillies in France. She duly obliged and went in to the winter fancied for the Epsom Oaks.

Her Classic season began in the Fred Darling Stakes at Newbury in April, where she proved not only that she had trained on, but also that she was a leading contender for the 1000 Guineas. Held up early, Sheikh Hamdan's filly came with a storming run to win most impressively by six lengths.

At Newmarket, Salsabil and Heart of Joy, the Nell Gwyn Stakes winner, fought out a thrilling finish. Running in to the dip, the latter was moving best of all, but Salsabil pressed on in the last furlong to win by three-quarters of a length.

Dunlop doubted her Oaks chances followings this performance but when, after long debate among connections, she was routed to Epsom, Salsabil again went off favourite ahead of Irish 1000 Guineas heroine In The Groove. If a tremendous battle was expected, it did not materialise, but the brilliance of Salsabil more than compensated. Tracking the leaders at Tattenham Corner, she stormed clear when Willie Carson asked for an effort to complete a five-length triumph. Her trainer later reported that despite his own fears, Sheikh Hamdan had been adamant she would stay the trip.

After her Epsom performance she passed up the Irish Oaks for a supplementary entry among the colts in the Irish Derby. At the Curragh, Salsabil went head-to-head with Deploy in the later stages, and was not found wanting, winning by three-quarters of a length after hitting the front 200 metres from home. In doing so, she become the first filly to win the Irish Derby since 1900.

Salsabil reappeared in September to claim the Prix Vermille at Longchamp, before a disappointing run in the Prix de l'Arc de Triomphe.

SALSABIL (b. 1987)	**Sadler's Wells (b. 1981)**	**Northern Dancer** — Nearctic / Natalma
		Fairy Bridge — Bold Reason / Special
	Flame of Tara (b. 1980)	**Artaius** — Round Table / Stylish Pattern
		Welsh Flame — Welsh Pageant / Electric Flash

317

Shadayid

gr. f by Shadeed – Desirable (Lord Gayle)

Tough and genuine, Sheikh Hamdan's homebred was also significant in that she was the first British Classic winner sired by a Maktoum-raced and owned stallion. Trained by John Dunlop, the striking grey filly was unbeaten as a two-year-old in three starts, including the Prix Marcel Boussac at Longchamp. This last victory began a career-long comparison with Salsabil, the great filly raced by the same owner, trainer and jockey combination.

Shadayid returned to the track in Newbury's Guineas test, the Fred Darling Stakes. Scarcely was jockey Willie Carson troubled as Shadayid trounced her peers by three lengths. She went into the 1000 Guineas as the shortest price favourite in three decades, and throughout looked worthy. Given her head at the dip, Shadayid ranged on and on and was good value for a two-length victory over Kooyonga.

Debate surrounded her ability to get a tough mile and a half in Epsom's Oaks. She didn't, but as so often in her unfolding career, Shadayid put in a gutsy performance finishing third to Jet Ski Lady and Shamshir, part of a Maktoum 1-2-3.

Clearly a mile was her trip and Shadayid reappeared in Royal Ascot's Coronation Stakes. After a match up the Ascot straight it was Kooyonga who got the better of the two. After claiming the runner-up spot again in a strong Sussex Stakes, Dunlop dropped his charge back to six furlongs for the Sprint Cup at Haydock. Again she produced a fine battling performance to finish third behind Polar Falcon.

Winless since the Guineas, her last British start was in the mile Queen Elizabeth II Stakes, where she finished a credible third.

A seventh place in the Breeders' Cup Mile at Churchill Downs, despite getting no sort of a run, was her last outing before she was retired to the paddocks. In her 11 career starts, this was the only occasion when the gutsy Shadayid finished out of the frame.

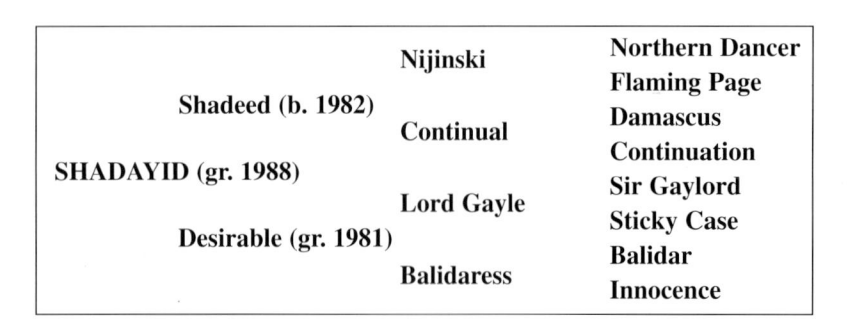

SHADAYID (gr. 1988)		
Shadeed (b. 1982)	Nijinski	Northern Dancer
		Flaming Page
	Continual	Damascus
		Continuation
Desirable (gr. 1981)	Lord Gayle	Sir Gaylord
		Sticky Case
	Balidaress	Balidar
		Innocence

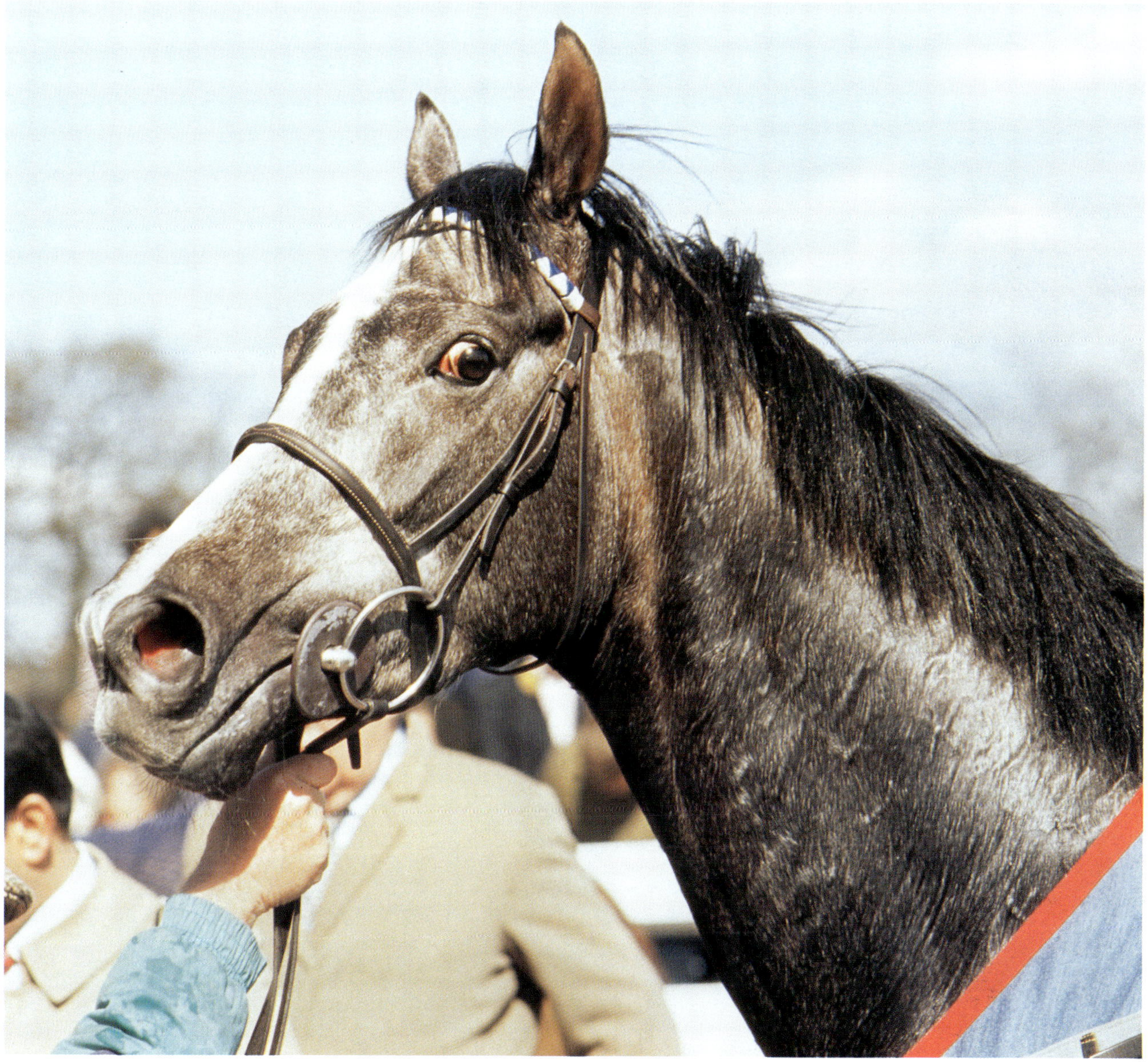

Shadeed

b. c by Nijinski — Continual (Damascus)

Enigmatic and highly strung, Shadeed was the Maktoum family's first 2000 Guineas winner and undoubtedly top class.Trained by Michael Stoute, the son of Nijinski fetched $800,000 as a yearling and proved well worth the investment.

The two-year-old appeared on the racecourse with a good reputation and after finishing third on his debut went on to take the Houghton Stakes.

When next seen in public the following spring in the Craven Stakes, Shadeed proved he had more than matured, now including in his armoury a strong flowing action and a champion's instinct. Sent off co-favourite, Shadeed trounced the field after bowling into the lead two furlongs from the line, still on the bridle. He crossed the line six lengths in front of Daimster with the reminder well behind.

A hot favourite for the 2000 Guineas, the only worry on the day of the race was his temperament and Shadeed went to the start early under Lester Piggott

When it came to the actual business of racing, however, Shadeed was a consummate professional. Tracking the pace for much of the way, Shadeed was still on the bridle when reaching the front two furlongs from the finish and held on in the last strides from a fast-finishing Bairn.

Thought to be capable of staying the extra half mile, Shadeed went to Epsom for the Derby well fancied but even allowing for his inability to get the distance he put in a ghastly performance. Returning to the Stoute yard, he showed signs of sickness and needed three months off to recover.

On his return, Stoute brought his star back to a mile for the Queen Elizabeth II Stakes and if anything, this was a better Shadeed than before. Chasing the pacemaker, Sheikh Maktoum's blue and white silks hit the front from the halfway point and as Shadeed opened up his powerful stride all his rivals were soon struggling. Having set a blistering pace, Shadeed tired close to home but was already out of the danger zone, claiming the contest by two and a half lengths from Arlington Million victor Teleprompter. This emphatic victory also proved to be the fastest over a mile during the season.

The year's outstanding miler was therefore fully entitled to take his place in the Breeders' Cup Mile in the autumn where he finished fourth to Cozzene, later promoted to third.

	Northern Dancer	Nearctic
Nijinsky (b. 1967)		Natalma
	Flaming Page	Bull Page
SHADEED (b. 1982)		Flaring Top
	Damascus	Sword Dancer
Continual (b/br. 1976)		Kerala
	Continuation	Forli
		Continue

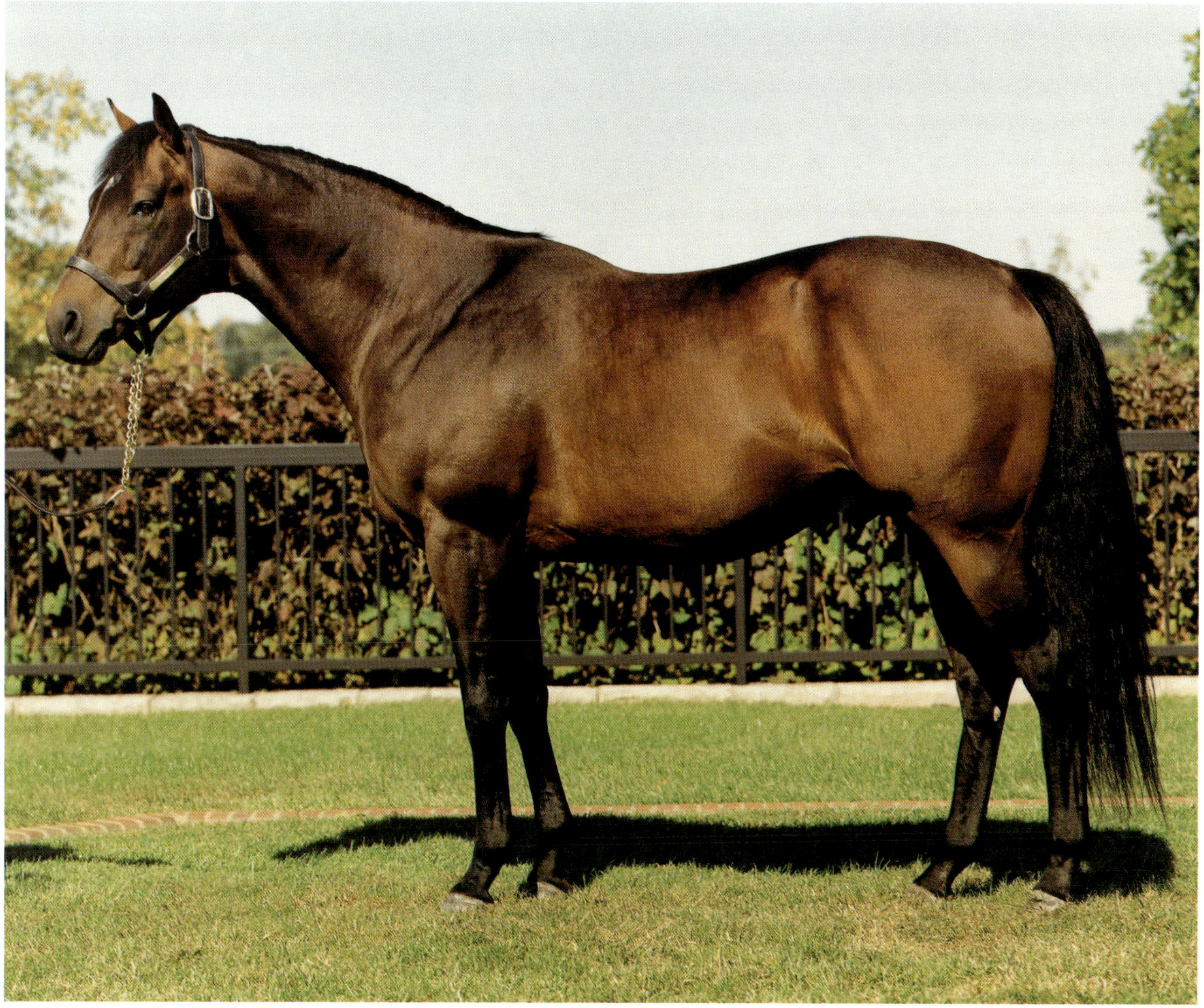

Sharmardal

b. c by Giant's Causeway — Helsinki (Machiavellian)

The tale of Shamardal could one day be made into a film. Having been offered at Keeneland as a foal in 2002, when he failed to sell with bidding reaching $485,000, the horse who was to become Shamardal was diagnosed as 'a grade three wobbler'. His breeders claimed insurance and the underwriters sold him on. He responded remarkably to treatment.

He was then offered at the Tattersalls Houghton Yearling Sale. However, his sale price of 50,000 guineas was among the lowest. The rest, as they say, is history.

He made his juvenile debut in a decent maiden at Ayr, sporting the colours of Abdulla Buhaleeba. He won by eight lengths. Next stop was Goodwood's Group Two Vintage Stakes, with subsequent Breeders' Cup Juvenile winner Wilko left trailing in second. Both those races were in July, with Joe Fanning in the saddle and this son of Giant's Causeway was not seen again until October and the Dewhurst Stakes. Over seven furlongs, but on soft ground, he never looked in any trouble in the colours of Gainsborough Stud. This time it was subsequent Eclipse Stakes winner Oratorio doing the chasing.

He finished the year as Champion Juvenile in Europe and was transferred to Godolphin. His sole defeat was suffered in the UAE Derby, his one run on dirt. Normal service was resumed with Frankie Dettori on board when winning both the French 2000 Guineas and Derby. Hurricane Run, whom he beat in the latter race, went on to win both the Irish Derby and Prix de l'Arc de Triomphe. The horse completed an unprecedented Group One treble when winning the St James's Palace Stakes but was sadly retired shortly afterwards due to injury.

Six wins from only seven starts and undefeated on grass. Few horses can have managed four Group One wins and his French 2000 Guineas, Derby and St James's Palace Stakes treble is unlikely to ever be emulated.

SHAMARDAL (b. 2002)	**Giant's Causeway (ch. 1997)**	
	Storm Cat	Storm Bird
		Terlingua
	Mariah's Storm	Rahy
		Immense
	Helsinki (b. 1993)	
	Machiavellian	Mr Prospector
		Coup De Folie
	Helen Street	Troy
		Waterway

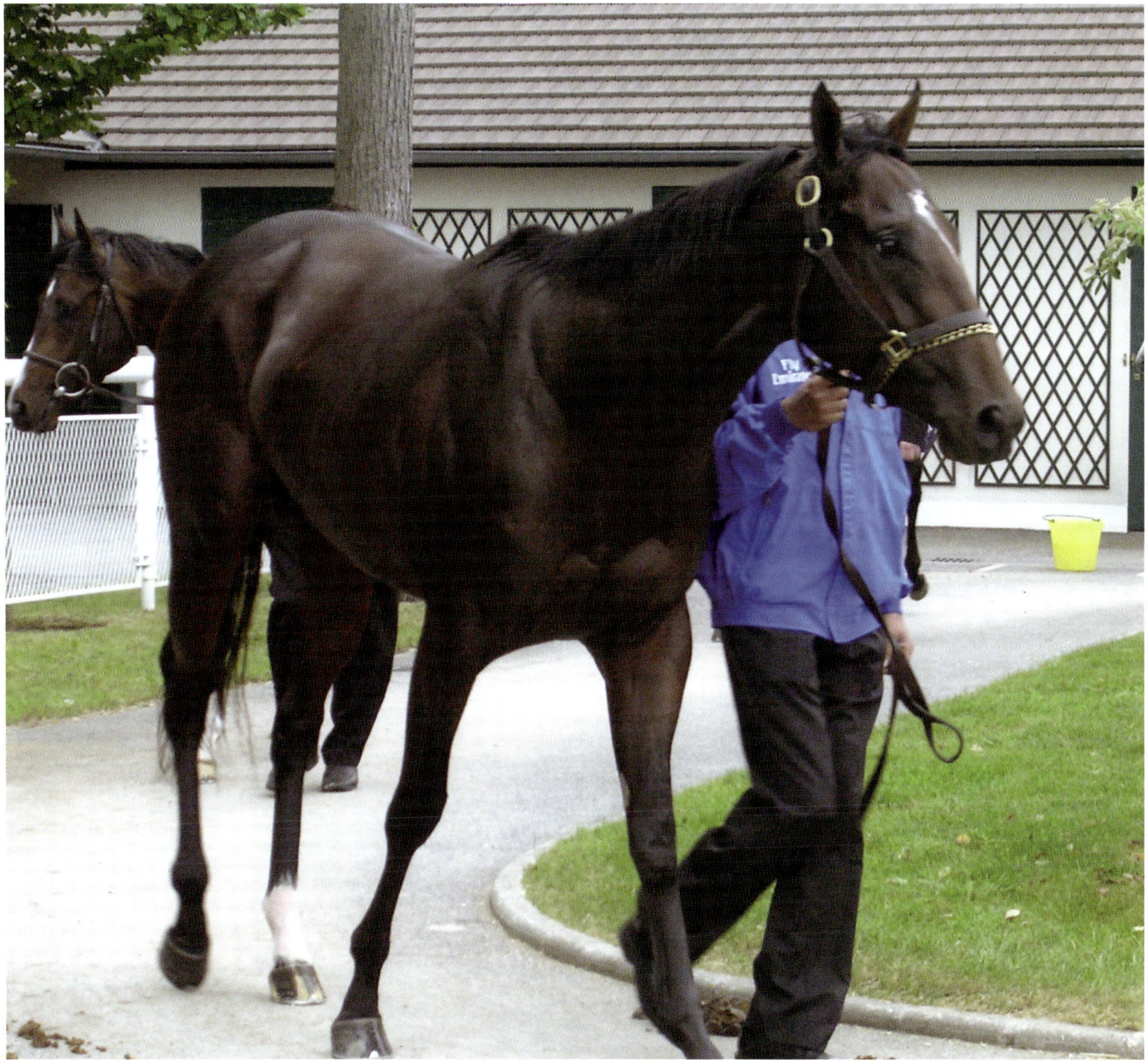

Sheikh Ahmed bin Mohammed Al Maktoum

Sheikh Ahmed bin Mohammed won the World Endurance Championship in 2002, becoming the youngest rider ever to do so, and the first Arabic or Asian world champion. In doing so he continued the fine tradition of his family in the saddle. He was also seen in the winner's enclosure twice at Nad Al Sheba after amateur races - in which he only contested five.

A natural horseman, his talent on horseback is hereditary, as is his hunger and desire to succeed. His maroon silks were first seen on the UAE racecourses in December 1994 with his first winner coming a month later. Since then they have been a regular fixture on UAE racecards, highlighted by the 2001/02 season when he had 15 winners. Another whose string has contracted somewhat in recent years, the 2005/06 still provided five winners and he was represented by Howick Falls on Dubai World Cup night.

His flagbearer in recent seasons has been the Purebred Arabian Royal Epic who provided the highlight of his owner's career thus far when winning a round of the prestigious Maktoum Challenge in 2005.

Unlike his brothers, his silks are not a regular sight on racecourses in Europe but his real claim to fame will always be his own ability in the saddle. Nobody will forget that day in September 2002 when he was crowned world champion, mastering the unfamiliar terrain and arguably the worst weather the competition had ever seen.

His 149 rivals, from 35 countries, were well beaten but it was his modesty at the end for which he should be remembered: "The race was very tough. It had all the best riders and the very best horses so to finish on top is really something. I honestly did not expect to win but I feel great and very proud."

The youngest rider in the event and part of a UAE team consisting of his two older brothers – Sheikh Rashid and Sheikh Hamdan – and his experienced father, he kept his composure to cross the finishing line without another rider in sight.

To achieve so much, so young, Sheikh Ahmed is typical of the Maktoums in his desire to succeed. So far, he has certainly done that.

With Superior creativity and ingenuity Quinting watches are designed as transparent watches with the mechanism ingeniously hidden in the case
Quartz movement. Platinum case and Strap

damas
THE ART OF BEAUTY.
Since 1907
Toll Free: 800 4916

Shantou

b. c by Alleged — Shaima (Shareef Dancer)

Shantou, whose dam produced two Maktoum Classic winners, Shareef Dancer and Oh So Sharp, was unraced as a two-year-old. With plenty of good home work, the colt was allowed to make his first racecourse outing in the heady heights of the Wood Ditton at Newmarket where he justified optimism with a good third, and followed that with second in a Chester Maiden. He reached the winner's spot at Sandown next time out.

Although Shantou was clearly making progress, it was with some surprise that he stood his ground in the entries and made an appearance in the Epsom Derby hardly two weeks later. A relative outsider, he belied his previous form in finishing third to Shaamit and Dushyantor.

With a great deal expected, he returned in the King Edward VII Stakes at Royal Ascot and showed little fight when finishing third. Entered in a Haydock listed event in July, the colt seemed disinclined to go on when asked to take up the running three furlongs out, finishing second.

Dropped in class again into a Windsor Conditions event, Shantou dealt relatively easily with his opposition, earning himself a place in the final Classic of the campaign, the St Leger at Doncaster. The race proved a wonderful advertisement for racing, Mons attempting to make all and the race seemingly all but over when Derby runner-up Dushyantor hit the lead under Pat Eddery. But from the pack came Shantou, staying on extremely well, and as the line neared steadily reached the leader's shoulder. A battle ensued, with Shantou just getting up on the line.

On his final start of the seaspm he won the Gran Premio Del Jockey-Club in Milan.

Returning as a four-year-old, Shantou looked superb in the Group One Grand Premio Di Milano in Milan. Defeating the useful Luso by one and a quarter lengths, he confirmed his well-being.

The colt returned to the racecourse in Britain facing a tough field in the Princess of Wales's Stakes. As his six rivals began to tire, Shantou was left to fight out a battle royale against Godolphin star Swain. Reaching the line with a head to spare, Shantou showed improved form and mettle to score from a top class opponent.

Later in the summer, he claimed third in the Geoffery Freer Stakes.

SHANTOU (b. 1993)	Alleged (b. 1974)	Houst The Flag — Tom Rolfe / Wavy Navy
		Princess Pout — Prince John / Determined Lady
	Shaima (b. 1988)	Shareef Dancer — Northern Dancer / Sweet Alliance
		Oh So Sharp — Kris / Oh So Fair

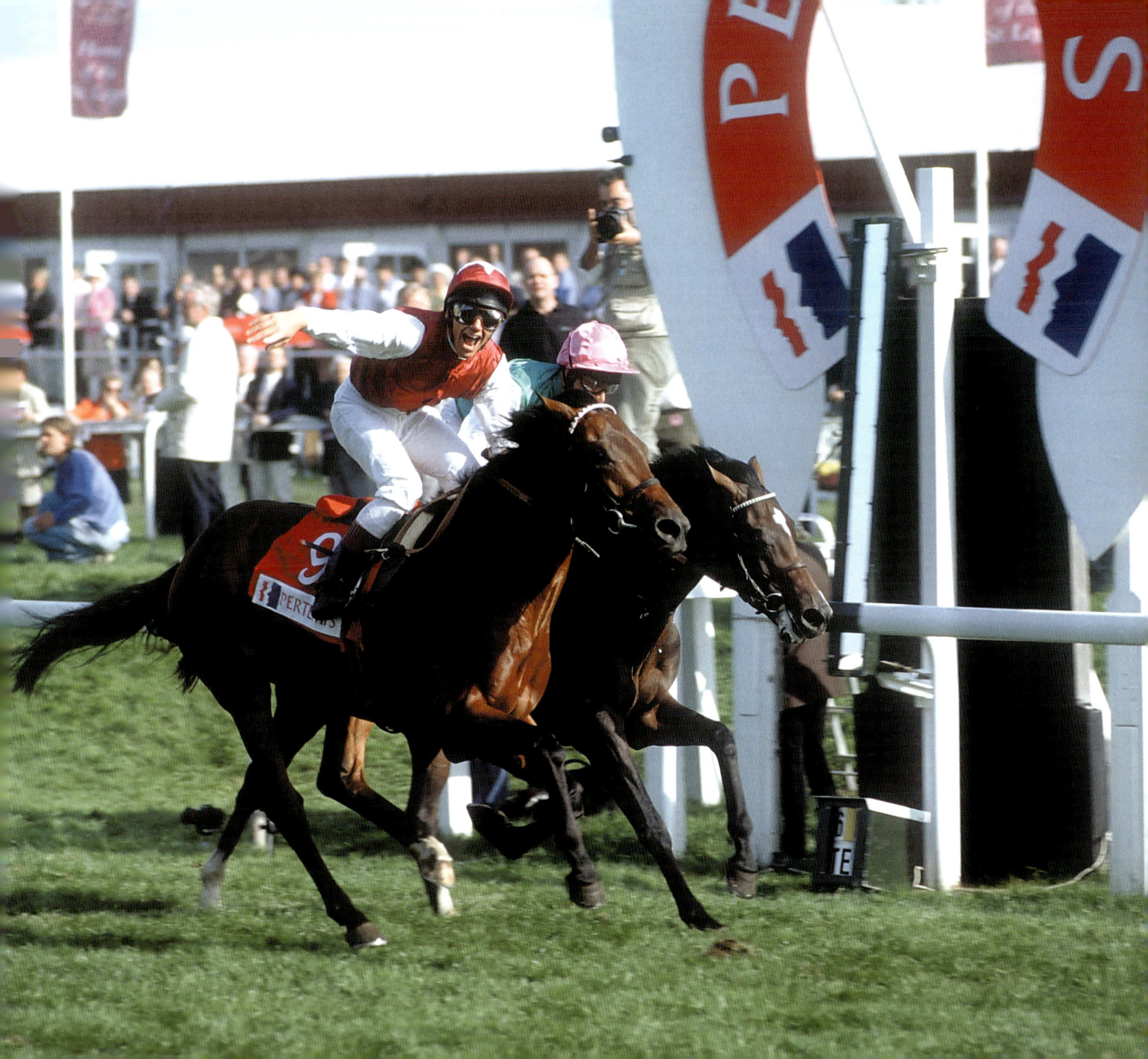
9

Shareef Dancer

b. c by Northern Dancer — Sweet Alliance (Sir Ivor)

Success, controversy and the mantle of being the first Maktoum-owned Derby winner all combine to make Shareef Dancer one of the most interesting animals to represent the family.

Trained by Michael Stoute, the colt made his juvenile debut in a six furlong Newmarket maiden, his success creating a favourable impression, one not necessarily spoilt by defeat in his only other start of the campaign, on unsuitably soft ground at Newmarket.

He returned to the racecourse the following spring in Sandown's Esher Cup with a big reputation, a shock second place when hot favourite later explained when he was found to be suffering from a sore throat.

Shareef Dancer was then thrown straight in against some of the best of his generation at Royal Ascot in the King Edward VII Stakes, on firm ground. His performance in winning was enough to earn a place in the Irish Derby.

The Irish classic proved a tremendously attractive running, including Prix du Jockey Club winner Caerleon and Epsom Derby winner Teenoso, the market sending Shareef Dancer off a distant third behind the two stars.

In a true-run race, Shareef Dancer was always moving easily a shade off the pace and, pushed along, moved to head the field with two furlongs remaining. For a fraction of a second the race could have gone to several contenders, but when Shareef Dancer lengthened the whole issue was beyond doubt in a handful of strides.

Rarely has a European Classic been won in such a comprehensive fashion. Shareef Dancer passed the Curragh finish line with three lengths to spare from Caerleon with Teenoso a further two back in third. In one stunning run, the colt established himself as the season's champion middle distance three-year-old and notably the third son of Northern Dancer to take Ireland's premier classic, alongside the likes of Nijinsky and The Minstrel.

Sadly this was to be the last racecourse appearance for Shareef Dancer for a variety of reasons and he was subsequently syndicated to stud for a reported valuation of $40 million.

SHAREEF DANCER (b. 1980)	**Northern Dancer (b. 1961)**	**Nearctic** — Nearco / Lady Angela
		Natalma — Native Dancer / Almahmoud
	Sweet Alliance (b. 1974)	**Sir Ivor** — Sir Gaylord / Attica
		Mrs Peterkin — Tom Fool / Legendera

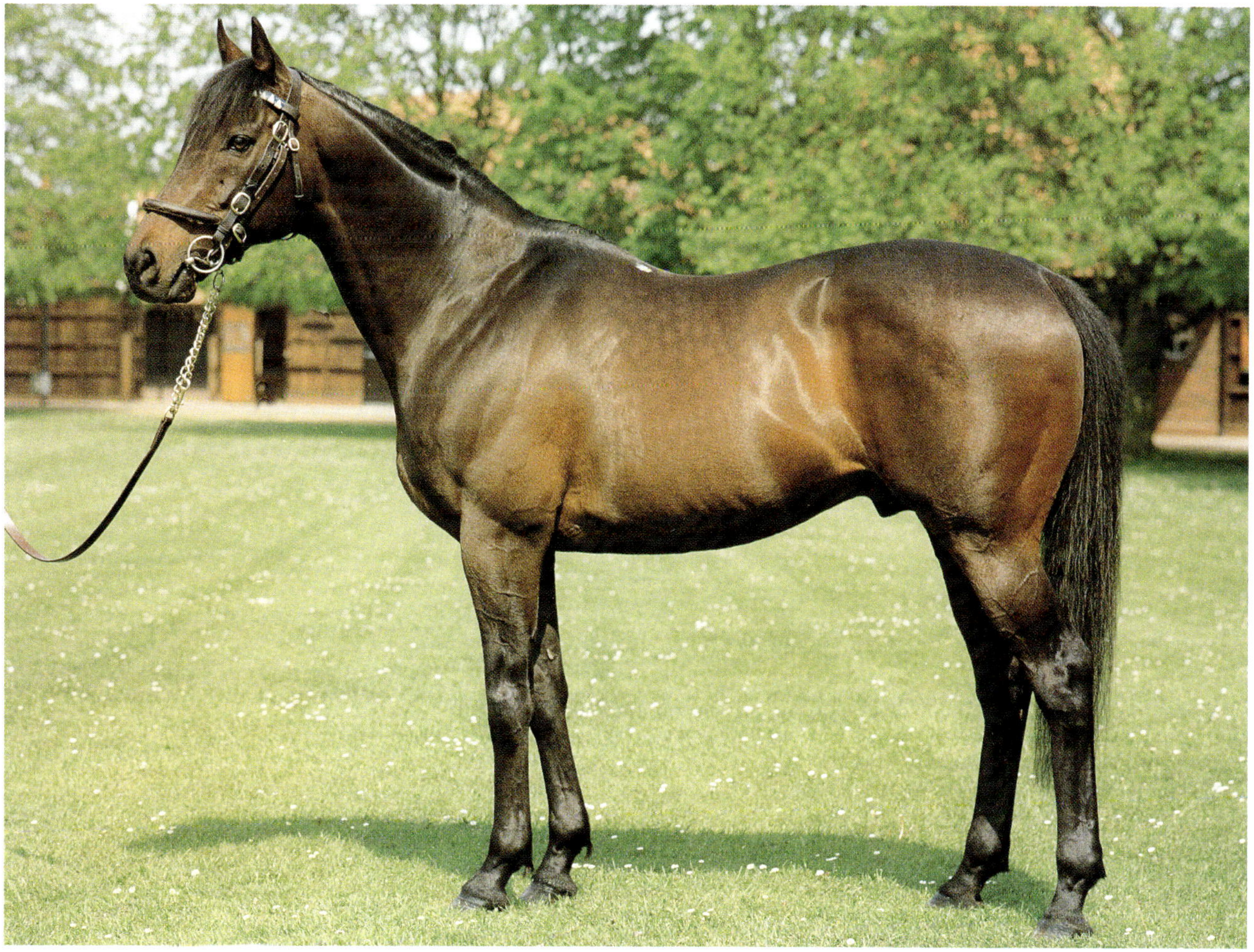

Singspiel

b. c by In The Wings — Glorious song (Halo)

The remarkable Singspiel is undoubtedly one of the best Thoroughbreds ever to go into training in Europe, with a record that shows Group/Grade One successes in four countries.

As a juvenile, he took a Chester maiden and a small race at Ascot. As a three-year-old he finished second to Pentire by a neck in the Thrèsher Classic Trial and then returned to the scene of his maiden success to claim fourth in the Chester Vase, before reeling off three second-place finishes in top company in the Grand Prix de Paris, Eclipse Stakes and Great Voltigeur.

Singspiel then won the Troy Stakes at Doncaster, and the colt stayed in training for the following year. Connections were again frustrated, but when Singspiel did score, he more than rewarded their perseverance.

On his reappearance he took the Gordon Richards Stakes at Sandown from Pilsudski and then added to his tally of seconds in both the Coronation Cup and Princess of Wales's Stakes. Singspiel regained that winning thread for the Select Stakes at Goodwood and travelled to North America to take the Canadian International at Woodbine by two lengths from Chief Bearhart. At the same track Singspiel finished second to Pilsudski in the Breeders' Cup Turf. That performance was enough to secure a place in the Japan Cup where he ran a superb race. With the colt running well throughout, Frankie Dettori launched him with masterful timing to claim the £2 million race.

After winning in Japan, it was with some confidence that connections took the colt to the Gulf for the $4 million Dubai World Cup, and he let no-one down. US challenger Siphon set a blistering pace but Jerry Bailey had his mount perfectly placed to pick off the leaders for what Sheikh Mohammed said was his dearest victory as an owner.

After a well-earned break, Singspiel returned to the track in June where he added the Coronation Cup, destroying Dushyantor by five lengths. At York, the colt faced the well-fancied Classic winner Bosra Sham, but once again proved himself a class above any rival in Britain.

On that form, Singspiel was considered Europe's outstanding chance for the Breeders' Cup Turf at Hollywood Park. However, it was not to be. The world champion disappeared into the early morning mist on one of his final pieces of work, only to reappear, limping, with a career-ending injury.

	Sadler's Wells	Northern Dancer
		Fairey Bridge
In The Wings (b. 1986)		Shirley Heights
	High Hawk	Sunbittern
SINGSPIEL (b. 1992)		Hail To Reason
	Halo	Cosmah
Glorious Song (b. 1976)		Herbager
	Ballade	Miss Swapsco

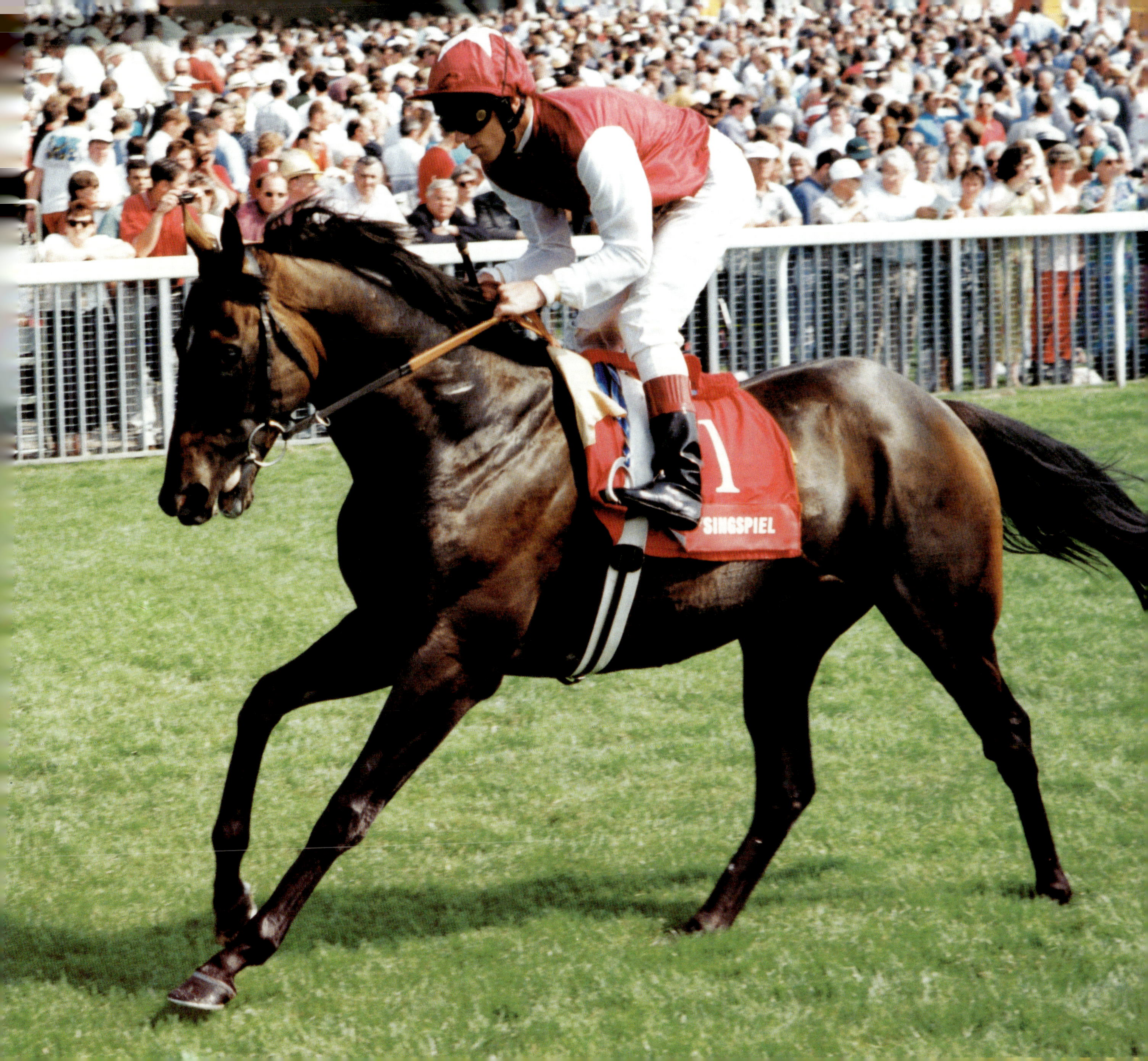
1
SINGSPIEL

Snow Bride

ch. f by Blushing Groom — Awaasif (Snow Knight)

Unbeaten in a pair of starts as a two-year-old, home-bred Snow Bride was widely seen as a potential Oaks filly going into the winter.

After producing some good work at home in the spring, the filly reappeared in Newmarket's Pretty Polly Stakes, sent off a well-supported favourite. But a fifth left notions of top class status in tatters. The subsequent discovery that she was in season at Newmarket in some way compensated, and Snow Bride was given every opportunity to get back on track next time out in the Musidora Stakes. She did just that—with the aid of a wonderfully judged ride by American Steve Cauthen.

Cauthen had the filly in front almost from the off and as she cruised into the straight began to up the pace. A good mover, her fluent action was soon in full flow and as she continued to stretch all her rivals, bar hot favourite Pilot, were soon toiling. Pilot threw down the gauntlet with 200 metres remaining and looked every inch the winner as she reached Snow Bride's shoulder, but with Cauthen's urging the daughter of Blushing Groom stayed on gamely and reached the line with half a length to spare.

Epsom provided a much stiffer test for Snow Bride, but again she looked to have a smart chance as Willie Carson opted to make use of her among the leading group. Three furlongs out Aliysa swept by with a run which would see her first past the post. Snow Bride stayed on strongly in the finish to claim second. The subsequent controversial disqualification of Aliysa would yet make Snow Bride the 1989 Oaks winner.

Three months later she returned to the track in the Prix Vermeille and produced a poor fourth.

Ascot's Princess Royal Stakes in October is a traditional meeting of top class three-year-old fillies, from early season Classic principals to late season developers, and Snow Bride came into the race with a great deal to prove. Top filly Princess Sobieska set off at a strong gallop to fully test her nine rivals. From early on, it was clear that Snow Bride was the only one who would have the stamina to mount a serious challenge. As they rounded the turn, Snow Bride upped the pressure and as they passed the one furlong marker began to draw alongside the leader, going on to claim the race by a length and a half.

SNOW BRIDE (ch. 1986)	Blushing Groom (ch. 1974)	Red God → Nasrullah / Spring Run
		Runaway Bride → Wild Risk / Aimee
	Awaasif (b. 1979)	Snow Knight → Firestreak / Snow Blossom
		Royal Statute → Northern Dancer / Queens Statute

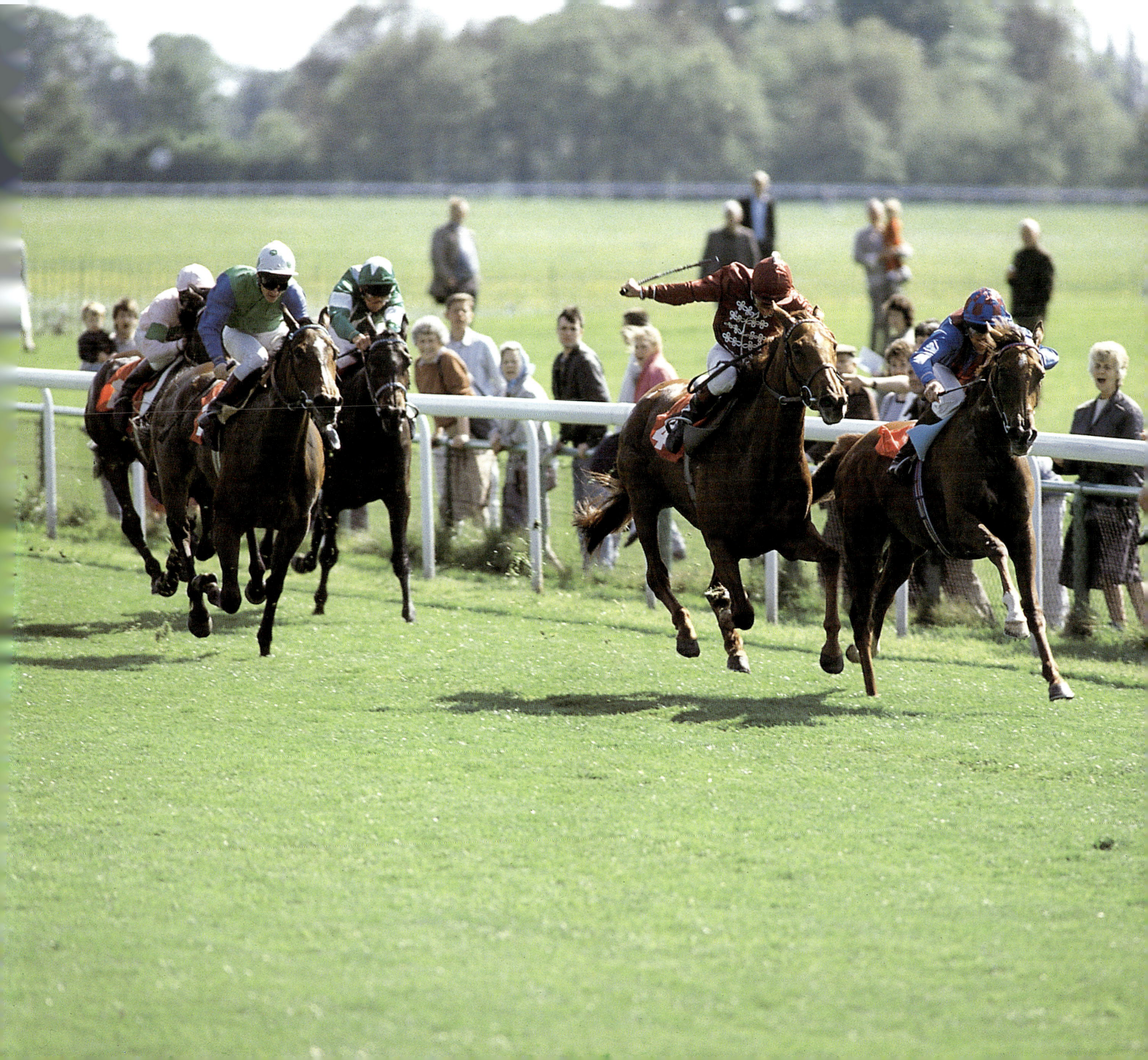

Sheikh Maktoum bin Mohammed Al Maktoum

Sheikh Maktoum bin Mohammed Al Maktoum is the Chairman of Dubai Technology and Media Free Zone Authority. In this capacity he is often seen opening exhibitions in the UAE and education also features in his diary — The Sheikh Maktoum bin Mohammed bin Rashid Al Maktoum Cambridge Awards presented annually to high achieving pupils, schools and inspirational teachers.

A keen sportsman, he sponsors many basketball, volleyball and football competitions, including the Dubai Pro Beach Soccer Tournament in 2001 and was heavily involved in the charity fun run in 2001 which raised Dhs. 405,000, divided between the directors of Dubai Centre for Special Needs, Al Noor Training Centre and Rashid Pediatric and Therapy Centre. In 2005 he was named Vice President of the Al Ahli Sports Club, of which his father is honorary President.

His brown and white colours in Britain have only been seen once in the last five years, when Beekeeper carried them in 2001. Purchased as a St Leger hopeful, he missed that race and went on to campaign for Godolphin but was back in Sheikh Maktoum's colours when eleventh in the Dubai City Of Gold.

He has always been a strong supporter of horse racing in the UAE although his maroon and white silks are not seen so often these days. He owned 16 winners in the 2001/02 season but only four in total during the four seasons to follow.

In 2000 he had two runners on Dubai World Cup night when Holy Pole lined up in the Golden Shaheen and Glad Master ran in the UAE Derby. The latter was to prove useful and won both the Al Shindagha Sprint and HH The President Cup in 2002. His colours were carried to victory in the inaugural 1996 Kahayla Classic on World Cup night by Yadeer, the same year that his Larrocha won the second round of the Maktoum Challenge. Other big race wins in the UAE have been supplied by Abreeze in the 1999 Jebel Ali Sprint, Grazalema in the 2000 Al Fahidi Fort and All The Way in the following year's Al Rashidiya.

In recent years, his thoroughbred interests have subsided and the majority of his runners have been in Purebred Arabian races.

BR01-97 Instrument
Power reserve, Automatic movement
Steel case, black dial with crocodile strap
Ref. BR0197-BL-ST

Bell & Ross

BR01-97 INSTRUMENT
www.bellross.com

damas
Les Exclusives

Toll Free: 800 4916

www.damasjewellery.com

Sonic Lady

b. f by Nureyev — Stumped (Owen Anthony)

A $500,000 yearling, Sonic Lady was immediately stamped as something special on her only outing as a two-year-old, when trotting up by a commanding seven lengths in the Blue Seal Stakes at Ascot. The Michael Stoute-trained filly returned to the racecourse in 1986 to trounce Lady Sophie by three lengths in the Nell Gwyn Stakes at Newmarket, a performance which marked her as favourite for the 1000 Guineas.

With confidence high for the Guineas, she was a different horse during the preliminaries, sweating profusely and unable to settle whereas during her first two outings she had been relaxed. In the event she ran well enough, laying down a brave challenge as Midway Lady took the race with Maysoon in second.

Stoute changed Sonic Lady's training regime in time for the Irish 1000 in an attempt to help her settle. At the Curragh she went through the preliminaries in a much easier fashion and was clearly superior to her rivals during the race itself, claiming the Classic by two and a half lengths from Lake Champlain.

Improving on each racecourse appearance at this stage, she claimed the Coronation Stakes at Royal Ascot and Childs Stakes at Newmarket, firmly establishing herself as the choice female performer of her generation.

Then came her biggest test, pitched against the colts in the Sussex Stakes at Goodwood where she was odds-on favourite. Walter Swinburn managed her nervous disposition well going to post and gave the filly a cracking ride. Held up well off the pace, she was given her head in the straight and came with a blistering wide run which claimed the race.

France was next and the Prix du Moulin where, facing a top-class field, she again failed to settle. The jockey's problems continued all the way to the straight and the filly was still unhappy at a point when she was passing beaten horses. When allowed to go on, Sonic Lady stretched herself and cleverly overhauled some class performers to win.

In view of that performance, she was clearly within her rights to hold a place in the Breeders' Cup. She took to the track at Santa Anita with hopes riding high, once again going to the post as favourite. For most of the way she travelled well, tracking Last Tycoon, but faded into seventh in the final stages, the first and only time during her career that she finished out of the frame.

SONIC LADY (b. 1983)	**Nureyev (b. 1977)**	**Northern Dancer**	Nearctic
			Natalma
		Special	Forli
			Thong
	Stumped (b. 1977)	**Owen Anthony**	Proud Chieftan
			Oweninny
		Luckhurst	Busted
			Lucasland

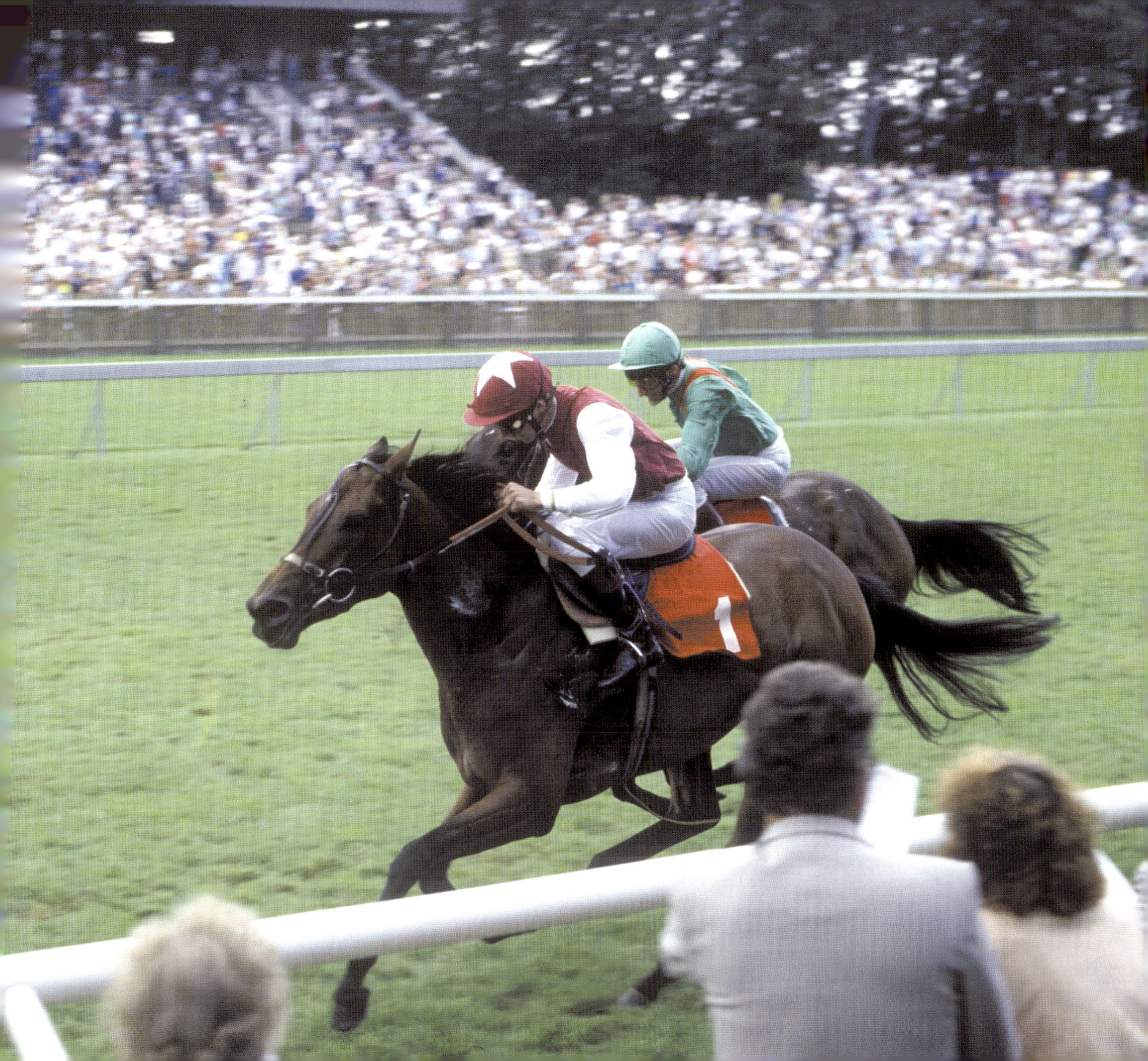
1

Soviet Star

b. c by Nureyev — Veruscha (Venture VII)

A $310,000 foal, Soviet Star was one of the first horses put into training in France for owner Sheikh Mohammed. After winning a maiden at Saint-Cloud as a juvenile for Andre Fabre, the Nureyev colt reappeared in Longchamp's Guineas trial the Prix Fontainebleau, winning well. This saw him installed as one of the leading fancies for the French 2000 Guineas, where European Free Handicap winner Noble Minstrel was also among starters. Under Greville Starkey, Soviet Star quickened well to win the Classic by one length.

After a pair of seconds in the Prix Jean Prat and Royal Ascot's St James's Palace Stakes, Soviet Star was back in Britain for his next start, the Sussex Stakes at Goodwood, where Starkey was seen at his very best in claiming victory.

In September the colt finished second to Miesque, in the Prix du Moulin De Longchamp, before rounding off the season with a third Group One success in the seven-furlong Prix de la Foret.

Soviet Star stayed in training and rewarded connections with a memorable four-year-old season, winning the Group Two mile with a splendid success under Cash Asmussen from Shady Heights, and a second in the Queen Anne Stakes.

Defeat brought an unexpected change of emphasis when Soviet Star next returned to Britain for a crack at the six furlong sprinters championship, Newmarket's July Cup. Possessing a good turn of foot for a mile horse, Soviet Star lined up against one of the best fields of specialist sprinters—and won. Appearing in tremendous condition, Soviet Star was settled by Asmussen just off pacemaker Governor General and as virtually the whole field came broadside 300 metres from the line, Soviet Star was certainly holding his place. Entering the distance, the American pressed the button and Soviet Star responded in strong fashion to sprint clear.

He came up against Miesque in the Prix de Moulin de Longchamp in September. Asmussen took his mount into the lead with two furlongs remaining, a lead he retained all the way to the line despite a dramatic challenge from Miesque.

His last start brought a fourth in the Queen Elizabeth II Stakes, only the second time in his career he finished out of the first two, and Soviet Star subsequently retired to stud.

SOVIET STAR (b. 1984)	**Nureyev (b. 1977)**	Northern Dancer	Nearctic
			Natalma
		Special	Forli
			Thong
	Veruschka	Venture VII	Relic
			Rose O'Lynn
		Marie d'Anjou	Vandale II
			Marigold

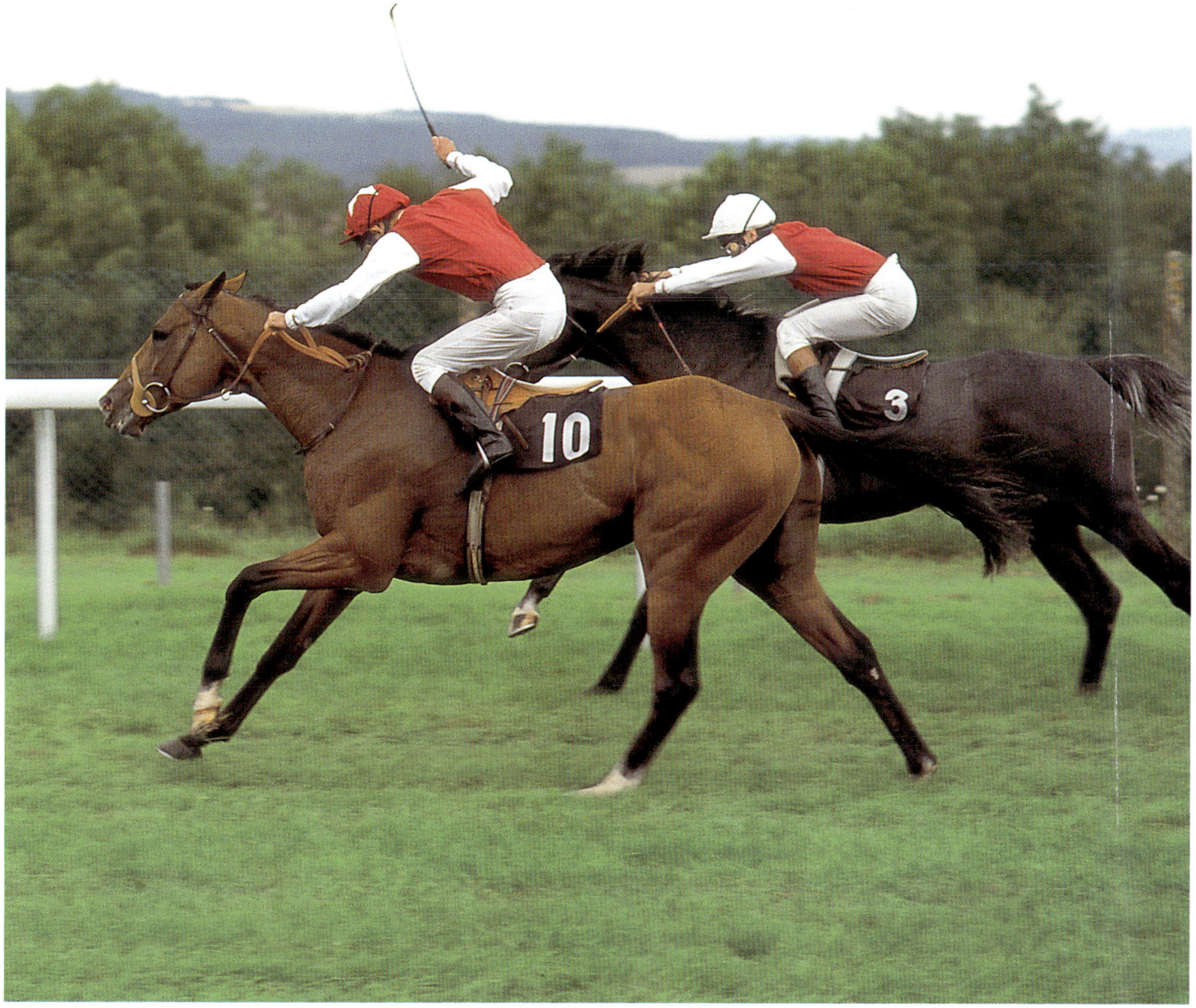
10
3

Street Cry

b. c by Machiavellian - Helen Street (Troy)

Street Cry had a pedigree that screamed champion. By leading sire Machiavellian, he is out of the Irish Oaks heroine Helen Street, a daughter of Derby winner Troy. Trained by Eoin Harty, Street Cry was a class two-year-old, whose finest run came when third in the Breeders' Cup Juvenile behind champions Macho Uno and Point Given.

Touted as a leading Kentucky Derby candidate, the colt shipped to Dubai where he won the UAE Guineas from Noverre and Count Dubois. Street Cry was then second in the UAE Derby, to stablemate Express Tour. Beaten just a head, Street Cry had the smart Lido Palace six lengths behind.

Looking in excellent shape, he was forced to miss the Kentucky Derby due to ankle problems. He resurfaced months later to run second to Evening Attire in the Discovery Handicap.

But it was as a four-year-old that the handsome bay finally fulfiled his promise. His thrashing of a field which included Sakhee in the Dubai World Cup was scintillating. When jockey Jerry Bailey asked Street Cry to lengthen his stride three furlongs out he soon put daylight between himself and the field. Sakhee came to challenge two out, but Street Cry cruised away to win comfortably.

Street Cry returned to America and on his first start won the Stephen Foster. Ridden by Jerry Bailey, Street Cry the lead at the top of the home straight and romped to a powerful victory in this $750,000 Churchill Downs event. This was another fluent win, over the smart performers Dollar Bill and Congaree. The winner also became the first horse to win both the Dubai World Cup and the Foster. Silver Charm (1998) and Captain Steve (2001) tried and failed. His final start came in the Whitney Handicap. In a strong field he ran second to the brilliant Left Bank.

On that he was warm favourite for the Breeders' Cup Classic, but suffered a recurrence of that ankle problem. Just before the Classic it was announced that he had retired.

He was sent to Jonabell alongside champions Cherokee Run and Holy Bull and had the talent to match his companions. Street Cry won his maiden by seven lengths, his first Graded Stakes by eight and a half, the Stephen Foster by six and a half, and the Dubai World Cup by a widening four and a half.

	Mr. Prospector	Raise A Native
Machiavellian (b. 1987)		Gold Digger
	Coup de Folie	Halo
STREET CRY (b. 1998)		Raise The Standard
	Troy	Petingo
Helen Street (b. 1982)		La Milo
	Waterway	Riverman
		Boulevard

DUBAI WORLD CUP
Fly Emirates
WORLD CUP
9
Dubai World Cup
2002

Sulamani

Hernando - Soul Dream (Alleged)

Sulamani has a special place in the annals of the short history of Godolphin. One of the most resilient, big-hearted and winning-most horses ever to represent the Dubai team, Sulamani became the organisation's 100th Group/Grade One winner when he claimed the Arlington Million in 2003.

Bred by the Niarchos family and trained by Pascal Bary, Sulamani was unraced at two years and debuted with a seventh. But from this inauspicious start the son of Hernando developed into a class act, claiming his next four races, all over 12 furlongs. Having gone on to win a conditions event and one listed race, Sulamani stormed the Prix du Jockey-Club, charging from last to first.

He reappeared to win a substandard Prix Niel, before finishing close up second to Marienbard in the Prix de l'Arc de Triomphe after his pacemaker failed and Sulamani wandered in the home straight. Eight days later Sheikh Mohammed purchased Sulamani and he transferred into the care of Godolphin. His career under Saeed bin Suroor began as it mostly continued, with a success. On Dubai World Cup day Sulamami won the Dubai Sheema Classic in convincing fashion.

After a below par fourth in the Grand Prix De Saint-Cloud, he returned to form with a second in the King George VI and Queen Elizabeth Diamond Stakes. Bin Suroor brought his charge back to 10 furlongs for the Grade One Arlington Million, when a disqualification for first-past-the-post Storming Home gave Sulamani the honours and Godolphin their 100. Sulamani now hit a rich vein of form and added a second US Grade One, the Turf Classic Invitation at Belmont Park, to his seasonal tally.

Somewhat hampered in the Breeders' Cup Turf at Santa Anita, Sulamani, it was announced, would remain in training at five.

Losing nothing in defeat during the early part of 2004, Sulamani was rewarded with his first Group One victory of the season in the Juddmonte International Stakes at York. Sulamani then brought the curtain down on a wonderful career with another brilliant performance to win the Canadian International at Woodbine, Toronto in October. He retired the winner of six Grade/Group One races in five different countries.

	Niniski	Nijinsky
Hernando (b. 1990)		Virginia Hills
	Whakilyric	Miswaki
SULAMANI (b. 1999)		Lyrism
	Alleged	Hoist The Flag
Soul Dream (br. 1990)		Princess Pout
	Normia	Northfields
		Mia Pola

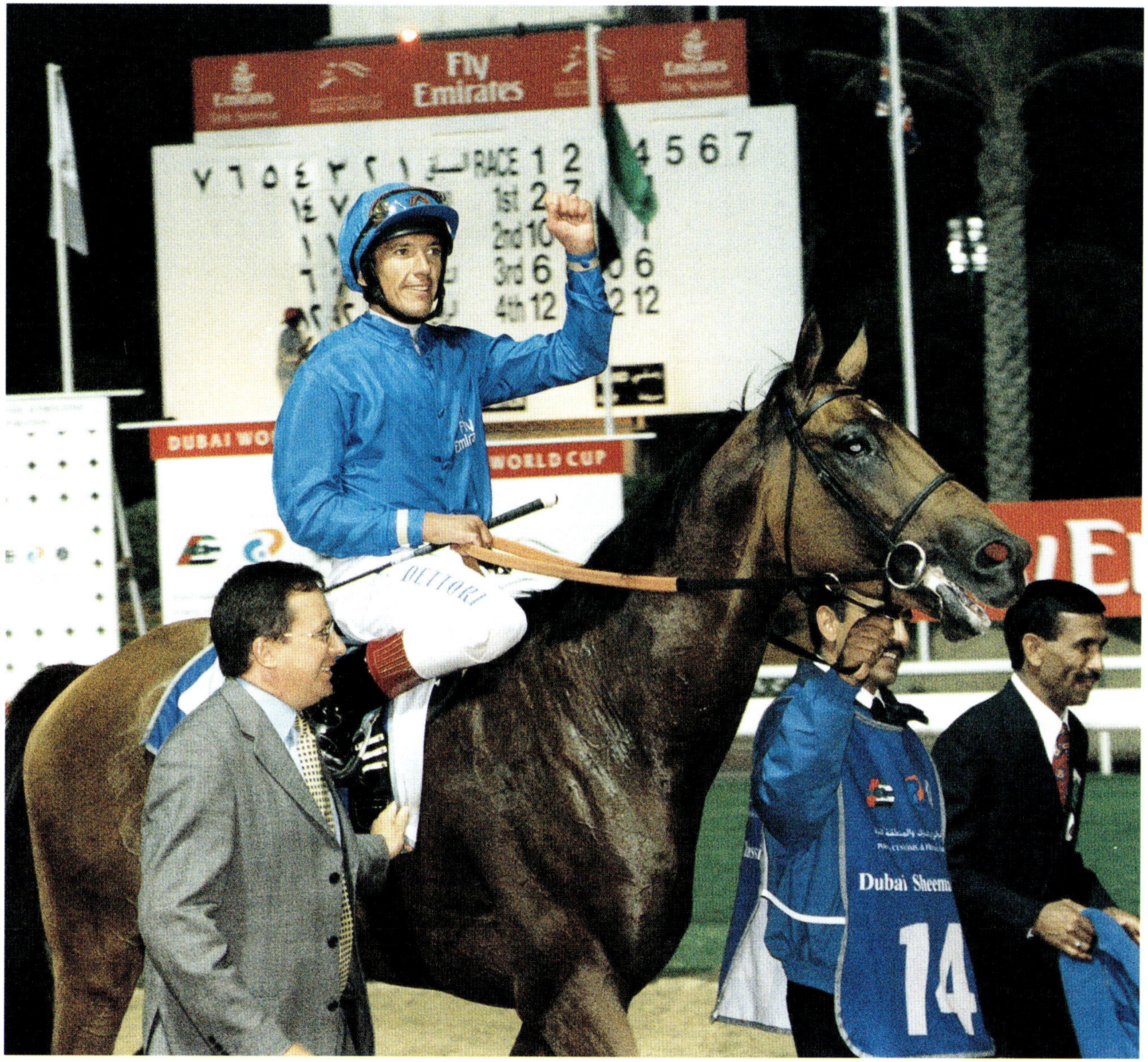
Fly Emirates
WORLD CUP
14

Sheikh Mohammed bin Obaid Al Maktoum

Sheikh Mohammed bin Obaid Al Maktoum has the distinction of achieving something few owners have been privileged to. In 1998 he saw his yellow colours with black spots carried to victory in the Epsom Derby by High-Rise. The son of High Estate won five of his 13 starts, including the Listed Dubai City of Gold at Nad Al Sheba. He was sent to the USA to continue his career in 2000 but was retired after succumbing to injury on his only start Stateside.

His dam, High Tern, was raced by Sheikh Mohammed, for whom he won two races and produced two foals, before she was given to cousin Sheikh Mohammed bin Obaid. She hails from the same family as High Hawk, who is the dam of In The Wings, whose seven wins included three in Group One company.

High Tern's first foal for Sheikh Mohammed bin Obaid was Jawaher. She is the dam of his Italian Oaks winner Zomaradah, herself the dam of Godolphin's Irish 2000 Guineas winner Dubawi - the best son of the legendary Dubai Millennium.

Sheikh Mohammed bin Obaid still has a handful of horses in training in Britain with Luca Cumani, who trained High-Rise for him before he joined Saeed Bin Suroor late in 1998. He has enjoyed a good start to the 2006 season with six winners from only 18 runners, having owned five winners in each of the previous two seasons.

He was a staunch supporter of UAE racing during its formative years, highlighted by 10 winners in the 1995/96 season. And Sheikh Mohammed bin Obaid was just as visible during this period off-course, where he attended racing regularly and worked to promote ownership among his countrymen and also managed affairs at Jebel Ali Racecourse.

However, Sheikh Mohammed bin Obaid has not had a runner in the UAE since 2000, the year High-Rise won the Dubai City of Gold and was third in the Sheema Classic. His Lost Soldier won the Godolphin Mile in both 1994 and 1995 but his silks have been absent from local racecourses since April 2000.

"Accuracy is everything when you climb Mt. Everest."

Jim Whittaker
- First American to reach the summit of Mt. Everest

"The top of the world is a very dangerous and unforgiving place. That's why, to avoid life threatening weather, you must start your descent on time. Which is why a dependable timepiece like a Ball Watch is so important in an environment that features truly adverse conditions."

The watch that once ran America's railroads now helps the world's explorers keep time. There is no timepiece that is as rugged and dependable.

- Anti-reflective sapphire cystal
- 5,000 Gs shock resistance
- 100 meter water resistance

Self-powered micro gas lights that glow 100 times brighter than luminous paint for more than 25 years

BALL
OFFICIAL RR STANDARD
Since 1891

Since 1891, accuracy under adverse conditions

Engineer Master Telemeter
Automatic Series

damas
THE ART OF BEAUTY.
Since 1907

Toll Free: 8004916

www.ballwatch.com

Sure Blade

b. c by Kris – Double Lock (Home Guard)

Tough and genuine, Sheikh Mohammed's Sure Blade was one of the finest milers in Britain during the mid-1980s when trained by Barry Hills. After claiming a maiden over the minimum distance, he rose in distance and class to add the Coventry Stakes and Champagne Stakes, before rounding off a pleasing debut campaign with a third to Huntingsdale in the Dewhurst Stakes.

Sure Blade wintered with expectations high that he was set to play a big part in races around a mile the following summer. Hills chose Thirsk's Classic Trial as a comeback target and although able to win the race it was clear that the soft ground played a significant part in taking the sting out of his performance. Subsequently he was placed to run on firmer ground.

The Classic trail inevitably led to Newmarket for the 2000 Guineas where Sure Blade ran a superb fifth in one of the decade's best Guineas, behind Dancing Brave, Green Desert and Sharood.

Sure Blade reappeared in the St James's Palace Stakes where he created a shock in defeating the front-running Green Desert, winning going away by two lengths.

With a niggling injury reportedly causing him to miss several intended mid-summer targets, Sure Blade eventually reappeared in the Ascot parade ring prior to the mile Queen Elizabeth II Stakes in September.

It was an impressive training feat by Hills that Sure Blade could return and win in this top class company. Taking on the likes of Teleprompter and Efisio, Sure Blade was nursed along almost from the start, but never lost his place and was soon making steady progress toward the head of the field. Teleprompter was showing the way as they reached two furlongs from the line, but Sure Blade was full of running as the line neared, taking up the lead and going on to record a remarkable success by three quarters of a length.

The colt seemed below par when running down the field in the Dubai Champion Stakes nearly a month later, pulling so hard early on that his race was lost well before the line. He was later retired to stud.

		Sharpen Up	Atan
			Rocchetta
	Kris (ch. 1976)		
		Doubly Sure	Reliance II
SURE BLADE (b. 1983)			Soft Angels
		Home Guard	Forli
			Stay At Home
	Double Lock (b. 1975)		
		St Padina	St Paddy
			Rose of Medina

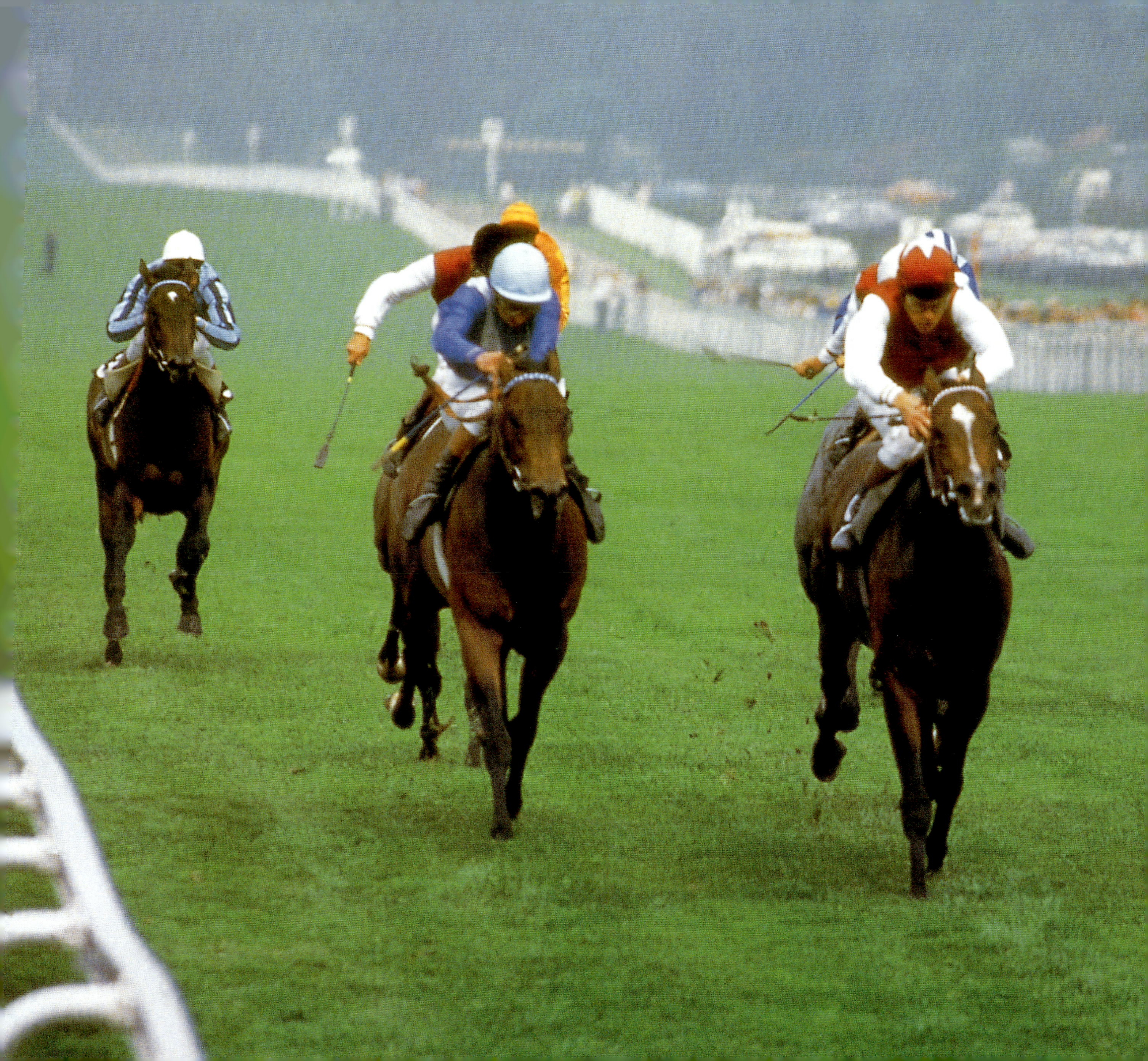

Susu

ch. m by Machiavellian — Home Truth (Known Fact)

Sheikh Rashid bin Mohammed Al Maktoum, like his father, is an out-and-out horseman. For Your Eyes Only, winner of the William Hill Mile at Goodwood, was the first class horse to represent him in Britain, while in the United Arab Emirates he has been served by a string of big race winners.

However, even at the outset of his time as a racehorse owner, Sheikh Rashid will know that few come as remarkable as his game mare Susu. In January 1997, having missed her two and three-year-old seasons, she appeared for the first time in a small maiden race at Nad Al Sheba. She was trounced. After dwelling in the stalls, she finished tailed off last of eight, the judge recording that she finished some 30 lengths behind the winner.

Despite that performance, Sheikh Rashid and trainer Satish Seemar persevered and were rewarded for their tenacity. Over the next 12 months, Susu put that debut behind her to come on in astonishing fashion. Seemar saddled her 10 times in the UAE, during which time she won five and finished second in the remainder. Near the end of this run of success, she was adjudged good enough to be thrown into Listed company on the turf at Abu Dhabi Equestrian and Racing Club in the 1998 staging of the The President's Cup. She had earned her place, but shocked many in the manner of her performance in the UAE capital, claiming the race with some style.

From maiden flop to listed winner was a remarkable feat, but Sheikh Rashid went on to give his gutsy mare a further chance to show her worth. At the end of the 1998/99 Gulf season, she shipped to Newmarket and the care of Sir Michael Stoute.

After a break following a long season, she made her bow in Britain as late as August in a listed race at Ascot, finishing seven lengths off the winner. Stoute next sent her north to Doncaster for the listed Kyoto Septre Stakes, where Susu showed her class. Not enjoying the clearest passage, she found space late and launched a strong kick that propelled her to victory.

She followed that up with an appearance in the Challenge Stakes where she took on a top quality field, and again she showed up surprisingly well. Only Lend A Hand proved better, and a number of big name group winners were left in Susu's wake.

Her next outing came in the Breeders' Cup Mile where she was never in contention.

	Mr Prospector	**Raise A Native**
		Gold Digger
Machiavellian (b. 1987)		**Halo**
	Coup De Folie	**Raise The St'd**
SUSU (ch. 1993)		**In Reality**
	Known Fact	**Tamerett**
Home Truth (ch. 1987)		**Be My Guest**
	Dance Card	**Ivor's Honey**

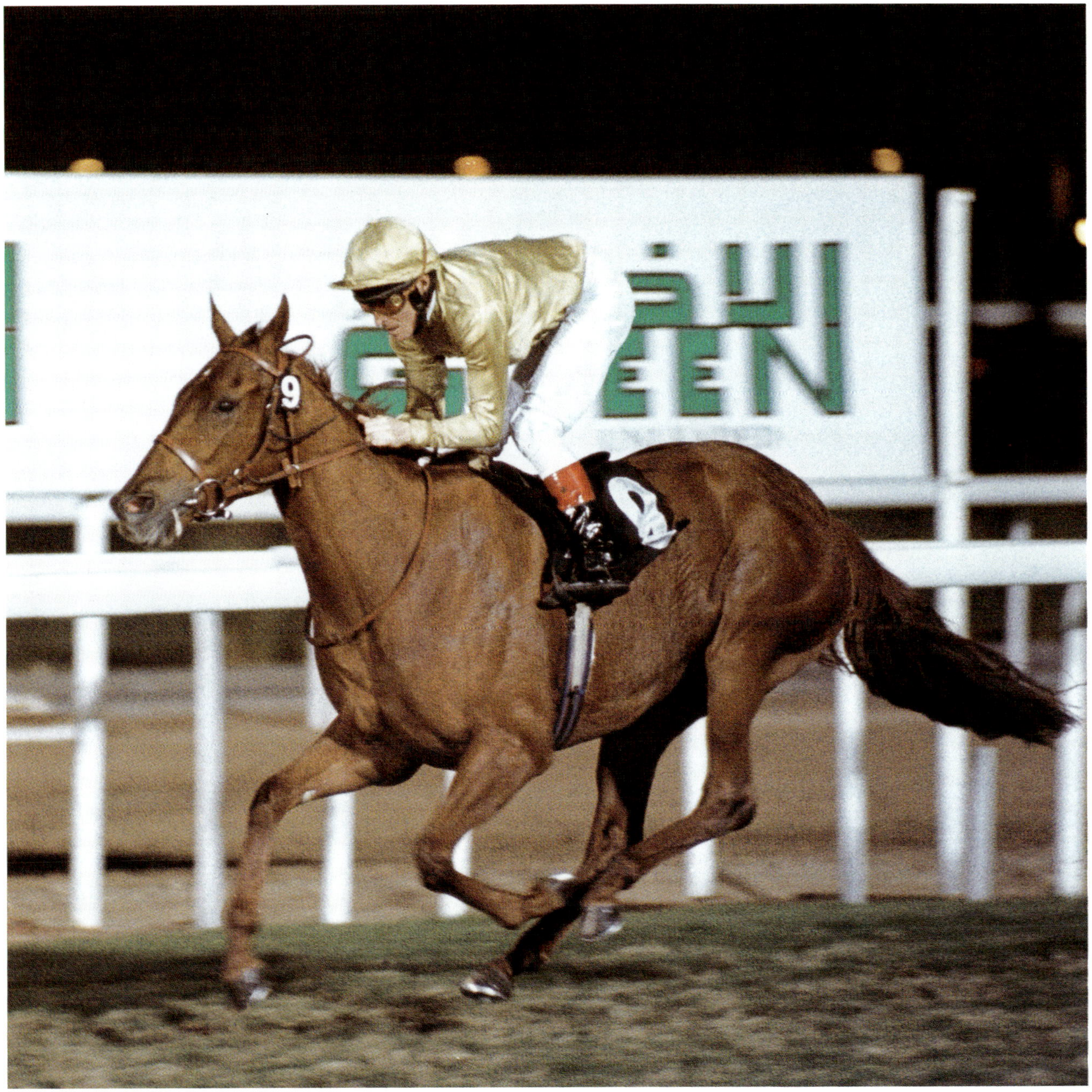
GREEN

Swain

b. c by Nashwan – Love Smitten (Key To The Mint)

Possibly the finest product of Maktoum Derby winner Nashwan's first two crops, Swain began his career with Andre Fabre. He was not raced as a juvenile. After debut success in a Saint Cloud maiden, he then won the listed Prix de Reux and the Group Two Grand Prix de Deauville.

Unbeaten, the colt was thrown in against the very best on his last outing of the campaign in the Prix de l'Arc de Triomphe where he put in a thrilling run to finish third.

He returned to finish third in the Prix Garnay the following season before an attempt at the Coronation Stakes. At Epsom, the Sheikh Mohammed pair of Swain and Singspiel drew well away to fight out the finish, the former getting up by a neck. After finishing second by a length to Helissio in the Grand Prix de Saint-Cloud and a success in the Prix Foy, Swain went into the Arc with hopes high, but finished fourth. His campaign ended with yet another brave performance when third to Pilsudski and Singspiel in the Breeders' Cup Turf, after which he joined Godolphin.

His reappearance came in the Princess of Wales's Stakes, where a head second to Shantou was no disgrace. However it was his performance in the King George VI and Queen Elizabeth Stakes that finally sealed his arrival. Swain ran a brilliant race to win by one length from Pilsudski.

After a seventh in the Arc, Swain was not seen again until the Dubai World Cup, where he ran arguably his bravest race in finishing a short head second to US superstar Silver Charm.

Swain made a quiet return to Britain in his first two outings, then bounced back to claim a second King George. He followed up by claiming the Irish Champion Stakes. His final racecourse appearance came in the Breeders' Cup Classic. Swain ran a superb race and was looking a winner when he veered across the track, losing ground. Godolphin's star finished less than a length third and, but for this quirk, would surely have won.

		Red God
	Blushing Groom	Runaway Bride
Nashwan (ch. 1986)		Bustino
	Height of Fashion	Highclere
SWAIN (b. 1992)		Graustark
	Key to the Mint	Key Bridge
Love Smitten (b. 1981)		Quadrangle
	Square Angel	Nangela

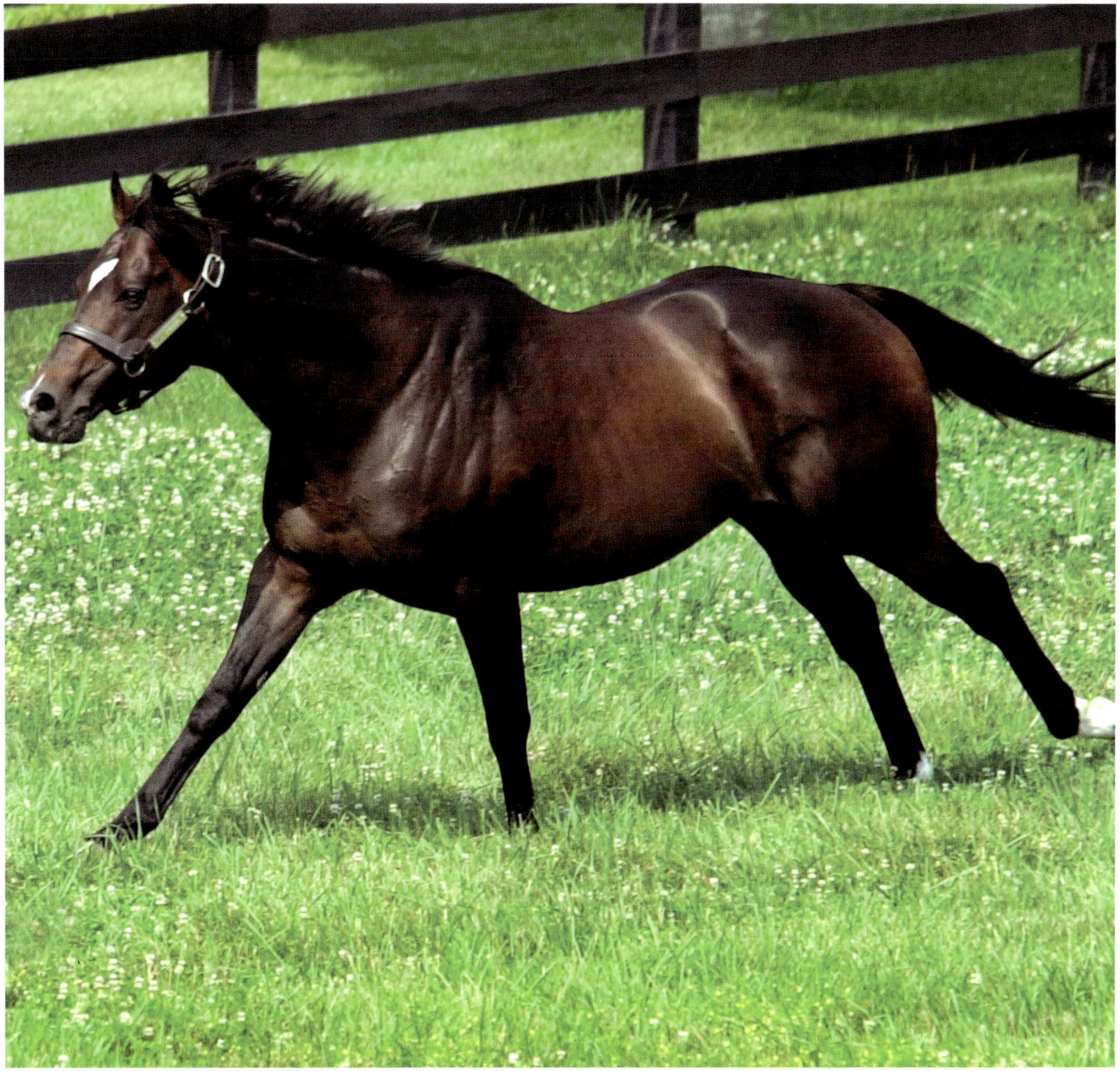

Touching Wood
b. c by Roberto — Mandera (Vaguely Noble)

Touching Wood was arguably the first top-class Maktoum-owned Thoroughbred, with wins in both English and Irish St Legers, and second in the Epsom Derby, highlighting a tremendous three-year-old season.

Trained by Tom Jones, this small colt was still a maiden when rated an outside chance in the Epsom Classic, where he stayed on strongly to finish three lengths second to Golden Fleece. That performance in the colours of Sheikh Maktoum earmarked him as a leading St Leger prospect and after finally breaking his maiden in the Welsh Derby at Chepstow, he made the frame in both the Gordon Stakes in July and Great Voltigeur Stakes in August

By August, Touching Wood did appear to be needing further and in the Great Voltigeur could have won but for being held up at the back during the early stages.

Following the latter performance, he was tried in blinkers at home, responded well, and would appear in both the English St Leger and Irish St Leger wearing headgear.

At Doncaster, Jones gave his star every chance, supplying Muslab as a pacemaker. This early leader setting a blistering pace that had most in the field labouring. As they rounded in to the straight Muslab and Touching Wood had left the 13 other runners well behind. Touching Wood took up the lead three furlongs out, sustaining a tremendous gallop all the way to the line. The colt recorded the fastest St Leger winning time since Bahrain in 1935, further underlining his class.

That performance had connections considering a trip to Longchamp for the Prix de l'Arc de Triomphe, but eventually he was routed to the Irish St Leger.

Billed as a battle between Touching Wood and Irish Oaks star Swiftfoot, the home performer was soon struggling in the wake of Touching Wood's relentless gallop and it was left to fellow British raider Father Rooney to follow him across the line.

In winning these two Classics, Touching Wood was the first horse to complete an English and Irish St Leger double since Trigo in 1929.

Hailed as a natural successor to staying champion Ardross, the colt was retired following his success at the Curragh.

TOUCHING WOOD (b. 1979)	**Roberto (b. 1969)**	Hail To Reason — Turn-to / Nothirdchance
		Bramalea — Nashua / Rarelea
	Mandera (b. 1970)	Vaguely Noble — Vienna / Noble Lassie
		Foolish One — Tom Fool / Miss Disco

Touching Wood wins the 1982 St Leger.

Sheikh Saeed bin Maktoum Al Maktoum

Sheikh Saeed bin Maktoum Al Maktoum will always be remembered as the owner of Lammtarra. He was bred to be a champion and certainly lived up to his pedigree. Lammtarra was only to run four times, winning his sole juvenile start for Alec Scott. Scott was sadly to be killed in a shooting incident and the horse moved to Saeed bin Suroor.

He made his seasonal reappearance, after a 302 day absence having suffered numerous training problems, in the Epsom Derby and carried his owner's green colours to a famous and emotional victory, breaking the race record in the process. He was the first horse since 1919 to win the race on seasonal debut.

The colt went on to claim the King George and Prix de l'Arc de Triomphe. Four runs and three Group 1 wins is an enviable record in anyone's language, especially for a new 19-year-old owner, at the time a university student.

Sheikh Saeed's colours have recorded just a handful of winners in the past five years in Britain, but are regular fixtures in the UAE where he owns the Jebel Ali Palace Stables and his horses have won about 125 races since racing started. The 2005/06 season saw his silks carried to victory on three occasions with 22 individual horses running for him. In recent years, he has been a great supporter of Arabian and breeds a lot of his own runners carrying the UAE prefix.

His Opportunist won twice at the 2005 Dubai International Racing Carnival and his eight winners in total that year, a far cry from his best of 19 in 1998/99, saw him finish eighth in the owner's list for number of winners. Other big local winners include Desert Conqueror in the Jebel Ali Mile of 1996, Kammtarra (Lammtarra's half-brother) in the both the first and last round of the Maktoum Challenge in 1997 and, arguably most famously, Key Of Luck in the Dubai Duty Free.

Although an accomplished horseman it is on the firing range where Sheikh Saeed has made a name for himself. He represented the UAE at shooting at the Olympics, one of four athletes to represent the country in the Sydney Olympics with skeet shooting his preferred discipline. He was a more than respectable ninth.

www.damasjewellery.com

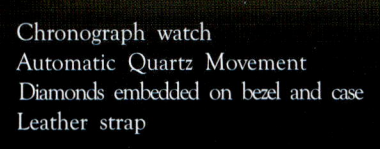

Chronograph watch
Automatic Quartz Movement
Diamonds embedded on bezel and case
Leather strap

damas
Les Exclusives

Toll Free: 800 4916

Unfuwain

b. c by Northern Dancer — Height of Fashion (Bustino)

Unfuwain enjoyed a promising juvenile season, finishing second in a Newbury maiden before getting off the mark at the same course.

Dick Hern brought his charge back in the Warren Stakes over the Derby distance at Epsom in April. Unfuwain's only trouble throughout the race was a momentary lack of balance rounding Tattenham Corner, but he recovered and strode away from the field to record a commanding 15 length success. Later he faced just three opponents in testing conditions for the Chester Vase and again won with plenty in hand.

Unfuwain returned to Epsom for the Derby as second favourite but ran a disappointing race, fading three furlongs out to finish seventh.

The colt was certainly back to his best in the Princess of Wales's Stakes at Newmarket in July, trouncing a good class field by 15 lengths. Following this, he returned to Group One action in the King George VI and Queen Elizabeth Diamond Stakes. Racing up with the leaders throughout, Willie Carson asked his mount to go on as they entered the straight and the colt responded strongly, running into a fine lead which looked enough for victory. Only the speedy turn of foot of Mtoto was enough to deny him.

He was not seen again on track until the autumn, taking his place in the Arc despite fears that the prevailing firm ground was far from suitable. Unfuwain was well in contention throughout and was sent on moments after the field entered the Longchamp straight. Forced to check slightly, the colt stayed on strongly but had to settle for fourth behind Tony Bin.

Unfuwain stayed in training at four and began a campaign which was primed toward the King George and Arc, with a powerful success in the John Porter EBF Stakes at Newbury and the Jockey Club Stakes at Newmarket.

Firm ground proved his undoing however. A dry summer keep him off the track for the remainder of the campaign and he was retired.

UNFUWAIN (b. 1985)	**Northern Dancer (b. 1961)**	Neartic → Nearco / Lady Angela
		Natalma → Native Dancer / Almahmoud
	Height of Fashion (b. 1979)	Bustino → Bustino / Ship Yard
		Highclere → Queen's Hussar / Highlight

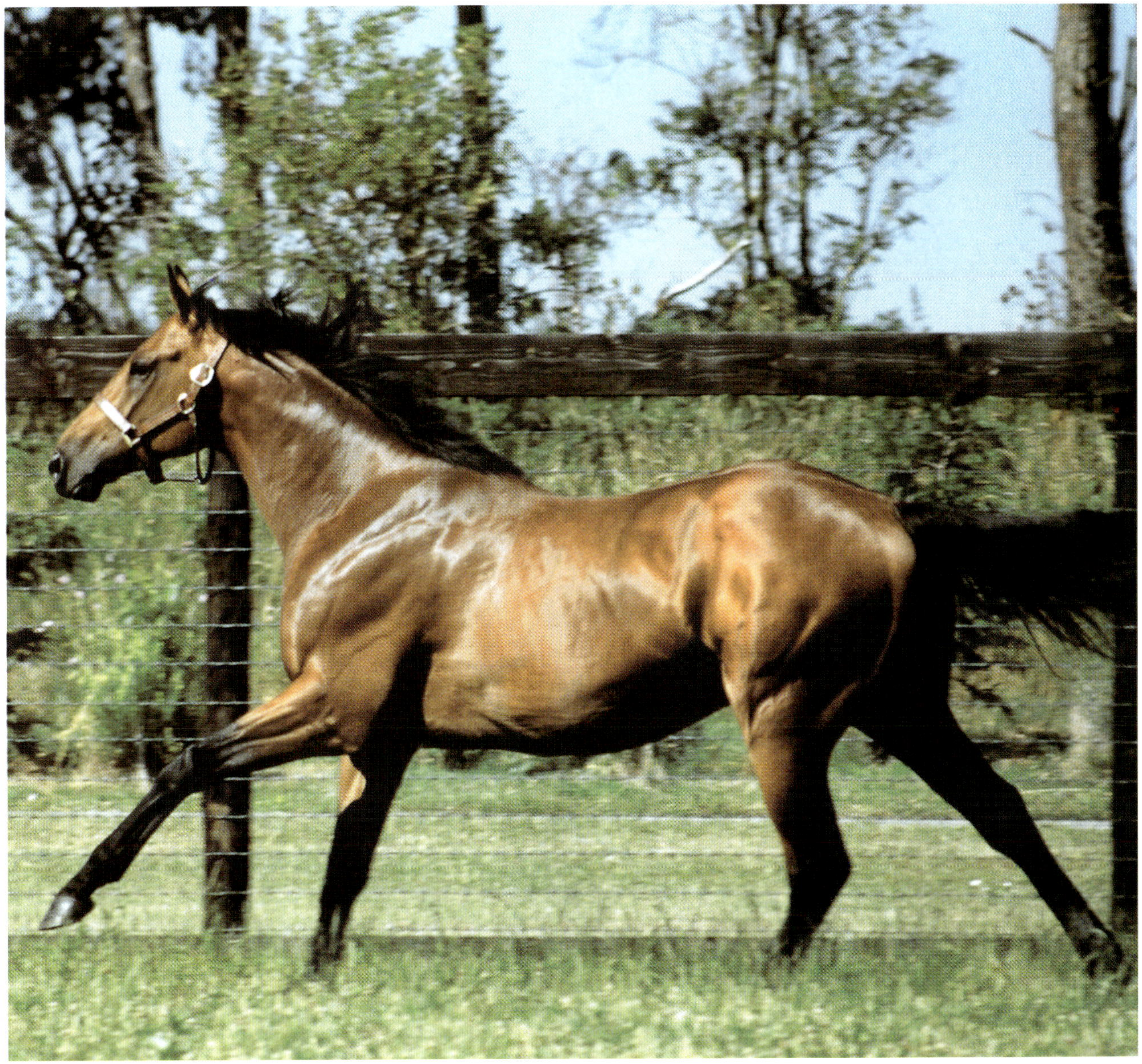

Wassl

b. c by Mill Reef — Hayloft III (Tudor Melody)

During his three-year-old campaign, Classic winner Wassl provided Sheikh Ahmed with a successful first season as an owner. With a sole juvenile appearance producing victory in a six-furlong event, a pedigree inclined toward speed and having shown a good turn of foot at home, expectations were that he would be a good proposition for the early season Classics.

Lazy at home and reportedly set to come on from the run, trainer John Dunlop found his charge not only fit, but very much a front-runner for the Classics when Wassl surprised all to land the Greenham Stakes at Newbury in April.

With that standard of performance, Wassl was one of the leading fancies when Dunlop saddled him at Newmarket in the 2000 Guineas. Sent off a well-supported third favourite, he disappointed connections to finish ninth behind Lomond. Though at a loss to explain such a below-standard performance, it was thought that having been drawn in stall one at Newmarket, Wassl, running effectively on his own, simply lost interest.

Dunlop kept faith and shipped Wassl to The Curragh for the Irish 2000 Guineas. Connections were indeed confident despite the fact that one of his nine opponents was Newmarket star Lomond. They were proved correct in their assessment.

Always kept prominent by Tony Murray, Wassl stayed on strongly at the finish after going on from halfway. Indeed, none were able to seriously test Sheikh Ahmed's first Classic star, the nearest at the line being Lomond, by three-quarters of a length.

Far from certain to stay a mile and a half, Wassl was given a chance in the Epsom Derby, but was found wanting. He tried again in the Irish equivalent and fared better, finishing fifth behind Shareef Dancer, before dropped to a mile for the Sussex Stakes in July, finishing second to Noalchaholic. Later in the campaign Wassl ran well in the Prix du Moulin de Longchamp and Joe McGrath Memorial Stakes at Leopardstown before disappointing in the Dubai Champion Stakes.

The colt, bucking a trend for Guineas winners to retire, stayed in training and more than justified his owner's decision on his seasonal reappearance. Wassl won his first race of the season for a third consecutive time, the Lockinge Stakes at Newbury in May. After further placed runs in the Queen Anne Stakes and Sussex Stakes he was retired.

WASSL (b. 1980)	**Mill Reef (b. 1968)**	Never Bend	Nasrullah
			Lalun
		Milan Mill	Princequillo
			Virginia Water
	Hayloft (b. 1973)	Tudor Melody	Tudor Minstrel
			Matelda
		Haymaking	Galivanter
			Haytime

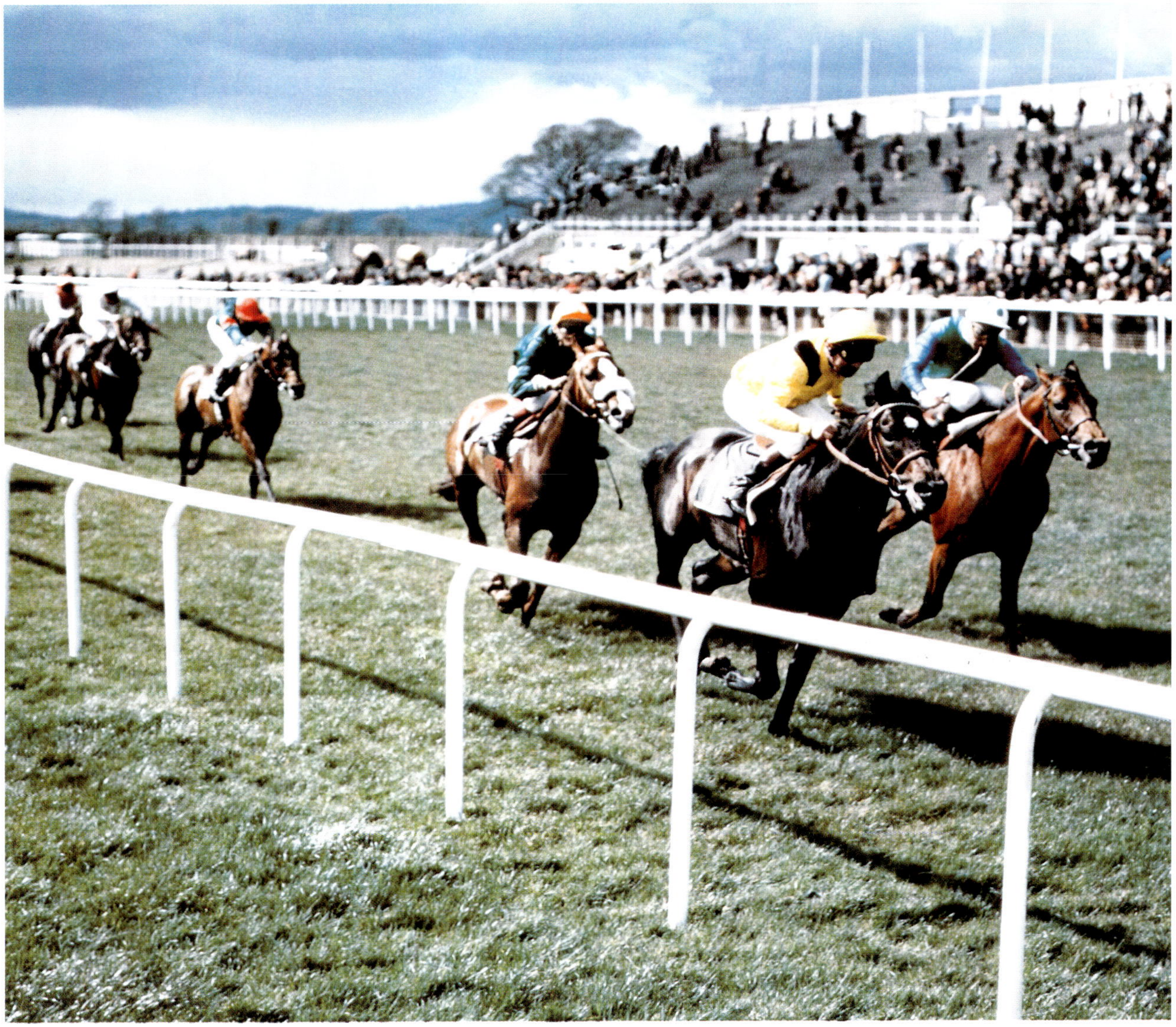

Zilzal

ch. c by Nureyev — French Charmer (Le Fabuleux)

In a racing career spanning just six races over five months, this Michael Stoute-trained star went from maiden to Breeders' Cup runner.

A $750,000 yearling, Zilzal went unraced as a two-year-old, making his bow in a minor Leicester maiden at three. The colt duly obliged with ease and considering the quality of opposition was noted as a tremendous prospect.

Connections routed Zilzal to the Jersey Stakes at Royal Ascot, where he put in a breathtaking display. A competitive field went along at a fast pace, but when moved to the front two furlongs out, Zilzal went away from his rivals for an easy victory over proven performers such as Russian Royal and Distant Relative. Despite a great deal of hype, Stoute opted to educate the leggy colt further, dropping him in class to score a pedestrian win in the Van Geest Stakes.

He was back in the best company next time out when entered in the Sussex Stakes at Goodwood, in what looked set to be one of the top mile races of the season, Zilzal facing the likes of Warning and stablemate Shaadi. The race proved to be a disappointment as the two other principals ran below par. Zilzal, however, ran a sensational and classy race. The colt claimed all the plaudits for a commanding performance, running up with a fast pace early and going on strongly 200 yards from the line. In recording a three-length success, Zilzal was first mooted as a candidate for the Breeders' Cup.

First though there was the matter of Polish President. The French three-year-old had run up a record of seven successes. The two came together in the Queen Elizabeth II Stakes at Ascot in September.

Zilzal jumped out and took the field along with his market rival tucked in behind. There was hardly a length in it as they turned into the straight but when Zilzal quickened Polish President always looked to be struggling and could not get on terms. Under hard driving the French star stayed on Zilzal's tail, until one furlong out when Sheikh Manna's star surged on to record a three-length success.

That performance booked a place in the Breeders' Cup Mile. Unfavourably drawn, he did nothing to help his chances with a slow start. A frantic pace and tight track had him fighting a loosing battle from the outset. He ran on gamely to finish sixth to Stainless, just two lengths adrift despite being hampered on the run in.

```
                                              Nearctic
                          Northern Dancer
                                              Natalma
         Nureyev (b. 1977)
                                              Forli
                          Special
                                              Thong
ZILZAL (ch. 1986)
                                              Wild Risk
                          Le Fabuleux
                                              Anguar
         French Charmer (ch. 1978)
                                              Bold Lad
                          Bold Example
                                              Lady Be Good
```

Acknowledgments

The Publishers would like to thank Shadwell for their continued support for this publication, now in its seventh edition. Without the backing of Shadwell this testimonial to the great Maktoum owned horses of the last thirty years would not have been possible. We would particilarly like to thank Mr. Mirza Al Sayegh for his continued insight and guidance.

Legends of the Turf, was produced with the assistance of Stephanie Fordham, Louise Chandler, Sheen McCarthy, Marie McClure, Marcus Tregoning, Enda Stanley, Briony Norris and Peter Kemp. A number of organisations also provided valuable resourses and efforts, including Khaleej Times, Emirates, Japanese Racing Association, British Racing Center, British Thoroughbred Breeders' Association, British Horseracing Board, Darley, Gainsborough Farm, Breeders' Cup Limited and The Bell Group.

For all their support, I acknowlegdge the contributions of the excellent people at Dubai Horse Racing Information Centre, especially Ayman Mahmood. At Media Prima, my thanks to Mohammed Mosleh, Leslie Cox and Kyra Wilson for the invaluable contribution. At Ibdaa Printing Press our thanks to Roni Khalife, Fouad Al Tawil, Jyotish Roy, Raj Lohia and Praveen V.

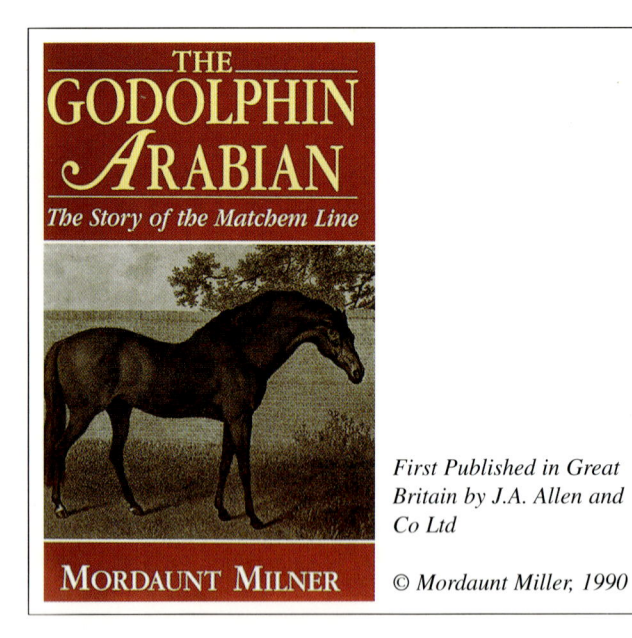

First Published in Great Britain by J.A. Allen and Co Ltd

© Mordaunt Miller, 1990

Primary Contributors: Jason Ford, Ian Carless, Paul Wilkin
Principal Photographers: David Hastings, Joy B. Gilbert, Trevor Jones, Andrew Watkins, Simon Anderton, Samantha Becks-Hampton, Randy Moore, PK Majeed
Design: Willow Design
Research and Production: Elie Moukarzel
Senior Editor: Barbara Saunders
Administration: Pratima Finch
Publishers: Ibdaa Printing Press, Dubai